ACT®
Advanced Practice
Prep for 36

KAPLAN

PUBLISHING

New York

D1441634

© 2017 by Kaplan, Inc.

Published by Kaplan Publishing, a division of Kaplan, Inc.
395 Hudson Street
New York, NY 10014

Printed in the United States of America

10 9 8 7 6 5 4 3 2 1

ISBN-13: 978-1-5062-2327-8

Kaplan Publishing print books are available at special quantity discounts to use for sales promotions, employee premiums, or educational purposes. For more information or to purchase books, please call the Simon & Schuster special sales department at 866-506-1949.

TABLE OF CONTENTS

UNIT 4: SCIENCE

UNIT 5: WRITING

K

INTRODUCTION TO THE ACT

Don't be scared of the ACT. Why? Because we know what's on the exam, and we know exactly how you should prepare for it. Kaplan has been teaching students how to succeed on the ACT for more than 75 years—longer than anyone else, period. Students who are working toward top scores know that they need to practice the most advanced concepts. If your goal is to earn a top score, this ACT Advanced Practice book will help you do just that!

ACT Structure

The ACT is 2 hours and 55 minutes long, or 3 hours and 35 minutes long if you choose to complete the optional Writing Test. It consists of a total of 215 scored multiple-choice questions and one optional essay.

Test	Allotted Time (min.)	Question Count
English	45	75
Math	60	60
Reading	35	40
Science	35	40
Writing (optional)	40	1
Total	175 *or* 215 (w/Writing)	215 *or* 216 (w/Writing)

ACT Scoring

ACT scoring can be pretty complex. The most important score is typically the Composite score (which is an unweighted average of the four major subject scores). This is the score used by most colleges and universities in the admissions and scholarship process. Though the subject scores can play a role in decisions or course placement at some schools, the reporting categories and domain scores usually aren't as important as the Composite score.

ACT scaled scores range from 1 to 36. Nearly half of all test takers score within a much narrower range: 17–23. If you earn a score of 24, you'll be in about the 74th percentile. That means that you did as well as or better than 74% of the test takers—in other words, you're in the top quarter of people who took the ACT.

Where and When to Take the ACT

The ACT is offered every year on multiple Saturday test dates. Typically, exams are offered in September, October, December, February, April, and June. (The February date is not available in the state of New York.) You can take the ACT multiple times. Some states offer special administrations of the ACT on different dates. Sunday tests are available by request for students requiring religious or other exemptions. The ACT is administered at high schools around the country that serve as testing centers. Your high school may or may not be a testing center. Check www.act.org for a list of testing centers near you. Note that you must register for the ACT approximately one month in advance to avoid paying a late fee.

HOW TO USE THIS BOOK

This book contains hundreds of practice questions. Each question is an ACT question type you will see on Test Day and provides you with plenty of opportunities to assess and practice your strengths and weaknesses before Test Day. Answering practice questions is important, but just as important is understanding why you got a particular question right or wrong. When you're done answering one or more questions, check out the detailed Answers and Explanations at the end of the book. These thorough explanations provide both the correct answers and strategic advice to help you practice thinking like an expert! In addition, every explanation includes the difficulty level of each question. All of this practice is geared toward one thing: getting you the most points on Test Day!

Follow these steps to get the most out of these practice questions:

1. Read the Test Overviews before beginning practice questions within that unit.

2. Assess your strengths and weaknesses. After you finish one set of practice questions, go to the back of the book to check your answers AND read the explanations for questions you missed as well as for questions on which you guessed.

3. Use the minutes per question or per passage rates for each Test to create timed practice question sets. For Math, you should think about how many minutes per question, while for English, Reading and Science, you should think about how many minutes per passage.

UNIT ONE

English

CHAPTER ONE

ACT English Test Overview

INSIDE THE ACT ENGLISH TEST

The English Test is 45 minutes long and includes 75 questions. The test includes five essays, or passages, each of which includes 15 questions. This means you only have 9 minutes to spend on each passage, or about 30–40 seconds on each question. Because time is limited, the Kaplan Method for ACT English will be invaluable in helping you answer the questions strategically within the time allowed.

The Format

English passages will be about a variety of subjects and may be written in numerous styles: persuasive, explanatory, narrative, etc. Recognizing the style of an English passage helps you focus on the questions as they relate to the passage's general purpose. Knowing the overarching aim of the passage will help you answer questions more efficiently and accurately.

✔ Expert Tip

Correct answers must be consistent with a passage's overall style.

Test Day Directions and Format

The directions on the English Test illustrate why there's an advantage to knowing them beforehand—they're long and complicated, and if you learn them now, then on Test Day, you'll already be racking up points while everyone else is reading the directions. The directions will look like this:

DIRECTIONS: In the five passages that follow, certain words and phrases are underlined and numbered. In the right-hand column, you will find alternatives for the underlined parts. In most cases, you are to choose the one that best expresses the idea, makes the statement appropriate for standard written English, or is worded most consistently with the style and tone of the passage as a whole. If you think the original version is best, choose NO CHANGE. In some cases, you will find in the right-hand column a question about the underlined part. You are to choose the best answer to the question.

You will also find questions about a section of the passage or about the passage as a whole. These questions do not refer to an underlined portion of the passage, but rather are identified by a number or numbers in a box.

For each question, choose the alternative you consider best and fill in the corresponding oval on your answer grid. Read each passage through once before you answer the questions that accompany it. For many questions, you must read several sentences beyond the underlined portion to determine the answer. Be sure that you have read enough ahead each time you answer a question.

Question Types

Most ACT English questions consist of underlined words, phrases, or sentences that are embedded within the passage itself. These questions follow the order of the passage and ask you to choose which answer choice best replaces the underlined portion (or to select "NO CHANGE"). Some questions within the passage will contain a question stem, which will correspond to either an underlined segment or a numbered box in the passage text. Other questions refer to the passage as a whole. These questions appear at the end of the passage after a box with the instructions, "Questions # and # ask about the preceding passage as a whole."

Outside Knowledge

The ACT English Test thoroughly covers rules from a variety of common English topics, mostly from courses students typically complete by the end of the 11th grade. The needed English "facts" are addressed in the introductory content for each of the English chapters in this book.

The Inside Scoop

The ACT is designed to test your understanding of the conventions of written English—including punctuation, usage, and sentence structure—and of general rhetorical skills. Rhetorical skills test more strategic concepts, like organizing the text and making sure it's consistently styled and concise.

The questions *do not* get harder as you proceed through the test.

Timing

Plan to spend 9 minutes on each passage. That way, when time is called, you should have looked at all 75 English questions and made sure you have gridded in at least a guess for every question.

Have an organized approach. Because of the passage-based format, we recommend that you *do not* skip around in the English Test. Move straight from beginning to end, answering all of the questions as you go. Unlike some sections, in English you'll usually have at least a sense of what the right answer should be rather quickly. Remember, though, that even the correct answer will start to sound wrong if you think about it too much!

Pay attention to the five minute warning. If you have no time left to even read the last few questions, choose the shortest answer for each one. Remember that "DELETE the underlined portion," when it appears, counts as the shortest answer. For questions not based on clarity, pick a "Letter of the Day" and just use that. No choice is more likely than any other, so pick one letter and use it for all questions you can't work on.

Scoring

You will receive an English subject score—from 1 to 36—for the entire English Test. This score will be averaged into your ACT Composite Score, equally weighted with your scores on the other three multiple-choice tests. You will also receive three other scores for the English Test based on specific knowledge and concepts. These are called reporting categories and consist of:

- Conventions of Standard English
- Production of Writing
- Knowledge of Language

QUICK TIPS

Mind-Set

- **When in doubt, take it out.** Make sure that everything is written as concisely as possible. If you think something doesn't belong in a sentence, it probably doesn't, so choose an answer that leaves it out. Between two grammatically correct and relevant choices, the shorter (more concise) one will always be right. Not just better—*right*.
- **Make sure it makes sense.** When switching phrases in and out, it's easy to correct grammar but lose logic. Consider sentence formation, making sure that sentences are complete, not fragments, and that ideas relate logically. For an answer to be correct in ACT English, it must create a sentence that is both logically *and* grammatically correct.
- **Trust your eyes and ears.** Mistakes in grammar often look or sound wrong—trust that instinct. Don't choose the answer that "sounds fancy." Choose the one that is *right*.

Special Strategies: If You Get Stuck . . .

A few questions will require you to rearrange the words in a sentence, the sentences in a paragraph, or even the paragraphs in a passage. Others may ask questions about the meaning of all or part of the passage or about its structure. Your approach to these questions should include three steps:

1. **Determine your task.** What are you being asked to do?
2. **Consider the passage as a whole.** Read the sentences around the numbered question to get the big picture; you need to know the points made there. Most passages will have a well-defined theme, laid out in a logical way, so choose the answer that expresses the arrangement of elements that best continues the "flow" of the passage.
3. **Predict your answer.** As you'll see again in the Reading Test, making a prediction will give you an idea of what the answer is before you look at the choices. It can be difficult to predict the exact answer to an English question, but knowing what to generally look for will keep you focused as you find the correct answer.

SMARTPOINTS BREAKDOWN

By studying the information released by the ACT, Kaplan has been able to determine how often certain topics are likely to show up on the test and, therefore, how many points, in general, these topics are worth on Test Day. If you master a given topic, you can expect to earn the corresponding number of SmartPoints on Test Day.

Here is a brief overview of what exactly to expect and how much of it you should be expecting.

Conventions of Standard English—19 Points

Conventions of Standard English questions make up 51–56% of the English Test. The questions in this category require an understanding of English grammar, usage, and mechanics. You will need to be able to identify errors, revise, and edit text.

Sentence Structure and Formation—8 Points

The test will require you to identify improper sentence structure and formation in a text. You'll need to make revisions to improve the text. Some concepts you will be tested on include, but are not limited to:

- Run-on sentences and fragments
- Misplaced modifiers
- Inappropriate grammatical shifts in the construction of verb and pronoun phrases

Punctuation—5 Points

The test will present common problems with standard English punctuation and require you to make revisions to improve the writing. Some concepts you will be tested on include, but are not limited to:

- Inappropriate use of punctuation within sentences
- Unnecessary punctuation
- Inappropriate use of possessive nouns and pronouns

Usage—6 Points

The test will present common problems with standard English usage and require you to make revisions to improve the writing. Some concepts you will be tested on include, but are not limited to:

- Errors in agreement between subject and verb, between pronoun and antecedent, and between modifiers and the word modified
- Errors in verb tense, pronoun case, and comparative and superlative modifiers
- Frequently misused words and idioms

Production of Writing—11 Points

Production of Writing questions make up 29–32% of the English Test. The questions in this category require an understanding of the purpose and focus of a piece of writing. You will need to be able to identify errors as well as to revise and edit text.

Organization, Unity, and Cohesion—5 Points

The test will require you to use various strategies to ensure that a text is logically organized, flows smoothly, and has an effective introduction and conclusion. Some concepts you will be tested on include, but are not limited to:

- Logical order of a text's information and ideas within each paragraph
- Logical order of a text's information and ideas within the passage as a whole
- Transition words, phrases, or sentences used to introduce, conclude, or connect information and ideas

Topic Development—6 Points

The test will require you to demonstrate an understanding of, and control over, the rhetorical aspects of texts. You'll need to identify the purposes and parts of texts, determine whether a text or part of text has met its intended goal, and evaluate the relevance of materials in terms of a text's focus. Some concepts you will be tested on include, but are not limited to:

- The effect of adding, revising, or deleting information within a passage
- Appropriate phrasing in relation to a passage's purpose, unity, or focus
- The purpose of an English passage, including whether the text accomplishes this purpose

Knowledge of Language—6 Points

Knowledge of Language questions make up 13–19% of the English Test. The questions in this category require you to demonstrate effective language use through ensuring precision and concision in word choice and through maintaining a consistent tone. You will need to be able to identify errors as well as to revise and edit text. Some concepts you will be tested on include, but are not limited to:

- Elements in a passage that are wordy, redundant, or not relevant to a passage's topic and purpose
- Exactness or content appropriateness of word choice
- Consistency of style and tone with a passage's purpose

CHAPTER TWO

Sentence Structure and Formation

GETTING STARTED

Sentence Structure and **Formation** questions assess your ability to construct correct sentences and to recognize poorly structured sentences. Study the question types below to learn how to approach them and the concepts that these questions test. Knowing the information that you'll need to answer the questions helps you identify the important clues in the passage that will lead you to the correct answers.

Fragments and Run-Ons

Run-ons and fragments create grammatically incorrect sentences. The ACT requires that you know the specific rules governing sentence construction.

Fragments

A complete sentence must have a subject and a predicate verb in an independent clause that expresses a complete thought. If any one of these elements is missing, the sentence is a fragment. You can recognize a fragment because the sentence does not make sense as written.

Missing Element	Example
Subject	*Running down the street.*
Predicate verb	*Seth running down the street.*
Complete thought	*While Seth was running down the street.*

Run-Ons

If a sentence has more than one independent clause, the clauses must be properly joined. Otherwise, the sentence is a run-on. There are three ways to correct a run-on such as *I recently learned how to cook a few basic dinners, I plan to try more difficult recipes soon.*

To Correct a Run-On	Example
Use a semicolon	*I recently learned how to cook a few basic dinners; I plan to try more difficult recipes soon.*
Make one clause dependent	*Because I recently learned how to cook a few basic dinners, I plan to try more difficult recipes soon.*
Add a FANBOYS conjunction: For, And, Nor, But, Or, Yet, So	*I recently learned how to cook a few basic dinners, and I plan to try more difficult recipes soon.*

✔ **Expert Tip**

A comma within or near the underlined segment is a clue that the sentence may be a run-on.

Parallelism

Parallelism questions on the ACT test your ability to revise sentences to create parallel structure. Items in a series, list, or compound must be parallel in form. Series, lists, and compounds may contain nouns, adjectives, adverbs, or verb forms.

Check for parallelism if the sentence contains:

Feature	Example	Parallel Form
A list	*Chloe **formulated** a question, **conducted** background research, and **constructed** a hypothesis before starting the experiment.*	3 verb phrases
A compound	***Hunting** and **fishing** were essential to the survival of Midwestern Native American tribes such as the Omaha.*	2 gerund verb forms
A correlative	*Kaylee remembered **to hydrate** and **to stretch** before the lacrosse game started.*	2 infinitive verb forms
A comparison	*Garrett enjoys a short **sprint** as much as a long-distance **run**.*	2 nouns
Related nouns	***Students** who review their practice **tests** are more likely to earn high **scores** on Test Day.*	3 related plural nouns

✔ **Expert Tip**

The noun closest to the verb may not be the subject of the sentence. Mentally "strip out" the modifiers between the subject and the verb when checking the person and number of the verb.

K

Modifiers

A modifier is a word or a group of words that describes, clarifies, or provides additional information about another part of the sentence. Modifier questions on the ACT require you to identify the part of a sentence being modified and use the appropriate modifier in the proper place. In many cases, an introductory phrase or clause will modify the first noun that follows. Use context clues in the passage to identify the correct placement of a modifier; a misplaced modifier can cause confusion.

Modifier/ Modifying Phrase	Incorrect	Correct
nearly	Andre **nearly** watched the play for four hours.	Andre watched the play for **nearly** four hours.
in individual containers	The art teacher handed out paints to students **in individual containers**.	The art teacher handed out paints **in individual containers** to students.
A scholar athlete	**A scholar athlete**, maintaining high grades in addition to playing soccer were expected of Maya.	**A scholar athlete**, Maya was expected to maintain high grades in addition to playing soccer.

> ✔ *Note*
>
> Verbs must be modified by adverbs. Adverbs usually end in *-ly*. It has become common usage to modify verbs with adjectives, but this is incorrect on the ACT. Use *"He drives slowly,"* not *"He drives slow."*

Shifts in Verb Tense and Pronoun Case

On the ACT English Test, you will be asked to identify and replace unnecessary shifts in verb tense and pronoun case. Because these shifts may occur within a single sentence or among multiple sentences, you will need to read around the underlined portion to identify the error. The underlined segment must logically match the other parts of the sentence as well as the passage as a whole.

Shifts in Verb Tense

Verb tense places the action or state of being described by the verb into a place in time: present, past, or future. Each tense has three forms: simple, progressive, and perfect.

Form	Past	Present	Future
Simple: Actions that simply occur at some point in time	*Connor* ***planted*** *vegetables in the community garden.*	*Connor* ***plants*** *vegetables in the community garden.*	*Connor* ***will plant*** *vegetables in the community garden.*
Progressive: Actions that are ongoing at some point in time	*Connor* ***was planting*** *vegetables in the community garden this morning before noon.*	*Connor* ***is planting*** *vegetables in the community garden this morning before noon.*	*Connor* ***will be planting*** *vegetables in the community garden this morning before noon.*
Perfect: Actions that are completed at some point in time	*Connor* ***had planted*** *vegetables in the community garden every year until he gave his job to Jasmine.*	*Connor* ***has planted*** *vegetables in the community garden since it started five years ago.*	*Connor* ***will have planted*** *vegetables in the community garden by the time the growing season starts.*

Shifts in Pronoun Case

Pronouns replace nouns in sentences. A pronoun must agree with the noun it is replacing in person and number. The ACT will test your ability to recognize and correct inappropriate shifts in pronoun usage.

> ✔ **Note**
>
> Do not shift between "you" and "one" unnecessarily. "You" refers to a specific person or group. "One" refers to an indefinite individual or group.

Person	Refers to	Singular Pronouns	Piural Pronouns
First person	the person speaking	*I, me, my*	*we, us, our*
Second person	the person spoken to	*you, your*	*you, your*
Third person	the person or thing spoken about	*he, she, it, him, her, his, hers, its*	*they, them, theirs*
Indefinite	a nonspecific person or group	*anybody, anyone, each, either, everyone, someone, one*	*both, few, many, several*

IMPROVING WITH PRACTICE

Step 1: Read Until You Can Identify the Issue

Always read the entire English passage, though you don't need to read slowly enough to remember all of the subject matter. This is particularly important for **Sentence Structure and Formation** questions because the best clues for the correct answers may be before or after the underlined segment or the numbered box.

Within the underlined segment, check for the following issues:

- If a verb is underlined, check the subject. Then check the tense of a nearby non-underlined verb in that same paragraph.
- If a pronoun is underlined, check the noun immediately preceding it.
- If a comma is underlined, check if there are independent clauses before and after it. If so, the sentence is a run-on and must be corrected.
- If a comma is underlined, check if the information preceding the comma is a modifying phrase. If so, the first noun following the comma must be what the modifier describes.
- If a modifier is underlined, check to be sure the modifier is as close as possible to the word it is modifying.

If you're not sure there's an issue, keep reading and then return to the question.

> ✔ *Expert Tip*
>
> **The best clue for the correct answer is frequently found either before or after the underlined segment. A non-underlined verb sets the tense for the entire sentence and/or paragraph, depending on the context, and a non-underlined antecedent determines the correct pronoun.**

Step 2: Answer the Questions

As you're practicing, refer back to the tips in the "Getting Started" section and answer questions one at a time, reviewing the Answer and Explanation for every question immediately after completing it. If you got the question correct, congratulate yourself, but take a moment to read the entire explanation to be sure you got the question right for the right reason. The explanation may even point out a more efficient way that you can use on a later question!

Step 3: Review Incorrect Answers

If you get the question incorrect . . . still congratulate yourself! You're about to learn something new that you'll be able to use to improve your performance on Test Day. Don't read the explanation yet; instead, try the question again.

If you get the question correct the second time, read the explanation to see if you solved the question in the most efficient way. Identify the mistake you made the first time, and determine how you're going to avoid making that mistake again.

> ✔ *Expert Tip*
>
> **Many top scoring students have an ACT notebook where they write down what they learn from every question. Doing this can be time-consuming, but it can also help you identify the types of mistakes you tend to make.**

If you get the question incorrect the second time, use the explanation to learn how to get the question correct. Work through the question again while following the explanation, and identify the steps you will need to take to get a similar question correct. Although the passages and questions will change, the concepts being tested will not. When you encounter unfamiliar questions, take note of them for future study sessions.

> ✔ *Note*
>
> **The ACT is a standardized test. While high-difficulty English questions are usually more diffi-cult to answer than low- or medium-difficulty questions, they are often similar in structure and purpose, and the same skills (listed in Chapter 1) are tested on every English Test. You actually can predict the types of questions you will see on Test Day!**

After all that work, it's time to move to the next question. Reviewing in this way will take time. However, improvement doesn't come from just doing lots and lots of questions; it comes from thinking through your approach and improving it with every question.

RAISING YOUR SCORE EVEN MORE

Here is one of the "secrets" to conquering the English Test: Because the ACT is a standardized test, there will always be clues that make one choice definitely correct and the other choices completely incorrect. It's never a matter of opinion.

The most important clues for **Sentence Structure** and **Formation** questions are listed in the "Improving With Practice" section above. To raise your score even more, look for:

- semicolons, since a non-underlined semicolon preceding an underlined segment means there must be an independent clause. However, keep in mind that an under-lined semicolon will often indicate a **Punctuation** question; these question types are covered in the next chapter.
- comparison keywords such as "than" or "as." Comparisons require parallel structure.
- modifiers. Carefully analyze every modifier. Modification errors are easy to miss be-cause your brain can figure out the meaning of the sentence, but on the ACT, the modifier must be placed as close as possible to the word it is modifying. For exam-ple, under "Getting Started" above, you knew it was the paints in the containers, but grammatically, the students were in the containers! The ACT requires precision, so look carefully for these types of errors.

PRACTICE QUESTIONS

The following test-like question sets provide an opportunity to practice reading Sentence Structure and Formation questions. While many of the questions pertain to Sentence Structure and Formation, some touch on other concepts tested on the English Test to ensure that your practice is test-like, with a variety of question types per passage.

PASSAGE I

The Right to Write

[1]

Going to see a play is a cultural tradition that has been passed on for thousands of years. Although theater is a form of art and entertainment, it is also a highly competitive business, especially for playwrights. Many plays are written, but it is only a select few are produced and seen by the public, and often with strings attached. Playwright José Rivera

is an example of a contemporary playwright that has fought for the right to have his work produced and seen in the way he intended it.

1. A. NO CHANGE
    B. there are only
    C. only
    D. there only is

2. F. NO CHANGE
    G. who
    H. which
    J. whom

[2]

Rivera was born in San Juan, Puerto Rico, in 1955, but his family moved to New York when he was four years old. Yet many of Rivera's relatives had already moved to the Bronx, a bustling neighborhood in New York, Rivera's father wanted to live in a place that felt more like a small town. So they moved to a quarter acre of land in Long Island, New York, which at the time had dirt roads and woods.

3. A. NO CHANGE
    B. Meanwhile,
    C. However,
    D. Although

[3]

From an early age, Rivera knew that he wanted to be a writer. As a kid, he wrote comic strips, a novel about baseball, and essays in response to <u>photographs, from</u> *Life* magazine. When he was in
4
middle school, he saw a play that inspired him

<u>when he saw the play that he wanted</u> to become a
5
playwright. He <u>writes</u> several plays during high
6
school and in college.

[4]

<u>Rivera, after graduating, returned to New York,</u>
7
<u>from college</u> determined to continue writing. He
7

worked at a bookstore and became <u>then</u> a copy
8
editor at a publishing company. Eventually, Rivera found an artistic home in a playwriting group called the Theater Matrix; the group met on Monday nights to share their work. One of <u>them</u>
9
he wrote and produced, *The House of Roman Iglesia*, received a good review by *The New York Times*. This

4. **F.** NO CHANGE
   G. photographs from
   H. photographs from:
   J. photographs; from

5. **A.** NO CHANGE
   B. that when he saw the play he wanted
   C. that he wanted when he saw that play
   D. DELETE the underlined portion.

6. **F.** NO CHANGE
   G. is writing
   H. has written
   J. wrote

7. **A.** NO CHANGE
   B. Rivera returned from college after graduating, to New York,
   C. After graduating from college, Rivera returned to New York,
   D. Rivera, from graduating, returned to New York,

8. **F.** NO CHANGE
   G. (Place before *became*)
   H. (Place before *publishing*)
   J. (Place after *company*)

9. **A.** NO CHANGE
   B. those
   C. the work
   D. the plays

was an important step in Rivera's <u>career receiving</u> a

₁₀

good review from a major publication led to more

work. The famous television producer Norman

Lear read the review and immediately offered

Rivera a job writing for Embassy Television in

California.

[5]

In order to make a living, Rivera accepted the

job. He learned a lot from the process of writing

for television shows, but there were sacrifices he

had to make. He missed writing plays and living

in New York. ⑪ Rivera also discovered that in the

entertainment business, he was often labeled and

identified by his ethnicity. Rivera was proud of his

cultural heritage but wanted to be acknowledged

for his talent.

[6]

After many years of hard work and perseverance,

Rivera has received the recognition he deserves

through countless productions of his plays and

the numerous awards he has won for playwriting.

Despite the challenges of show business, José Rivera

<u>has became</u> an important playwright whose work

₁₂

has an impact on audiences worldwide.

10. **F.** NO CHANGE

   G. career, receiving

   H. career; receiving

   J. career receiving.

11. If the writer wanted to reinforce the main point made in Paragraph 5, which sentence would she add here?

   A. He also missed the reward of owning his work, because his writing became the property of the television shows.

   B. California is a beautiful state with a variety of places to visit, from beaches to major cities.

   C. He had the opportunity to write for television shows such as *Family Matters* and *Eerie, Indiana*.

   D. While in California, he became a founding member of a theater company in the city of Los Angeles.

12. **F.** NO CHANGE

   G. is became

   H. has become

   J. have become

Questions 13–15 ask about the preceding passage as a whole.

13. The most logical placement of Paragraph 3 is
   A. where it is now.
   B. after Paragraph 1.
   C. after Paragraph 4.
   D. after Paragraph 5.

14. The writer is considering adding the following sentence:

   The contrast between small-town and city life became an influence on Rivera's work.

   The best placement for this detail is in:
   F. Paragraph 1.
   G. Paragraph 2.
   H. Paragraph 5.
   J. Paragraph 6.

15. Does this essay successfully describe the challenges faced by playwrights in the entertainment business?
   A. The essay is not successful; it is a neutral biography of the playwright José Rivera.
   B. The essay is not successful; it portrays playwriting as a fun and rewarding career.
   C. The essay is successful; it describes playwriting as an impossible dream for only the very lucky.
   D. The essay is successful; it demonstrates the challenges through the life and work of José Rivera.

PASSAGE II

The Dream of the American West

As the sun <u>was slowly rising</u> over the Atlantic
Ocean and painted New York harbor a spectacular
fiery orange, I started my old Toyota's engine. At
this early hour, there was still some semblance of
the night's tranquility left on the city sidewalks,
but I knew that, as the minutes ticked by,
<u>the streets would flood with humanity.</u> I smiled

<u>with</u> the thought that soon all the wonderful chaos
of New York City would be disappearing behind

me as I <u>embarked on my trip to the other side of</u>
the country.

16.
F. NO CHANGE
G. rising slowly
H. rose slowly
J. continued to rise

17. The author wants to contrast the statement about the quiet of the night streets with a related detail about the daytime activity. Assuming that all of the choices are true, which of the following best accomplishes that goal?
A. NO CHANGE
B. some people might appear.
C. everything would be different.
D. the tranquility would be unbroken.

18.
F. NO CHANGE
G. along with
H. at
J. all because of

19.
A. NO CHANGE
B. embarked on this journey across
C. traveled to the other side of
D. traveled across

As the morning sun climbed into the sky,
20

I shuddered with excitement to think that my final
21
stop would be in California, where the sun itself
21
ends its journey across America. Like the sun,
21
however, I still had quite a journey before me.

I had been planning this road trip across the United States for as long as I could remember. In my life, I had been fortunate enough to see some of the most beautiful countries in the world. However, it had always bothered me that although I'd stood in the shadow of the Eiffel Tower, mar-
22
veled in the desert heat at the Pyramids of Giza,
22
I'd never seen any of the wonders of my own country, except those found in my hometown of New York City. All of that was about to change.

As I left the city, the tall buildings began to
23
give way to smaller ones, then to transform into
23
the quaint rows of houses that clustered the
23
crowded suburbs. Trees and grass, then the yellow-
23
green of cornfields and the golden wash of wheat

20. Which of the following alternatives to the underlined portion would NOT be acceptable?

   F. At sunrise,

   G. Watching the morning sun climb into the sky,

   H. The morning sun climbed into the sky,

   J. As the sun rose,

21. The writer is considering revising this sentence by deleting the underlined portion. If she did so, the paragraph would primarily lose:

   A. information about the reasons for the writer's trip.

   B. information about the writer's destination.

   C. a description of the writer's planned route.

   D. a comparison between the sunrise in New York and the sunset in California.

22. **F.** NO CHANGE

   G. Eiffel Tower and had marveled in the desert heat at the Pyramids of Giza,

   H. Eiffel Tower and marveled in the desert heat at the Pyramids of Giza

   J. Eiffel Tower, and had marveled, in the desert heat, at the Pyramids of Giza

23. Given that all are true, which of the following provides the most effective transition between the third paragraph and the description of the Midwest in the fourth paragraph?

   A. NO CHANGE

   B. In fact, there were changes on the horizon almost immediately.

   C. My excitement hadn't diminished.

   D. I realized that people who lived in other areas might feel the same way about visiting New York.

were slowly replacing the familiar mazes of cement
24
and steel. My world no longer stretched vertically
24

24. Assuming that all are true, which of the following provides information most relevant to the main focus of the paragraph?

F. NO CHANGE

G. appearing before me.

H. racing past my window.

J. becoming monotonous.

toward the sky, it now spread horizontally toward
25
eternity. For two days, I pushed through the wind-whipped farmlands of Mid-America, hypnotized by the beauty of the undulating yet unbroken lines. At night, the breeze from my car would stir the wheat fields to dance beneath the moon, and the silos hid in the shadows, quietly imposing their simply serenity upon everything.
26

25. A. NO CHANGE

B. the sky but it now spread

C. the sky; it now spread

D. the sky spreading

26. F. NO CHANGE

G. simple

H. simplest

J. simpler

Then, as the night's shadows gave way to
27
light, there seemed to be a great force rising to

27. A. NO CHANGE

B. nights shadows

C. shadows from the night

D. night shadow

meet the sun as it made its reappearance.
28

28. F. NO CHANGE

G. sun as it reappeared

H. reappearing sun

J. sun as it was also rising

Still, I had no idea what I was looking at. Then,
29

29. A. NO CHANGE

B. Even so,

C. At first,

D. Eventually,

there was no <u>mistaking it.</u> The unbroken lines of
₃₀
Mid-America had given way to the jagged and
majestic heights of the Rockies and the gateway to
the American West.

PASSAGE III

My Cousin Nicola

My father and his two younger brothers
emigrated from Italy to New York in the early
1970s. Only their older sister Lucia, <u>which</u> was
₃₁
already married, remained behind in their small

home <u>town, this village</u> lies in the shadow of
₃₂
Mount Vesuvius. Growing up in America, my
cousins and I were as close as brothers and sisters,

but we hardly <u>known</u> our family across the Atlantic.
₃₃
When I was a young child, my parents and I went
to Italy to visit Aunt Lucia and her family for a

week. I first met my cousin <u>Nicola however,</u> I
₃₄
remember that we were not only about the same

age, <u>and</u> we also got along well. But because
₃₅

30. F. NO CHANGE
    G. mistake to be made.
    H. chance to mistake it.
    J. having made a mistake.

31. A. NO CHANGE
    B. whom
    C. who
    D. she who

32. F. NO CHANGE
    G. town, it can be seen where it
    H. town it
    J. town that

33. A. NO CHANGE
    B. knew
    C. had knew
    D. been known

34. F. NO CHANGE
    G. Nicola, so then
    H. Nicola because
    J. Nicola then.

35. A. NO CHANGE
    B. so
    C. but
    D. then

<u>I being</u> so young, I remember little else. I hadn't
seen him again up until this last summer.

Nicola decided that he wanted to join the
Italian Air Force after finishing high school. Before
beginning his service, though, he wanted to travel
for a bit. <u>He had never been to America, even
though so many of his relatives live here, but he
had been to England already.</u> When the rest of the

cousins heard the news, they were <u>ecstatic</u>. Most of

them had never met Nicola or, like me, <u>hadn't seen
him, since we were kids;</u> they were eager to get to
know him.

Two weeks later, we picked Nicola up at JFK
Airport. Right away, I was surprised by his height.
I am the tallest of all the cousins in America, and
Nicola was easily a couple of inches taller than me.

36. **F.** NO CHANGE
    G. I, who was
    H. I was
    J. I,

37. Assuming that each choice is true, which one
    provides the most relevant information about
    Nicola's travel plans?
    A. NO CHANGE
    B. He had never been to America, so he
    called my father and asked if he could
    come spend the summer with us in
    New York.
    C. He had never been to America, which is
    most easily reached from Italy by plane.
    D. Because it was expensive for his whole
    family to travel overseas, Nicola had
    never been to America before.

38. Three of these choices indicate that the
    cousins looked forward to meeting Nicola.
    Which choice does NOT do so?
    F. NO CHANGE
    G. excited
    H. apprehensive
    J. thrilled

39. **A.** NO CHANGE
    B. hadn't seen him since we were kids
    C. hadn't seen him since we were kids;
    D. hadn't seen, him since we were kids,

In addition to our height, he and I had another similarity: we were both musicians. The moment I saw the acoustic guitar slung over his shoulder, I knew he and I would get along just fine. None of them plays an instrument, and I always thought
₄₀

40. **F.** NO CHANGE
    G. us
    H. the Americans
    J. my American cousins

that I was the only musician in the family (even
₄₁
though some relatives have lovely singing voices).
₄₁
I was happy to find out I was wrong.

    Throughout that summer, Nicola and I shared the gift of music. We would sing and play our guitars long into the night, only stopping when my mother came downstairs and forced us to quit. We liked many of the same bands, and we taught each other to play our favorite songs. Taught to him as a
₄₂
child before she passed away in Italy, I was taught
₄₂
by him the Italian folk songs of our grandmother
₄₂
more importantly.
₄₂
    It was through those songs that I truly connected to the beauty of our ancestry. On the night before Nicola returned to Italy, my father

would have thrown a big party for all of the relatives.
₄₃

41. **A.** NO CHANGE
    B. in the family, which has at least 20 members that I know of.
    C. in the family.
    D. DELETE the underlined portion (ending the sentence with a period).

42. **F.** NO CHANGE
    G. Teaching him as a child before she passed away, our grandmother in Italy more importantly taught to me many of the Italian folk songs.
    H. Teaching him as a child, more importantly, by our grandmother in Italy, I was taught by him many Italian folk songs.
    J. More importantly, however, he taught me many of the Italian folk songs our grandmother in Italy had taught him as a child before she passed away.

43. **A.** NO CHANGE
    B. will have thrown
    C. threw
    D. throws

Nicola and I played the folk songs of <u>our grandmothers</u> country for the American side of our family. When we were done, my Uncle Vittorio had a tear in his eye. Since coming to America so long ago, he had never been able to return to Italy. In the music and our singing, Nicola and I brought the beautiful country back to Uncle Vittorio.

44. **F.** NO CHANGE
    G. our grandmother's
    H. our grandmothers'
    J. are grandmother's

Question 45 asks about the preceding passage as a whole.

45. Suppose the writer's goal had been to write a personal narrative that emphasizes the value of family. Would this passage accomplish this purpose?

    A. Yes, because it shows how connecting with distant family can be meaningful.
    B. Yes, because it shows how much closer the narrator is to Nicola than to his American cousins.
    C. No, because the narrator and Nicola are not closely related.
    D. No, because the passage does not mention any family members besides Nicola.

ANSWERS AND EXPLANATIONS

The Right to Write

1. C   Difficulty: Medium

Category: Sentence Structure and Formation

Getting to the Answer: Be aware of phrases like *it is only*, because they add no real meaning to the sentence and provide no clear antecedent for the pronoun. *It is only* is unnecessary here. Choice (C) eliminates the unnecessary language and makes the second clause subordinate. Choices B and D both use incorrect grammatical structure.

2. G   Difficulty: Medium

Category: Usage

Getting to the Answer: Use *who* or *whom* to refer to a person. The underlined word refers to José Rivera; the correct pronoun is *who*, because José Rivera is a person. Choice (G) is correct. *Which*, in H, is incorrect when used to refer to a person. Choice J uses the objective case *whom*; you wouldn't say "him has fought for the right," so "whom has fought for the right" is incorrect.

3. D   Difficulty: Medium

Category: Transitions

Getting to the Answer: Remember to read for logic, as well as grammar and usage. This sentence inappropriately uses the coordinating conjunction *Yet*. *Although*, a subordinating conjunction that introduces subordinate clauses, is the best choice here. Choice (D) is correct. Choice B is inappropriate for the context. Choice C cannot be used as a conjunction.

4. G   Difficulty: Low

Category: Punctuation

Getting to the Answer: A comma should not be inserted between a preposition and its object. The concluding conjunction *and* completed the list of the different things Rivera wrote. The direct object, *photographs*, and the indirect object, Life *magazine*, are part of one thought. Choice (G) is the correct answer. Choice H uses a colon, which is only correct when it follows an independent clause in order to introduce some information. Choice J uses a semicolon, which is only correct when used to connect two independent clauses.

5. D   Difficulty: Low

Category: Concision

Getting to the Answer: When DELETE is an option, read the underlined selection for relevance. Eliminate answer choices that contain redundant language. It is redundant to use "he saw a play" and "when he saw the play" together; (D) eliminates the redundancy. Choices A, B, and C all contain redundant language.

6. J   Difficulty: Low

Category: Sentence Structure and Formation

Getting to the Answer: When a verb is underlined, check to see if the tense is correct. The simple present tense, *writes*, is used in this sentence to describe an event that happened in the past. The correct tense here is the simple past tense, *wrote*, as in (J). Choice G uses the present continuous tense, and H uses the present perfect tense, but the sentence describes something that happened in the past.

7. C   Difficulty: High

Category: Sentence Structure and Formation

Getting to the Answer: Remember to read for logic, as well as grammar and usage. In the underlined portion, the subject and predicate are split by misplaced prepositional phrases. The subject is *Rivera*, and the predicate is "returned to New York determined to continue writing." The prepositional phrase, "After graduating from college," modifies the action. Choice (C) is the correct answer. Choices B and D both contain misplaced modifiers.

8. G   Difficulty: Low

Category: Sentence Structure and Formation

Getting to the Answer: When you need to consider moving information, read it into the passage at the suggested points to determine its logical placement. *Then* modifies *became*, so (G) is the correct answer. Choice F is awkward, and H and J are illogical.

9. D   Difficulty: Medium

Category: Ambiguity

Getting to the Answer: A pronoun must clearly refer to its antecedent. In A, it is unclear to whom or what *them* refers. The last plural entity was the group of people, but that does not make sense in the context. Choice B is unclear for the same reasons. While C and (D) both clearly refer to Rivera's writing, it makes more sense to refer to "one of the plays" than "one of the work," because *work* is singular. Choice (D) is correct.

10. H   Difficulty: Medium

Category: Punctuation

Getting to the Answer: When the only difference in the answer choices is punctuation, remember your tested rules. A semicolon is used to join independent clauses closely related in meaning. Choice (H) is the correct answer. Choice G is incorrect because a comma cannot join two independent clauses without a conjunction. Choice J is incorrect because the period is placed in the middle of the predicate.

11. A   Difficulty: Medium

Category: Supporting Material

Getting to the Answer: Read question stems and the paragraph that is being added to carefully. Often, all four answer choices to Supporting Material questions will be somewhat relevant to the passage, but only one will fulfill the specific requirements of the question. The question asks for a detail that supports Paragraph 5, which is about the sacrifices

Rivera had to make to be a writer. Choice (A) is the only answer choice that supports this idea. Choices B and C are incorrect because they are off topic and do not support the main idea. Choice D is incorrect because it describes the writing he did for television as an opportunity, which is a positive change.

12. H   Difficulty: Medium

Category: Sentence Structure and Formation

Getting to the Answer: When a verb is underlined, check to see if the tense is correct. The correct tense here is the past continuous tense, *has become*, as in (H). *Has became* is an incorrect construction, making F incorrect. Choice G uses *is*, which cannot be used with *became*. Choice J uses the past continuous tense, but José Rivera is singular, not plural as *have* would imply.

13. A   Difficulty: Medium

Category: Passage Organization

Getting to the Answer: When you need to consider moving information, first read it to determine the main idea. Then consider the context of this information in the essay as a whole to determine its logical placement. The paragraph describes the early years in Rivera's schooling when he discovered he wanted to be a writer. In the essay as a whole, this information is in the right sequence; the paragraph before describes his childhood and the paragraph after describes his employment as an adult. Choice (A) is the correct answer. Choices B, C, and D would place the information out of sequence.

14. G   Difficulty: Medium

Category: Passage Organization

Getting to the Answer: The first sentence of a paragraph typically introduces the topic of the paragraph, so look for the paragraph that contains details related to the sentence in question. Paragraph 2 describes Rivera's upbringing and contrasts the "bustling neighborhood of the Bronx" with the "dirt roads and woods" of Long Island. Choice (G) is the correct answer. Choices F, H, and J can be eliminated because the detail does not support the main idea of any of these paragraphs.

15. D Difficulty: Medium

Category: Writer's Purpose

Getting to the Answer: By determining the main idea of the passage, you can quickly eliminate two answer choices. The main idea of the essay is that being a playwright is challenging, but there are people like José Rivera who have succeeded despite the odds. Choice (D) is the correct answer. Choice A is incorrect because the essay is persuasive, not merely biographical. Choice B is incorrect because it conveys the opposite of what the passage is arguing. Choice C is too extreme; the passage portrays playwriting as challenging, but not impossible.

The Dream of the American West

16. H Difficulty: Medium

Category: Sentence Structure and Formation

Getting to the Answer: Verbs in a compound should be in the same tense. The compound verb in this clause is "was . . . rising . . . and painted." Since the second verb is in the past tense, the first should be as well, so F is incorrect; (H) is correct. Choice G uses the gerund verb form without the necessary helping verb. Choice J is unnecessarily wordy.

17. A Difficulty: Medium

Category: Writer's Purpose

Getting to the Answer: Read English Test question stems carefully. Often, all of the choices will be relevant and grammatically correct, but only one will fulfill the requirements of the stem. This question stem asks for a detail that shows a contrast between the quiet night streets and the daytime activity. The original text does this best. The verb in B does not convey the difference in the streets at these two times as well as *flood* in (A). Choice C is too general. Choice D does not provide the necessary contrast.

18. H Difficulty: Medium

Category: Usage

Getting to the Answer: Use your Kaplan resources to familiarize yourself with commonly tested idioms. Although all four answer choices form idioms that would be correct in some contexts, one smiles *at* someone or something; (H) is correct.

19. D Difficulty: Medium

Category: Concision

Getting to the Answer: When you don't spot an error in grammar or usage, look for errors in style. Choice A is a wordy way of saying *traveled across*, (D). Choices B and C are unnecessarily wordy as well.

20. H Difficulty: Low

Category: Sentence Structure and Formation

Getting to the Answer: Read question stems carefully. This one asks which answer choice would NOT be acceptable, which means that three of the choices will be correct in context. Choices F, G, and J are appropriate introductory clauses, but (H) is an independent clause, which makes the sentence a run-on.

21. B Difficulty: Medium

Category: Supporting Material

Getting to the Answer: Use your Reading skills for questions like this one that ask for the function of a detail. The underlined portion tells us that the writer's journey will end in California. Choice (B) is correct. The underlined selection does not mention the reasons for the writer's trip, describe her route, or make any comparisons, so A, C, and D are incorrect.

22. G Difficulty: Medium

Category: Punctuation

Getting to the Answer: Use commas in a list or series only if there are three or more items. Since the writer only mentions two places she has been, the first comma here is incorrect; eliminate F. Choice (G) corrects this without introducing any additional errors. Choice H eliminates the incorrect comma but removes the one at the end of the selection, which is needed to separate the introductory clause from the rest of the sentence. Choice J does not address the error.

23. A   Difficulty: Medium

Category: Transitions

Getting to the Answer: To identify the most effective transition, you'll need to read both paragraphs. Paragraph 3 is about how the author has traveled to foreign countries but, within the United States, only knows New York City. Paragraph 4 describes her drive through the Midwest. The text as written takes the reader from New York City (tall buildings) to the less populated areas, leading to the description of the cornfields. Choice (A), NO CHANGE, is the correct choice here. Choice B misstates the passage; the cornfields didn't appear *almost immediately*, but gradually. Choices C and D do not provide appropriate transitions between the paragraphs.

24. F   Difficulty: Medium

Category: Supporting Material

Getting to the Answer: When you're asked to identify the *most relevant* choice, use context clues. The paragraph is about the change the author experiences as she drives from New York across the country. That contrast is clear in the passage as written; (F) is the correct choice here. Choices G and H do not relate to the paragraph's topic. Choice J is opposite; the writer describes many different settings, which is the opposite of *monotonous*.

25. C   Difficulty: Medium

Category: Sentence Structure and Formation

Getting to the Answer: There are a number of ways to correct a run-on sentence, but only one answer choice will do so without introducing any additional errors. Each of the clauses in this sentence is independent; (C) corrects the run-on by replacing the comma with a semicolon. Choice B omits the comma necessary with the coordinating conjunction *but*.

Choice D loses the contrast between the clauses that is present in the original.

26. G   Difficulty: Medium

Category: Usage

Getting to the Answer: When a single adverb is underlined, you are most likely being tested on idioms. Determine what is being modified. The underlined portion modifies the noun *serenity*, so it should be an adjective. Eliminate F. Choices H and J compare this serenity to other states of being, but there is no such comparison in the passage. Choice (G) is correct.

27. A   Difficulty: Medium

Category: Punctuation

Getting to the Answer: Only two apostrophe uses are tested on the ACT: possessive nouns and contractions. The noun here is possessive; the apostrophe is used correctly in (A). Choice B uses the plural *nights* instead of the possessive. Choice C is unnecessarily wordy and uses the idiomatically incorrect "shadows from the night." Choice D changes the meaning of the sentence.

28. H   Difficulty: Medium

Category: Concision

Getting to the Answer: If you don't spot a grammar or usage error, check for errors in style. As written, this sentence is unnecessarily wordy, so F is incorrect; (H) provides the best revision. Choices G and J are still unnecessarily wordy.

29. C   Difficulty: Medium

Category: Transitions

Getting to the Answer: When a transition word or clause is underlined, determine the relationship between the ideas being connected. Look at the relationship between the sentences in this paragraph. The ideas are presented chronologically—that is, in the order in which they happened. Choice (C), *At first*, is the best transition into this series of events. Choices A and B imply contradiction or quali-fication, which is incorrect in context. Choice D implies that a lot went on prior to the writer's not having any idea what she was looking at, but this is presented as the first in a series of events.

30. F   Difficulty: High

Category: Sentence Structure and Formation

Getting to the Answer: The correct answer will rarely be longer than the original selection. This question requires no change, so (F) is correct. The pronoun's antecedent appears in the previous sentence ("what I was looking at") and the *-ing* verb form is used correctly. Choices G, H, and J are wordy; addi-tionally, G introduces the passive voice unnecessarily.

My Cousin Nicola

31. C   Difficulty: Medium

Category: Usage

Getting to the Answer: Use *who* or *whom* to refer to a person. The underlined word begins a descrip-tion of Lucia; the correct pronoun is *who*, because Lucia is a person. Choice (C) is correct. *Which*, in A, is incorrect when used to refer to a person. Choice B uses the objective case *whom*; you wouldn't say "*her* was already married," so "*whom* was already married" is incorrect. *She who*, in D, makes the sen-tence unnecessarily wordy and awkward.

32. J   Difficulty: Medium

Category: Sentence Structure and Formation

Getting to the Answer: Independent clauses should either be joined by a semicolon or connected with a coordinating conjunction; otherwise, one of the clauses must be made subordinate. As written, the sentence is a run-on. None of the answer choices offers a semicolon or a comma and a coordinating conjunction, but (J) makes the second clause depen-dent by using *that*. Choices G and H do not address the run-on error.

33. B   Difficulty: Medium

Category: Sentence Structure and Formation

Getting to the Answer: Use context to determine appropriate verb tenses. This sentence uses the simple past tense *were* and doesn't indicate any time shift, so the simple past tense *knew* makes the most sense. Choice (B) is correct. Choice A uses the past participle *known* without the necessary help-ing verb *had*. Choice C incorrectly uses *had knew*; the past participle of *know* is *known*. Choice D uses *been known* without the necessary helping verb *had*; it also creates a sentence that is grammatically incorrect.

34. J   Difficulty: Medium

Category: Transitions

Getting to the Answer: Remember to read for logic, as well as grammar and usage. This sentence inappropriately uses the contrast word *however*. Choice (J) correctly uses *then*, a transition word indi-cating time. Choices G and H use cause-and-effect transitions, which are inappropriate in context.

35. C   Difficulty: Medium

Category: Usage

Getting to the Answer: When an idiomatic con-struction begins with *not only*, it must conclude with *but also*. Only (C) correctly completes the idiom. *And*, A, *so*, B, and *then*, D, all fail to correctly complete the idiom.

36. H   Difficulty: Medium

Category: Sentence Structure and Formation

Getting to the Answer: The *-ing* form can serve several functions; when used as a verb, it requires a helping verb to be correct. *I being* here is grammati-cally incorrect; (H) substitutes the correct verb form *was*. Choice G creates a grammatically incorrect sen-tence, and J omits the verb.

37. B   Difficulty: Medium

Category: Writer's Purpose

Getting to the Answer: With Writer's Purpose questions like this one, you need to identify the choice that matches the purpose stated in the question stem. The question asks you to select the sentence that gives the most relevant information about Nicola's travel plans. Only (B) tells you about Nicola's plans; he intends to spend the summer with his family in New York. Choice A mentions Nicola's trip to England, which is out of scope for the passage. Choice C provides general information about the easiest way to travel from Italy to America, but it doesn't tell you anything about Nicola's specific plans to visit America. Choice D also focuses on the past, explaining why Nicola had not previously come to America; this doesn't match the question stem's call for information about Nicola's travel plans.

38. H   Difficulty: Medium

Category: Precision

Getting to the Answer: Always read question stems carefully; it's easy to miss an important word like NOT or EXCEPT. The question asks for the word that does NOT show that the cousins looked forward to meeting Nicola. The only negatively charged word here is *apprehensive*, which suggests that the cousins feared Nicola's arrival. Choice (H) is correct. Choices F, G, and J all use positively charged words that indicate the cousins were looking forward to Nicola's visit.

39. C   Difficulty: Medium

Category: Punctuation

Getting to the Answer: A phrase set off between commas must be nonessential: that is, the sentence must still make sense without it. As written, this sentence treats the phrase "hadn't seen him" as nonessential, but "like me, since they were kids" does not make sense—this phrase must remain in the sentence. Choice (C) eliminates the incorrect

comma without introducing any additional errors. Choices B and D create run-on sentences; additionally, D incorrectly inserts a comma between a verb and its object.

40. J   Difficulty: High

Category: Ambiguity

Getting to the Answer: When a pronoun is underlined, first determine to what or whom it refers. In this case, the reference is unclear. The last plural noun is *musicians*, but that refers to the narrator and Nicola, who do play instruments. Eliminate F. Choice G clearly refers to the narrator and Nicola, so it should also be eliminated. Choice H is ambiguous: to which Americans does the sentence refer? Choice (J) correctly identifies the group mentioned earlier in the paragraph: the narrator's American cousins.

41. C   Difficulty: Medium

Category: Concision

Getting to the Answer: The shortest answer isn't always correct—D omits a phrase necessary for the sentence to make sense. Choices A and B include information irrelevant to the topic of the writer meeting Nicola. That leaves (C), which eliminates the irrelevant information without losing the logic of the sentence.

42. J   Difficulty: Medium

Category: Sentence Structure and Formation

Getting to the Answer: As a general rule, descriptive phrases modify the nouns that immediately follow them. As written, this sentence tells us that *I* was "Taught to him before she passed away in Italy." Choice (J) is the most concise and logical version of this sentence. Choice G incorrectly indicates that the grandmother, not Nicola, taught the songs to the writer. Choice H gives the introductory phrase no logical noun to modify, making its grammatical structure incorrect.

43. C   Difficulty: Low

Category: Sentence Structure and Formation

Getting to the Answer: A verb is underlined, so start by checking to see if the tense is correct. The simple past tense is used in this paragraph: *shared* and *connected*. The correct tense here is the simple past *threw*, as in (C). Choice A uses the conditional tense "would have thrown," but the sentence describes something the writer's father actually did, not something hypothetical. Choice B uses the future perfect tense, but the sentence describes something that happened in the past, not an upcoming event. Choice D uses the present tense, but the action happened in the past.

44. G   Difficulty: Low

Category: Punctuation

Getting to the Answer: "Possessive versus plural" questions can often be answered quickly: does the sentence refer to more than one grandmother or something belonging to a grandmother? This sentence is discussing the country that *belongs* to the grandmother, so an apostrophe is needed to make *grandmother* possessive. Only (G) does this without introducing an additional error. Choice F is missing the necessary apostrophe; *grandmothers* is plural, not possessive. Choice H uses the plural possessive *grandmothers'*, but only one grandmother is discussed in the paragraph. Choice J corrects the punctuation error but substitutes the homophone *are* for the plural possessive pronoun *our*.

45. A   Difficulty: Medium

Category: Writer's Purpose

Getting to the Answer: When asked about the purpose of the passage as a whole, consider its topic and tone. The narrator describes a personal experience getting to know his cousin from Italy. The tone is positive, emphasizing their similarities and ending with a scene in which family members are touched emotionally by the singing of family folk songs. Thus, the passage accomplishes the stated purpose; eliminate C and D. Choice B is a distortion; the differences between Nicola and the narrator's American cousins are not the reason the essay accomplishes the stated purpose. Thus, (A) is correct.

CHAPTER THREE

Punctuation and Usage

GETTING STARTED

Punctuation and **Usage** questions test your knowledge of a variety of punctuation marks, pronouns, agreements, comparatives, and idioms. Study the question types below to learn how to approach them and the concepts that these questions test. Knowing the information that you'll need to answer the questions helps you identify the important clues in the passage that will lead you to the correct answers.

Punctuation

Within-Sentence Punctuation

The ACT English Test requires you to identify and correct inappropriate commas, semicolons, colons, and dashes when they are used to indicate breaks in thought within a sentence.

You can recognize **Punctuation** questions because the underlined portion of the text will include at least one punctuation mark. The answer choices will move that punctuation mark around, replace it with another punctuation mark, or remove it altogether. When you identify a **Punctuation** question, check to make sure the punctuation is used correctly in context.

Commas

Use commas to . . .	Example
Separate independent clauses connected by a FANBOYS conjunction (For, And, Nor, But, Or, Yet, So)	*Jess finished her homework earlier than expected, so she started a project that was due the following week.*
Separate an introductory or modifying phrase from the rest of the sentence	*Knowing that soccer practice would be especially strenuous, Tia spent extra time stretching beforehand.*
Set off three or more items in a series or list	*Jeremiah packed a sleeping bag, a raincoat, and a lantern for his upcoming camping trip.*
Separate nonessential information from the rest of the sentence	*Professor Mann, who is the head of the English department, is known for the extensive assignments in his courses.*
Separate an independent and dependent clause	*Tyson arrived at school a few minutes early, which gave him time to organize his locker before class.*

✔ *Expert Tip*

When you see an underlined comma, ask yourself, "Could the comma be replaced by a period or a semicolon?" If yes, the comma is grammatically incorrect and needs to be changed.

Semicolons

Use semicolons to . . .	Example
Join two independent clauses that are not connected by a FANBOYS conjunction	*Gaby knew that her term paper would take at least four more hours to write; she got started in study hall and then finished it at home.*
Separate items in a series or list if those items already include commas	*The team needed to bring uniforms, helmets, and gloves; oranges, almonds, and water; and hockey sticks, pucks, and skates.*

✔ *Expert Tip*

When you see an underlined semicolon, ask yourself, "Could the semicolon be replaced by a comma?" If yes, the semicolon is grammatically incorrect and needs to be changed. If the semicolon is separating two independent clauses and can be replaced with a period, it is grammatically correct.

Colons

Use colons to . . .	Example
Introduce and/or emphasize a short phrase, quotation, explanation, example, or list	*Sanjay had two important projects to complete: a science experiment and an expository essay.*

Dashes

Use dashes to . . .	Example
Indicate a hesitation or a break in thought	*Going to a history museum is a good way to begin researching prehistoric creatures—on second thought, heading to the library would likely be much more efficient.*
Set off explanatory elements within a sentence	*Rockwell's Space Transportation Systems Division handled all facets—design, development, and testing—of the reusable orbiter.*

✔ *Expert Tip*

When you see an underlined colon or dash, ask yourself, "Has the author included a new idea by introducing or explaining something, or by breaking his or her thought process?" If yes, the punctuation is often grammatically correct.

Unnecessary Punctuation

The ACT will ask you to recognize instances of unnecessary punctuation, particularly commas.

Do NOT use a comma to . . .	Incorrect	Correct
Separate a subject from its predicate	*The diligent student council, meets every week.*	*The diligent student council meets every week.*
Separate a verb from its object or its subject, or a preposition from its object	*The diligent student council meets, every week.*	*The diligent student council meets every week.*
Set off elements that are essential to a sentence's meaning	*The, diligent student, council meets every week.*	*The diligent student council meets every week.*
Separate adjectives that work together to modify a noun	*The diligent, student council meets every week.*	*The diligent student council meets every week.*

✔ *Expert Tip*

To determine whether information is nonessential, read the sentence without the information. If the sentence still makes sense and has the same intended meaning without the omitted words, then those words need to be set off with punctuation.

Possessive Nouns, Pronouns, and Apostrophes

Possessive nouns and pronouns refer to something that belongs to someone or something. Each follows different rules, and the ACT will test the rules for both. The ACT will also require you to identify both the singular and plural forms.

Possessive Nouns and Pronouns

To spot errors in possessive noun or pronoun construction, look for . . .	Example
Two nouns in a row	*The **professor's lectures** were both informative and entertaining.*
Pronouns with apostrophes	*It is in **one's** best interest to plan ahead.*
Words that sound alike	*The three friends decided to ride **their** bicycles to the park over **there** where **they're** going to enjoy a picnic lunch.*

Apostrophes

Use an apostrophe to . . .	Example
Indicate the possessive form of a single noun	*My oldest **sister's** soccer game is on Saturday.*
Indicate the possessive form of a plural noun	*My two older **sisters'** soccer games are on Saturday.*
Indicate a contraction (e.g., *don't, can't*)	***They've** won every soccer match this season.*

✔ *Expert Tip*

To check whether *it's* is appropriate, replace it in the sentence with *it is* or *it has*. If the sentence no longer makes sense, *it's* is incorrect.

The tree frog blends perfectly into its surroundings. When it holds still, it's nearly invisible.

Usage

Agreement

Subject-Verb Agreement

A verb must agree with its subject in person and number:

Singular: *The apple tastes delicious.*

Plural: *Apples taste delicious.*

The noun closest to the verb is not always the subject: *The chair with the cabriole legs is an antique.* The singular verb in this sentence, *is*, is closest to the plural noun *legs*. However, the verb's actual subject is the singular noun *chair*, so the sentence is correct as written.

Only the conjunction *and* forms a compound subject requiring a plural verb form:

> *Saliyah and Taylor are in the running club.*
>
> *Either Saliyah or Taylor is in the running club.*
>
> *Neither Saliyah nor Taylor is in the running club.*

✔ Expert Tip

When there are two pronouns or a noun and a pronoun in a compound structure, drop the other noun or pronoun to confirm which case to use. For example: *Leo and me walked into town.* Would you say, "Me walked into town"? No, you would say, "I walked into town." Therefore, the correct case is subjective, and the original sentence should read: *Leo and I walked into town.*

Pronoun-Antecedent Agreement

A pronoun is a word that takes the place of a noun. Pronouns must agree with their antecedents not only in person and number but also in gender.

Gender	Example
Feminine	*Because Yvonne had a question, **she** raised her hand.*
Masculine	*Since **he** had lots of homework, Rico started working right away.*
Neutral	*The rain started slowly, but then **it** became a downpour.*
Unspecified	*If a traveler is lost, **he** or **she** should ask for directions.*

Modifier Agreement

A modifier is a word or group of words that describes, clarifies, or provides more information about another part of the sentence.

Adjectives are single-word modifiers that describe nouns and pronouns: *Ian conducted an **efficient** lab experiment.*

Adverbs are single-word modifiers that describe verbs, adjectives, or other adverbs: *Ian **efficiently** conducted a lab experiment.*

Verbs, Pronoun Case, Comparative/Superlative

Verbs

Verb tense indicates when an action or state of being took place: past, present, or future. Each tense has three forms: simple, progressive, and perfect. Don't worry about the names of verb tenses, just their correct usage.

	Past	Present	Future
Simple: Actions that occur at some point in time	*She **studied** two extra hours before her math test.*	*She **studies** diligently.*	*She **will study** tomorrow for her French test.*
Progressive: Actions that are ongoing at some point in time	*She **was studying** yesterday for a French test today.*	*She **is studying** today for her math test tomorrow.*	*She **will be studying** tomorrow for her physics test next week.*
Perfect: Actions that are completed at some point in time	*She **had studied** two extra hours before she took her math test yesterday.*	*She **has studied** diligently every day this semester.*	*She **will have studied** each chapter before her physics test next week.*

Pronoun Cases

There are three pronoun cases, each of which is used based on the context of the sentence.

Case	Pronouns	Example
Subjective: The pronoun is used as the subject	I, you, she, he, it, we, you, they, who	*Rivka is the student **who** will lead the presentation.*
Objective: The pronoun is used as the object of a verb or a preposition	me, you, her, him, it, us, you, them, whom	*With **whom** will Rivka present the scientific findings?*
Possessive: The pronoun expresses ownership	my, mine, your, yours, his, her, hers, its, our, ours, their, theirs, whose	*Rivka will likely choose a partner **whose** work is excellent.*

✔ *Expert Tip*

To determine whether who or whom is correct, replace who/whom with a name (or names) and then the appropriate pronoun. If he, she, or they is correct, use *who*. If him, her, or them is correct, use *whom*. For example: *The teacher, [who/whom] studied in France, speaks three languages.* Change the sentence: *John speaks three languages.* Then, change the name to the appropriate pronoun: *He speaks three languages.* Therefore, the correct case is subjective, and the original sentence should read: *The teacher, who studied in France, speaks three languages.*

K

Comparative/Superlative

When comparing like things, use adjectives that match the number of items being compared. When comparing two items or people, use the comparative form of the adjective. When comparing three or more items or people, use the superlative form.

Comparative (two items)	Superlative (three or more items)
better, more, newer, older, shorter, taller, worse, younger	best, most, newest, oldest, shortest, tallest, worst, youngest

✔ **Expert Tip**

Be on the lookout for clues that will force the comparative. A comparison between "twins" or a "pair," for example, requires the comparative.

Idioms

An idiom is a combination of words that must be used together to convey either a figurative or literal meaning. Idioms are tested in three ways on the ACT:

1. Proper Preposition Usage in Context: The preposition must reflect the writer's intended meaning.

   *She waits **on** customers.*
   *She waits **for** the bus.*
   *She waits **with** her friends.*

2. Idiomatic Expressions: Some words or phrases must be used together to be correct.

   *Simone will **either** bike **or** run to the park.*
   ***Neither** the principal **nor** the teachers will tolerate tardiness.*
   *This fall, Shari is playing **not only** soccer **but also** field hockey.*

3. Implicit Double Negatives: Some words imply a negative and therefore cannot be paired with an explicit negative.

   *Janie **can hardly** wait for vacation.*

Frequently Tested Prepositions	Idiomatic Expressions	Words That Can't Pair with Negative Words
at	as . . . as	barely
by	between . . . and	hardly
for	both . . . and	scarcely
from	either . . . or	
of	neither . . . nor	
on	just as . . . so too	
to	not only . . . but also	
with	prefer . . . to	

IMPROVING WITH PRACTICE

Step 1: Read Until You Can Identify the Issue

Always read the entire English passage, though you don't need to read slowly enough to remember all of the subject matter. This is particularly important for **Punctuation** and **Usage** questions because the best clues for the correct answers may be before or after the underlined segment or the numbered box. Be sure to identify the issue by checking:

- any underlined punctuation mark;
- any underlined pronouns;
- any comparison keywords before, after, or within the underline; and
- any of the "Frequently Confused Words" from the list above.

If you're not sure there's an issue, keep reading and then return to the question.

Step 2: Answer the Questions

As you're practicing, refer back to the tips in the "Getting Started" section and answer questions one at a time, reviewing the Answer and Explanation for every question immediately after completing it. If you got the question correct, congratulate yourself, but take a moment to read the entire explanation to be sure you got the question right for the right reason. The explanation may even point out a more efficient way that you can use on a later question!

Step 3: Review Incorrect Answers

If you get the question incorrect . . . still congratulate yourself! You're about to learn something new that you'll be able to use to improve your performance on Test Day. Don't read the explanation yet; instead, try the question again.

If you get the question correct the second time, read the explanation to see if you solved the question in the most efficient way. Identify the mistake you made the first time, and determine how you're going to avoid making that mistake again.

> ✔ *Expert Tip*
>
> Many top scoring students have an ACT notebook where they write down what they learn from every question. Doing this can be time-consuming, but it can also help you identify the types of mistakes you tend to make.

If you get the question incorrect the second time, use the explanation to learn how to get the question correct. Work through the question again while following the explanation, and identify the steps you will need to take to get a similar question correct. Although the passages and questions will change, the concepts being tested will not. When you encounter unfamiliar questions, take note of them for future study sessions.

> ✔ *Note*
>
> The ACT is a standardized test. While high-difficulty English questions are usually more difficult to answer than low- or medium-difficulty questions, they are often similar in structure and purpose, and the same skills (listed in Chapter 1) are tested on every English Test. You actually can predict the types of questions you will see on Test Day!

After all that work, it's time to move to the next question. Reviewing in this way will take time. However, improvement doesn't come from just doing lots and lots of questions; it comes from thinking through your approach and improving it with every question.

RAISING YOUR SCORE EVEN MORE

Here is one of the "secrets" to conquering the English Test: Because the ACT is a standardized test, there will always be clues that make one choice definitely correct and the other choices completely incorrect. It's never a matter of opinion.

The most important clues for **Punctuation** and **Usage** questions are listed in the "Improving With Practice" section above. To raise your score even more, use the following tips:

- Memorize the uses of a comma listed above and check the list systematically whenever a comma is underlined.
- Mentally "strip out" modifying phrases, especially prepositional phrases, when checking subject-verb agreement. Ask yourself, "Who or what is performing the action of the verb?"
- Check underlined pronouns to be sure there is only one antecedent, and that the antecedent is the noun closest to the pronoun.
- Check modifiers to be sure they are as close as possible to the word they're modifying.
- "Than" and "as" are keywords that indicate a comparison. Use the comparative (*-er*) when comparing two people or items; use the superlative (*-est*) when comparing three or more: *"Mary is the taller of the twins"* and *"John is the tallest singer in the chorus."*

PRACTICE QUESTIONS

The following test-like question sets provide an opportunity to practice reading Punctuation and Usage questions. While many of the questions pertain to Punctuation and Usage, some touch on other concepts tested on the English Test to ensure that your practice is test-like, with a variety of question types per passage.

PASSAGE I

Root for the Home Team?

If you are young and love football, it is advantageous to live near a large sporting-goods store that carries a wide variety of paraphernalia from different teams. My daughter and I visit our local store at least once a year to buy another new football jersey for yet another team. Although my daughter is a fan of our <u>city</u> professional team, she
1
frequently changes her jersey to match that of her favorite player.

A free agent is a professional football player who is no longer under contract with a team, which means he can choose the team <u>which</u> he
2
wants to play. In the NFL today, players can

1. **A.** NO CHANGE
   B. city's
   C. cities
   D. cities'

2. **F.** NO CHANGE
   G. at which
   H. for which
   J. DELETE the underlined portion.

become free agents easily. ③ Things were much different when I was growing up. My favorite player

was on the same team for his entire <u>career I had</u> one jersey. My daughter has bought over eight team jerseys in the past six years! At seventy-five dollars a shirt, this is not a sustainable trend.

There are many disadvantages to <u>free agency. When my</u> daughter and I went to pre-season training practice to get a preview of this year's home team, we constantly consulted the team roster to figure out the new line-up, because there were so many new players. At one point, a number of fans even started to cheer for a <u>player who, was no longer with the team,</u> because they did not realize someone new was wearing his number.

3. The writer is considering adding a comma and the following to the end of the preceding sentence:

> so they often switch teams many times in their careers.

Should the writer make this addition?

A. Yes, because it adds an interesting detail about why players become free agents.

B. Yes, because it provides a necessary link between being a free agent and switching teams.

C. No, because it distracts from the focus on the parent-daughter relationship.

D. No, because it is irrelevant to the point being made about free agents.

4. F. NO CHANGE
   G. career, so I had
   H. career, because I had
   J. career, and then I had

5. A. NO CHANGE
   B. free agency: for when my
   C. free agency, when my
   D. free agency when my

6. F. NO CHANGE
   G. player who was no longer with the team
   H. player, who was no longer, with the team
   J. player who was no longer, with the team

A second disadvantage of free agency is having some camaraderie and cohesion. Football is the ultimate team sport, in which players must

7.
  A. NO CHANGE
  B. lack of
  C. total
  D. wholehearted

depend upon each other to win. A team

8.
  F. NO CHANGE
  G. to win on each other
  H. upon winning with each other
  J. DELETE the underlined portion.

trains strategizes and plays together for months. The players learn each other's strengths and weaknesses. Eleven players are on the field at one time,

9.
  A. NO CHANGE
  B. trains, strategizes, and plays,
  C. trains strategizes, and plays
  D. trains, strategizes, and plays

and their goal is to stop the other team from progressing down the field. If any one of those eleven

10.
  F. NO CHANGE
  G. because their goal
  H. yet their goal
  J. or their goal

players leaves the team, it disrupt the dynamics and cohesion that the entire team has worked together to build.

11.
  A. NO CHANGE
  B. disrupted
  C. disrupts
  D. disrupting

A third disadvantage is the loss of team dynasties. When I was a teenager, my home team made the playoffs for three years in a row. Since free agency was introduced, our team has not made it back to the playoffs for ten years. When the team

12.
  F. NO CHANGE
  G. A loss is the third disadvantage
  H. A disadvantage is the third loss
  J. The third loss is a disadvantage

did return <u>10 years later,</u> my daughter fell in love
₁₃
with both the team and our star quarterback. That

player moved to another team; <u>because</u> our
₁₄
home team has not had a winning season since

he left, his new team has won the Super Bowl

for the last two years. 15

13. **A.** NO CHANGE
    B. to the Super Bowl
    C. 10 years' later
    D. DELETE the underlined portion.

14. **F.** NO CHANGE
    G. however
    H. therefore
    J. while

15. Which of the following sentences, if added, would best conclude the essay?

    A. Football is a great sport that will never decrease in popularity.

    B. Free agency has a variety of benefits, but the negatives outweigh the positives.

    C. Free agency allows players to change teams frequently, which has made it increasingly difficult to root for a home team that never stays the same.

    D. One thing will never change, and that is the home team.

PASSAGE II

The Bear Mountain Bridge

When the gleaming Bear Mountain Bridge officially opened to traffic on Thanksgiving Day in
<u>1924, it</u> was known as the Harriman Bridge, after
  16
Edward H. Harriman, wealthy philanthropist and
patriarch of the family most influential in the

bridge's construction. Before <u>they were</u> constructed,
                                   17
there were no bridges spanning the Hudson River
south of Albany. By the early 1920s, the ferry ser-
vices used to transport people back and forth
across the river had become woefully inadequate.
In February of 1922, in an effort to alleviate some
of the burden on the ferries and create a permanent link across the Hudson, the New York State
Legislature <u>had authorized</u> a group of private in-
                 18
vestors, led by Mary Harriman, to build a bridge.
The group, known as the Bear Mountain Hudson
Bridge Company (BMHBC), was allotted thirty
years to <u>build, construct, and maintain</u> the struc-
                                      19
ture, at which time the span would be handed over
to New York State.

The BMHBC invested almost $4,500,000 into
the suspension bridge and hired the world-renowned

16. **F.** NO CHANGE
    G. 1924; it
    H. 1924. It
    J. 1924 and it

17. **A.** NO CHANGE
    B. the bridges were
    C. it was
    D. it were

18. **F.** NO CHANGE
    G. authorized
    H. was authorized
    J. would authorize

19. **A.** NO CHANGE
    B. build and construct and maintain
    C. construct and maintain
    D. construct, and maintain

design team <u>of Howard Baird and George Hodge</u> as
20

architects. 21 Baird and Hodge enlisted the help of

John A. Roebling and Sons, <u>who were</u> instrumental
22
in the steel work of the Brooklyn Bridge and would
later work on the Golden Gate and George
Washington Bridges.

Amazingly, the bridge took only twenty
months and eleven days to complete, and not one
life was lost. 23 It was a technological marvel and
would stand as a model for the suspension bridges
of the future. At the time of the Harriman Bridge's
completion, it was, at 2,257 feet, the longest
single-span steel suspension bridge in the world.

20. F. NO CHANGE
    G. of Howard Baird, and George Hodge
    H. of Howard Baird and, George Hodge
    J. of, Howard Baird and George Hodge

21. The purpose of including the cost of the bridge is to:
    A. provide a piece of information critical to the point of the essay.
    B. insert a necessary transition between the second and third paragraphs.
    C. add a detail contributing to the reader's understanding of the magnitude of the project.
    D. provide an explanation of how the group raised money to invest in the bridge.

22. F. NO CHANGE
    G. who was
    H. a company
    J. a company that had been

23. If the writer were to delete the preceding sentence, the essay would lose primarily:
    A. information about how long the project had been expected to take.
    B. a warning about the dangers of large-scale construction projects.
    C. crucial information about the duration of the project.
    D. a necessary transition between Paragraphs 3 and 4.

Therefore, the two main cables used in the suspension were 18 inches in diameter, and each contained 7,752 individual steel wires wrapped in 37 thick strands. If completely unraveled, the single wires in both cables would be 7,377 miles longer. The bridge links Bear Mountain on the western bank of the Hudson to Anthony's Nose on the eastern

side, it lies so precisely on an east-west plane that one can check a compass by it. It carries Routes 6 and 202 across the Hudson and is the point of river crossing for the Appalachian Trail.

In an attempt to recoup some of its investment after the bridge opened, the BMHBC charged an exorbitant toll of eighty cents per crossing. Even with the high toll, however, it operated at a loss for thirteen of its first sixteen years. Finally it was acquired, more than ten years earlier than planned, by the New York State Bridge Authority. The bridge was renamed the Bear Mountain Bridge. Moreover,

24. F. NO CHANGE
    G. Nonetheless, the
    H. At the same time, the
    J. The

25. A. NO CHANGE
    B. long.
    C. in total length.
    D. lengthy.

26. F. NO CHANGE
    G. side, lies
    H. side, lying
    J. side; and it lies

27. A. NO CHANGE
    B. opened the BMHBC charged
    C. opened: the BMHBC charged
    D. opened; the BMHBC charged

28. F. NO CHANGE
    G. In contrast
    H. Besides that fact
    J. Today

the Bear Mountain Bridge sees <u>more than</u> six mil-
₂₉
lion vehicles cross its concrete decks each year.

29. **A.** NO CHANGE

  B. over

  C. even more than

  D. a higher amount than

Question 30 asks about the essay as a whole.

---

30. Suppose the author had been assigned to write a brief history of bridge building in the United States. Would this essay successfully fulfill that requirement?

  F. Yes, because it provides information on the entire process from the initial funding through the opening of the bridge.

  G. Yes, because Bear Mountain Bridge is historically significant.

  H. No, because it focuses on only one bridge.

  J. No, because the essay is primarily concerned with the financial aspects of building and maintaining the bridge.

PASSAGE III

The Handsome Bean

On the ground floor of the apartment building where, I live, the Handsome Bean coffee shop is almost always bustling with customers. During the warm months, the shop sets up outdoor tables on the sidewalk, and the chatter of conversation mixed with the aroma of coffee often floats in through my window to wake me in the mornings. Next to the Handsome Bean is a used bookstore, and the two shops share many of the same customers. People come to find a book and stay to enjoy a cup of coffee. Across the street from the building is the neighborhood Little League field. [32] The

Handsome Bean often sponsors a local team. During the games, the coffee shop offers a discount to parents whose children are competing across the

31.
A. NO CHANGE
B. building where I live,
C. building, where I live
D. building where I live

32. The purpose of including the location of the Little League field is to:
F. introduce the kind of team the Handsome Bean sponsors.
G. transition from a discussion of the Handsome Bean to a discussion of baseball.
H. add a detail that helps the reader picture the scene.
J. downplay the importance of the Handsome Bean.

33.
A. NO CHANGE
B. had sponsored
C. was a sponsor of
D. supported

street. [34] It is a pleasure to have as a neighbor a

34. At this point, the writer wants to add a sentence that provides additional detail about the customers who come to the Handsome Bean. Which of the following sentences would best achieve the writer's purpose?

    F. In addition to this discount, the shop offers all patrons a punch card to receive a tenth coffee for free.

    G. The shop also sells ice cream, so it often gets very crowded with children and parents after the Little League games are over.

    H. The Handsome Bean also provides uniforms for an elementary school soccer team.

    J. The Little League field doesn't have a concession stand, so the coffee shop doesn't have much competition for the parents' business.

business that <u>children. And adults</u> enjoy so much.
                       35

35.   **A.** NO CHANGE

    B. children and adults

    C. children and that adults

    D. children. Adults

<u>Over the past few years, I have become friends</u>
                      36
<u>with Mary, the owner of the shop.</u> The store's main
            36
counter is a century-old antique that Mary bought

36. Which choice most effectively leads the reader into the topic of this paragraph?

    F. NO CHANGE

    G. Mary, the shop's owner, has a great appreciation for history.

    H. The Handsome Bean has only been open for a couple of years, but the owner, Mary, has taken great care to make it look like it has been there for decades.

    J. Before Mary, the shop's owner, opened the Handsome Bean, the space had been unoccupied for six months.

and restored to its <u>originally conditional</u>, and the
                        37

photos that adorn the back wall <u>depicts</u> our town
                                    38
during the 1920s and 1930s. My favorite detail of
the shop, however, is the original tin ceiling. One
afternoon, while staring at the intricate patterns
etched into the tin tiles, I noticed a name camou-
flaged within the ornate design: Harvey. I pointed
it out to Mary, and she said the original owner of
the building was named Harvey Wallaby. Her guess
was that he had probably written it there more
than 70 years ago. ³⁹ That night after the coffee
shop had closed, Mary and I etched our names into
the ceiling right next to Harvey's, hoping that our
names would similarly be discovered in the far-off
future.

On Friday nights, the Handsome Bean has live

entertainment, usually in the <u>form of, a</u> band or a
                                    40
poetry reading. For a small-town coffee shop, the

37. **A.** NO CHANGE
    B. original conditional
    C. original condition
    D. conditionally original

38. **F.** NO CHANGE
    G. depict
    H. has depicted
    J. shows

39. The writer is considering deleting the sen-
    tence below from the passage:

    Her guess was that he had probably written
    it there more than 70 years ago.

    If the writer were to delete this sentence, the
    essay would primarily lose:

    A. an additional detail about the building
    that houses the coffee shop.

    B. a depiction of the action taken by Mary
    and the writer.

    C. an emphasis on the original owner's
    influence.

    D. a description of the shop's interior.

40. **F.** NO CHANGE
    G. form; of a
    H. form, of a
    J. form of a

Handsome Bean attracts a <u>good amount</u> of talented
41

musicians and poets. <u>It being that I am amazed by the</u>
42
<u>performances, they</u> transpire within its cozy walls.
42

[1] The clientele of the coffee shop is as varied as the selection of flavored brews. [2] In the mornings, the Handsome Bean is abuzz with the 9-to-5 crowd stopping in for some java before heading off to work. [3] During the day, the tables are home to local artists lost in their thoughts and cappuccinos. [4] The evening finds the Handsome Bean filled with bleary-eyed college students loading up on caffeine so they can cram all night for their upcoming exams or <u>finishing</u> their research papers with
43
looming due dates. [5] Then there's me, sitting in the corner, maybe talking to Mary or reading the paper, smiling at the thought that the best cup of coffee in town is found right beneath my bedroom window. [6] In the afternoons, a group of high school <u>students who</u> stops by to have an ice cream
44

cone or an egg cream. 45

41. **A.** NO CHANGE
    B. better amount
    C. better number
    D. good number

42. **F.** NO CHANGE
    G. Amazing the performances, it is that I know they
    H. I am amazed by the performances that
    J. Amazing the performances, they

43. **A.** NO CHANGE
    B. finish
    C. finishes
    D. finalizing

44. **F.** NO CHANGE
    G. students that
    H. students, and they
    J. students

45. For the sake of logic and coherence, Sentence 6 should be placed:
    A. where it is now.
    B. before Sentence 2.
    C. before Sentence 4.
    D. before Sentence 5.

ANSWERS AND EXPLANATIONS

Root for the Home Team?

1. B   Difficulty: Low

Category: Punctuation

Getting to the Answer: The possessive form of most singular nouns is formed by adding 's. Context tells us that the singular possessive, not the plural, form is needed here. Choice (B) retains the singular form and places the apostrophe correctly. Choice C creates the plural of the noun and does not show possession. Choice D creates the plural possessive of the noun, but the context is referring to one city.

2. H   Difficulty: Medium

Category: Usage

Getting to the Answer: Be sure to read ACT passages for logic as well as grammatical correctness. The word *which* modifies *team*, and a preposition is necessary. Choice (H) is the correct answer, because it adds the preposition *for*. Choice G introduces an incorrect preposition. Omitting the selection, as J suggests, changes the meaning of the sentence. The player is not choosing which team to play against, but rather which team to join.

3. B   Difficulty: High

Category: Supporting Material

Getting to the Answer: When asked whether information should be added, consider whether the new information is relevant. If it is relevant, consider what it adds. The narrator brings up the topic of free agents in order to explain why the daughter continues to need new jerseys, so the fact that being a free agent leads players to switch teams is relevant; the team-switching is the reason the daughter's favorite players keep changing jerseys. Thus, C and D are incorrect. Choice A is also incorrect; the new information tells us a result, not a cause, of becoming a

free agent. Choice (B) accurately describes the reason the information should be added—namely, that it provides the missing link.

4. G   Difficulty: Medium

Category: Sentence Structure and Formation

Getting to the Answer: A complete sentence must have a subject and predicate verb that express a complete thought. In this case, there are two subjects and predicates that create a run-on sentence and an incomplete thought. Choice (G) properly uses the conjunction *so* to join two independent clauses expressing connected thoughts. Choice H creates a grammatically correct sentence, but it suggests an illogical cause-and-effect relationship. Choice J creates an illogical sentence; presumably, the narrator had one jersey while his or her favorite player was on the team, not after.

5. A   Difficulty: Low

Category: Sentence Structure and Formation

Getting to the Answer: Make sure independent clauses are properly separated. The sentences in question are correctly separated by a period because they express two separate, complete thoughts. This matches (A). Choice B is incorrect because, while the colon draws the reader's attention to a specific point directly related to what precedes it, the words *for when* makes the sentence structure awkward. The first sentence says there are *many* disadvantages to free agency, but the information in the second sentence expresses only one disadvantage. Choice C is incorrect because the comma separates two independent clauses. Choice D is incorrect because it also creates a run-on.

6. G   Difficulty: Medium

Category: Punctuation

Getting to the Answer: When a word or phrase is set off from the rest of the sentence with commas, the sentence must make sense without that phrase. The sentence is grammatically incorrect as written.

A comma incorrectly separates *who* from the remainder of the phrase. Choice (G) corrects this by removing the comma. Choices H and J maintain an incorrect use of a comma, which breaks up the thought.

7. B   Difficulty: Medium

Category: Precision

Getting to the Answer: The answer choices have different meanings, which indicates that you are being tested on precision. Choose the answer that makes the most sense in context. The sentence introduces a disadvantage related to camaraderie and cohesion. Because those are both good things, it would be a disadvantage to be without them. Choice (B) conveys this meaning. Choice A is too neutral to make sense, whereas C and D are too positive.

8. F   Difficulty: Low

Category: Usage

Getting to the Answer: When DELETE is an option, first determine if the underlined information is necessary to the meaning of the sentence. The underlined information is necessary to the sentence, which means J can be eliminated. In the correct answer, (F), *upon* correctly precedes the direct object *each other*. Choice G uses incorrect prepositions, *to* and *on*, and separates the direct object from *depend*. Choice H is illogical; the players depend on each other, not on winning.

9. D   Difficulty: Low

Category: Punctuation

Getting to the Answer: A list must be set off with serial commas. Choice (D) is the correct answer because it correctly places the commas between each item. Choice A is incorrect because it omits the commas. Choice B is incorrect because it uses a comma to separate the adverb *together* from the verb it modifies, *plays*. Choice C is incorrect because the comma that separates the first item from the second is missing.

10. F   Difficulty: Low

Category: Transitions

Getting to the Answer: When determining whether two thoughts are correctly combined, check for the logic of the transition as well as proper grammar and punctuation. Because the players' attempt to block the other team is not a result of the number of players, the cause-and-effect transition *because* is inappropriate; eliminate G. No contrast is needed, making H incorrect. *Or* does not make sense in context; it would be illogical for the team either to have eleven players on the field or to try to stop the other team from progressing. Thus, J is incorrect. The sentence is correct as written, so (F) is the correct answer.

11. C   Difficulty: Low

Category: Usage

Getting to the Answer: When a verb is underlined, check to see if it matches the subject. The subject, *it*, is singular, requiring the plural verb *disrupts*, (C). Choice A requires a plural subject, B makes an unwarranted shift to past tense, and D creates a fragment.

12. F   Difficulty: Medium

Category: Sentence Structure and Formation

Getting to the Answer: Make sure modifying phrases are placed so as to modify logical things. Choice (F) is the correct answer because it concludes the sequence of three major disadvantages to free agency and correctly modifies "the loss of team dynasties." Choice G is incorrect because *loss* should modify *team dynasties*. Choices H and J are incorrect because the adverb *third* should modify *disadvantage*, not *loss*.

13. D   Difficulty: Medium

Category: Concision

Getting to the Answer: Read the sentence without the underlined information to see if it still makes sense, and eliminate answer choices that contain redundant language. In the context of the paragraph, the sentence still makes sense without the underlined information. Choice (D) is the correct answer. Choice B contains redundant language. Adding an apostrophe to *years* in C is grammatically incorrect, and the phrase is redundant.

14. J   Difficulty: High

Category: Transitions

Getting to the Answer: Remember to read for logic, as well as grammar and usage. Choice (J) is the only choice that logically connects ideas in this sentence by setting up the contrast between the simultaneous failure of the home team and the success of the player's new team. Choice F is incorrect because it creates a causal relationship between the home team failing and the player's new team winning (as a result of the home team's failure). Choices G and H cannot introduce dependent clauses, making the sentence ungrammatical.

15. C   Difficulty: Medium

Category: Passage Organization

Getting to the Answer: Read question stems carefully. Often, incorrect answer choices will be consistent with the passage but fail to answer the question posed. The question stem is looking for the choice that best reflects the main idea of the essay. This paragraph concerns the author's dislike of what free agency has done to his or her experience of football; choice (C) makes this point best. Choice A is a general opinion that does not relate to the specific argument in the essay. Choice B is incorrect because the author does not describe any benefits of free agency. Choice D is incorrect because it takes the opposite point of view from the main point of persuasion in the essay.

The Bear Mountain Bridge

16. F   Difficulty: Medium

Category: Punctuation

Getting to the Answer: An introductory phrase should be separated from the rest of the sentence by a comma. This introductory phrase is set off by a comma; the sentence is correct as written, (F). Choices G and H incorrectly treat the introductory phrase as an independent clause. Choice J incorrectly connects a dependent and an independent clause with the conjunction *and*.

17. C   Difficulty: Medium

Category: Usage

Getting to the Answer: When a pronoun is underlined, check whether it matches its antecedent. The underlined portion refers to the bridge, so the correct answer will be singular; eliminate A and B. Choice D contains a subject-verb agreement error; the singular *it* requires the singular *was*. Choice (C) is correct.

18. G   Difficulty: Medium

Category: Sentence Structure and Formation

Getting to the Answer: Make sure verb tenses make sense within the chronology of the passage. The past perfect is used in this sentence, but this tense is only correct when used to describe one past action completed before another. That is not the case here, so F is incorrect; (G) correctly replaces the verb with its past-tense form. Choice H changes the meaning of the sentence (the legislature did the authorizing; it wasn't authorized by someone else) and creates a sentence that is grammatically incorrect. Choice J uses a conditional verb phrase, which is inappropriate in context.

19. C   Difficulty: Low

Category: Concision

Getting to the Answer: When the underlined selection contains a compound, check to see if the words mean the same thing. If so, the correct answer choice will eliminate one of them. *Build* and *construct* mean the same thing, so you can eliminate A and B right away. The only difference between (C) and D is a comma, which is incorrect in a compound; eliminate D.

20. F   Difficulty: Medium

Category: Punctuation

Getting to the Answer: Where the only difference among the answer choices is comma placement, remember your tested rules. This sentence needs NO CHANGE, (F). Choice G incorrectly places a comma between items in a compound. Choice H places a comma after the conjunction in a compound, which is also incorrect. Choice J incorrectly inserts a comma between a preposition and its object.

21. C   Difficulty: Medium

Category: Writer's Purpose

Getting to the Answer: Read the sentence without the material in question to determine what it adds to the paragraph and therefore why it was included. Looking at the paragraph as a whole, you can see that the author mentions the amount of money invested, the prominence of the architects, and the accomplishments of the firm the architects brought in to help. Removing one of these details detracts from that description; (C) is the best choice here. Choice A can be eliminated because this is not the only detail that supports the larger point; in and of itself, it's not critical. Removing this one phrase wouldn't impact the transition, as B suggests. Choice D is a trap. The segment in question does concern finances, but the text only mentions the amount of money invested, not how it was raised.

22. J   Difficulty: High

Category: Usage

Getting to the Answer: On the ACT, "who" will only be correct when used to refer to people. Despite the fact that it's named after a person, "John A. Roebling and Sons" is the name of a company, so "who" isn't appropriate. That eliminates F and G. Choice H might be tempting because it's shorter than (J), but when choice H is read in the sentence, it creates a grammatical problem: "a company . . . and would later" requires another verb. Choice (J) is correct.

23. D   Difficulty: Medium

Category: Supporting Material

Getting to the Answer: Consider context when you're asked about the role a piece of text plays. A question that asks what would be lost if text were deleted is really just asking for the function of that text. If you read the paragraphs before and after the sentence in question, you'll see that what is missing is a clear transition; (D) is correct. Choice A distorts the meaning of the sentence, which discusses how long the project actually took, not how long it was expected to take. Choice B is out of scope; danger is only mentioned in this one sentence and then only to say that no lives were lost constructing the bridge. Choice C overstates the significance of the detail regarding construction time.

24. J   Difficulty: Medium

Category: Transitions

Getting to the Answer: When transition words are underlined, focus on the relationship between the sentences or clauses they combine. The preceding sentence talks about the length of the bridge, and the sentence in which the underlined segment appears goes on to describe the cables in more detail. Since the second isn't a result of the first, you can eliminate F. Choice G inaccurately suggests an inconsistent or contradictory relationship between the sentences. Choice H is illogical; these are facts about the bridge, not events occurring simultaneously. The best choice here is no transition at all, as in (J).

25. B   Difficulty: Low

Category: Usage

Getting to the Answer: When you're tested on Usage, incorrect answer choices may have the wrong word in context. They may also be wordy or passive. *Longer* means a comparison: one thing is longer *than* something else. Since this sentence doesn't offer a comparison, *longer* can't be correct. Eliminate A. Choices (B) and C are both grammatically correct in context, but C is unnecessarily wordy. *Lengthy*, in D, is not correct when used to describe a specific length.

26. H   Difficulty: Medium

Category: Sentence Structure and Formation

Getting to the Answer: When the underlined portion contains a comma, check for a run-on. Because the comma separates two independent clauses, F is incorrect. Choice G eliminates the subject of the second clause, so it is incorrect. Choice J incorrectly combines a semicolon and a FANBOYS conjunction. Choice (H) makes the second clause dependent and correctly separates the clauses with a comma. Choice (H) is correct.

27. A   Difficulty: Medium

Category: Punctuation

Getting to the Answer: Introductory phrases and clauses should be set off from the rest of the sentence by a comma. The comma here is used correctly, so no change is needed; (A) is correct. Choice B eliminates the comma, making the sentence difficult to understand. Both the colon in C and the semicolon in D would work only if the first clause were independent, which it is not.

28. J   Difficulty: Medium

Category: Transitions

Getting to the Answer: When a transition word is underlined, check to see what ideas are being connected by the transition. The previous sentence mentions that the bridge was renamed, and the sentence beginning with the underlined portion switches to the present tense to describe the number of vehicles that cross the bridge daily. There is no logical contrast between these ideas, so G and H can be eliminated. Choice F indicates a continuation of the previous thought, but that does not fit the context; eliminate it. Choice (J) is correct, because it transitions from the past-tense description in the previous sentence to the present-tense description of the bridge's daily activity.

29. A   Difficulty: Medium

Category: Usage

Getting to the Answer: Use *over* for physical location and *more than* for numbers or amounts. This sentence is correct as written, (A). Choice B replaces *more than* with *over*, which, despite its common usage, is actually a preposition that indicates location, not amount. Choice C is unnecessarily wordy. Choice D is also wordy and uses *amount*, which is incorrect for a countable noun like *vehicles*.

30. H   Difficulty: Medium

Category: Writer's Purpose

Getting to the Answer: As you read ACT English passages, develop a sense of the topic or *big idea*, just like you do in Reading; this question format is very common on the ACT. This passage is about one specific bridge, so it would not satisfy the requirement set out in the question stem. You can therefore eliminate F and G right away. Now turn to the reasoning. Choice J misstates the topic of the passage; (H) is correct.

The Handsome Bean

31. B   Difficulty: Medium

Category: Punctuation

Getting to the Answer: When the only difference in the answer choices is the use of commas, focus on sentence structure. Are there items in a list that need to be separated by commas? A nonessential phrase that needs to be set off from the rest of the sentence with a pair of commas? An introductory phrase or clause that needs to be separated from the rest of the sentence? This sentence treats the phrase *I live* as nonessential, but removing it creates a sentence fragment. Choice (B) properly places a comma between the introductory phrase describing the location of the Handsome Bean coffee shop and the sentence's independent clause. Choice C creates an introductory clause with no noun to modify, which is grammatically incorrect. Choice D fails to set off the introductory phrase from the body of the sentence, making the sentence difficult to understand.

32. F   Difficulty: Medium

Category: Writer's Purpose

Getting to the Answer: When you're asked the purpose of including a detail, read around that detail for context. By describing the proximity of the Little League field, the writer provides a context for the teams the Handsome Bean often sponsors. Without this information, the following sentence would not fit well in context. Thus, (F) is correct. There is no change of topic, so G is incorrect. While the information helps the reader picture the scene, H misses the function of introducing the sponsored team in the following sentence. Choice J does not match the tone of the passage, which portrays the Handsome Bean positively.

33. A   Difficulty: Low

Category: Sentence Structure and Formation

Getting to the Answer: Use context to determine the answers to questions with underlined verbs. The verbs in this paragraph are in the present tense: *come, stay, is,* and *offers.* The present tense *sponsors* is correct, so no change is needed, (A). Choice B uses the past perfect *had sponsored,* incorrectly suggesting that the coffee shop sponsored the Little League team before another past event. Choices C and D use the past tense, which is inconsistent with the rest of the paragraph.

34. G   Difficulty: Medium

Category: Supporting Material

Getting to the Answer: Read question stems carefully. Often, all four answer choices to Supporting Material questions will be relevant to the passage, but only one will fulfill the specific requirements of the question. The question asks for additional detail about the customers who come to the coffee shop. Only (G) focuses on customers—the parents and children who come for ice cream after the Little League games. Choice F focuses on an additional discount provided by the coffee shop, not on the customers of the shop. Choice H provides a detail about another sport supported by the coffee shop; this doesn't match the purpose stated in the question stem. Choice J provides more information about the Little League field, not about the coffee shop's customers.

35. B   Difficulty: Medium

Category: Sentence Structure and Formation

Getting to the Answer: When the end of one sentence and the beginning of the next are underlined, consider whether one or both are sentence fragments. As written, both of these sentences are fragments, since neither expresses a complete thought. Choice (B) correctly combines the two fragments into a single sentence. Choice C is unnecessarily wordy. Choice D does not address the error.

36. H   Difficulty: Medium

Category: Passage Organization

Getting to the Answer: Remember the first step in the Kaplan Method: read the passage and identify the issue. Here, you need to select the sentence that best introduces the topic of the paragraph, so you'll need to read the paragraph. The paragraph describes the antique décor of the coffee shop—its "century-old" counter, the photos from the 1920s and 1930s, and the "original tin ceiling." Choice (H) effectively leads into this description by explaining that the owner wants the shop to "look like it has been there for decades." Choice F focuses on the friendship between the writer and Mary; this doesn't connect with the details of the antique counter, old photos, and original tin ceiling. Choice G is too general; (H) provides a more specific reason for the decorating decisions Mary has made. Choice J explains that the space was vacant before the Handsome Bean opened, but this doesn't introduce the description of the décor.

37. C   Difficulty: Low

Category: Usage

Getting to the Answer: The object of a preposition must be a noun, pronoun, or gerund (-*ing* verb form functioning as a noun). For this sentence to make sense, the noun *condition* is required as the object of *to*. Since nouns can only be modified by adjectives, (C) is correct. Choices A and B use the adjective *conditional* as the object of the preposition, which is grammatically incorrect. Although *original* can function as a noun, it could not then be modified by an adverb, so D is incorrect.

38. G   Difficulty: Medium

Category: Usage

Getting to the Answer: The ACT will often separate a tested verb from its subject with an intervening phrase or clause. Make sure that you've correctly identified the subject with which an underlined verb must agree. As in many sentences on the ACT, a description separates the subject and verb here; the subject of the verb *depicts* is the plural *photos*. The plural form *depict* is needed; (G) is correct. Choices H and J do not address the error; additionally, H introduces an unwarranted verb tense change.

39. A   Difficulty: High

Category: Supporting Material

Getting to the Answer: To answer this type of question, focus on the function of the sentence. What purpose does it serve in the paragraph? The sentence provides the reader with the information

that the building is at least 70 years old. Therefore, if the sentence were deleted, you would lose information about the age of the building. Choice (A) is correct. Choice B refers to Mary and the writer etching their names in the ceiling, but the sentence does not describe this action. Choice C relates the sentence to the influence of the original owner; however, the time at which Harvey etched his name has little to do with his influence on Mary, the writer, or anyone else. Choice D treats the sentence as a description of the interior of the coffee shop, but no description of the ceiling is given in this sentence.

40. J   Difficulty: Medium

Category: Punctuation

Getting to the Answer: A comma should not be inserted between a preposition and its object. This sentence requires no comma; (J) is correct. Choice G uses a semicolon, which is only correct when used to connect two independent clauses. Choice H treats "usually in the form" as a nonessential phrase. However, deleting this phrase does not leave a logical sentence, so H is incorrect.

41. D   Difficulty: Medium

Category: Usage

Getting to the Answer: Use *number* for items that are countable and *amount* for quantities that are not. The talented musicians and poets are countable, so *number* should be used instead of *amount*. Since the number of talented performers isn't compared to anything, *good* is the correct adjective. The answer is (D). Choices A and B use *amount* where *number* would be correct; additionally, Choice B uses the comparative adjective *better*, but nothing is compared here. Choice C also uses *better*, which is correct only in a comparison.

42. H   Difficulty: Medium

Category: Concision

Getting to the Answer: Be aware of phrases like "It being that"; they add no real meaning to the sentence and provide no clear antecedent for the pronoun. "It being that" is unnecessary here, but eliminating it creates a run-on sentence. Choice (H) eliminates the unnecessary language and makes the second clause subordinate. Choices G and J both use incorrect grammatical structure.

43. B   Difficulty: Medium

Category: Sentence Structure and Formation

Getting to the Answer: Elements in a compound must be parallel in structure. The conjunction "or" creates a compound: students load up on caffeine "so they can cram all night . . . or finishing their research papers." Choice (B) makes the two verbs, *cram* and *finish*, parallel. Choices C and D do not address the parallelism error.

44. J   Difficulty: Medium

Category: Sentence Structure and Formation

Getting to the Answer: A sentence may have multiple nouns and verbs and still be a fragment. A complete sentence requires a subject and a verb in an independent clause that expresses a complete thought. The subject here is "a group of high school students," but the clause "who stops by to have an ice cream cone or an egg cream" describes the students without providing a predicate verb. Choice (J) eliminates the pronoun, making *stops* the predicate verb. Choice G does not address the error and incorrectly uses *that* to refer to people. Choice H creates an error in subject-verb agreement; the plural pronoun *they* does not agree with the verb *stops*.

45. C   Difficulty: Medium

Category: Passage Organization

Getting to the Answer: When you need to add or move information, read the new information into the passage at the suggested points to determine its logical placement. The paragraph describes different customers at the coffee shop throughout a typical day, starting in the morning and ending in the evening. This sentence talks about customers who come to the coffee shop in the afternoon, so it should be placed between Sentence 3, which talks about daytime customers, and Sentence 4, which describes customers in the evening. Choice (C) is correct. Choices A and D both place the information about customers in the afternoon after information about customers in the evening. Choice B places the information about afternoon customers before the information about morning customers.

CHAPTER FOUR

Organization, Unity, and Cohesion

GETTING STARTED

Study the **Organization**, **Unity**, and **Cohesion** question types below to learn how to approach them and the concepts that these questions test. Knowing the information that you'll need to answer the questions helps you identify the important clues in the passage that will lead you to the correct answers.

Organization, Unity, and Cohesion

Organization, **Unity**, and **Cohesion** questions require you to assess the logic and coherence of an English passage. These questions differ in scope; you might be asked to organize the writing at the level of a sentence, a paragraph, or even an entire passage.

Transitions

If a transition word is underlined, you must determine the writer's intended meaning and find the transition that best conveys this meaning. Writers use transitions to show relationships such as contrast, cause and effect, continuation, emphasis, and chronology. Knowing which types of words convey each type of transition will help you choose the correct word on Test Day.

Contrast Transitions	Cause-and-Effect Transitions	Sequential Transitions	Emphasis Transitions
although, but, despite, even though, however, in contrast, nonetheless, on the other hand, rather than, though, unlike, while, yet	as a result, because, consequently, since, so, therefore, thus	after, also, before, first (second, etc.), furthermore, in addition	certainly, in fact, indeed, that is

Passage Organization

Organizing Ideas

Some **Organization** questions ask you to either reorder the sentences in a paragraph or reorder the paragraphs in a passage to ensure that information and ideas are logically conveyed. When reordering, begin by determining which sentence or paragraph most logically introduces the paragraph or passage, respectively.

Adding Information

Some **Organization** questions ask you to insert new ideas into a passage. When inserting new information into a passage, begin by determining which paragraph of the passage most logically accompanies the new idea. If more than one answer choice includes the paragraph you have in mind, plug in each new idea to see how it fits within the context. Choose the answer that best reflects the writer's tone and purpose.

Opening, Transitional, and Closing Sentences

Some **Organization** questions task you with improving the beginning or ending of a paragraph or passage. The transition words, phrases, or sentences must be used effectively not only to connect information and ideas but also to maintain logical structure. To answer these questions effectively, determine the writer's intended purpose, eliminate answer choices that do not reflect this purpose, and choose the most correct and relevant option.

> ✔ **Note**
>
> While concision is important, it is not the primary goal when answering **Organization, Unity,** and **Cohesion** questions. Instead, focus on picking answer choices that make the most sense logically, given your understanding of the writer's tone and purpose.

IMPROVING WITH PRACTICE

Step 1: Read Until You Can Identify the Issue

Always read the entire English passage, though you don't need to read slowly enough to remember all of the subject matter. This is particularly important for **Organization, Unity,** and **Cohesion** questions because the best clues for the correct answers may be before or after the underlined segment or the numbered box. Be sure to identify:

- the main idea of each paragraph;
- the author's opinion or tone; and
- any keywords, especially transition and timing keywords. These may be before, after, or within the underlined segment.

If you're not sure there's an issue, keep reading and then return to the question.

Step 2: Answer the Questions

As you're practicing, refer back to the tips in the "Getting Started" section and answer questions one at a time, reviewing the Answer and Explanation for every question immediately after completing it. If you got the question correct, congratulate yourself, but take a moment to read the entire explanation to be sure you got the question right for the right reason. The explanation may even point out a more efficient way that you can use on a later question!

Step 3: Review Incorrect Answers

If you get the question incorrect . . . still congratulate yourself! You're about to learn something new that you'll be able to use to improve your performance on Test Day. Don't read the explanation yet; instead, try the question again.

If you get the question correct the second time, read the explanation to see if you solved the question in the most efficient way. Identify the mistake you made the first time, and determine how you're going to avoid making that mistake again.

> **✔ Expert Tip**
>
> **Many top scoring students have an ACT notebook where they write down what they learn from every question. Doing this can be time-consuming, but it can also help you identify the types of mistakes you tend to make.**

If you get the question incorrect the second time, use the explanation to learn how to get the question correct. Work through the question again while following the explanation, and identify the steps you will need to take to get a similar question correct. Although the passages and questions will change, the concepts being tested will not. When you encounter unfamiliar questions, take note of them for future study sessions.

> **✔ Note**
>
> **The ACT is a standardized test. While high-difficulty English questions are usually more difficult to answer than low- or medium-difficulty questions, they are often similar in structure and purpose, and the same skills (listed in Chapter 1) are tested on every English Test. You actually can predict the types of questions you will see on Test Day!**

After all that work, it's time to move to the next question. Reviewing in this way will take time. However, improvement doesn't come from just doing lots and lots of questions; it comes from thinking through your approach and improving it with every question.

RAISING YOUR SCORE EVEN MORE

Here is one of the "secrets" to conquering the English Test: because the ACT is a standardized test, there will always be clues that make one choice definitely correct and the other choices completely incorrect. It's never a matter of opinion.

For **Organization**, **Unity**, and **Cohesion** questions, these clues include:

- transition keywords, such as those listed above;
- timing keywords, such as "first," "then," "later," and "finally"; and
- underlined pronouns, such as "this" or "these." Always ask yourself, "What is 'this'?" and then substitute that idea back into the sentence. The noun to which the pronoun refers must be clearly and grammatically connected to the pronoun.

✔ *Expert Tip*

Time spent identifying the clues not only saves time evaluating the choices but also improves your accuracy. Always find the clues first!

For questions asking about introductions, evaluate each choice by reading it strictly on its own. If any part of the sentence is unclear when you read the sentence in isolation, it is not a good introductory sentence.

For questions asking about conclusions, the correct choice will not bring in any new ideas, but it will effectively summarize the paragraph or the passage.

PRACTICE QUESTIONS

The following test-like question sets provide an opportunity to practice reading Organization, Unity, and Cohesion questions. While many of the questions pertain to Organization, Unity, and Cohesion some touch on other concepts tested on the English Test to ensure that your practice is test-like, with a variety of question types per passage.

PASSAGE I

The Toughest Task in Sports

[1]

I've often heard others make the comment that the hardest single act in all of sports is to hit a major league fastball. I'm not going to deny that hitting a ball traveling at upwards of 95 miles per hour is a daunting task, but I can think of something even tougher than taking a major league at-bat: stopping a crank shot in lacrosse. <u>Football quarterbacks facing oncoming defensive</u>₁ <u>linemen are also in a difficult position.</u>₁

1. **A.** NO CHANGE
    B. Also in a challenging position are football quarterbacks facing oncoming defensive linemen.
    C. (Football quarterbacks also face a daunting task when they are rushed by defensive linemen.)
    D. DELETE the underlined portion.

[2]

Lacrosse <u>that is</u>₂ often referred to as "the fastest sport on two feet," and with good reason. The game

2. **F.** NO CHANGE
    G. which has been
    H. is
    J. DELETE the underlined portion.

is often <u>brutally</u>, and the best players normally
₃

possess a bit of <u>toughness and</u> a bit of finesse. Using
₄
sticks known as "crosses" to pass a hard rubber ball

back and forth through the air, players on two

teams sprint around a field; <u>they then attempted</u> to
₅
set up a shot on the opposing team's goal. As in

hockey or soccer, the only thing that stands be-

tween the ball and the goal is the goalkeeper.

Using just his body and his crosse, the goalie must

protect the six-foot by six-foot goal from being

penetrated by a ball that is less than eight inches in

circumference.

[3]

    This brings me to the heart of my argument. A

regulation lacrosse ball is almost an inch narrower

than a regulation baseball, with an unstitched,

smooth rubber surface. The fastest baseball pitch

on record was clocked at 100.9 mph, <u>because</u> only
₆
a handful of major league pitchers can approach

even the upper nineties in speed. In men's lacrosse,

because the crosse acts as a lever, the fastest crank

shots on <u>goal, can</u> reach 110 mph. Even at the high
₇
school level, crank shots of more than 90 mph

3. **A.** NO CHANGE
   B. brutal
   C. brute
   D. brutality

4. **F.** NO CHANGE
   G. toughness; and
   H. toughness
   J. toughness, and,

5. **A.** NO CHANGE
   B. they must attempt
   C. one then attempts
   D. one must attempt

6. **F.** NO CHANGE
   G. before
   H. though
   J. moreover,

7. **A.** NO CHANGE
   B. goal, can,
   C. goal can
   D. goal can,

made by high school players are not uncommon.
8
Unlike a baseball pitcher throwing his fastball from a fixed position on the mound, a lacrosse player

may shoot from anywhere on the field. [9] This means that a lacrosse goalie may be asked to stop a crank shot from only six feet away! To make the

goalie's job even more absurd, a lacrosse player
10
may shoot from over his shoulder, from his side, or drop his stick down and wind up from the ground.

On top of that, the best players often employ a
11
variety of fakes, and most have the ability to shoot left-handed or right-handed, depending upon their angle to the goal.

8. F. NO CHANGE
    G. made by these high school players
    H. shot by high school players
    J. DELETE the underlined portion.

9. The writer is considering adding a comma and the following information to the end of the preceding sentence:
    which is usually grass.
    Should the writer make this addition?
    A. Yes, because it allows the reader to picture the field.
    B. Yes, because it adds a detail that supports the rest of the sentence.
    C. No, because it distracts from the focus on the game.
    D. No, because it weakens the claim in the following sentence.

10. F. NO CHANGE
    G. insurmountable
    H. harrowing
    J. difficult

11. Of the following possible replacements for the underlined portion, which would be LEAST acceptable?
    A. In addition,
    B. On the other hand,
    C. Furthermore,
    D. What's more,

[4]

Like hitting a major league fastball, stopping a
                                              12
crank shot in lacrosse is tough. Both of these
          12

endeavors, however, require the same set of skills.
                       13
One must possess superlative athleticism, great

hand-eye coordination, and catlike quickness.

Above all, you must be fearless.
           14

12. Which choice is the most effective and logical transition from the topic of Paragraph 3 to the topic of Paragraph 4?

F. NO CHANGE

G. The combination of these unknown variables makes stopping a crank shot in lacrosse tougher than hitting a major league fastball.

H. Though baseball is less challenging than lacrosse, both sports require tremendous skill and dedication from athletes.

J. There is little question that stopping a crank shot in lacrosse is among the toughest tasks an athlete can face.

13. A. NO CHANGE

B. requires

C. required

D. would have required

14. F. NO CHANGE

G. one must be

H. they must be

J. he must have been

Question 15 asks about the preceding passage as a whole.

15. Suppose that the writer had wanted to write an essay comparing the strategies used by baseball pitchers and lacrosse goalies. Would this essay fulfill the writer's goal?

A. Yes, because the writer compares both sports throughout the essay.

B. Yes, because the writer details the challenges that lacrosse goalies face.

C. No, because the writer does not provide any specific details about baseball pitchers.

D. No, because the writer focuses on comparing the difficulty of hitting a ball pitched by a major league pitcher to the difficulty of blocking a crank shot in men's lacrosse.

PASSAGE II

The Swallows of San Juan Capistrano

[1]

The oldest building still in use in California is the Mission at San Juan Capistrano, the seventh in the chain of California missions built by Spanish priests in the late eighteenth and early nineteenth centuries. The mission has gained fame as the <u>well-known summer residence</u> of the swallows
16

of San Juan Capistrano. ⑰

[2]

[1] For centuries, these cliff swallows have migrated to and from California every year in a cloud-like formation. [2] The swallows leave the town of San Juan Capistrano, halfway between San Diego and Los Angeles, around October 23. [3] They then journey 7,000 miles to spend the winter in Argentina. [4] Every spring, the birds faithfully return from Argentina to nest and <u>for bearing</u> their young in the valley near the mis-
18
sion. [5] On March 19, mission bells ring, a fiesta is

16. **F.** NO CHANGE
    G. seasonal residence for the summer
    H. summer residence
    J. residential summer home

17. The primary purpose of this paragraph is to:
    A. introduce the story of the founding of the mission.
    B. transition into a discussion of the architecture of the mission.
    C. set the scene for a discussion of the swallows.
    D. persuade the reader that the mission is important.

18. **F.** NO CHANGE
    G. with bearing
    H. bearing
    J. bear

K

held, and a parade <u>snaking</u> through the streets as
throngs of locals and tourists celebrate the birds'
return.

[3]

According to legend, the swallows were seeking refuge from an innkeeper who had destroyed
their muddy <u>nests when they discovered</u> the mission. Biologists have a different explanation for

how the birds <u>might of</u> developed their fondness

for the mission. <u>Although</u> observing the swallows'
behavior and noting that the birds build their nests
out of mud, biologists have postulated that the
swallows really chose the mission due to its
proximity to two rivers. These rivers provide the
swallows with ample mud for building their

19. **A.** NO CHANGE
 B. snaked
 C. snakes
 D. is snaking

20. **F.** NO CHANGE
 G. nests when discovering
 H. nests, when
 J. nests, when finding

21. **A.** NO CHANGE
 B. might have
 C. may of
 D. may

22. **F.** NO CHANGE
 G. Indeed
 H. After
 J. Before

funnel-like nests <u>of which</u> they return year after
₂₃

year. 24

[4]

[1] One aspect of the legend, however, rings
true. [2] The swallows, sensing that they will be
protected within the mission walls, return to the
compound every spring. [3] <u>Despite this,</u> beyond
₂₅
the church walls, the entire city has sought to protect the swallows. San Juan Capistrano municipal
ordinances declare the city a bird sanctuary and
outlaw the destruction or damaging of swallow
nests.

[5]

[1] Although the <u>community clearly</u> sees
₂₆
the importance of providing a home for the swallows, some problems have arisen in recent years.
[2] Due to the city's growth and development, the
number of insects has declined, causing many of
the swallows to locate farther from the mission in

23. **A.** NO CHANGE
    B. to which
    C. by which
    D. which

24. Of the following true statements, which is the
best choice to insert here in order to further
support the biologists' explanation that the
swallows chose the mission because of its
proximity to two rivers?
    F. The swallows will repair a damaged nest
    instead of building an entirely new nest.
    G. The rivers also supply insects upon which
    the swallows feed.
    H. Both rivers are also home to a
    wide variety of fish.
    J. The location of the mission near the
    rivers also provides other advantages for
    the swallows.

25. **A.** NO CHANGE
    B. Finally
    C. In fact
    D. Next

26. **F.** NO CHANGE
    G. community, clearly
    H. community clearly,
    J. community clear

the town center and closer to the open areas where their food source thrives. [3] Large groups of swallows have found other nesting sites in the area, usually in the hills due to disruptions from
27

recent restorations of the old, historic buildings at
28
the mission. [4] Fortunately, city and mission officials have started to respond to these problems.

[5] For example, to attempt at enticing the birds
29
back home, mission workers have strewn insects about the mission's grounds.

27. **A.** NO CHANGE
    B. area; usually in the hills,
    C. area—usually in the hills—
    D. area, having been usual in the hills,

28. **F.** NO CHANGE
    G. old and historic
    H. historic
    J. olden times

29. **A.** NO CHANGE
    B. in an attempt to entice
    C. in an attempt's enticement
    D. in an attempt of enticing

Question 30 asks about the preceding passage as a whole.

---

30. The writer is considering adding the following sentence to further explain how residents of San Juan Capistrano feel about the swallows:

    > Many residents and visitors miss the huge clouds of swallows descending upon the mission as in the past decades.

    The most logical place to insert this sentence would be directly after:

    F. Sentence 5 in Paragraph 2.
    G. Sentence 3 in Paragraph 4.
    H. Sentence 1 in Paragraph 5.
    J. Sentence 3 in Paragraph 5.

PASSAGE III

My Old-Fashioned Father

My father, though he is only in his early 50s, is stuck in his old-fashioned ways. He has a general mistrust of any innovation or technology that he

can't immediately grasp and he always tells us, that if something isn't broken, then you shouldn't fix it.

He has run a small grocery store in town, and if you were to look at a snapshot of his back office taken when he opened the store in 1975, you

would see that not much has changed since. He is the most disorganized person I know and still uses

a pencil and paper to keep track of his inventory. His small office is about to burst with all the various documents, notes, and receipts he has

31. **A.** NO CHANGE
    B. ways he has a
    C. ways having a
    D. ways, and still has a

32. **F.** NO CHANGE
    G. tells us, that,
    H. tells us that,
    J. tells us that

33. **A.** NO CHANGE
    B. was running
    C. runs
    D. ran

34. **F.** NO CHANGE
    G. not be likely to see very much that has changed since.
    H. be able to see right away that not very much has changed since.
    J. not change very much.

35. Assuming that all are true, which of the following additions to the word "inventory" is most relevant in context?
    A. inventory of canned and dry goods.
    B. inventory, refusing to consider a more current method.
    C. inventory, which he writes down by hand.
    D. inventory of goods on the shelves and in the storeroom.

accumulated over the <u>years, his filing cabinets</u> have
₃₆
long since been filled up. The centerpiece of all the
clutter is his ancient typewriter, which isn't even
electric. In the past few years, Father's search for
replacement typewriter ribbons has become an increasingly difficult task, because they are no longer
being produced. He is perpetually tracking down
the few remaining places that still have these
antiquated ribbons in their dusty inventories.
When people ask him why he doesn't upgrade his
equipment, he tells them, "Electric typewriters
won't work in a blackout. All I need is a candle
and some paper, and I'm fine." Little does Father
<u>know, however, is that</u> the "upgrade" people are
₃₇
speaking of is not to an electric typewriter but to a
computer.

[1] Hoping to bring Father out of the dark
ages, <u>my sister, and I</u> bought him a brand new
₃₈
computer for his fiftieth birthday. [2] We offered to
help him to transfer all of his records onto it and to

teach him how to use it. [3] <u>Eagerly,</u> we told him
₃₉
about all the new spreadsheet programs that would
help simplify his recordkeeping and organize his

<u>accounts; and</u> emphasized the advantage of not
₄₀
having to completely retype any document when
he found a typo. [4] Rather than offering us a look
of joy for the life-changing gift we had presented
him, however, he again brought up the blackout

36. **F.** NO CHANGE
    G. years; his filing cabinets
    H. years, and besides that, his filing
    cabinets
    J. years and since his filing cabinets

37. **A.** NO CHANGE
    B. know, besides, that
    C. know, however, that
    D. know, beyond that,

38. **F.** NO CHANGE
    G. me and my sister
    H. my sister and I
    J. my sister and I,

39. **A.** NO CHANGE
    B. On the other hand,
    C. In addition
    D. Rather,

40. **F.** NO CHANGE
    G. accounts and
    H. accounts and,
    J. accounts, we

scenario. [5] To Father, this is a concrete argument, although our town hasn't had a blackout in five years, and that one only lasted an hour or two. 41 42

My father's state-of-the-art computer now serves as a very expensive bulletin board for the hundreds of adhesive notes he uses to keep himself

41. The purpose of including this fact about the town's blackout history is to:

    A. make the father appear delusional.

    B. suggest that the father's reasons not to update his technology are ill-founded.

    C. add an interesting detail to set the scene.

    D. foreshadow an event that occurs later in the story.

42. The author wants to include the following statement in this paragraph:

> We expected it to save him a lot of time and effort.

The most logical placement for this sentence would be:

    F. before Sentence 1

    G. after Sentence 1

    H. after Sentence 4

    J. after Sentence 5

organized. <u>Sooner than later,</u> we fully expect it will
               43
completely disappear under the mounting files and

43.   **A.** NO CHANGE

    B. Sooner rather than later,

    C. Sooner or later,

    D. As soon as later,

papers in the back office. <u>In the depths of that</u>
                        44
<u>disorganized office, the computer will join the</u>
                        44
<u>cell phone my mom gave him a few years ago.</u>
                        44

44.   **F.** NO CHANGE

    G. Deep in the disorganization of that office's, the computer will join the cell phone my mom gave him a few years back.

    H. In the disorganized depths of the office, the computer will soon be joined by the cell phone my mom gave him a few years ago.

    J. The computer will join the cell phone my mom gave him a few years back in the disorganized depths of that office.

Interestingly enough, every once in a while, that completely forgotten cell phone will ring from under the heavy clutter of the past. 45

45. Which of the following would provide the most appropriate conclusion for the passage?

A. It's hard to say what else might be lost in there.

B. We tell my father it's a reminder that he can't hide from the future forever.

C. We have no idea who might be calling.

D. Maybe one day I will try to find it and answer it.

ANSWERS AND EXPLANATIONS

The Toughest Task in Sports

1. D   Difficulty: Low

Category: Concision

Getting to the Answer: When DELETE is an option, read the underlined selection for relevance. The first paragraph compares the challenge of hitting a major league fastball to that of stopping a crank shot in lacrosse. The rest of the passage focuses on lacrosse, returning to the comparison to baseball in the third and fourth paragraphs. The description of quarterbacks is out of scope, so it should be deleted, (D). Choices B and C also concern the challenge faced by quarterbacks.

2. H   Difficulty: Medium

Category: Sentence Structure and Formation

Getting to the Answer: The words *that* and *which* often begin dependent clauses; when one of these words is included in an underlined portion, make sure it doesn't create a sentence fragment. As written, this sentence has no predicate verb. *Lacrosse* is the subject, but "is often referred to" is the verb for the clause that begins with *that* and describes *Lacrosse*. Removing *that* makes "is often referred to" the main verb; (H) is correct. Choices G and J do not correct the fragment error.

3. B   Difficulty: Medium

Category: Usage

Getting to the Answer: An adverb can modify a verb, adjective, or another adverb; it cannot be used to modify a noun. Here, the adverb *brutally* is used to modify the noun *game*. The adjective form *brutal* in (B) is correct. Although *brute*, C, can be used as an adjective, it is incorrect in this context. Choice D uses *brutality*, which is a noun, where the adjective form is needed.

4. F   Difficulty: Medium

Category: Punctuation

Getting to the Answer: When the main difference in the answer choices is punctuation, remember your tested rules. A comma is not needed to separate two items connected with *and*. No change is needed, making (F) correct. Choice G uses a semicolon, which would only be correct if an independent clause followed it. Choice H omits the conjunction, making the meaning of the sentence unclear. Choice J inserts a comma after *and*; commas are incorrect after the conjunctions in compounds.

5. B   Difficulty: High

Category: Sentence Structure and Formation

Getting to the Answer: A pronoun and a verb are underlined, so you have several things to check. Make sure that the pronoun has a clear antecedent and is used consistently. Then make sure that the verb agrees with its subject and is in the correct tense. The pronoun *they* correctly refers to the *players*, but this paragraph is written in the present tense (*is, possess, stands, sprint*). The present tense *attempt* in (B) is correct. Choice A incorrectly uses the past tense. Choices C and D both incorrectly use the pronoun *one*, which does not agree with its plural antecedent *players*.

6. H   Difficulty: Medium

Category: Transitions

Getting to the Answer: The underlined portion is a transition word, so check whether the sentence is logically and grammatically correct. The transition connects the fastest recorded pitch speed with the fact that few pitchers can pitch at speeds in the upper nineties. The first idea is not the result of the second, so F is incorrect. The passage is citing statistics where no temporal relationship is implied; eliminate G. Choice J turns the sentence into a run-on. Choice (H) correctly contrasts the fastest recorded pitch with the idea that few pitchers come close to that record.

7. C   Difficulty: High

Category: Punctuation

Getting to the Answer: If you're not sure how to approach a tough Punctuation question, try boiling the sentence down to its basics. Identify the subject and verb in each clause. Remember that a single comma should not separate a subject from its verb. Eliminate the introductory phrase and dependent clause from this sentence, and you're left with "the fastest crank shots on goal, can reach 110 mph." The subject is *crank shots*, and the verb is *can reach*. There should be no comma separating them, so (C) is correct. Choice A treats "the fastest crank shots on goal" as a nonessential phrase, but the sentence does not make sense without it. Choice B inserts two commas, treating *can* as nonessential. However, *can* is a necessary part of the verb phrase *can reach*. Choice D places the comma between the two verbs in the verb phrase, which will never be correct.

8. J   Difficulty: Medium

Category: Concision

Getting to the Answer: Always consider redundancy when DELETE is an answer choice. "By high school players" is redundant in a sentence that begins "Even at the high school level." Choice (J) removes the redundant language. Choices G and H both contain redundancies.

9. C   Difficulty: Low

Category: Supporting Material

Getting to the Answer: When asked whether to add new information, first consider whether it is relevant. The information about the composition of the field is not relevant to the point about the difficulty of stopping a lacrosse shot. Eliminate A and B. Choice (C) accurately describes the irrelevance of the new information, so it is correct.

10. J   Difficulty: High

Category: Precision

Getting to the Answer: When the answer choices are all single words with similar meanings, you are likely being tested on Precision. Choose the word that best describes the challenging job of the goalie. Choice F does not fit; to be *absurd* is to be ridiculous or meaningless, which does not apply to the goalie's job. Choice G is incorrect because a task cannot be *more* insurmountable; if it is insurmountable, the task cannot be done, and there is no way to have a higher degree of that failure. A *harrowing* event is deeply disturbing. While the goalie's job is challenging, we do not get a sense that the narrator is disturbed by the job. Rather, the narrator seems in awe of lacrosse goalies. Thus, H is incorrect. Choice (J), *difficult*, accurately describes the goalie's job.

11. B   Difficulty: Low

Category: Transitions

Getting to the Answer: Think about what relationships these transitions depict. The preceding sentence gives an explanation of why a lacrosse goalie has a difficult task. This sentence adds to that explanation, telling you that players can make fake moves to trick the goalie. Choices A, C, and D all use transitions that indicate one idea is being added to another. Only (B) indicates a different relationship; "On the other hand" suggests a contrast between the ideas in the two sentences.

12. G   Difficulty: Medium

Category: Passage Organization

Getting to the Answer: When asked to connect paragraphs, be sure you read through them, considering both subject matter and tone. The keyword *however* in the second sentence of Paragraph 4 tells you that there must be some sort of contrast between the first and second sentences. The second sentence also refers to "Both of these endeavors," so the sentence in question should discuss both hitting a major league pitch and blocking a crank shot. Only (G) meets both of these requirements. Choices F and H do not provide the contrast indicated by *however*; additionally, the slang phrase *is tough* in F is inconsistent with the tone of the rest of the passage. Choice J does not mention hitting a major league pitch, making "Both of these endeavors" in the second sentence illogical.

13. A   Difficulty: Medium

Category: Usage

Getting to the Answer: Get in the habit of matching verbs with their subject nouns. Since the subject of the underlined verb is the plural *Both*, this sentence needs no change, (A). Choice B is singular and does not agree with the plural subject *Both*. Choice C changes the verb to the past tense, but the passage is in the present tense. Choice D uses the conditional *would have*, but there is nothing conditional or hypothetical about the writer's opinion.

14. G   Difficulty: Medium

Category: Sentence Structure and Formation

Getting to the Answer: A pronoun is underlined, so the issue may be pronoun-antecedent agreement, ambiguity, or a pronoun shift. Check context clues. The preceding sentence uses the third-person pronoun *One*. Because the underlined sentence adds a thought to the preceding sentence, the pronouns should be consistent. This makes (G) correct. Choice F uses the second-person pronoun *you*. Choice H shifts to the third-person plural *they*. Choice J shifts from *One* to *he*; it also illogically changes the verb tense.

15. D   Difficulty: Medium

Category: Writer's Purpose

Getting to the Answer: This type of question requires you to determine the main idea of the passage. Your Reading skills will come in handy here. In the first paragraph, the writer argues that "stopping a crank shot in men's lacrosse" is "even tougher than

taking a major league at-bat." All of the following details support this position. Choice (D) correctly identifies the main idea of the passage. Choices A and B are both automatically out, because the passage does not go into any depth about the strategies employed by baseball pitchers. Choice C is incorrect because the passage provides details in Paragraph 3 about the speeds achieved by baseball pitchers.

The Swallows of San Juan Capistrano

16. H   Difficulty: Medium

Category: Concision

Getting to the Answer: The underlined selection may repeat something said elsewhere in the sentence, so take the whole sentence into consideration before choosing an answer. This sentence already indicates that the mission *gained fame*, so it is unnecessary to repeat that it is *well-known*. Eliminate F. Choice G unnecessarily uses the adjective *seasonal* along with *summer*; summer is a season, so you can eliminate G. Choice J describes the *home* as *residential*, but a home is, by definition, residential. Choice (H) is the only choice that eliminates all redundant language.

17. C   Difficulty: Low

Category: Writer's Purpose

Getting to the Answer: When asked about the purpose of a paragraph, consider both its topic and the surrounding context. Read further in the passage if necessary. The topic of the paragraph is the Mission at San Juan Capistrano, which is famous as a summer home for swallows. The following paragraph discusses the migration of these swallows, and they are the focus of the rest of the passage. Choice (C) describes the purpose of introducing these swallows. Choices A, B, and D are irrelevant to the purpose of the passage.

18. J   Difficulty: Medium

Category: Sentence Structure and Formation

Getting to the Answer: Items in a compound must be parallel in form. The two verbs joined by *and* in the original sentence are *nest* and *bearing*. Only (J) provides the needed parallel verb. Choices F, G, and H all use the *-ing* form, violating the rules of parallel structure.

19. C   Difficulty: Medium

Category: Sentence Structure and Formation

Getting to the Answer: Items in a series or list require parallel structure. There are three verbs in this series. The first two verbs, *ring* and *is*, are in the simple present tense, so the underlined verb should be also. Choice (C) is correct. Choices A, B, and D all violate the rules of parallel structure.

20. F   Difficulty: Medium

Category: Sentence Structure and Formation

Getting to the Answer: NO CHANGE will be the answer to about 25% of English Test questions. This sentence is correct as written, so (F) is the answer. The past tense verb *discovered* used after the past progressive *were seeking* indicates that the birds found the mission while in the process of looking for *refuge*. Choices G and J omit the pronoun *they*, suggesting that it was the innkeeper, not the birds, who found the mission. Choice H creates a grammatically incorrect sentence.

21. B   Difficulty: Low

Category: Usage

Getting to the Answer: The preposition *of* cannot be part of a verb phrase. The preposition *of* in the original version should actually be the verb *have*. Choice (B) corrects this error. Choices A and C both use the preposition *of* instead of the verb *have*. Choice D omits the verb *have*, leaving the grammatically incorrect *may developed*.

22. H   Difficulty: Medium

Category: Transitions

Getting to the Answer: When a transition word is underlined, determine what two ideas are being connected. Here, the transition word connects the discovery that the birds create their nests out of mud and the idea that the swallows chose the mission because it was near rivers. The following sentence explains that the rivers are a source of mud, so these ideas are not in contrast; eliminate F. *Indeed* cannot be used to create a subordinate clause, making G ungrammatical. It would make more sense for the biologists to postulate about the reason the swallows wanted to live near rivers after discovering that they needed mud for their nests, so (H) is correct.

23. B   Difficulty: Low

Category: Usage

Getting to the Answer: Many Usage questions will present you with four grammatically correct idioms; use context to determine which is correct. *Of which*, A, *to which*, (B), and *by which*, C, are all proper idioms, but the only one that makes sense in context is (B): the swallows *return to* their nests. Choice D omits the preposition, incorrectly suggesting that the birds return the nests to some person or place.

24. G   Difficulty: Medium

Category: Supporting Material

Getting to the Answer: When an English Test question has a question stem, read it carefully. Frequently, all of the answer choices will be both consistent and relevant, but only one will fulfill the requirements of the stem. Only one sentence gives a specific reason for the swallows choosing the mission based on its location near two rivers. Choice (G) explains that the rivers provide a food supply for the swallows, which is a logical reason for the swallows to live nearby. Choice F provides information about swallow nest-building, not about swallows choosing the mission based on its location near the rivers. Choice H provides a detail about the rivers, but it is unclear how this detail relates to the swallows. Choice J is a generalization; it doesn't tell you anything specific about the other advantages provided by the rivers.

25. C   Difficulty: Medium

Category: Transitions

Getting to the Answer: The underlined portion is a transitional phrase, so check for errors in both logic and grammar. The previous sentence describes the swallows returning to the mission for protection, and the sentence with the underlined portion explains that the whole city protects the swallows. Choice A includes a contrast transition, which is illogical here; both ideas involve protecting the swallows. Choices B and D are sequential transitions, which do not make sense in context. The idea that the whole city protects the swallows serves to reinforce that they can return to the mission for protection, making the emphasis transition in (C) correct.

26. F   Difficulty: Medium

Category: Punctuation

Getting to the Answer: Remember your tested comma rules; no other uses will be correct on the ACT. The sentence is correct as written; no change is needed, (F). Choices G and H both incorrectly insert a comma between the noun *community* and its verb *sees*. Choice J uses an adjective (*clear*), instead of an adverb, to modify the verb *sees*.

27. C   Difficulty: Medium

Category: Punctuation

Getting to the Answer: Dashes may be used to offset supplementary material within a sentence. Here, "usually in the hills" is descriptive information about *the area*. Such descriptive phrases can be offset from the main sentence with commas or dashes; (C) correctly uses dashes to offset and emphasize the phrase. Choice A omits one of the commas necessary to correctly offset the phrase. Choice B uses a

semicolon, but the second clause is not independent. Choice D is awkward and unnecessarily wordy.

28. H   Difficulty: Medium

Category: Concision

Getting to the Answer: Two words that convey the same information are redundant and incorrect on the ACT. All historic buildings are old, so F and G are both incorrect. Choice J is unnecessarily wordy. Choice (H) is the most concise answer and is therefore correct.

29. B   Difficulty: Medium

Category: Usage

Getting to the Answer: Some idioms will be properly constructed but incorrect in context. The phrase *in an attempt* requires the infinitive verb form; (B) is correct. Choice A uses *to attempt at*, which is idiomatically incorrect. Choices C and D change the infinitive *to attempt* to the noun *an attempt*; this creates an illogical sentence in C and an idiomatically incorrect one in D.

30. J   Difficulty: Medium

Category: Passage Organization

Getting to the Answer: Since NO CHANGE is not offered as an option, you'll need to find the most logical place to insert the new sentence. Paragraph 5 discusses the problems that "have arisen in recent years," so this sentence about a problem with the swallows belongs in Paragraph 5; eliminate F and G. Sentences 2 and 3 in Paragraph 5 explain the specific problems that are leading to a decline in the swallow migration. It is reasonable that one result of the changes discussed in Sentences 2 and 3 would be the lack of "huge clouds of swallows descending upon the mission as in the past decades." The best placement for the new sentence is after Sentence 3 in Paragraph 5; (J) is correct.

My Old-Fashioned Father

31. A   Difficulty: Low

Category: Sentence Structure and Formation

Getting to the Answer: When a period appears in the underlined portion, check to see if each sentence is complete. Here, each sentence is complete and correct; therefore (A), NO CHANGE, is correct. Choice B creates a run-on sentence. Choices C and D create sentences that are awkward and overly wordy.

32. J   Difficulty: Medium

Category: Punctuation

Getting to the Answer: The ACT tests very specific punctuation rules. If punctuation is used in a way not covered by these rules, it will be incorrect. No commas are required in the underlined selection; (J) is correct. Choices F, G, and H all contain unnecessary commas.

33. C   Difficulty: Medium

Category: Sentence Structure and Formation

Getting to the Answer: When a verb is underlined, make sure it places the action properly in relation to the other events in the passage. This passage is written primarily in the present tense; *runs*, (C), is the correct answer here. Choices A and B use verb tenses that do not make sense in context. The past tense verb in D is inconsistent with the rest of the passage.

34. F   Difficulty: Medium

Category: Concision

Getting to the Answer: Very rarely will a correct answer choice be significantly longer than the original selection. The underlined selection is grammatically and logically correct, so check the answer choices for a more concise version. You can eliminate G and H, both of which are wordier than the original. Choice J may be tempting because it's shorter than the underlined selection, but it

changes the meaning of the sentence; the back office, not the reader, is what hasn't changed. Choice (F) is correct.

35. B   Difficulty: Medium

Category: Supporting Material

Getting to the Answer: When an English Test question contains a question stem, read it carefully. More than one choice is likely to be both relevant and correct, but only one will satisfy the conditions of the stem. This paragraph deals with the author's father's refusal to give up his old-fashioned ways. Choice (B) is the most consistent choice. Choices A and D describe the items being inventoried, which is irrelevant to the point of the paragraph. Choice C is redundant; since we already know he uses paper and pencil to keep his inventory, it's understood that he's writing it by hand.

36. G   Difficulty: Medium

Category: Sentence Structure and Formation

Getting to the Answer: Commas cannot be used to combine independent clauses. Here, the comma connects two independent clauses. Choice (G) correctly replaces the comma with a semicolon. Choice H corrects the run-on error but is unnecessarily wordy. Choice J leaves the meaning of the second clause incomplete.

37. C   Difficulty: High

Category: Sentence Structure and Formation

Getting to the Answer: Beware of answer choices that make changes to parts of the selection that contain no error; these choices will rarely be correct. As written, this sentence uses incorrect grammatical structure; the verb *is* is incorrect here, so you should eliminate A. Choice (C) eliminates it without introducing additional errors. Choices B and D correct the sentence's grammatical error, but neither uses the necessary contrast transition to relate this sentence to the one before it.

38. H   Difficulty: Low

Category: Punctuation

Getting to the Answer: Commas are used in a series of three or more; they are incorrect in compounds. "My sister and I" is a compound; no comma is needed, so F is incorrect. Choice (H) corrects the error without adding any new ones. Choice G uses the incorrect pronoun case; because you wouldn't say "me bought him a brand new computer," *me* is incorrect in the compound as well. Choice J incorrectly separates the sentence's subject and its predicate verb with a comma.

39. A   Difficulty: High

Category: Transitions

Getting to the Answer: When a transition word or phrase is underlined, make sure it properly relates the ideas it connects. The underlined word is the transition between the offer to help transfer records and the information about other ways the computer could be helpful. The second sentence is a continuation of the first, so you can eliminate B and D, both of which suggest a contrast. Choosing between (A) and C is a little more difficult, but remember that new errors may be introduced in answer choices. *In addition* in C would be acceptable if it were followed by a comma, but as written, it's incorrect. Choice (A) is correct.

40. G   Difficulty: Medium

Category: Punctuation

Getting to the Answer: Semicolons can only combine independent clauses. Here, the second clause is not independent, so the semicolon is incorrect; eliminate F. Choice (G) correctly eliminates the semicolon. Choice H incorrectly places a comma after the conjunction. Choice J creates a run-on sentence.

41. B   Difficulty: High

Category: Writer's Purpose

Getting to the Answer: When asked about the purpose of particular information, consider the purpose of the larger section. This paragraph describes the father's resistance to technology, which stems in part from his desire to be able to work even in blackout conditions. The information about the town's history shows that blackout conditions seldom occur, making the father's reason a bad one. Choice (B) reflects this reasoning, and it is correct. Choice A is too extreme; the father's reason may be poor, but that does not make him delusional. Choices C and D do not relate to the purpose of the paragraph.

42. G   Difficulty: Medium

Category: Passage Organization

Getting to the Answer: When asked to add new information, read it into the passage at the points suggested to choose its most logical placement. There are three pronouns in this new sentence; clarity requires that it be placed somewhere that these pronouns have logical antecedents. Placing it after Sentence 1, as (G) suggests, gives each pronoun a clear antecedent: *we* is the author and his sister, *him* is their father, and *it* is the computer. Choice F puts the siblings' hopes about how a computer could help their father before the information that they bought him one. Choice H's placement makes the antecedent for *it* Father's *blackout scenario*, which doesn't make sense in context. Placing the new sentence where Choice J suggests gives the pronoun the antecedent *blackout*, which is also illogical.

43. C   Difficulty: Medium

Category: Usage

Getting to the Answer: Idiom questions often offer more than one idiomatically correct answer choice; use context to determine which is appropriate. "Sooner than later" is idiomatically incorrect, so you should eliminate A; these are comparison words, but nothing is compared here. Both B and (C) offer proper idioms, but (C) is the one that's appropriate here. Choice D is also idiomatically incorrect.

44. F   Difficulty: Medium

Category: Sentence Structure and Formation

Getting to the Answer: Remember to read for logic as well as for grammar and usage. The best version of this sentence is the way it is written; (F) is correct. Choice G redundantly uses the possessive *office's* where possession has already been indicated by *of*. Choice H misstates the information in the passage; the writer's father received the cell phone before the computer. Choice J incorrectly indicates that "the disorganized depths of that office" is where the

writer's father received his cell phone, not where the cell phone ended up, which is opposite of the writer's intended meaning.

45. B   Difficulty: Low

Category: Passage Organization

Getting to the Answer: When asked to add information, consider both subject matter and tone. This essay is about the author's father's resistance to technology. Choice (B) concludes the essay by referencing something stated at the beginning: that the writer's father tries to *hide* from the future. Choices A, C, and D, while relevant to the paragraph, do not provide strong conclusions to a passage about the father's aversion to technology.

CHAPTER FIVE

Topic Development and Knowledge of Language

GETTING STARTED

Study the **Topic Development** and **Knowledge of Language** question types below to learn how to approach them and the concepts that these questions test. Knowing the information that you'll need to answer the questions helps you identify the important clues in the passage that will lead you to the correct answers.

Topic Development

Topic Development questions test your ability to determine why a passage is written and whether particular information helps accomplish that purpose. There are two subcategories within **Topic Development**: Supporting Material and Writer's Purpose.

Supporting Material questions may ask you to:

- evaluate whether material maintains the focus and unity of the passage;
- identify the purposes of parts of the passage; or
- determine the effect of adding, revising, or deleting information.

Writer's Purpose questions may ask you to:

- determine whether a sentence or a paragraph has met the writer's intended goal, or

- determine whether an entire passage has met the writer's intended goal.

> ✔ *Note*
>
> **Remember, if any part of a choice does not match the passage, the entire choice is incorrect.**

Supporting Material

Focus and Unity

When determining the focus, or the author's subject matter and particular emphasis within that subject matter, of a passage, ask yourself what the passage is discussing. Often, the first paragraph and the topic sentences of the remaining paragraphs reveal the main focus of the passage.

In order to be unified, a passage must maintain a consistent focus on its subject matter. Information that is not relevant to the focus of the passage should be deleted. Keep in mind that each paragraph has its own main idea and all the information in the paragraph should relate to this main idea. Even information that relates to the overall subject of the passage should be deleted if it does not match the focus of the paragraph in which it appears.

Purpose

Once you've determined a passage's focus, identifying the purpose of the passage or a portion of the passage will be much easier. To determine the purpose of a passage, ask yourself what the author is trying to achieve by writing the passage. The writer selects particular wording and examples to support the focus of the passage while maintaining a consistent tone and purpose.

Effect of Adding, Revising, or Deleting Information

When asked about adding or revising a selection, consider what new information the selection provides and whether that information: (a) matches the writer's focus and (b) helps express the purpose of the sentence or paragraph. When asked about deleting a selection, consider what the passage might be missing if the proposed revision were made. To answer these questions, read the passage both ways—with and without the proposed change—to see which sounds more cohesive. Be sure to read the sentences before and after the proposed revision to best assess the change in context.

> ✔ **Expert Tip**
>
> When the question has a question stem, you are not being tested on concision, or expressing an idea in the fewest words possible, even when asked about deleting information. The test shows no preference for deleting information on Topic Development questions, so don't automatically think that deleting is the best option! When you see a question stem, focus on relevance rather than concision.

Writer's Purpose

Some **Topic Development** questions ask explicitly about the purpose of a part of the passage or the passage as a whole. When asked which choice best accomplishes the purpose of a part of the passage, consider the scope and function of that part. For example, a good conclusion is designed to summarize the passage, and a good paragraph transition clearly connects the ideas between the paragraphs.

Some questions ask whether the essay as a whole accomplishes a certain purpose. These questions appear at the end of the passage. In order to answer these questions, consider the overall purpose and scope of the passage. Is the passage meant to persuade the reader, or is it more neutral and explanatory? What is the main topic of the passage? Be careful not to select answer choices that are either too narrow or too broad. For example, a passage discussing the history of European fairy tales could not accurately be described as an essay on the history of literature; that description is too broad. On the other hand, describing it as an essay on one particular fairy tale would be too narrow. Incorrect answer choices that are too narrow often describe the focus of one paragraph but do not capture the scope of the entire passage.

Knowledge of Language

Good writing must be concise, precise, and consistent in tone. The ACT rewards your ability to identify and correct these Knowledge of Language issues.

Concision

A concise sentence includes no unnecessary words: avoid phrasing that is wordy or redundant. Each word must contribute to the meaning of the sentence; otherwise, it should be eliminated.

Wordy/Redundant Sentence	Concise Sentence
The superb musical score **added enhancement to the experience of** the play's development.	The superb musical score **enhanced** the play's development.
I **did not anticipate** the **surprising, unexpected** plot twist.	I **did not anticipate** the plot twist.
The students **increased some of their knowledge of** Tuscan architecture.	The students **learned about** Tuscan architecture.

Precision

Words should convey their meaning precisely, so be on the lookout for language that is vague or ambiguous. The ACT rewards your ability to distinguish between clear and unclear language.

Words within passages should be not only necessary but also relevant to the main point of the paragraph in which they occur. Make sure that no sentence includes phrases that detract from the main point. If "DELETE the underlined portion" is an answer choice, ask yourself whether the underlined portion enhances the meaning and clarity of the passage.

Ambiguous Pronouns

A pronoun is ambiguous if its antecedent (the noun to which it refers) is either missing or unclear. The ACT tests your ability to identify and correct both of these issues. When you see an underlined pronoun, make sure you can identify the noun to which it refers and check whether the pronoun clearly refers to that noun.

Ambiguous Pronoun Use	Clear Pronoun Use
Anthony walked with Cody to the ice cream shop, and **he** bought a banana split.	Anthony walked with Cody to the ice cream shop, and **Cody** bought a banana split.

Word Choice

Some questions test your knowledge of the correct word to use in context. The ACT does not primarily test difficult vocabulary; rather, the ACT tests your ability to identify whether the author has used the correct word(s) to convey the intended meaning. The ACT may explicitly ask you to identify which choice conveys a certain meaning. The test may also ask you to identify how well a sentence fits with the main point of the paragraph. Make sure the underlined portion or answer choice clearly conveys the intended meaning and fits with the rest of the content.

Style and Tone

An author's style and tone are conveyed by word choice, rhetorical devices, and sentence structure. An author may write informally, as though speaking with friends; academically, as though speaking to experts; or persuasively, as though trying to convince the reader. The ACT requires you to revise a text to ensure that its style and tone are consistent. Some Style and Tone questions have question stems, whereas others do not. Even if the question lacks a question stem, check to ensure that the wording matches the style and tone of the passage as a whole.

Style

An important element of style is the voice of the passage: whom the passage is directed toward and whether the author refers to himself or herself. One indicator of style is the type of pronouns the author uses.

Style	Pronoun Use in Passage
Somewhat informal	First-person pronouns such as *I* and *my*
More informal	Second-person pronouns such as *you* and *your*
Formal	Third-person pronouns such as *one* and *one's*

Different voices are appropriate for different subject matter and purposes. Within a passage, style—including how it is expressed with pronouns—must be consistent.

Tone

Tone includes the features of the text that reflect the author's point of view. The tone of the text should match the author's purpose. For example, the phrase "this mind-blowing new treatment" might fit well in a passage whose purpose is to recommend a course of action, but it would not fit the tone of a passage whose purpose is to give an objective description of the treatment. Some Tone questions include a question stem that asks which choice best maintains the essay's tone. Whether or not there is a question stem, make sure that the underlined portion matches the overall purpose and the author's point of view.

IMPROVING WITH PRACTICE

Step 1: Read Until You Can Identify the Issue

Always read the entire English passage. This is particularly important for **Topic Development** questions because these will frequently test your understanding of the entire passage. This is particularly important for **Knowledge of Language** questions because the best clues for the correct answers may be before or after the underlined segment or the numbered box. Be sure to identify:

- the main idea of each paragraph,
- the author's opinion/tone, and
- any keywords, especially transition and timing keywords.

You may have to read well after the underlined segment or question marker to be able to identify the issue. If you're not sure there's an issue, keep reading and then return to the question.

Step 2: Answer the Questions

As you're practicing, refer back to the tips in the "Getting Started" section and answer questions one at a time, reviewing the Answer and Explanation for every question immediately after completing it. If you got the question correct, congratulate yourself, but take a moment to read the entire explanation to be sure you got the question right for the right reason. The explanation may even point out a more efficient way that you can use on a later question!

Step 3: Review Incorrect Answers

If you get the question incorrect . . . still congratulate yourself! You're about to learn something new that you'll be able to use to improve your performance on Test Day. Don't read the explanation yet; instead, try the question again.

If you get the question correct the second time, read the explanation to see if you solved the question in the most efficient way. Identify the mistake you made the first time, and determine how you're going to avoid making that mistake again.

> ✔ **Expert Tip**
>
> Many top scoring students have an ACT notebook where they write down what they learn from every question. Doing this can be time-consuming, but it can also help you identify the types of mistakes you tend to make.

If you get the question incorrect the second time, use the explanation to learn how to get the question correct. Work through the question again while following the explanation, and identify the steps you will need to take to get a similar question correct. Although the passages and questions will change, the concepts being tested will not. When you encounter unfamiliar questions, take note of them for future study sessions.

> ✔ **Note**
>
> The ACT is a standardized test. While high-difficulty English questions are usually more difficult to answer than low- or medium-difficulty questions, they are often similar in structure and purpose, and the same skills (listed in Chapter 1) are tested on every English Test. You actually can predict the types of questions you will see on Test Day!

After all that work, it's time to move to the next question. Reviewing in this way will take time. However, improvement doesn't come from just doing lots and lots of questions; it comes from thinking through your approach and improving it with every question.

RAISING YOUR SCORE EVEN MORE

Here is one of the "secrets" to conquering the English Test: because the ACT is a standardized test, there will always be clues that make one choice definitely correct and the other choices completely incorrect. It's never a matter of opinion.

> ✔ **Expert Tip**
>
> Time spent identifying the clues not only saves time evaluating the choices but also improves your accuracy. Always find the clues first!

For questions asking about the purpose or effect of a feature, re-read the feature absolutely literally and describe that information in your own words. Then, match your description to the choices.

For questions asking about introductions, evaluate each choice by reading it strictly on its own. If any part of the sentence is unclear when you read the sentence in isolation, it is not a good introductory sentence.

For questions asking about conclusions, the correct choice will not bring in any new ideas, but it will effectively summarize the paragraph or the passage.

PRACTICE QUESTIONS

The following test-like question sets provide an opportunity to practice reading Topic Development and Knowledge of Language questions. While many of the questions pertain to Topic Development and Knowledge of Language, some touch on other concepts tested on the English Test to ensure that your practice is test-like, with a variety of question types per passage.

PASSAGE I

Signature of the Time

[1] The home of Tyler Gregory looks like an abandoned bureaucratic archive. [2] Almost all of the available space <u>being crammed with old books or</u>
₁
covered with folios and documents. [3] Dr. Gregory, a psychologist, first began collecting old documents as a hobby. [4] What was initially a <u>hobby quickly became a life's</u> passion and devotion.
₂
[5] Predictably, several papers in Dr. Gregory's collection, which includes a faded but detailed inn

receipt, <u>is</u> signed by John Hancock. [6] Proudly
₃
displayed, the John Hancock documents

<u>had represented</u> Dr. Gregory's work: graphology.
₄
[7] Unlike other rare and vintage document

1. **A.** NO CHANGE
   B. was crammed with old books or is
   C. is crammed with old books or
   D. crammed with old books or

2. **F.** NO CHANGE
   G. hobby, quickly became a life's
   H. hobby quickly became a life's,
   J. hobby: quickly became a life's

3. **A.** NO CHANGE
   B. are
   C. was
   D. DELETE the underlined portion.

4. **F.** NO CHANGE
   G. represent
   H. represented
   J. would have represented

enthusiasts, Dr. Gregory collects only documents

that bear famous signatures. ⑤

Graphology, a growing field, is used to authen-
        6
ticate documents in court trials and other legal

proceedings, but it has other, less familiar uses as

well. Psychologists can use graphology to analyze

a patient's psyche. Many patients cannot explain

their problems, but psychologists have techniques
                                              7
to help patients learn to express themselves.
                    7
Psychologists and graphologists have noted that

handwriting is a subconscious expression of inner

thoughts. Many of the issues involuntarily revealed

by a subject's handwriting remain unknown to the

subject herself. Unlike the patients of most

psychologists use graphology, however, Dr. Gregory's
          8
subjects are dead. Dr. Gregory once practiced clinical

5. To maintain the logic and coherence of this
   paragraph, Sentence 7 should be placed:

   A. where it is now.

   B. after Sentence 1.

   C. after Sentence 3.

   D. after Sentence 4.

6. Which of the following true choices provides
   information that is most relevant and mean-
   ingful to the essay in its entirety?

   F. NO CHANGE

   G. or handwriting analysis,

   H. which has been practiced for decades,

   J. as a professional endeavor,

7. After reviewing the essay, the writer wants to
   insert a statement at this point that would
   lead into the next sentence. Given that all
   of the choices are true, which one best
   accomplishes the writer's purpose?

   A. NO CHANGE

   B. and this is one reason they seek help
      from professionals.

   C. but their handwriting often can.

   D. so analyzing the psyche can be
      challenging.

8. F. NO CHANGE

   G. used to

   H. who use

   J. being used

psychology in the past, but his interest in graphology is a more historical one. He studies the handwriting of historical figures, hoping to better
understand their personalities. Dr. Gregory's interest in historical personalities stems from an inter-
disciplinary desire to apply psychological theories
to the explanation of historical events. Historians
and political scientists have long sought to apply psychology and its theories to their work, but they have
not always met with success. While such theories as
organizational psychology and cognitive dissonance
have illuminated some historical decisions, they have
done so neither definitively nor broadly. The scarcity
of information regarding the personalities of historical figures has been the biggest obstacle. ⑩

Unlike current in-depth information from
multiple media sources, scarcely any record exists
of the private personalities and lives of history's

greatest figures. ⑪ The records that do exist paint

9. **A.** NO CHANGE
    B. psychology for a time,
    C. psychology at an earlier period in his life,
    D. psychology,

10. The primary purpose of mentioning
    psychology in this paragraph is to:
    F. provide introductory information about
    Dr. Gregory.
    G. explain its relation to graphology.
    H. discuss the psychology of preserving
    historical documents.
    J. downplay its importance in
    understanding personalities.

11. If the writer were to delete the previous
    sentence, the paragraph would primarily lose:
    A. a motivation for Dr. Gregory's interest in
    graphology.
    B. an important detail about the difficulty in
    applying psychological theories to
    historical figures.
    C. a reason for the broad agreement about
    the analyses of historical figures.
    D. a cause for the friends of well-known
    figures to write accounts of them.

skewed <u>pictures, for they</u> come almost entirely
₁₂
from friends, enemies, or the historical figures
themselves. Thus, Dr. Gregory uses graphology to
study and understand the personalities and inner
lives of important men and women who lived so
long ago.

Dr. Gregory, along with most graphologists,
believes that a person's signature reveals more
about that person's personality than normal handwriting. The signature legally and traditionally
conveys the mark of an individual. This supports
Dr. Gregory's <u>belief that</u> the shape of a signature
₁₃
also serves as a psychological stamp. According to

Dr. Gregory, a person <u>has been</u> both consciously
₁₄
and unconsciously imprinting key aspects of his
personality while he forms a signature. Those
aspects have led Dr. Gregory to infer many personal details about historical figures. Such details
are now being used by historians in their analyses
of historical decisions.

12. Of the following alternatives to the underlined portion, which choice would NOT be
acceptable?

F. pictures; they

G. pictures. They

H. pictures, as they

J. pictures they

13. A. NO CHANGE

B. belief, that

C. belief that,

D. belief: that

14. F. NO CHANGE

G. had been

H. will be

J. is

> Question 15 asks about the preceding passage as a whole.

15. Suppose the writer had intended to write a short essay about an example of one area of study influencing another area of study. Would this essay achieve the writer's goal?

A. Yes, because the essay explains how personality traits determined through analyzing a historical individual's handwriting can be used to form a psychological study of such figures and their roles in historical events.

B. Yes, because the essay compares the research process of graphologists to the research process of historians.

C. No, because the essay focuses on Dr. Gregory's personal life rather than his area of study.

D. No, because the essay does not discuss the findings of historians who have applied psychological theories to historical figures and events.

PASSAGE II

Traveling at the Speed of Sound

The term "supersonic" refers to anything that travels faster than the speed of sound. When the last of the supersonic Concorde passenger planes made its final trip across the Atlantic in <u>November of 2003, an interesting</u> chapter in
₁₆
history was finally closed. The fleet of supersonic Concorde SSTs, or "Supersonic Transports,"

<u>they were</u> jointly operated by Air France and
₁₇
British Airways, had been making the intercontinental trip across the Atlantic for almost thirty years. These amazing machines cruised at Mach 2, more than twice the speed of sound. They flew <u>to a height</u> almost twice that of standard passenger
₁₈
airplanes. The Concorde routinely made the trip from New York to London in less than three hours and was much more expensive than normal transatlantic flights. <u>Furthermore,</u> the majority of the passengers
₁₉
who traveled on the Concorde were celebrities or the extremely wealthy, it also attracted ordinary people who simply wanted to know how it felt to travel faster than the speed of sound. Some would save money for years just to gain that knowledge.

What is the speed of sound? Many people are surprised to learn that there is no fixed answer to this question. The speed <u>that</u> sound travels through
₂₀
a given medium depends on a number of factors.

16. **F.** NO CHANGE
    G. November, of 2003 an interesting
    H. November of 2003 an interesting
    J. November of 2003; an interesting

17. **A.** NO CHANGE
    B. those were
    C. which were
    D. which being

18. **F.** NO CHANGE
    G. at an altitude
    H. toward an altitude
    J. very high

19. **A.** NO CHANGE
    B. Despite
    C. Though
    D. Along with

20. **F.** NO CHANGE
    G. to which
    H. at which
    J. where

To understand the speed of sound, we must first understand what a "sound" really is. 21

The standard dictionary definition of sound is "a vibration or disturbance transmitted, like waves through water, through a material medium such as a gas." Our ears are able to pick up those sound

waves and <u>convert</u> them into what we hear. This means that the speed at which sound travels through

gas <u>directly depends on what gas it is traveling through, and the temperature and pressure of the gas.</u> When discussing aircraft breaking the speed of sound, that gas medium, of course, is air. As air

temperature and pressure decrease <u>with altitude</u>, so does the speed of sound. An airplane flying at the speed of sound at sea level is traveling roughly at

21. The purpose of this paragraph, as it relates to the surrounding paragraphs, is primarily to:

A. provide an example of the main idea before continuing discussion of that idea.

B. transition from a discussion of certain aircraft to the science behind them.

C. present a counterargument to the main thesis before refuting that counterargument.

D. transition from the general topic of aircraft to a story about specific airplanes.

22. Which of the following alternatives to the underlined portion would be the LEAST acceptable?

F. change

G. translate

H. alter

J. transform

23. A. NO CHANGE

B. depends directly on the type, temperature, and pressure of the gas it is traveling through.

C. directly depends on what gas it is, and also on the temperature and pressure of that gas.

D. depends directly on the type, temperature, and pressure of the gas.

24. F. NO CHANGE

G. with height

H. with a drop in altitude

J. at higher altitudes

761 mph; <u>however</u> when that same plane climbs
₂₅
to 20,000 feet, the speed of sound is only about
707 mph. This is why the Concorde's cruising
attitude was so much higher than that of a regular
passenger aircraft; <u>planes can reach supersonic</u>
₂₆
<u>speeds more easily at higher altitudes.</u>
₂₆

In the years since the Concorde <u>has been</u>
₂₇
decommissioned, only fighter pilots and astronauts
have been able to experience the sensation of

breaking "the sound barrier." <u>But that is all about</u>
₂₈
<u>to change very soon.</u> Newer and faster supersonic
₂₈
passenger planes are being developed that will be
technologically superior to the Concorde and
much cheaper to operate. <u>Now,</u> supersonic passen-
₂₉
ger travel will be available not only to the rich and

famous, <u>but also be for</u> the masses, so they, too, can
₃₀
experience life at supersonic speeds.

25. **A.** NO CHANGE
    B. however,
    C. and so,
    D. even so

26. Given that all are true, which of the following
    provides the most logical conclusion for this
    sentence?
    F. NO CHANGE
    G. they're much faster.
    H. they use much more fuel than regular
       aircraft.
    J. they're rarely visible because they fly
       above the cloud cover.

27. **A.** NO CHANGE
    B. came to be
    C. was
    D. had been

28. **F.** NO CHANGE
    G. Soon, however, that is about to change.
    H. Soon, however, that will change.
    J. That is about to change soon.

29. **A.** NO CHANGE
    B. Nearby,
    C. Soon,
    D. Upcoming,

30. **F.** NO CHANGE
    G. but also be available to
    H. but also to
    J. but for

PASSAGE III

A Screenwriting Career

Wanting to have success as a Hollywood
screenwriter, if you do, you should be aware of the
difficulties that come along with this career and its
development. Very few budding screenwriters
attain success by selling, let alone producing, their
screenplays. On the other hand, even successful
screenwriters report living stressful and dissatisfied, though wealthy, lives.

    The first difficulty encountered by budding
screenwriters is the lack of a formal career path. A
recent college graduate cannot approach the career
center at his or her school or find time for
extracurricular activities. While several successful

31. **A.** NO CHANGE
    B. If you want to succeed as a Hollywood
       screenwriter,
    C. Whether or not wanting to succeed as a
       Hollywood screenwriter,
    D. Having decided if you want to or not
       succeed as a Hollywood screenwriter,

32. **F.** NO CHANGE
    G. For this reason
    H. Nowadays
    J. Furthermore

33. Assuming that all are true, which choice is
    the most logical and appropriate in context?
    A. NO CHANGE
    B. read the classified ads in order to find
       screenwriting opportunities.
    C. understand the difficulties of his or her
       chosen career.
    D. stumble into an opportunity to work in
       the field.

screenwriters have written guides that outline possibilities for success, their proposed suggestions only highlight the <u>fruitlessness</u> of their experiences.
₃₄

34. Which choice best conveys that there is no one path to becoming a screenwriter?
   F. NO CHANGE
   G. difficulty
   H. rewards
   J. disparity

Unlike its value in other professional pursuits, <u>a college education was</u> not necessarily a career
₃₅
boost for a budding screenwriter. In fact, a college education can have the reverse effect on a screen-writer. The academic study of literature or film may help a budding screenwriter to produce higher quality work, but such an education delays its recipient from competing in the film industry. <u>This also tends to hold true for actors.</u> While a
₃₆
college graduate spends his or her late teens and early twenties studying, the budding screenwriters

35. **A.** NO CHANGE
   B. a college education has been
   C. a college education is
   D. it is, a college education

36. **F.** NO CHANGE
   G. Actors also find this to be true for themselves.
   H. This has similar repercussions for actors.
   J. DELETE the underlined portion.

who do not attend college <u>begins honing</u> their craft
₃₇
and competing for work several years earlier. In a

37. **A.** NO CHANGE
   B. begins to hone
   C. begin honing
   D. has begun honing

career path that usually requires years to develop, late entry can create a substantial disadvantage. 38

38. Suppose the writer had intended to write a paragraph discouraging those interested in writing screenplays from pursuing a college education. Does the paragraph fulfill this purpose?

F. Yes, because it mentions the value of education.

G. Yes, because it provides reasons why pursuing an education can be harmful.

H. No, because the author does not express an opinion about the value of education.

J. No, because the focus is on screenwriting rather than education.

Moreover, the debt of a college education acquired at a prestigious school may lead many young screenwriters to surrender early to the allure of steady, if not glamorous, work and pay. Those without college educations often cannot escape to

"fallback" careers; this lack of options bolsters their drive to succeed. Furthermore, those without college educations are less averse to the low-wage

jobs, aspiring screenwriters are forced to take in order to pay living expenses while saving blocks of time to hone their craft.

The very few screenwriters who succeed often find that's the realities of their day-to-day lives are far different from their glamorous preconceptions and the media's idealistic portrayals. While they can earn very high salaries, successful Hollywood screenwriters often feel more stressed and power-

39. A. NO CHANGE

B. though universities offer work-study programs to help students pay for school, many graduate with debt; this burden

C. the burden of student loans

D. student loans which

40. F. NO CHANGE

G. careers; this,

H. careers so, this

J. careers this

41. A. NO CHANGE

B. jobs, these aspiring screenwriters

C. jobs aspiring, screenwriters,

D. jobs that aspiring screenwriters

42. F. NO CHANGE

G. that the realities of there

H. there the realities of their

J. that the realities of their

less than they did when they struggled. A Hollywood screenwriter's reputation always hinges on
the success of his or her last screenplay. <u>It</u> produces
a high level of stress and pressure to
₄₃

43. **A.** NO CHANGE
    B. This volatile situation
    C. The screenplay
    D. They

<u>continually produce more and better</u> work.
₄₄
Furthermore, the Hollywood hierarchy places stu-
dio executives, producers, directors, and star actors
above screenwriters in both pay and importance.
Thus, even the most successful screenwriters must
yield creative power to individuals who often have
very little knowledge of the craft of screenwriting.

44. **F.** NO CHANGE
    G. churn out improving and increasing
    H. be more productive and improved
    J. raising the stakes of

Regardless of the hardships of initially succeeding and then thriving in the screenwriting profession, young people move to Los Angeles every year
to pursue this career. If <u>one is among these people,</u>
₄₅
please research and learn as much as possible about
the vicissitudes as well as the potential triumphs of
this profession.

45. **A.** NO CHANGE
    B. one is among them
    C. finding yourself among these people
    D. you are among these people

ANSWERS AND EXPLANATIONS

Signature of the Time

1. C **Difficulty:** Medium

Category: Sentence Structure and Formation

Getting to the Answer: Remember that an *-ing* verb form by itself cannot serve as the predicate (main) verb in a sentence. As written, this sentence is a fragment. Choice (C) corrects this error by replacing *being* with *is* and does not introduce any additional errors. Choice B uses verb tenses inconsistently. Choice D does not address the error.

2. F **Difficulty:** Medium

Category: Punctuation

Getting to the Answer: Remember the tested punctuation rules. If punctuation isn't needed for one of those reasons, it will be incorrect on the ACT. This sentence is correct as written, (F); no additional punctuation is needed in the underlined portion. Choice G incorrectly places a comma between the subject "What was initially a hobby" and the verb phrase *quickly became*. Choice H incorrectly places a comma between a possessive noun (which functions grammatically as an adjective) and the noun it modifies. Choice J uses a colon, but what follows is not a brief definition, explanation, or list of what comes before.

3. B **Difficulty:** Medium

Category: Usage

Getting to the Answer: Don't fall for the common test makers' trick of putting a singular noun near a verb with a plural subject. Always determine the correct subject of an underlined verb. The subject of the verb *is* is not the singular *receipt* that immediately precedes it, but the plural *papers* ("several papers…is signed by John Hancock"). The underlined verb must be in the plural form; (B) is correct.

Choices A and C both use singular verb forms, which do not agree with the plural subject. Choice D eliminates the verb, creating a sentence fragment.

4. G **Difficulty:** Medium

Category: Sentence Structure and Formation

Getting to the Answer: The past perfect verb tense is only correct when describing an action that was completed prior to another stated past action. Checking context, you can see that the verbs used to describe Dr. Gregory's collection of signatures are all in the present tense: *includes* and *are* (the correction to the underlined *is* in question 3). The verb here should also be in the present tense; (G) is correct. Choice F uses the past perfect, but there is no stated past action here to justify this tense. Choice H uses the past tense, which is inconsistent with the rest of the description of the collection. Choice J uses the conditional, but there is nothing hypothetical about the meaning of the Hancock documents.

5. D **Difficulty:** Medium

Category: Passage Organization

Getting to the Answer: When you need to determine the best placement for a sentence, look for keywords that show how the sentence relates to other ideas in the paragraph. Sentence 7 identifies the type of documents that Dr. Gregory collects, and Sentences 5 and 6 specifically describe some of those documents. The keyword *Predictably* in Sentence 5 tells you that Sentence 7 should come right before Sentence 5; it is only predictable for Dr. Gregory to have documents signed by Hancock if it has already been stated that Dr. Gregory collects famous signatures. Choice (D) is correct. Choice A disrupts the logical general-to-specific order set up in the paragraph; it also interrupts the transition between Sentence 6, which gives the name of Dr. Gregory's field, and the beginning of Paragraph 2, which provides an explanation of that field. Choice B interrupts the description of Dr. Gregory's home. Choice C interrupts the explanation of how Dr. Gregory's interest in collecting documents developed.

6. G   Difficulty: Medium

Category: Supporting Material

Getting to the Answer: Since NO CHANGE is offered as an answer choice, you must first decide whether a change is warranted. If so, you must then decide what the change should be. Graphology is discussed throughout the essay, so a definition of the term would be relevant and helpful to readers. Choice (G) provides this definition. The other choices do not provide information related to the topic discussed in the rest of the essay—the analysis of the handwriting of historical figures.

7. C   Difficulty: Medium

Category: Writer's Purpose

Getting to the Answer: Remember the first step of the Kaplan Method: read until you have enough information to identify the issue. To determine the best transition to the following sentence, you must first read that sentence. The sentence following the underlined portion explains how psychologists and graphologists use handwriting. Only (C) mentions handwriting, identifying it as a tool to diagnose patients' problems. This is the most logical lead-in to the next sentence. Choice A changes the focus from handwriting to the general topic of how patients learn to express themselves. Choice B similarly moves the topic to an explanation of why patients seek help; this doesn't lead in to the next sentence's explanation of how psychologists use handwriting. Choice D is too general; it doesn't lead in to the specific information of why handwriting analysis can be helpful.

8. H   Difficulty: Medium

Category: Sentence Structure and Formation

Getting to the Answer: As written, the sentence contains an incomplete first clause. The idea of using graphology needs to be properly connected to the psychologists who use it for the sentence to be complete. Choice (H) properly connects these ideas; it is the psychologists who use graphology. Choice G

changes the meaning of the sentence; the sentence is about those who use graphology, not those who are accustomed to it. Choice J creates a grammatically incorrect sentence by forming the phrase "psychologists being used graphology."

9. D   Difficulty: Medium

Category: Concision

Getting to the Answer: If a sentence is grammatically correct, check for errors in style. The sentence already tells you that "Dr. Gregory *once* practiced clinical psychology," so there is no need to repeat the information that this occurred "in the past." Choice (D) eliminates this redundant language. Choices B and C both contain unnecessary language.

10. G   Difficulty: Medium

Category: Writer's Purpose

Getting to the Answer: The purpose of a part of the passage will always fit with the overall purpose. The passage discusses Dr. Gregory's interest in graphology, focusing on his use of graphology on historical documents. Thus, we can expect the information about psychology to relate to graphology, and it does; the paragraph explains that graphology can be used to determine a person's psychology. Choice (G) is correct. Choice F is incorrect because Dr. Gregory has already been introduced at this point in the passage. Choice H distorts the text; the focus is on learning about historical figures, not the people who preserve historical documents. Choice J is incorrect as well; the author mentions challenges in understanding historical figures' personalities, but that does not mean psychology is generally unimportant in understanding personalities.

11. B   Difficulty: High

Category: Supporting Material

Getting to the Answer: When considering the effect of deleting material, think about what information it adds to the surrounding text. The sentence says that few records exist of the lives and personalities of historical figures, thus reinforcing the idea in the previous paragraph that it is difficult to apply psychological theories to historical figures. Choice (B) accurately reflects this idea. Choice A is out of scope; the passage does not suggest that Dr. Gregory turns to graphology because he cannot use other means to analyze historical figures. Choice C is the opposite of true; the lack of records is a reason there is not broad agreement. Choice D is a distortion; the passage does not suggest that the lack of historical records led friends of historical figures to write about them.

12. J   Difficulty: Medium

Category: Sentence Structure and Formation

Getting to the Answer: You need to find the choice that is NOT acceptable; in other words, the correct answer will create an error in the sentence. It is not acceptable to connect two independent clauses, such as the ones in this sentence, without the proper punctuation and/or conjunction. Choice (J) creates a run-on sentence. Choice F correctly uses a semicolon to connect two independent clauses. Choice G forms two complete sentences. Choice H keeps the second clause dependent, replacing *for* with *as*.

13. A   Difficulty: Medium

Category: Punctuation

Getting to the Answer: Don't expect to find a grammatical or stylistic error in every underlined selection. About 25% of your English Test questions will require no change. No punctuation is needed here; the sentence is correct as written, (A). Choice B incorrectly inserts a comma before *that*, which is used here as a conjunction. Choice C incorrectly uses a comma after *that*; commas are not correct after conjunctions. Choice D uses a colon, which would be appropriate only if it also eliminated *that*, but it does not.

14. J   Difficulty: High

Category: Sentence Structure and Formation

Getting to the Answer: Use context to make sure verb tenses properly sequence the actions discussed in a sentence. As indicated by the word *while*, the two actions in this sentence take place at the same time. The second verb, *forms*, is in the present tense, so the underlined verb should also be in the present tense. Choice (J) is correct. Choices F and G both put the action of "imprinting key aspects of his personality" in the past; this would only make sense if the rest of the sentence were also in the past tense. Choice H indicates that the action of "imprinting key aspects of his personality" takes place in the future, not *while* he "forms a signature."

15. A   Difficulty: High

Category: Writer's Purpose

Getting to the Answer: To make sure you understand the question, take a moment to put it in your own words. Here, you might rephrase the questions as "Does the essay talk about how one area of study can influence another?" The essay explains how Dr. Gregory, a psychologist, has used graphology to identify personality traits in historical figures; the essay concludes by explaining that these "details are now being used by historians in their analyses of historical decisions." This satisfies the condition of the question stem, so you can eliminate both "no" answers, C and D. Now move on to the reasoning. Choice (A) is an accurate paraphrase of the main idea of the essay. Choice B is incorrect because the essay does not compare different research processes.

Traveling at the Speed of Sound

16. F   Difficulty: Low

Category: Punctuation

Getting to the Answer: Commas are used to combine an independent and a dependent clause. This sentence is correct as written, (F), with the comma properly placed after the introductory clause. Choice

G places the comma incorrectly; *of 2003* is part of the introductory clause. Choice H omits the necessary comma. Choice J incorrectly uses a semicolon between a dependent and an independent clause.

17. C   Difficulty: Medium

Category: Sentence Structure and Formation

Getting to the Answer: The underlined portion introduces nonessential information, so it should not form an independent clause. Choices A and B both make the clause an independent one; they should be eliminated. The passage is in the past tense, making the present tense verb in D incorrect. Choice (C) is correct.

18. G   Difficulty: Medium

Category: Precision

Getting to the Answer: Precision questions require you to look at context; frequently, words will have similar meanings but be used differently. *Height* means "the distance from the top to the bottom of something"; *altitude* means "height above sea level." Since *altitude* is correct in this context, you can eliminate F. Choices (G) and H both use *altitude*, but "at an altitude" is the correct idiom here; (G) is correct. Choice J creates a grammatically incorrect sentence.

19. C   Difficulty: High

Category: Transitions

Getting to the Answer: When a transition word is underlined, check the logic of the transition as well as the grammar and punctuation. The sentence contrasts the famous and wealthy passengers with passengers who were ordinary people. Eliminate A and D because they do not express contrast. While B presents a contrast, it is grammatically incorrect. *Despite* creates a dependent clause requiring an *-ing* or *-ed* verb form, which is not present in the sentence. Choice (C) is correct, both logically and grammatically.

20. H   Difficulty: High

Category: Usage

Getting to the Answer: Words like *that*, which are commonly misused in everyday speech, can make a question more challenging. Sound doesn't travel a speed, it travels *at* a speed; eliminate F. Only (H) makes the correction. Sound doesn't travel *to* a speed, as in G; *where*, J, will only be correct on the ACT when used to indicate location or direction.

21. B   Difficulty: Medium

Category: Writer's Purpose

Getting to the Answer: When asked about the purpose of a paragraph in relation to others, take a few seconds to summarize the paragraph in question, the one before it, and the one after it. The previous paragraph introduced the topic of supersonic aircraft. The paragraph in question transitions to questions of science, which are then discussed in the following paragraph. Choice (B) is correct. The paragraph does not provide an example or a counterargument, making A and C incorrect. The passage does not move from the general topic to a specific story, making D incorrect.

22. H   Difficulty: Medium

Category: Precision

Getting to the Answer: Read English Test question stems carefully. This one asks for the LEAST acceptable alternative, which means that three of the choices will be correct in the sentence. All of the answer choices mean *change*, so read each of them into the sentence. "Change them into," "translate them into," and "transform them into" are all appropriate usage, but "alter them into" is not because it changes the meaning. Choice (H) is correct here.

23. D   Difficulty: High

Category: Concision

Getting to the Answer: Look for constructions that repeat words unnecessarily; these will be incorrect on the ACT. The sentence tells us that the speed at which sound travels through gas depends on three things: what kind of gas it is, the temperature, and the pressure; "it is traveling through" is redundant, so A is incorrect. Choice (D) is the most concise answer, and it does not lose any of the meaning of the underlined selection. Choices B and C do not address the error.

24. J   Difficulty: High

Category: Ambiguity

Getting to the Answer: Don't choose the shortest answer if it fails to make the writer's meaning clear. "Air temperature and pressure decrease with altitude" isn't clear; *air temperature* and *pressure* themselves do not have altitude, and we're not told to what the altitude is referring, so F is incorrect. Choice (J) makes the writer's meaning clear; when altitudes are higher, the decrease in temperature and pressure occur. Choice G does not address the error and even compounds it by replacing *altitude* with *height*. Choice H contradicts the facts in the passage; higher, not lower, altitudes have this effect.

25. B   Difficulty: Medium

Category: Punctuation

Getting to the Answer: Beware of answer choices that make unnecessary changes to the sentence. The information provided in the two clauses contrasts, so *however* is correct, but it requires a comma to separate it from the rest of the clause. Eliminate A. Choice (B) is correct. Choice C creates an inappropriate cause-and-effect relationship between the clauses. Choice D does not address the punctuation error.

26. F   Difficulty: Medium

Category: Passage Organization

Getting to the Answer: When you're asked to choose the most logical conclusion, first determine the sentence's function within the paragraph. The first half of this sentence previews a reason that the Concorde cruises at a higher altitude than regular planes, and it ties that reason back to the contrast between the speed of sound at two different altitudes. You need, then, a conclusion to the sentence that both explains why the planes would fly higher and does so in light of the information about altitude in the preceding sentence. The best choice here is (F); the original version of the sentence is the most logical. Choice G doesn't provide a reason; it simply repeats information that has already been stated. Choice H is out of scope; fuel consumption isn't mentioned in the passage. Choice J is a result of the plane's higher altitude, not its cause.

27. C   Difficulty: High

Category: Sentence Structure and Formation

Getting to the Answer: The use of *since* creates a specific marking point in the past and requires a verb that does the same. You need a simple past verb with *since*; (C) is correct. Choice A uses a tense that indicates an action that is ongoing, but the decommissioning of the Concorde has been completed. Choice B is unnecessarily wordy. The past perfect in D is only correct when used to indicate one past action completed prior to another stated past action, which is not the case here.

28. H   Difficulty: Medium

Category: Concision

Getting to the Answer: The phrases *about to* and *very soon* are redundant, making F, G, and J all incorrect. Furthermore, sentences beginning with coordinating (FANBOYS) conjunctions will not be correct on the ACT, which is an additional error in F. Only (H) correctly removes the redundancy.

29. C   Difficulty: Medium

Category: Transition

Getting to the Answer: When a transition word is underlined, check to see if it makes sense in the context. The sentence discusses upcoming advances to supersonic travel. Choice A places the advances in the present, which does not match the future-tense *will* later in the sentence. Choice B is about location rather than time, which does not fit the context. Choices (C) and D both refer to a future time, but only (C) makes sense in context. The answer must be an adverb in order to describe when the advances will take place, but *Upcoming*, choice D, is an adjective. Choice (C) is therefore correct.

30. H   Difficulty: Medium

Category: Sentence Structure and Formation

Getting to the Answer: Here, the items combined by "not only . . . but also" are "to the rich and famous" and "be for the masses." These items are correlated in the sentence, but they are not parallel in structure; eliminate F. Choices G and J do not address the error in parallel structure. Choice (H) corrects the error.

A Screenwriting Career

31. B   Difficulty: Medium

Category: Concision

Getting to the Answer: Look for the answer choice that expresses the sentence's idea in the clearest, most concise way. The clearest version here is (B): "If you want to succeed as a Hollywood screenwriter." This is grammatically correct and sets up the if–then relationship between the clauses. Choice A is awkward and unnecessarily wordy. Choices C and D create sentences that are grammatically incorrect.

32. J   Difficulty: Medium

Category: Transitions

Getting to the Answer: When a transition word or phrase is underlined, check for the logic of the transition and then for correct grammar and punctuation. The paragraph discusses the difficulties of pursuing a career in screenwriting, and the previous sentence mentions one difficulty. The sentence containing the underlined portion discusses another difficulty: that those who obtain these careers are stressed and dissatisfied. Although the sentence mentions these people being wealthy, it does so in contrast to the main part of the sentence, which is a disadvantage of pursuing this career. Thus, the sentence is a continuation of the idea that this career is challenging, making (J) correct. Choice F incorrectly contrasts the ideas. The first difficulty does not provide a reason for the second, making G incorrect. Choice H is irrelevant, because time is not being discussed.

33. B   Difficulty: Medium

Category: Supporting Material

Getting to the Answer: Don't forget to read for logic as well as for grammar and usage. The preceding sentence explains that screenwriters don't have "a formal career path." The first part of the sentence in question gives an example of what a formal career path might involve—going to a school career center for help. The correct answer will provide another example along these lines. Someone with a formal career path can find job opportunities in the classified ads, but a screenwriter cannot. Choice (B) is correct. Choice A refers to *extracurricular activities*, which is out of scope for a sentence concerning a career path. There's no reason to believe that a college graduate can't understand how difficult it is to become a screenwriter, as C suggests. Choice D is an example of something involved in an *informal* career path, not a formal one.

34. J   Difficulty: Medium

Category: Precision

Getting to the Answer: When asked which choice best conveys a certain meaning, choose the answer that conveys that meaning most precisely. The only choice that conveys the difference in how successful screenwriters have achieved their success is (J). The other choices convey either the challenges, as in F and G, or the benefits, as in H.

35. C   Difficulty: Medium

Category: Sentence Structure and Formation

Getting to the Answer: A passage should not change tense for no reason. The passage is in the present tense, making the past tense verb in A incorrect. There is no reason to discuss the ongoing nature of a college education in the past, so the verb tense in B is incorrect. Choice D creates a grammatically incorrect sentence. Choice (C), with the present tense, is correct.

36. J   Difficulty: Low

Category: Concision

Getting to the Answer: When "DELETE the underlined portion" is an option, read the underlined selection for relevance. The topic of this paragraph, and the entire essay, is the career of screenwriting. No matter how it is worded, a sentence about an acting career is out of scope. This sentence should be deleted, (J).

37. C   Difficulty: Medium

Category: Usage

Getting to the Answer: The ACT often separates a subject from its verb with an intervening phrase or clause containing another noun. Although the singular noun *college* is closer to the verb *begins* in this sentence, its subject is the plural *screenwriters*. The verb needs to be in the plural form, which eliminates all answer choices but (C). Choice B does not address the error. *Has begun* in D is also singular.

38. G   Difficulty: Medium

Category: Writer's Purpose

Getting to the Answer: When asked if a paragraph fulfills a certain purpose, consider its topic and scope. The topic of this paragraph is pursuing a college education on the path to becoming a screenwriter, and the author expresses the judgment that a college education can delay entry into the screenwriting profession. Thus, the paragraph does fulfill the goal of discouraging aspiring screenplay writers from pursuing a college education. Eliminate H and J. Choice F is opposite; mentioning the value of education does not discourage people from pursuing an education. Choice (G) is correct.

39. C   Difficulty: Medium

Category: Concision

Getting to the Answer: Be wary of answer choices that are significantly longer than the underlined selection; they will rarely be correct. As written, the underlined portion is unnecessarily wordy and the phrase "at a prestigious school" is misleading, since it is not just some colleges that the writer deems irrelevant for screenwriters. Choice (C) corrects this error by focusing only on the student loans. Choice B is much wordier than the original and includes irrelevant information about "work-study programs." Choice D creates a sentence fragment.

40. F   Difficulty: Medium

Category: Punctuation

Getting to the Answer: To check if a semicolon is correctly used, try replacing it with a period and making the second clause a separate sentence. If two complete sentences are formed, then the semicolon is correct. A semicolon is correctly used here to join two independent clauses. No change is needed, (F). Choice G incorrectly inserts a comma between *this* and the noun it modifies. Choice H incorrectly places a comma after *so*; a comma should be placed before a coordinating conjunction. Choice J creates a run-on sentence.

41. D   Difficulty: Medium

Category: Punctuation

Getting to the Answer: If you're unsure about punctuation, read the sentence without the descriptive words and phrases to focus on its structure. Stripped of some of the descriptive phrases, this sentence becomes easier to deal with: "Those without college educations are less averse to the jobs, aspiring screenwriters are forced to take." There is no reason for a comma here. Choice (D) correctly uses *that* to indicate that the phrase "aspiring screenwriters are forced to take" is meant to modify *jobs*. Choice B creates a run-on sentence. Choice C incorrectly treats *screenwriters* as inessential information.

42. J   Difficulty: Low

Category: Usage

Getting to the Answer: Many words can function as more than one part of speech; use context to help you eliminate choices that use these words incorrectly. The word *that's* in the underlined selection is a contraction of the pronoun *that* and the verb *is*, but context tells us that this sentence requires *that* to be used as a conjunction. Choice (J) uses *that* correctly and does not introduce any new errors. Choice G replaces the correct possessive pronoun *their* with its homophone *there*; familiarize yourself with the correct uses of *their*, *there*, and *they're* before Test Day. Choice H creates a grammatically incorrect sentence.

43. B   Difficulty: Medium

Category: Ambiguity

Getting to the Answer: When a pronoun is underlined, always determine to what it refers. We know that something about the described scenario produces stress, but the exact referent is unclear, making A incorrect. Choice D is similarly unclear. Choice C incorrectly identifies the screenplay as the source of the stress; the stress is caused by the writer's situation, not the screenplay. Choice (B) correctly identifies the situation as the source of the stress, removing the ambiguity.

44. F   Difficulty: Medium

Category: Usage

Getting to the Answer: About one in four English Test questions will require no change. This sentence is correct as written, (F). Choice G illogically states the screenwriter's work must be *increasing*. Choice H suggests that screenwriters face pressure to "be . . . work," which does not make sense. Choice J is idiomatically incorrect; *to raise*, not *to raising*, is the correct infinitive.

45. D   Difficulty: Medium

Category: Style and Tone

Getting to the Answer: When some answer choices contain *you* and others contain *one*, determine which pronoun matches the style of the passage. This passage never uses *one*, but it does use *you* in the first sentence. Furthermore, the remainder of the sentence directly addresses the reader with *please*. Eliminate A and B. Choice (D) is more straightforwardly worded than C, so (D) is correct.

UNIT TWO

Math

CHAPTER SIX

ACT Math Test Overview

INSIDE THE ACT MATH TEST

The Math Test is 60 minutes long and includes 60 questions. That works out to 1 minute per question, but you'll wind up using more time on some questions and less on others.

The Format

All of the Math questions have the same basic multiple-choice format, with a stand-alone question and five possible answers (unlike questions on the other subject tests, which have only four choices each). Occasionally, you may encounter a set of two or three questions that share a table, graph, or other relevant information.

The questions cover a wide range of math topics, from pre-algebra to coordinate geometry and even a little bit of trigonometry. More emphasis is placed on earlier-level math skills (such as order of operations, working with variables, solving basic equations, and geometry) and less on higher-level math (such as sequences, logarithms, and matrices).

Test Day Directions and Format

Here's what the Math directions will look like:

DIRECTIONS: Solve each problem, choose the correct answer, and then fill in the corresponding oval on your answer document.

Do not linger over problems that take too much time. Solve as many as you can; then return to the others in the time you have left for this test.

You are permitted to use a calculator on this test. You may use your calculator for any problems you choose, but some of the problems may best be done without using a calculator.

> Note: Unless otherwise stated, all of the following should be assumed:
>
> 1. Illustrative figures are NOT necessarily drawn to scale.
>
> 2. Geometric figures lie in a plane.
>
> 3. The word *line* indicates a straight line.
>
> 4. The word *average* indicates arithmetic mean.

When it comes to directions on the ACT, the golden rule is this: don't read anything on Test Day you already know! Familiarize yourself with everything now to save time later.

The Math directions don't really tell you much anyway. Of the four special notes at the end of the Math directions, #2, #3, and #4 almost go without saying. Note #1 is pretty important, though—while this rule "bends" a little bit when you have to guess, it's important to know that your eyes *don't* tell you what you need to know about figures; you really do have to do the math. What a figure *looks like* won't reliably get you the right answer.

Question Types

The types of questions you'll see on the ACT can be divided into three main types—those that include a diagram (or for which you need to draw one), story problems, and concept questions.

Diagram Questions

About one-third of the Math questions either give you a diagram or describe a situation that should be diagrammed. For these questions, the diagrams are crucial—you don't get any points for solving questions in your head, so draw *everything* out.

Example

1. The figure below contains five congruent triangles. The longest side of each triangle is 4 meters long. What is the area of the whole figure in square meters?

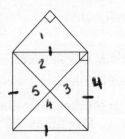

4·5 = 20

    A. 12.5

    B. 15

    C. 20

    D. 30

    E. Cannot be determined from the given information

Getting to the Answer: The key to this question is to let the diagram tell you what you need to know: each triangle represents one-quarter of the area of the square, and the sides of the *square* are 4 meters (you can figure this out because the top side of the square is the hypotenuse of the triangle that makes the "roof"). Because the area of a square can be found by squaring its side length, the area of the square is 16 square meters. Thus, each triangle has an area that is one-fourth as much, or 4 square meters. Because the whole figure consists of *five* triangles, each with area 4, the total area is 5 × 4 = 20 square meters. The answer is (C).

> ✔ *Expert Tip*
>
> In ACT Math questions, the choice "cannot be determined" is rare. When it does appear, it's rarely the right answer, and is almost always incorrect in a question that comes with a diagram or for which you can draw one.

Story Problems

About another third of the Math questions are story problems, which are also referred to as modeling questions. Here's an example:

Example

2. Evan drove halfway home at 20 miles per hour, then sped up and drove the rest of the way at 30 miles per hour. What was his average speed for the entire trip?

    F. 20 miles per hour
    G. 22 miles per hour
    H. 24 miles per hour
    J. 25 miles per hour
    K. 28 miles per hour

Getting to the Answer: A good way to comprehend—and resolve—a story problem like this is to think of a real situation like the one in the story. Imagining an actual trip with miles and speeds may make the question more approachable. For example, what if Evan had 60 miles to drive? (You should pick a distance that's easily divisible by both rates.) He would go 30 miles at 20 mph, then 30 miles at 30 mph. How long would it take? Consider each leg of the trip: 30 miles at 30 mph is 1 hour, and 30 miles at 20 mph is 1.5 hours. That's a total of 60 miles in 2.5 hours; 60 divided by 2.5 gives an average speed of 24 mph. The correct answer is (H).

> ✔ *Expert Tip*
>
> Don't let variables or abstract stories confuse you. When you see them, stay calm and make them simpler by putting real numbers in for the variables. You'll learn more about this Picking Numbers strategy a bit later.

Concept Questions

Finally, about one-third of ACT Math questions directly ask you to demonstrate your knowledge of specific math concepts.

Example

3. If angles *A* and *B* are supplementary, and the measure of angle *A* is 57°, what is the measure, in degrees, of angle *B*?

    A. 33
    B. 43
    C. 47
    D. 123
    E. 147

$$\begin{array}{r} 180 \\ -\ 57 \\ \hline 123 \end{array}$$

Getting to the Answer: This question requires that you know the concept of supplementary angles: two angles are *supplementary* when they form a straight line—in other words, when they add up to 180°. Thus, question 3 boils down to this: what number, added to 57, makes 180? The answer is (D), 123.

These three types of Math questions, of course, will be discussed more fully in the Math chapters that follow.

Outside Knowledge

The ACT Math Test thoroughly covers rules from a variety of common Math topics, mostly from courses students typically complete by the end of the 11th grade. The needed math "facts" are addressed in the strategic discussion throughout the math chapters in this book.

The Inside Scoop

The ACT Math Test is designed to measure problem solving and logical reasoning, along with basic computational skills. Covered topics include:

- Rates, percents, proportions, and unit conversion
- Number properties
- Number operations
- Algebra
- Functions
- Graphing
- Geometry and trigonometry
- Statistics and probability

Although Math questions aren't ordered in terms of difficulty, questions drawn from elementary or middle school curricula tend to come earlier in the test, while those from high school curricula tend to come later. But this doesn't mean that the easy questions come first and the hardest ones come later. We've found that high school subjects tend to be fresher in most students' minds than things they were taught years ago, so you may actually find the later questions easier.

When You're Running Out of Time

If at some point you realize you have more questions left than you have time for, be willing to skip around, looking for questions you understand right away. Pick your points and concentrate on the questions you have the best chance of correctly answering. Just be sure to grid an answer—even if it's just a wild guess—for every question.

Scoring

You will receive a Math subject score—from 1 to 36—for the entire Math Test. This score will be averaged into your ACT Composite Score, equally weighted with your scores on the other three major subject tests. You will also receive eight other scores based on specific knowledge and concepts. These are called reporting categories and consist of:

- Integrating Essential Skills
- Preparing for Higher Mathematics, which also includes separate scores for Number and Quantity, Algebra, Functions, Geometry, and Statistics and Probability
- Modeling

QUICK TIPS

Mind-Set

- **The end justifies the means.** Your goal is to get as many points as possible, not to demonstrate how great you are at any particular math area, or show all your work, or get all the "hard" questions—just to get points, plain and simple. That means getting as many correct answers as you can as quickly as possible. If the best way to get this done is to do straightforward questions in a straightforward way, that's fine. But many questions can be solved faster by using Kaplan Strategies, such as Backsolving and Picking Numbers, which will make you both faster and more accurate.

- **Take time to save time.** It sounds paradoxical, but to go your fastest on the Math Test, you sometimes have to slow down. Don't just dive in headlong, wildly crunching numbers or manipulating equations without first giving the question some thought. Remember your priority is the whole section, not just one particular question.

- **When in doubt, shake it up.** ACT Math questions are not always what they seem at first glance. Sometimes all you need is a new perspective to break through the disguise. Take a step back and look at the question another way.

Special Strategies: If You Get Stuck . . .

If after a few moments of thought you find you still can't come up with a reasonable way of doing the problem, try one of these techniques:

- **Restate.** When you get stuck, try looking at the question from a different angle. Try rearranging the numbers, changing decimals to fractions, changing fractions to decimals, multiplying out numbers, factoring problems, redrawing a diagram, or doing anything that might help you to look at the information you've been given a bit differently.

- **Remove the disguise.** Find out what the question is really asking—it might not be obvious at first glance.

- **Try eyeballing.** Even though the directions warn you that diagrams are "not necessarily" drawn to scale, eyeballing is a surprisingly effective guessing strategy. You won't be able to get specifics without doing the math, sometimes, but you will be able to rule some answers out or get a better idea of what you're looking for.

SMARTPOINTS BREAKDOWN

By studying the information released by the ACT, Kaplan has been able to determine how often certain topics are likely to show up on the test, and, therefore, how many points these topics are worth on Test Day. If you master a given topic, you can expect to earn the corresponding number of SmartPoints on Test Day.

Here is a brief overview of what exactly to expect and how much of it you should be expecting.

Essential Skills—14 Points

Approximately 40–43% of the Math Test will be Essential Skills questions. These questions test your knowledge and skill level associated with concepts you likely learned in middle school. Topics include but are not limited to:

- Numbers and operations
- Rates, percents, proportions, and unit conversion
- Expressions and equations
- Basic geometry
- Basic statistics and probability

Many of the concepts that you'll see in Essential Skills questions will also be present in Higher Math questions—the questions in the latter group will just be more advanced and will require more steps to arrive at a final solution. For example, an Essential Skills question may involve finding the mean of a list of numbers. A related Higher Math question may involve calculating a mean from a bar graph or a frequency table—the underlying concept is the same, but getting to the final answer requires significantly more work and finesse.

Higher Math—22 Points

Approximately 57–60% of the test will consist of Higher Math questions. These questions capture the mathematics that you most likely learned more recently, or are learning right now, in high school. This category is divided into the five subcategories described next.

Number and Quantity—3 Points

Number and Quantity questions make up about 7–10% of the Math Test. These questions test your knowledge of the real and complex number systems. You will need to understand, reason about, and use numerical quantities in various forms, including integer and rational exponents, and matrices and vectors. Number and Quantity questions require that you understand the behavior of numbers, particularly evens and odds and positives and negatives. These questions are ripe for Picking Numbers, which will be discussed in the next chapter. You'll also need to use properties of divisibility, such as factors, multiples, and prime numbers. Tested operations include all parts of the PEMDAS order of operations (parentheses, exponents, multiplication, division, addition, and subtraction). Rarer questions test basic knowledge of radical and imaginary numbers.

Algebra—5 Points

Algebra questions make up about 12–15% of the Math Test and extensively test your ability to solve for an unknown quantity given a wide range of information of varying complexity. The simplest questions are pulled from elementary algebra and require you to solve for a single variable. They build up to more advanced algebra, asking you to solve systems of equations, equations involving absolute value, inequalities, and quadratic equations. These questions also test your ability to write the equation of a line given certain types of information. The slope-intercept form of a line is the most important equation to remember here, and slope in general is paramount. You may even see radical and rational expressions and equations sprinkled in among the more typical polynomial equations.

Functions—5 Points

Functions questions make up about 12–15% of the Math Test. You'll need to know how to interpret function notation and recognize the different ways in which functions can be represented. You will also be tested on function operations, which include adding, subtracting, multiplying, dividing, and finding compositions. Questions in this category will also involve using functions to solve problems about real world scenarios and describing important features of graphs of functions. The types of functions you may see include but are not limited to linear, polynomial, radical, rational, exponential, logarithmic, trigonometric, and piecewise functions. Finally, the Functions category includes questions involving arithmetic and geometric sequences.

Geometry—5 Points

Geometry includes coordinate geometry, plane geometry, and solid geometry. Geometry questions make up about 12–15% of the Math Test. These questions test your ability to graph equations and inequalities in the coordinate plane and to solve problems related to lines, angles, and figures. Triangles—specifically right triangles—and circles are the two most commonly tested shapes, but you can expect to see questions on a variety of polygons, as well as complex 2-D and simple 3-D shapes. The test will ask you to break down complex figures into recognizable shapes and use problem-solving skills to transfer information throughout a figure. Fortunately, as on the rest of the ACT Math Test, the number of rules to remember is limited. The test will ask questions that require knowledge of the Midpoint and Distance formulas, and occasionally you will need to work with the graphs of simple shapes such as triangles and circles in the coordinate plane.

Statistics and Probability—4 Points

Statistics and Probability questions make up about 8–12% of the Math Test. These questions test your ability to interpret and/or use data presented in a variety of forms. Common questions include finding or using averages and describing or analyzing the center or spread of a set of data. You'll also see questions involving counting techniques, such as combinations and permutations, as well as questions about Venn diagrams. Finally, you'll have to calculate simple and conditional probabilities that are based on a description of a scenario, data presented in a two-way table or other type of chart or graph, or a probability distribution function.

A Note About Modeling

Together, Essential Skills and Higher Math questions make up 100% of the Math Test. However, there is a third category, Modeling, to be aware of, although it doesn't have a Smart-Points value associated with it. The test makers have indicated that more than 25% of the test will involve modeling, but don't let this fact intimidate you. *Modeling* just means using mathematical equations, graphs, diagrams, scatterplots, etc. to represent real-world scenarios. Word problems certainly fit within this category, but you'll also see some concept questions that fit within the Modeling category. Every modeling question will also be counted in the reporting categories described earlier.

CHAPTER SEVEN

Number and Quantity

PRACTICE QUESTIONS

The following test-like questions provide an opportunity to practice Number and Quantity questions.

1. Two vectors are given by $v_1 = \langle 7, -3 \rangle$ and $v_2 = \langle a, b \rangle$. If $v_1 + v_2 = \langle 5, 5 \rangle$, then what is the value of a?

   A. -2 *(circled)*
   B. 2
   C. 5
   D. 8
   E. 12

2. Which of the following is equivalent to $\dfrac{(3.0 \times 10^4)(8.0 \times 10^9)}{1.2 \times 10^6}$?

   F. 2.0×10^6
   G. 2.0×10^7
   H. 2.0×10^8 *(circled)*
   J. 2.0×10^{30}
   K. 2.0×10^{31}

   (handwritten) $\dfrac{24}{1.2} = 20 \times 10^7$

   2.0×10^8

3. A certain dining room set is discounted 20% on Monday and then discounted another 20% on Tuesday. What is the total percent discount applied to the price of the dining room set on Monday and Tuesday?

   A. 20%
   B. 36% *(circled)*
   C. 40% *(crossed out)*
   D. 50%
   E. 55%

   (handwritten) If it was $100 on monday. → $80
   anothe 20% = 64
   ∴ $\dfrac{100 - 64}{100} \cdot 100 = 36\%$

4. Which of the following matrices is equal to the matrix product $\begin{bmatrix} -2 & 0 \\ 1 & -3 \end{bmatrix} \times \begin{bmatrix} 2 \\ 2 \end{bmatrix}$?

   F. $\begin{bmatrix} -4 & 0 \\ 2 & -6 \end{bmatrix}$ *(circled)*
   G. $\begin{bmatrix} -4 & 2 \\ 2 & -6 \end{bmatrix}$
   H. $\begin{bmatrix} 0 & 0 \\ 0 & 0 \end{bmatrix}$
   J. $\begin{bmatrix} -4 \\ -4 \end{bmatrix}$
   K. $\begin{bmatrix} -4 \\ -6 \end{bmatrix}$

5. Which of the following is equivalent to the product $\left(\sqrt{8} + \sqrt{6}\right)\left(\sqrt{8} - \sqrt{6}\right)$?

   A. 1
   B. 2 *(circled)*
   C. $\sqrt{7}$
   D. $\sqrt{14}$
   E. 7

   (handwritten) $8 - \sqrt{48} + \sqrt{48} - 6$
   $8 - 6 = 2$

6. If $x \geq 0$ and $y < 0$, which of the following MUST be true?

   F. $xy > 0$ $x \geq 0$

   G. $xy < 0$

   H. $xy = 0$ $y < 0$

   J. $xy \geq 0$

   K. $xy \leq 0$

7. The number of executives at a large company, by division, can be modeled using the following matrix.

Marketing	Human Resources	Operations	Legal
20	12	40	10

   The company is downsizing and the head of Human Resources estimates the proportion of current executives who will be laid off within the next year. The estimates are shown in the following matrix.

   $$\begin{array}{c} \text{Marketing} \\ \text{Human Resources} \\ \text{Operations} \\ \text{Legal} \end{array} \begin{bmatrix} 0.3 \\ 0.5 \\ 0.2 \\ 0.4 \end{bmatrix}$$

   Given these matrices, what is the head of Human Resources' estimate of the number of current executives in these departments who will be laid off within the next year?

   A. 24

   B. 27

   C. 30

   D. 32

   E. 36

8. What fraction lies exactly halfway between $\frac{4}{5}$ and $\frac{5}{6}$?

   F. $\frac{5}{7}$

   G. $\frac{9}{10}$

   H. $\frac{13}{15}$

   J. $\frac{23}{30}$

   K. $\frac{49}{60}$

9. On a map, $\frac{1}{2}$ inch represents an actual distance of 5 miles. What is the actual area, in square miles, of a rectangular region that is $4\frac{1}{3}$ inches by 5 inches on the map?

   A. $53\frac{2}{3}$

   B. $107\frac{1}{3}$

   C. $541\frac{2}{3}$

   D. $2{,}166\frac{2}{3}$

   E. $4{,}377\frac{2}{3}$

10. If u and v are vectors such that $u = \langle 2,0 \rangle$ and $v = \langle 0,-2 \rangle$, which of the following represents $u + v$?

    F. $\langle -2,-2 \rangle$

    G. $\langle -2,2 \rangle$

    H. $\langle 0,0 \rangle$

    J. $\langle 2,-2 \rangle$

    K. $\langle 2,2 \rangle$

11. When $-1 \leq a \leq 1$ and $-4 \leq b \leq 3$, what is the greatest possible value of the expression $a \times b$?

    A. 4

    B. 3

    C. 2

    D. -3

    E. -12

12. There are three feet in a yard. If 2.5 yards of fabric cost $4.50, what is the cost per foot?

    F. $ 0.60

    G. $ 0.90

    H. $ 1.50

    J. $ 1.80

    K. $11.25

13. What is the value of $-1\begin{bmatrix} 4 & 3 \\ 2 & 1 \end{bmatrix} + 2\begin{bmatrix} 1 & 2 \\ 3 & 4 \end{bmatrix}$?

    A. $\begin{bmatrix} -2 & -1 \\ -4 & -7 \end{bmatrix}$

    B. $\begin{bmatrix} -1 & -2 \\ -3 & -4 \end{bmatrix}$

    C. $\begin{bmatrix} -2 & 1 \\ 3 & 4 \end{bmatrix}$

    D. $\begin{bmatrix} -2 & 1 \\ 4 & 7 \end{bmatrix}$

    E. $\begin{bmatrix} 1 & 2 \\ 3 & 4 \end{bmatrix}$

14. A piece of letter-sized paper is $8\frac{1}{2}$ inches wide and 11 inches long. Suppose you want to cut strips of paper that are $\frac{5}{8}$ inch wide and 11 inches long. What is the maximum number of strips of paper you could make from 1 piece of letter-sized paper?

    F. 5

    G. 6

    H. 12

    J. 13

    K. 14

15. A long-distance phone company offers a rate plan that charges $0.10 per minute for up to 200 minutes per month, and $0.15 for each minute over 200 minutes. If you talk for 250 minutes in one month, how much will you be charged?

    A. $20.00

    B. $25.00

    C. $27.50

    D. $30.00

    E. $37.50

16. If x^n is the simplified form of the expression below, what is the value of n?

    $$\frac{\sqrt[3]{x} \times x^{\frac{5}{2}} \times x}{\sqrt{x}}$$

    F. $\frac{3}{10}$

    G. $\frac{5}{6}$

    H. $\frac{7}{6}$

    J. $\frac{7}{3}$

    K. $\frac{10}{3}$

17. The numbers 84 and 96 are both divisible by n, a real positive integer. Neither 18 nor 16 is divisible by n. What is the sum of the digits of n?

    A. 1
    B. 3
    C. 4
    D. 5
    E. 6

18. If $3x - 2y = 5$, what is the value of $\dfrac{8^x}{4^y}$?

    F. 10
    G. 25
    H. 32
    J. 50
    K. 64

19. Liza drove at an average speed of 40 miles per hour for 2 hours and then increased her average speed by 25% for the next 3 hours. Her average speed for the 5 hours was r miles per hour. What is the value of r?

    A. 44
    B. 45
    C. 46
    D. 47
    E. 48

20. If $i^2 = -1$, which of the following is a square root of $8 - 6i$?

    F. $3 + i$
    G. $3 - i$
    H. $3 - 4i$
    J. $4 + 3i$
    K. $4 - 3i$

21. In a crew race, Ashwin rowed 0.8 miles in 5 minutes and 20 seconds. How many miles per hour did he row?

    A. 4
    B. 5
    C. 7
    D. 9
    E. 10

22. Given that $i = \sqrt{-1}$, which of the following shows the product $\left(2 + \sqrt{-9}\right)\left(-1 + \sqrt{-4}\right)$ written in the form $a + bi$?

    F. $-8 + i$
    G. $-8 - i$
    H. $4 + i$
    J. $4 - i$
    K. $8 + i$

23. Which of the following sets of numbers has the property that the sum of any two numbers in the set is also a number in the set?

    I. The set of even integers
    II. The set of odd integers
    III. The set of prime numbers

    A. I only
    B. III only
    C. I and II only
    D. I and III only
    E. I, II, and III

24. If the vector u is given by $u = \langle u_1, u_2 \rangle$ and $-\dfrac{2}{3}u = \langle 12, -24 \rangle$, what is the value of $u_1 + u_2$?

    F. -24
    G. -18
    H. 8
    J. 12
    K. 18

25. Michelle is pulling gummy worms out of a bag that only has green and orange gummy worms in it. In her first handful, she pulled out 10 orange worms and 6 green worms. Setting these worms aside, she pulled out a second handful, and 40% of these were orange. After both handfuls, 50% of all the worms pulled were orange. How many worms did Michelle pull out in her second handful if she only pulled whole worms?

    A. 20
    B. 26
    C. 30
    D. 36
    E. 40

26. What is the smallest possible value for the product of two real numbers that differ by 8 ?

    F. -64
    G. -16
    H. -8
    J. 0
    K. 16

27. If $\begin{bmatrix} 2x & 9 \\ x & -5 \end{bmatrix} + \begin{bmatrix} 6 & 3y \\ y & 8 \end{bmatrix} = \begin{bmatrix} 2 & 15 \\ z & 3 \end{bmatrix}$, what is the value of z ?

    A. -2
    B. 0
    C. 2
    D. 4
    E. 12

28. Marvin has two saltwater fish tanks in his home. One has tangs and angelfish in a ratio of 5 to 2. The second tank has tangs and puffers in a ratio of 2 to 3. Marvin wants to put a tank in his office with angelfish and puffers using the same ratio he has at home to make it easier to buy food for them in bulk. What ratio of angelfish to puffers should he use?

    F. 2:3
    G. 2:5
    H. 5:2
    J. 5:7
    K. 4:15

29. If $x > 1$, then which of the following must be true?

    A. $\dfrac{\sqrt{x}}{x} - 1 < 0$
    B. $\dfrac{x}{\sqrt{x}} < 1$
    C. $2\sqrt{x} < x$
    D. $\sqrt{x} + x > x^2$
    E. All of the choices are true.

30. In complex numbers, where $i^2 = -1$, what is the simplified form of the expression $\dfrac{(2i + 2)^2}{(2i - 2)^2}$?

    F. $\dfrac{i+1}{i-1}$
    G. $\dfrac{i}{4}$
    H. $\dfrac{4}{i}$
    J. 1
    K. -1

ANSWERS AND EXPLANATIONS

1. A **Difficulty:** Medium

Category: Number and Quantity

Getting to the Answer: Don't let the vector notation scare you. Adding vectors works exactly as you would expect it to: to add two vectors, add the corresponding components. The question only asks about the value of a, so focus on the first entries only: $7 + a = 5$, which gives $a = 5 - 7$, or -2. Choice (A) is correct.

2. H **Difficulty:** Medium

Category: Number and Quantity

Getting to the Answer: When multiplying and dividing numbers written in scientific notation, you can separate the plain numbers from the powers of 10. This allows you to use rules of exponents to simplify the powers of 10.

$$\frac{\left(3.0 \times 10^4\right)\left(8.0 \times 10^9\right)}{1.2 \times 10^6} = \frac{3 \times 8}{1.2} \times \frac{10^4 \times 10^9}{10^6}$$
$$= \frac{24}{1.2} \times 10^{4+9-6}$$
$$= 20 \times 10^7 = 2.0 \times 10^8$$

This matches (H).

3. B **Difficulty:** Medium

Category: Number and Quantity

Getting to the Answer: This is a great question for Picking Numbers. Remember, you should start with 100 to make your calculations easier.

If the original cost is $100, then Monday's cost is equal to $100(0.8) = $80 and Tuesday's cost is equal to $80(0.8) = $64.

$$\text{Percent change} = \frac{\$100 - \$64}{\$100} \times 100\% = 36\%.$$

Choice (B) is correct.

4. J **Difficulty:** Medium

Category: Number and Quantity

Getting to the Answer: To multiply two matrices, the sizes (# of rows by # of columns) must match in a certain way. Here, the size of the first matrix is 2×2 and the size of the second is 2×1. If you multiply a 2×2 matrix by a 2×1 matrix (which is possible because the middle dimensions match), the result will be a 2×1 matrix (the outer dimensions when the sizes are written as a product). This means you can eliminate F, G, and H, which are all 2×2 matrices. To multiply the matrices, multiply each element in the first row of the first matrix by the corresponding element in the second matrix and add the products. Then repeat the process using the second row of the first matrix:

$$\begin{bmatrix} -2 & 0 \\ 1 & -3 \end{bmatrix} \cdot \begin{bmatrix} 2 \\ 2 \end{bmatrix} = \begin{bmatrix} -2(2) + 0(2) \\ 1(2) + (-3)(2) \end{bmatrix} = \begin{bmatrix} -4 \\ -4 \end{bmatrix}$$

Choice (J) is correct.

5. B **Difficulty:** Medium

Category: Number and Quantity

Getting to the Answer: You could use FOIL right away (just as you would when multiplying two binomials), or you could simplify $\sqrt{8}$ before you FOIL to keep the size of the numbers small. If you happen to notice that the two factors resemble the terms in a difference of squares, you might conclude that the first option will be quicker (because the middle two terms are going to cancel anyway):

$$\left(\sqrt{8} + \sqrt{6}\right)\left(\sqrt{8} - \sqrt{6}\right)$$
$$= 8 - \sqrt{48} + \sqrt{48} - 6$$
$$= 8 - 6 = 2$$

Choice (B) is correct.

6. K   Difficulty: Medium

Category: Number and Quantity

Getting to the Answer: Picking Numbers works well for number properties questions. Because $x \geq 0$ and $y < 0$, let $x = 2$ and $y = -3$, which gives $xy = -6$.

Choice F: $-6 > 0$ False. Eliminate F.

Choice G: $-6 < 0$ True. Keep G for now.

Choice H: $-6 = 0$ False. Eliminate H.

Choice J: $-6 \geq 0$ False. Eliminate J.

Choice (K): $-6 \leq 0$ True. Keep (K) for now.

You have narrowed your choices to G and (K). To eliminate further, pick different numbers: try $x = 0$ and $y = -2$, which gives $xy = 0$.

Choice G: $0 < 0$ False. Eliminate G.

Choice (K) is correct.

7. A   Difficulty: Medium

Category: Number and Quantity

Getting to the Answer: Even if you're not sure how to perform operations on matrices, you can probably reason out the answer. The number of people who will leave Marketing is $0.3(20) = 6$. You can compute the number for each department, then add them all together. This will give you the same result as multiplying the matrices.

$$\begin{bmatrix} 20 & 12 & 40 & 10 \end{bmatrix} \begin{bmatrix} 0.3 \\ 0.5 \\ 0.2 \\ 0.4 \end{bmatrix}$$

$$= 20(0.3) + 12(0.5) + 40(0.2) + 10(0.4)$$
$$= 6 + 6 + 8 + 4 = 24$$

Choice (A) is correct.

8. K   Difficulty: Medium

Category: Number and Quantity

Getting to the Answer: On Test Day, you will be able to approach many questions using a number of methods. For each question, use the method that you are most comfortable with and that will lead you to the correct answer choice most quickly. For this question, restate the fractions in the question stem so they have a common denominator: $\frac{4}{5}$ and $\frac{5}{6}$ are equivalent to $\frac{24}{30}$ and $\frac{25}{30}$. To find the fraction halfway between these two fractions, restate them again with a larger common denominator, so the numerators are not sequential: $\frac{24}{30}$ and $\frac{25}{30}$ are equivalent to $\frac{48}{60}$ and $\frac{50}{60}$. The fraction that is halfway between these numbers is $\frac{49}{60}$, (K).

9. D   Difficulty: Medium

Category: Number and Quantity

Getting to the Answer: Scales are just proportions. The scale given is $\frac{1}{2}$ inch $= 5$ miles. Set up a proportion to determine the distances (the length and the width of the rectangular region) involved in the question:

$$\frac{\frac{1}{2}\text{inch}}{5 \text{ miles}} = \frac{4\frac{1}{3}\text{inches}}{x \text{ miles}}$$

$$\left(\frac{1}{2}\right)x = \left(4\frac{1}{3}\right)(5)$$

$$\frac{1}{2}x = 21\frac{2}{3}$$

$$x = 21\frac{2}{3} \times 2 = 43\frac{1}{3}\text{miles}$$

Now repeat this process for the other dimension using the same proportion:

$$\frac{\frac{1}{2}\text{inch}}{5 \text{ miles}} = \frac{5 \text{ inches}}{y \text{ miles}}$$

$$\frac{1}{2}y = (5)(5)$$

$$\frac{1}{2}y = 25$$

$$y = 25 \times 2 = 50 \text{ miles}$$

To find the area of the rectangular region, multiply the two dimensions:

$$\left(43\frac{1}{3}\text{ miles}\right)(50\text{ miles}) = 2{,}166\frac{2}{3}\text{ square miles, which}$$

is (D).

10. J   Difficulty: Medium

Category: Number and Quantity

Getting to the Answer: Adding vectors is very straightforward. Add the first coordinates together and add the second coordinates together:

$$u + v = \langle 2 + 0, 0 + (-2)\rangle = \langle 2, -2\rangle$$

Choice (J) is correct.

11. A   Difficulty: Medium

Category: Number and Quantity

Getting to the Answer: Pick Numbers for questions like this. Because the operation involved is multiplication, you can focus on the endpoints of the ranges given. Multiply all combinations of the endpoints and choose the greatest possible product. Because a falls between -1 and 1, use those endpoints for a, and because b falls between -4 and 3, use those endpoints for b:

$$a \times b = -1 \times (-4) = 4$$

$$a \times b = -1 \times 3 = -3$$

$$a \times b = 1 \times (-4) = -4$$

$$a \times b = 1 \times 3 = 3$$

The greatest possible product of a and b is 4, which is (A).

12. F   Difficulty: Medium

Category: Number and Quantity

Getting to the Answer: Writing out the units on conversion questions will help you avoid mistakes. First find the cost per yard: $\dfrac{4.50\text{ dollars}}{2.5\text{ yards}} = 1.80\dfrac{\text{dollars}}{\text{yard}}$.

Then find the cost per foot (notice that yards cancel):

$$1.80\frac{\text{dollars}}{\text{yard}} \cdot \frac{1\text{ yard}}{3\text{ feet}} = 0.60\frac{\text{dollars}}{\text{foot}}$$

Choice (F) is correct.

13. D   Difficulty: Medium

Category: Number and Quantity

Getting to the Answer: Matrices behave exactly as you would expect (except when multiplying one matrix by another), so don't let this question intimidate you. The numbers in front of the matrices (-1 and 2) are called scalars, and you simply multiply each entry in the matrix by the scalar (just like distributing inside a set of parentheses):

$$-1\begin{bmatrix} 4 & 3 \\ 2 & 1 \end{bmatrix} + 2\begin{bmatrix} 1 & 2 \\ 3 & 4 \end{bmatrix} = \begin{bmatrix} -4 & -3 \\ -2 & -1 \end{bmatrix} + \begin{bmatrix} 2 & 4 \\ 6 & 8 \end{bmatrix}$$

To add the two resulting matrices, simply add the corresponding entries (the numbers that sit in the same spots):

$$\begin{bmatrix} -4 & -3 \\ -2 & -1 \end{bmatrix} + \begin{bmatrix} 2 & 4 \\ 6 & 8 \end{bmatrix} = \begin{bmatrix} -4+2 & -3+4 \\ -2+6 & -1+8 \end{bmatrix}$$

$$= \begin{bmatrix} -2 & 1 \\ 4 & 7 \end{bmatrix}$$

Choice (D) is correct.

14. J   Difficulty: Medium

Category: Number and Quantity

Getting to the Answer: To divide by a fraction, multiply by its reciprocal. The piece of paper is $8\frac{1}{2}$ inches wide. To find the number of $\frac{5}{8}$ inch wide strips of paper you can cut, divide:

$$8\frac{1}{2} \div \frac{5}{8} = \frac{17}{2} \div \frac{5}{8} = \frac{17}{2} \times \frac{8}{5} = \frac{136}{10} = \frac{68}{5} = 13.6$$

Thus, you can make 13 strips of paper that are $\frac{5}{8}$ inch wide and 11 inches long, and you will have a small, thin strip of paper left over. Choice (J) is correct.

15. C   Difficulty: Medium

Category: Number and Quantity

Getting to the Answer: Pay attention to units when you are working with rates. If you talk for 250 minutes, you will be charged $0.10 per minute for 200 minutes, and $0.15 per minute for the additional 50 minutes:

$(\$0.10 \times 200) + (\$0.15 \times 50) = \$20.00 + \$7.50 = \$27.50$

Choice (C) is correct.

16. K   Difficulty: High

Category: Number and Quantity

Getting to the Answer: Write each factor in the expression in exponential form (using fractional exponents for the radicals). Then use exponent rules to simplify the expression. Add the exponents of the factors that are being multiplied and subtract the exponent of the factor that is being divided:

$$\frac{\sqrt[3]{x} \cdot x^{\frac{5}{2}} \cdot x}{\sqrt{x}} = \frac{x^{\frac{1}{3}} \cdot x^{\frac{5}{2}} \cdot x^{1}}{x^{\frac{1}{2}}}$$

$$= x^{\frac{1}{3}+\frac{5}{2}+1-\frac{1}{2}} = x^{\frac{2}{6}+\frac{15}{6}+\frac{6}{6}-\frac{3}{6}}$$

$$= x^{\frac{20}{6}} = x^{\frac{10}{3}}$$

The question states that n is the power of x, so the value of n is $\frac{10}{3}$. That matches (K).

17. B   Difficulty: High

Category: Number and Quantity

Getting to the Answer: "Divisible by" means the same as "is a factor of," so think of all of the integers that are factors of both 84 and 96; they are 1, 2, 3, 4, 6, and 12. Now, 1, 2, 3, 4, and 6 are all factors of either 18 or 16, so they can be eliminated. The only integer left is 12. The digits of 12 (1 and 2) add up to 3, making (B) the correct answer.

18. H   Difficulty: High

Category: Number and Quantity

Getting to the Answer: Whenever a question gives you one expression (or equation) and asks for another unusual one (rather than the value of one or both of the variables), look for any possible relationship between the two. Also look for relationships between the numbers in the expressions so you can simplify if possible. Here, start by manipulating the expression $\frac{8^x}{4^y}$ so that the numerator and denominator have the same base. This will allow you to combine the exponents. Because 8 and 4 are both multiples of 2, you can rewrite the numerator and the denominator as powers of 2 and then simplify the expression using rules of exponents (when you divide powers of the same base, subtract the exponents):

$$\frac{8^x}{4^y} = \frac{(2^3)^x}{(2^2)^y} = \frac{2^{3x}}{2^{2y}} = 2^{3x-2y}$$

Now look carefully—the expression in the exponent is the same as the left-hand side of the equation given in the question. You are told that $3x - 2y = 5$, which means you can replace the new exponent $(3x - 2y)$ with 5, making 2^5, which simplifies to 32, (H).

19. C   Difficulty: High

Category: Number and Quantity

Getting to the Answer: The average speed is the total distance traveled divided by the total hours traveled. Liza drove at 40 miles per hour for 2 hours, for a total of 40×2, or 80 miles. If she increased her speed by 25%, then she increased her speed by $0.25\,(40) = 10$, so her new speed was $40 + 10 = 50$ miles per hour. So she drove at 50 miles per hour for the next 3 hours, for a total of $50 \times 3 = 150$ miles. She went 80 miles and then 150 miles, for a total of 230 miles, and she drove for 2 hours and then for 3 hours, for a total of 5 hours. Liza's average rate for the trip was 230 miles divided by 5 hours, or 46 miles per hour, making (C) the correct answer.

20. G   Difficulty: High

Category: Number and Quantity

Getting to the Answer: Taking the square root of a complex number is not a concept you are likely to have learned, so you'll need to work backward to answer this question. Square the answer choices (using FOIL) until you find one that gives you $8 - 6i$. Start with F:

$$(3 + i)^2 = (3 + i)(3 + i)$$
$$= 9 + 6i + i^2$$
$$= 9 + 6i - 1$$
$$= 8 + 6i$$

That's not it, but it's close, so try (G) next.

$$(3 - i)^2 = (3 - i)(3 - i)$$
$$= 9 - 6i + i^2$$
$$= 9 - 6i - 1$$
$$= 8 - 6i$$

Choice (G) is correct.

21. D   Difficulty: Medium

Category: Number and Quantity

Getting to the Answer: When calculating rates, be sure to use the correct units. It takes Ashwin 5 minutes and 20 seconds, or $5\frac{1}{3}$ minutes, to row 0.8 miles. Set this up as a proportion:

$$\frac{5\frac{1}{3}\text{ minutes}}{0.8\text{ miles}} = \frac{60\text{ minutes}}{x\text{ miles}}$$
$$\left(5\frac{1}{3}\right)x = 0.8 \times 60$$
$$\frac{16}{3}x = 48$$
$$x = 48 \times \frac{3}{16} = 9$$

Choice (D) is correct.

22. F   Difficulty: High

Category: Number and Quantity

Getting to the Answer: Each of the factors in this product has two terms, so they behave like binomials. This means you can use FOIL to find the product. To avoid messy numbers, simplify the two radicals first using the definition of i. Write each of the numbers under the radicals as a product of -1 and the number, take the square roots, and then FOIL the resulting expressions. You'll also need to use the property that $i^2 = -1$:

$$\left(2 + \sqrt{-9}\right)\left(-1 + \sqrt{-4}\right) = \left(2 + \sqrt{-1 \times 9}\right)\left(-1 + \sqrt{-1 \times 4}\right)$$
$$= (2 + 3i)(-1 + 2i)$$
$$= -2 + 4i - 3i + 6i^2$$
$$= -2 + i + 6(-1)$$
$$= -8 + i$$

Choice (F) is correct.

23. A   Difficulty: High

Category: Number and Quantity

Getting to the Answer: Picking Numbers is the easiest, fastest way to answer this question. Choose a pair of numbers from each set and add them together. If you are unable to prove immediately that a set does not have the property described in the question stem, you may want to choose another pair. In set I, if you add 2 and 4, you get 6. Adding 12 and 8 gives you 20. Adding -2 and 8 gives you 6. Because each sum is a member of the set of even integers, set I seems to be true. For set II, adding 3 and 5 yields 8, which is not an odd integer. Therefore, II is not true. Finally, if you add two primes, say 2 and 3, you get 5. That example is true. If you add 3 and 5, however, you get 8, and 8 is not a prime number. Therefore, only set I has the property, and the answer is (A).

24. K   Difficulty: High

Category: Number and Quantity

Getting to the Answer: Even if you know absolutely nothing about vectors, you can answer this question. The $-\frac{2}{3}$ is called a scalar, and it behaves the same way any number being multiplied by a quantity does: multiply the scalar by each of the numbers that represents each of the two components of the vector. Be careful, though—the question gives the products, so you actually need to set up an equation for each component and solve:

$$-\frac{2}{3}u_1 = 12 \rightarrow u_1 = -\frac{3}{2} \times 12 = -18$$

$$-\frac{2}{3}u_2 = -24 \rightarrow u_2 = -\frac{3}{2} \times -24 = 36$$

Now find the sum of u_1 and u_2, which is $-18 + 36 = 18$, (K).

25. A   Difficulty: High

Category: Number and Quantity

Getting to the Answer: Read the word problem carefully to isolate the key details that will lead you to the correct answer. In the question, Michelle pulls gummy worms from the bag twice. For the answer to be correct, 50% of all worms pulled must be orange after Michelle's second handful. Therefore, the total number of orange worms pulled must equal the total number of gummy worms that have a different color.

The correct choice represents the number of worms pulled in her second handful, 40% of which are orange. Because Michelle only pulled whole worms, you can eliminate B and D right away, as 40% of 26 or 36 does not result in a whole number. Backsolve the remaining choices, starting with C:

If Michelle pulled 30 worms the second time, $30 \times 40\% = 12$ of them would be orange. Therefore, she would have $12 + 10 = 22$ orange worms and $(30 - 12) + 6 = 24$ worms of other colors. Because $22 \neq 24$, eliminate C.

You could try either (A) or E. Let's start with E: $40 \times 40\% = 16$ orange worms. Therefore, Michele has $16 + 10 = 26$ orange worms and $(40 - 16) + 6 = 30$ worms of other colors. Because $26 \neq 30$, eliminate E.

Now for (A): $20 \times 40\% = 8$ orange worms. Michelle has $8 + 10 = 18$ orange worms and $(20 - 8) + 6 = 18$ worms of other colors. Then $18 = 18$, so (A) is the correct answer.

26. G   Difficulty: High

Category: Number and Quantity

Getting to the Answer: Sometimes trial-and-error is the best way to approach a question. Try a few different values for the two numbers. Let the answer choices be clues as to which numbers you experiment with. To get the smallest possible product, you want to have a negative product. That means that one of the factors will have to be negative, and the other will have to be positive. Don't forget that the factors differ by 8. So, use numbers that are close to zero. You'll find that 4 and -4 give you the smallest possible product, -16. Choice (G) is correct.

27. B   Difficulty: High

Category: Number and Quantity

Getting to the Answer: To add matrices of the same size, add corresponding entries (entries that sit in the same spot). Here, you can use the upper-left entries to find x, the upper-right entries to find y, and the lower-left entries to find z as follows:

$$2x + 6 = 2 \rightarrow x = -2$$
$$9 + 3y = 15 \rightarrow y = 2$$
$$x + y = z \rightarrow z = -2 + 2 = 0$$

Choice (B) is correct.

28. K   Difficulty: High

Category: Number and Quantity

Getting to the Answer: You need to find the ratio of angelfish to puffers. You're given two ratios: tangs to angelfish and tangs to puffers.

Both of the given ratios contain tangs, but the tang amounts (5 and 2) are not the same. To directly compare them, find a common multiple (10). Multiply each ratio by the factor that will make the number of tangs equal to 10:

tangs to angelfish: (5:2) × (2:2) = 10:4

tangs to puffers: (2:3) × (5:5) = 10:15

Now that the number of tangs is the same in both ratios, you can merge the two ratios to compare angelfish to puffers directly: **4**:10:**15**. So the proper ratio of angelfish to puffers is 4:15, which matches (K).

29. A   Difficulty: High

Category: Number and Quantity

Getting to the Answer: This is a great question for Picking Numbers. Take a peek at the answer choices to see that you'll want to pick a value of x that is a perfect square (so you can take the square root). The question states that $x > 1$, and the next perfect square is 4, so let $x = 4$.

Try (A): $\frac{\sqrt{4}}{4} - 1 = \frac{2}{4} - 1 = -\frac{1}{2}$, which is less than 0, so keep (A).

Try B: $\frac{4}{\sqrt{4}} = \frac{4}{2} = 2$, which is not less than 1, so eliminate B and E.

Try C: $2\sqrt{4} = 2 \times 2 = 4$, which is equal to *but not less than* 4, so eliminate C.

Try D: $\sqrt{4} + 4 = 2 + 4 = 6$, which is not greater than 4^2, so eliminate D.

Choice (A) is correct.

30. K   Difficulty: High

Category: Number and Quantity

Getting to the Answer: You don't have to know anything about complex numbers ahead of time. All the information you need is in the question stem. Treat i as a variable, write the squared binomials as repeated multiplication, FOIL, and replace i^2 with -1 whenever it appears:

$$\frac{(2i+2)^2}{(2i-2)^2} = \frac{(2i+2)(2i+2)}{(2i-2)(2i-2)}$$

$$= \frac{4i^2 + 4i + 4i + 4}{4i^2 - 4i - 4i + 4}$$

$$= \frac{4(-1) + 8i + 4}{4(-1) - 8i + 4}$$

$$= \frac{8i}{-8i} = -1$$

Choice (K) is correct.

CHAPTER EIGHT

Algebra

PRACTICE QUESTIONS

The following test-like questions provide an opportunity to practice Algebra questions.

1. For all $x \neq 8$, $\dfrac{x^2 - 11x + 24}{8 - x} = ?$

   A. $3 - x$ $(x - 8)(x - 3)$

   B. $8 - x$

   C. $x - 3$ $x = 8, 3$

   D. $x - 8$ $x \neq 8 \therefore x - 3$

   E. $x - 11$

2. If r, s, and t represent nonzero values such that $r = \dfrac{s}{t}$, which expression must be equivalent to rs?

   doesn't ask to isolate from the orig. formula

   F. $\dfrac{s}{t}$ $(s)r = \dfrac{s}{t}(s)$

   G. $\dfrac{r}{t^2}$ $rs = \dfrac{s^2}{t}$

   H. st

   J. $\dfrac{s^2}{t}$

   K. $\dfrac{1}{t}$

3. For what values of x is $x^2 + 9 < 0$?

   A. $x < -3$ $(x - 3)(x + 3) < 0$

   B. $x > 3$ $x = \pm 3$

   C. $-3 < x < 3$

   D. $x < -3$ or $x > 3$

   E. There are no values of x for which the inequality is true.

4. If $|x| = -2x + 1$, then $x = ?$

   F. -1 $|x| = -2x + 1$

   G. $-\dfrac{1}{3}$

   H. 0 $3x = 1$

   J. $\dfrac{1}{3}$ $x = \dfrac{1}{3}$

   K. 1

5. For all $x \neq 0$, $\dfrac{x^2 + 2x^2 + 3x^2}{x^2} = ?$

   A. 3 $\dfrac{x^2(2 + 3)}{x^2}$

   B. 6

   C. $3x$

   D. $6x^2$

   E. $6x^4$

6. If the equation of a line is $3x - 5y = 20$, what is the slope of the line?

    F. -5

    G. $-\dfrac{3}{5}$

    H. $\dfrac{3}{5}$

    J. $\dfrac{5}{3}$

    K. 5

(handwritten: $3x - 20 = 5y$; $\dfrac{3}{5}x - 4 = y$; $y = mx + b$; $m = \dfrac{3}{5}$ *)*

7. Which of the following is a factor of $6x^2 - 13x + 6$?

    A. $2x + 3$

    B. $3x - 2$

    C. $3x + 2$

    D. $6x - 2$

    E. $6x + 2$

(handwritten: $6x^2 - 9x - 4x + 6$; $3x(2x - 3) + 2(2x - 3)$; $(3x - 2)(2x - 3)$ *)*

8. What is the value of a if $\dfrac{1}{a} + \dfrac{2}{a} + \dfrac{3}{a} + \dfrac{4}{a} = 5$?

    F. $\dfrac{1}{2}$

    G. 2

    H. 4

    J. $12\dfrac{1}{2}$

    K. 50

9. For what value of x would the following system of equations have an infinite number of solutions?

$$\begin{cases} 4a - b = 4 \\ 16a - 4b = 8x \end{cases}$$

    A. 2

    B. 4

    C. 6

    D. 16

    E. 24

(handwritten: $4a = 4 + b$; $4a - b = b$; $16a - 4(4a - 4) = 8x$ *)*

10. Morris is offered two different jobs as a salesperson. At company A, he will earn a base salary of $300 per week, plus a commission of $20 per sale. At Company B, he does not have a base salary, but will earn $35 per sale. If s is positive and represents the number of total sales, for what values of s will Morris earn more at Company A than Company B?

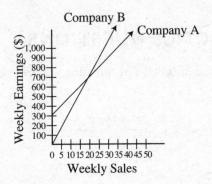

    F. $s > 20$

    G. $s \geq 20$

    H. $s \leq 20$

    J. $s < 20$

    K. $s \geq 0$

11. If the number line below shows the range of possible values for some number b, which of the following shows the same possible values for b ?

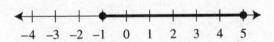

    A. $|b - 1| \leq 5$

    B. $|b - 2| \leq 3$

    C. $|b - 2| \leq 5$

    D. $|b - 5| \leq 1$

    E. $|b - 5| \leq 2$

12. If (x,y) is the solution of the system of equations below, what is the product of xy?

$$-x + y = 3$$
$$-3x + y = -5$$

F. -28

G. -15

H. -4

J. 15

K. 28

13. Which of the following values of x satisfy the equation $|2x - 6| = -4$?

A. -1

B. 1

C. 5

D. 1 and 5

E. There are no values of x for which the equation is true.

14. What is the x-coordinate of the point in the standard (x,y) coordinate plane at which the two lines $y = 4x + 10$ and $y = 5x + 7$ intersect?

F. 3

G. 4

H. 7

J. 10

K. 22

15. A number line contains points W, X, Y, and Z. Point X is between points W and Y. Point Z is between Y and X. Which of the following inequalities must be true?

A. $XY < WX$

B. $XZ < WX$

C. $XZ < YZ$

D. $YZ < WX$

E. $YZ < XY$

16. Which of the following is parallel to $4x + 3y = 15$?

F. $y = -\dfrac{4}{3}x - 5$

G. $y = \dfrac{3}{4}x + 5$

H. $y = \dfrac{3}{4}x - 5$

J. $y = \dfrac{4}{3}x + 5$

K. $y = 3x + 5$

17. The larger of two numbers is six less than triple the smaller one. The sum of four times the larger and twice the smaller is 77. If x represents the smaller number, which of the following equations determines the correct value for x?

A. $2(3x - 6) + 4x = 77$

B. $2(3x + 6) + 4x = 77$

C. $(12x - 6) + 2x = 77$

D. $4(3x - 6) + 2x = 77$

E. $4(3x + 6) + 2x = 77$

18. Which equation represents the line that is parallel to $y = 4x + 7$ and passes through $(-5,1)$?

F. $y = x + 20$

G. $y = -5x - 19$

H. $y = 4x + 19$

J. $y = -4x + 20$

K. $y = 4x + 21$

19. For what value of x is the equation $\sqrt[3]{4x - 12} + 25 = 27$ true?

A. -5

B. -1

C. -2.5

D. 5

E. 6.5

20. How many points do the graphs of all three equations below have in common?

$$x = y + 8$$
$$-x = y - 8$$
$$6x = 2y + 4$$

F. 0

G. 1

H. 2

J. 3

K. Infinitely many

21. The expression $\dfrac{12x + 6}{3x - 1}$ is equivalent to which of the following?

A. -2

B. 9

C. $4 - \dfrac{6}{3x - 1}$

D. $\dfrac{4}{3x - 1} - 6$

E. $4 + \dfrac{10}{3x - 1}$

22. In the figure below, line l has the equation $y = x$. Line m is perpendicular to l and intercepts the x-axis at $(3,0)$. Which of the following is an equation for m?

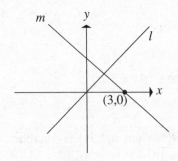

F. $y = x + 3\sqrt{2}$

G. $y = x + 3$

H. $y = -x + 3$

J. $y = -x + 3\sqrt{2}$

K. $y = -3x + 3$

23. For what values of x is $x^2 - 5x - 24 > 0$?

A. $-8 < x < -3$

B. $-8 < x < 3$

C. $-3 < x < 8$

D. $-8 > x$ or $x > 3$

E. $-3 > x$ or $x > 8$

24. Which of the following expressions is equivalent to $\dfrac{\sqrt{3 + x}}{\sqrt{3 - x}}$ for all x such that $-3 < x < 3$?

F. $\dfrac{3 - x}{3 + x}$

G. $\dfrac{3 + x}{3 - x}$

H. $\dfrac{-3\sqrt{3 + x}}{\sqrt{3 - x}}$

J. $\dfrac{\sqrt{9 - x^2}}{3 - x}$

K. $\dfrac{x^2 - 9}{3 + x}$

25. What is the solution to the system of equations shown here?

$$\begin{cases} -0.5x + 0.5y = 1.5 \\ -0.75x + 0.25y = -1.25 \end{cases}$$

A. $(-8, -5)$

B. $(-4, -1)$

C. $(3, -5)$

D. $(4, 7)$

E. $(8, 11)$

26. For what value of a would the following system of equations have no solution?

$$\begin{cases} -x + 6y = 7 \\ -5x + 10ay = 32 \end{cases}$$

    F. $\dfrac{5}{3}$

    G. 3

    H. 6

    J. 30

    K. 60

27. If $(x^{3b-1})^2 = x^{16}$ for all x, then $b = $?

    A. 1

    B. $\dfrac{5}{3}$

    C. $\dfrac{5}{4}$

    D. 3

    E. $\dfrac{16}{3}$

28. If the solutions to the equation $2x^2 + bx - 20 = 0$ are $x = -\dfrac{5}{2}$ and $x = 4$, what is the value of b ?

    F. -10

    G. -3

    H. 3

    J. 4

    K. 10

29. Which of these shows that y varies inversely as x and directly as the square of z ?

    A. $y = \dfrac{kx^2}{z}$

    B. $y = \dfrac{kz^2}{x}$

    C. $y = \dfrac{kx}{z^2}$

    D. $y = kxz^2$

    E. $y = kx^2z$

30. If $\left(\sqrt{a}\sqrt{b}\right)^4 = 5b^2$, such that a and b are nonzero real numbers, then a could be which of the following?

    F. -5

    G. $-\sqrt[4]{5}$

    H. $\dfrac{1}{5}$

    J. $\sqrt[4]{5}$

    K. $\sqrt{5}$

31. If $a = 6c + 7$ and $b = 3 - 2c$, which of the following expresses a in terms of b ?

    A. $a = \dfrac{16 - b}{3}$

    B. $a = \dfrac{17 - b}{2}$

    C. $a = 16 - 3b$

    D. $a = 25 - 12b$

    E. $a = 6b + 7$

32. Which of the following is NOT a factor of the polynomial $x^4 - x^3 - 13x^2 + x + 12$?

    F. $x - 6$

    G. $x - 4$

    H. $x - 1$

    J. $x + 1$

    K. $x + 3$

33. Which of these is NOT a factor of $x^6 - 81x^2$?

    A. $x + 9$

    B. $x^2 + 9$

    C. x^2

    D. $x - 3$

    E. $x + 3$

34. How many integers are in the solution set of $|5x + 3| < 9$?

F.   0

G.   2

H.   3

J.   4

K.   Infinitely many

35. If $(a - b)^2 = 81$ and $ab = \frac{3}{2}$, then $a^2 + b^2 = ?$

A. -18

B.   18

C.   27

D.   84

E.   90

36. For positive real numbers x, y, and z, which of the following expressions is equivalent to $x^{\frac{2}{3}} y^{\frac{1}{4}} z^{\frac{5}{2}}$?

F. $\sqrt[3]{x^2 y z^5}$

G. $\sqrt[4]{x^2 y z^5}$

H. $\sqrt[6]{x^2 y z^5}$

J. $\sqrt[6]{x^4 y^2 z^{10}}$

K. $\sqrt[12]{x^8 y^3 z^{30}}$

37. In the system of equations below, r and s are constants. If the system has infinitely many solutions, what is the value of $\frac{r}{s}$?

$$\begin{cases} rx + sy = 7 \\ 10x + 15y = -4 \end{cases}$$

A. $-\frac{7}{4}$

B. $-\frac{3}{2}$

C. $-\frac{2}{3}$

D. $\frac{4}{7}$

E. $\frac{2}{3}$

38. If $g = 4q + 3$ and $h = 2q - 8$, what is g in terms of h ?

F. $g = \frac{h + 8}{2}$

G. $g = \frac{4h + 11}{2}$

H. $h = \frac{g - 3}{4}$

J. $2h + 11$

K. $2h + 19$

39. What is the value of $2a + b$ given that $4a^2 + 6ab + 2b^2 = 40$ and $a + b = 5$?

A.   4

B.   5

C.   6

D.   7

E.   8

40. How many integer values of x satisfy the inequality $|2x + 5| > 11$?

    F. None

    G. Two

    H. Three

    J. Four

    K. Infinitely many

41. If $x^2 + 4x - 9 = 0$, which of the following is a possible value of x ?

    A. -7

    B. $-2 - \sqrt{52}$

    C. $-2 \pm \dfrac{\sqrt{52}}{2}$

    D. $2 \pm \dfrac{\sqrt{52}}{2}$

    E. 7

42. Which of the following is equivalent to the expression shown below?

$$\frac{1}{\dfrac{1}{x+2} - \dfrac{1}{x+4}}$$

    F. $\dfrac{2}{x^2 + 6x + 8}$

    G. $\dfrac{6}{x^2 + 6x + 8}$

    H. $\dfrac{x^2 + 6x + 8}{6}$

    J. $\dfrac{x^2 + 6x + 8}{2}$

    K. $\dfrac{x^2 + 6x + 8}{4}$

43. If $x > 0$ and $y > 0$, $\dfrac{\sqrt{x}}{x} + \dfrac{\sqrt{y}}{y}$ is equivalent to which of the following?

    A. $\dfrac{2}{\sqrt{xy}}$

    B. $\dfrac{\sqrt{x} + \sqrt{y}}{\sqrt{xy}}$

    C. $\dfrac{x + y}{xy}$

    D. $\dfrac{\sqrt{x + \sqrt{y}}}{\sqrt{x + y}}$

    E. $\dfrac{x + y}{\sqrt{xy}}$

44. What value of x satisfies the equation $\dfrac{6}{5}\sqrt{2x + 1} - 2 = -\dfrac{2}{5}$?

    F. $-\dfrac{6}{5}$

    G. $-\dfrac{1}{2}$

    H. $\dfrac{7}{18}$

    J. $\dfrac{5}{8}$

    K. $\dfrac{8}{5}$

45. Charles earned a score of 76 on a recent 50-question multiple-choice exam. The scoring for the exam was such that each correct answer earned +5 points, each incorrect answer earned −1 point, and each unanswered question received 0 points. What is the maximum number of questions Charles could have answered correctly?

    A. 15

    B. 18

    C. 21

    D. 23

    E. 25

ANSWERS AND EXPLANATIONS

1. A   Difficulty: Medium

Category: Algebra

Getting to the Answer: To factor a quadratic expression, find factors of the last term that, when added together, equal the middle term. The factors of 24 that add to -11 are -8 and -3. Also keep in mind that $(a - b)$ is equivalent to $-(b - a)$.

$$\frac{x^2 - 11x + 24}{8 - x} = \frac{(x - 8)(x - 3)}{8 - x}$$
$$= \frac{-(8 - x)(x - 3)}{8 - x}$$
$$= -(x - 3)$$
$$= 3 - x$$

This matches (A).

2. J   Difficulty: Medium

Category: Algebra

Getting to the Answer: When you manipulate an equation, you may only multiply or divide on the same side by expressions that are equal to one, or on opposite sides by expressions that will cancel each other out. Start with the given equation, and manipulate the equation until you get rs on one side of the equation. The other side of the equation will be your answer.

First, multiply both sides by s:

$$r = \frac{s}{t}$$
$$r(s) = \frac{s}{t} \times s$$
$$rs = \frac{s^2}{t}$$

Choice (J) is correct.

3. E   Difficulty: Medium

Category: Algebra

Getting to the Answer: Don't be fooled—the left side of this inequality cannot be factored (because of the $+$ between the terms), so you need to approach this question a bit differently. Think of what the graph would look like: The expression on the left is the standard quadratic (x^2) shifted up 9 units. Its graph, therefore, is a parabola (a U shape) that opens upward and has a minimum value of 9. (Note that parabolas will be covered in more detail in later chapters.) This means the graph never drops below the x-axis (which is where $y = 0$), so $x^2 + 9$ will never be less than 0. Choice (E) is correct.

You could also think about this algebraically: A number squared is either positive or 0 (if the number happens to be 0), and adding 9 to a number squared will certainly result in a positive number. Thus, $x^2 + 9$ is definitely a positive number and will never be less than 0.

4. J   Difficulty: Medium

Category: Algebra

Getting to the Answer: On Test Day, Backsolving can be a real time saver. Try it whenever you're not sure how to set up or solve an equation. Backsolving works very well here, because it's tricky to solve equations with absolute values in them. Start with H:

$$|0| = -2(0) + 1$$
$$0 \neq 1$$

Eliminate H. Now try (J).

$$\left|\frac{1}{3}\right| = -2\left(\frac{1}{3}\right) + 1$$
$$\frac{1}{3} = -\frac{2}{3} + \frac{3}{3}$$
$$\frac{1}{3} = \frac{1}{3}$$

Choice (J) works.

To solve this problem algebraically, you'll need to look at both possible values of $|x|$. If x is positive, then $|x|$ equals x. If x is negative, then $|x|$ equals $-x$. Try both possibilities:

$$x = -2x + 1$$
$$3x = 1$$
$$x = \frac{1}{3}$$

Now check this solution.

$$\left|\frac{1}{3}\right| = -2\left(\frac{1}{3}\right) + 1$$
$$\frac{1}{3} = \frac{-2}{3} + 1 = \frac{1}{3}$$

This works. Now try the other possibility.

$$-x = -2x + 1$$
$$x = 1$$

Now check this solution.

$$|1| = -2(1) + 1$$
$$1 \neq -1$$

This does not work. The only solution is $x = \frac{1}{3}$.

5. B   Difficulty: Medium

Category: Algebra

Getting to the Answer: All the terms in the numerator are like terms, so add them together. Then cancel powers of x to simplify the expression:

$$\frac{x^2 + 2x^2 + 3x^2}{x^2} = \frac{6x^2}{x^2} = 6$$

Choice (B) is correct.

6. H   Difficulty: Medium

Category: Algebra

Getting to the Answer: The slope-intercept form of a line is $y = mx + b$, where m is the slope and b is the

y-intercept. The quickest way to get to the answer is by rewriting the given equation in this form:

$$3x - 5y = 20$$
$$-5y = -3x + 20$$
$$y = \frac{-3x}{-5} + \frac{20}{-5}$$
$$y = \frac{3}{5}x - 4$$

The slope of the line given by this equation is the coefficient of x, which is $\frac{3}{5}$. Choice (H) is correct.

7. B   Difficulty: Medium

Category: Algebra

Getting to the Answer: Think "reverse FOIL": To factor $6x^2 - 13x + 6$, you need a pair of binomials whose "first" terms will give you a product of $6x^2$ and whose "last" terms will give you a product of $+6$. Because the middle term of the original expression is negative, the two last terms must both be negative. You know that one of the factors is among the answer choices, so you can use them in your trial-and-error effort to factor. You know you're looking for a factor with a minus sign in it, so the answer is either (B) or D.

Try (B) first: Its first term is $3x$, so the other factor's first term would have to be $2x$ (to get that $6x^2$ in the product). Choice (B)'s last term is -2, so the other factor's last term would have to be -3. Check to see whether the factors $(3x - 2)$ and $(2x - 3)$ work:

$$(3x - 2)(2x - 3) = 3x(2x) + 3x(-3) + (-2)(2x) + (-2)(-3)$$
$$= 6x^2 - 9x - 4x + 6$$
$$= 6x^2 - 13x + 6$$

It works, so (B) is correct. There's no need to check D. Note that you could also use grouping to factor the expression; you will find the correct answer either way.

8. G **Difficulty:** Medium

Category: Algebra

Getting to the Answer: The four fractions on the left side of the equation are all ready to be added since they already have a common denominator: a.

$$\frac{1}{a} + \frac{2}{a} + \frac{3}{a} + \frac{4}{a} = 5$$
$$\frac{1+2+3+4}{a} = 5$$
$$\frac{10}{a} = 5$$
$$10 = 5a$$
$$a = 2$$

Choice (G) is correct.

9. A **Difficulty:** Medium

Category: Algebra

Getting to the Answer: A system of equations has an infinite number of solutions when both equations represent the same line. So, you just have to find the value of x that will make the second equation equivalent to the first one. Compare the two equations. The left side of the second equation is 4 times the left side of the first equation. If the term on the right side of the second equation is also 4 times the term on the right side of the first equation, the two equations will be equivalent.

$$4(4a - b) = 4(4)$$
$$16a - 4b = 16$$

So:

$$16 = 8x$$
$$2 = x$$

Choice (A) is correct. Note that you could also write each equation in slope-intercept form and find the value of x that makes the y-intercepts the same.

10. J **Difficulty:** Medium

Category: Algebra

Getting to the Answer: The point where the two graphs intersect represents the point where the two equations have equal values. The graph for company A is above the graph for company B between 0 and 20 sales. The graphs intersect at 20 sales, so the range where he will earn more at Company A than Company B is $s < 20$, which matches (J).

11. B **Difficulty:** Medium

Category: Algebra

Getting to the Answer: One approach to this question is to solve each of the answer choices to get a range of values for b and then see which one gives you the same range as that shown in the figure. A faster approach is to think of absolute value as a distance. You can see that the values in the figure are centered at 2 and include everything up to and including 3 units away from the center. Therefore, the distance between b and 2 must be less than or equal to 3, so $|b - 2| \leq 3$. Choice (B) is correct.

12. K **Difficulty:** Medium

Category: Algebra

Getting to the Answer: One way to find the solution to the given system is to use the combination method. To eliminate the y terms, multiply the top equation by -1:

$$\begin{cases} -x + y = 3 \\ -3x + y = -5 \end{cases} \Rightarrow \begin{aligned} -1(-x + y = 3) \\ -3x + y = -5 \end{aligned}$$

Now add the equations to eliminate y, and solve the resulting equation for x:

$$x - y = -3$$
$$\underline{-3x + y = -5}$$
$$-2x = -8$$
$$x = \boxed{4}$$

Next, substitute this value for x in either equation to find the value of y:

$$-\boxed{x} + y = 3$$
$$-\boxed{4} + y = 3$$
$$y = 7$$

The product of $xy = 4 \times 7 = 28$, which is (K).

13. E   Difficulty: Medium

Category: Algebra

Getting to the Answer: There is no math to be done here. If you recall that absolute value represents distance on a number line and therefore cannot be negative, you'll immediately see that there are no values of x for which the equation is true (because the right-hand side is -4). Choice (E) is correct.

14. F   Difficulty: Medium

Category: Algebra

Getting to the Answer: The intersection of two lines is simply the one (x,y) point that makes both equations true. You can solve this like any system of equations.

$$4x + 10 = 5x + 7$$
$$10 = x + 7$$
$$3 = x$$

Choice (F) is correct. If you had accidentally solved for the y-coordinate, you would have gotten K. Look out for traps like this in coordinate geometry questions.

15. E   Difficulty: Medium

Category: Algebra

Getting to the Answer: If the test maker doesn't give you a diagram, make a sketch! Your sketch of the number line should place Z between X and Y, thus the distance between Y and Z must be less than the distance between X and Y. Choose (E).

16. F   Difficulty: Medium

Category: Algebra

Getting to the Answer: Parallel lines have the same slope, so find the slope of the given line and then compare it to each of the answer choices. To find the slope, isolate y (so the equation is written in slope-intercept form):

$$4x + 3y = 15$$
$$3y = -4x + 15$$
$$y = -\frac{4}{3}x + 5$$

The slope of the original line is $-\frac{4}{3}$. The only choice with the same slope is (F).

17. D   Difficulty: Medium

Category: Algebra

Getting to the Answer: When you're translating from English to math, it's easiest to first translate literally (word by word) and then simplify the expression. Be careful: "6 less than x" means $x - 6$, not $6 - x$.

Smaller number $= x$
Larger number $= 3x - 6$
Four times the larger $= 4(3x - 6)$
Sum of four times the larger and twice the smaller $= 4(3x - 6) + 2x$

This sum is supposed to be 77, so $4(3x - 6) + 2x = 77$, which is (D).

18. K   Difficulty: Medium

Category: Algebra

Getting to the Answer: Parallel lines have equal slopes, and the slope of the given line is 4, so the correct answer must be either H or (K). Find the correct y-intercept using the slope-intercept equation and the given point:

$$y = 4x + b$$
$$1 = 4(-5) + b$$
$$1 = -20 + b$$
$$21 = b$$

Therefore, the equation of the line is $y = 4x + 21$. Choice (K) is the correct answer.

19. D   Difficulty: High

Category: Algebra

Getting to the Answer: Solving equations that involve radicals may seem daunting, but they work just like other equations. In fact, they're usually easier to solve than quadratic equations because you don't have to worry about factoring. As a general rule, you need to: 1) isolate the radical part; 2) eliminate the radical by squaring both sides of the equation if the radical is a square root, cubing both sides if it's a cube root, and so on; and 3) isolate the variable. To solve the equation here, the steps are:

$$\sqrt[3]{4x - 12} + 25 = 27$$
$$\sqrt[3]{4x - 12} = 2$$
$$\left(\sqrt[3]{4x - 12}\right)^3 = 2^3$$
$$4x - 12 = 8$$
$$4x = 20$$
$$x = 5$$

Choice (D) is correct. Note that you could also use Backsolving to answer this question.

20. F   Difficulty: High

Category: Algebra

Getting to the Answer: Equations share points when the same values of x and y work for all of the equations involved. Start with the first two equations. Rewrite the second so that both equations have the same term on one side, then set them equal to each other:

$$-x = y - 8$$
$$x = -y + 8$$
$$x = y + 8$$
$$-y + 8 = y + 8$$
$$-y = y$$

This is only true when y equals 0. Plug $y = 0$ into either equation and solve for x:

$$x = y + 8$$
$$x = 0 + 8$$
$$x = 8$$

The point $(8, 0)$ is shared between the first two equations. Does it work in the third?

$$6x = 2y + 4$$
$$6(8) = 2(0) + 4$$
$$48 = 4$$

That's not true, so this point is not shared between all three equations. There are no points that work in every equation, so (F) is correct.

21. E   Difficulty: High

Category: Algebra

Getting to the Answer: This question is actually more difficult than it appears at first. To find the equivalent expression, you need to divide $12x + 6$ by $3x - 1$ because the expression is already as simplified as it can get in its current form (nothing to add, subtract, multiply, or even factor out and cancel). Be careful here—you cannot just cancel out the x's in the numerator and denominator because they are each part of a quantity that includes addition and/or subtraction; instead, you must use polynomial long division.

$$3x - 1 \overline{)12x + 6} \quad \begin{array}{c} 4 \\ \end{array}$$
$$\underline{-(12x - 4)}$$
$$10$$

Remember, when you have a remainder, place it over the divisor (which, in a fraction, is the denominator). Therefore, the correct answer is $4 + \dfrac{10}{3x - 1}$, which matches (E).

22. H   Difficulty: High

Category: Algebra

Getting to the Answer: When lines in the coordinate plane are perpendicular, the slopes of the two lines are negative reciprocals. Because m is perpendicular to l, and l has a slope of 1, the slope of m must be -1. That eliminates F, G, and K. To distinguish between (H) and J, you'll need to find the y-intercept of line m. Because the slope is -1, the line goes down 1 unit for every unit it goes to the right. You can also think of it as going up 1 unit for every unit it goes to the left. Start at $(3,0)$ and count units until you reach the y-axis: $(3,0)$, $(2,1)$, $(1,2)$, $(0,3)$. The y-intercept of line m is 3, so (H) is correct.

23. E **Difficulty:** High

Category: Algebra

Getting to the Answer: You can't solve a quadratic inequality the same way you do a linear inequality because the squared term changes the sign of negative values of x. Instead, you need to factor the left side of the inequality and then think about what "> 0" means numerically or picture the graph (which happens to be easier in this case). The left side factors to $(x + 3)(x - 8)$, so the graph is a parabola that crosses the x-axis at -3 and $+8$ and opens upward (because the coefficient of the squared term is positive). Now think about the parts of the graph that lie *above* the x-axis (because you want > 0), which are the parts to the left of $x = -3$ and to the right of $x = 8$. Using symbols, this translates to $x < -3$ (which can also be written as $-3 > x$) or $x > 8$. This matches (E). Note: You can also graph $y = x^2 - 5x - 24$ in your graphing calculator to find the parts that lie above the x-axis.

24. J **Difficulty:** High

Category: Algebra

Getting to the Answer: Take a quick look at the answer choices before simplifying an expression like this one. Notice that only one of these choices contains a radical sign in its denominator. So when you simplify the expression, try to eliminate that radical sign. Your calculations should look something like this:

$$\frac{\sqrt{3+x}}{\sqrt{3-x}} \times \frac{\sqrt{3-x}}{\sqrt{3-x}} = \frac{\sqrt{(3+x)(3-x)}}{\sqrt{(3-x)^2}}$$

$$= \frac{\sqrt{9-3x+3x-x^2}}{3-x} = \frac{\sqrt{9-x^2}}{3-x}$$

Choice (J) is correct.

25. D **Difficulty:** High

Category: Algebra

Getting to the Answer: There are several ways to solve a system of equations. Before choosing a method, eliminate the decimals (multiply the top equation by 2 and the bottom equation by 4).

$$-0.5x + 0.5y = 1.5 \rightarrow -x + y = 3$$
$$-0.75x + 0.25y = -1.25 \rightarrow -3x + y = -5$$

To solve using combination, you can eliminate the y terms by multiplying the top equation by -1:

$$\begin{cases} -1(-x + y = 3) \\ -3x + y = -5 \end{cases} \Rightarrow \begin{matrix} x - y = -3 \\ -3x + y = -5 \end{matrix}$$

Now add the equations to eliminate y, and solve the resulting equation for x:

$$\begin{array}{r} x - y = -3 \\ -3x + y = -5 \\ \hline -2x = -8 \\ x = 4 \end{array}$$

You can eliminate A, B, C, and E, because none has 4 as the x-coordinate, making (D) the correct answer. If you're not sure, you can substitute this value into either equation to find the exact value of y:

$$-x + y = 3$$
$$-4 + y = 3$$
$$y = 7$$

The solution is $(4,7)$, making (D) the correct choice.

26. G **Difficulty:** High

Category: Algebra

Getting to the Answer: If a system of equations has no solution, there are no values of x and y that make both equations true. Graphically, that means the two linear equations never intersect and are therefore parallel (have the same slope but different *y*-intercepts). Write both equations in slope-intercept form, then set the slopes equal and solve for *a*:

$$-x + 6y = 7$$
$$6y = x + 7$$
$$y = \boxed{\frac{1}{6}}x + \frac{7}{6}$$
$$-5x + 10ay = 32$$
$$10ay = 5x + 32$$
$$y = \boxed{\frac{5}{10a}}x + \frac{32}{10a}$$

$$\frac{1}{6} = \frac{5}{10a}$$
$$10a = 30$$
$$a = 3$$

The correct answer is (G).

27. D   Difficulty: High

Category: Algebra

Getting to the Answer: This question is not as difficult as it may appear. It's primarily testing your knowledge of rules of exponents. When an exponent is raised to another exponent, multiply the exponents. Because the variable you want to solve for is part of an exponent, try to make the bases the same so that you can compare the exponents.

$$\left(x^{3b-1}\right)^2 = x^{16}$$
$$x^{6b-2} = x^{16}$$

Now that the bases are the same, set up an equation comparing the exponents:

$$6b - 2 = 16$$
$$6b = 18$$
$$b = 3$$

That matches (D).

28. G   Difficulty: High

Category: Algebra

Getting to the Answer: Understanding the connection between solutions to an equation and factors of an expression is the key to answering this question. The solution $x = -\frac{5}{2}$ results from the factor $(2x + 5)$, and the solution $x = 4$ results from the factor $(x - 4)$. Multiply these two factors together (using FOIL) to get $2x^2 - 3x - 20$. This matches the given equation, so the value of *b* must be -3, which is (G).

29. B   Difficulty: High

Category: Algebra

Getting to the Answer: Recall the different types of variations. To write a joint variation, write both parts of the variation together. Because *y* varies inversely as *x*, begin by writing $y = \frac{k}{x}$. Because *y* also varies directly as the square of *z*, or z^2, the equation $y = \frac{kz^2}{x}$ shows both variations, so (B) is correct.

30. K   Difficulty: High

Category: Algebra

Getting to the Answer: This question looks impossible to solve because there are two variables and only one equation. This is usually a tipoff that one of the variables will disappear once the equation is simplified a bit. Here, part of the given expression is written in radical notation and part is written using exponents, so begin by rewriting everything using exponents. To do this, recall that $\sqrt{a}$ can be written as $a^{\frac{1}{2}}$. After rewriting the radical numbers, you can simplify using rules of exponents.

$$\left(\sqrt{a}\sqrt{b}\right)^4 = 5b^2$$

$$\left(a^{\frac{1}{2}}b^{\frac{1}{2}}\right)^4 = 5b^2$$

$$a^{\left(\frac{1}{2}\times 4\right)} b^{\left(\frac{1}{2}\times 4\right)} = 5b^2$$

$$a^2 b^2 = 5b^2$$

$$a^2 = 5$$

$$a = \pm\sqrt{5}$$

The positive solution matches (K).

31. C   Difficulty: High

Category: Algebra

Getting to the Answer: To get a in terms of b, you'll first need to get c in terms of b, because c is the variable the two equations have in common.

$$b = 3 - 2c$$

$$b + 2c = 3$$

$$2c = 3 - b$$

$$c = \boxed{\frac{3-b}{2}}$$

$$a = 6\boxed{c} + 7$$

$$a = 6\left(\frac{3-b}{2}\right) + 7$$

$$a = 3(3 - b) + 7$$

$$a = 9 - 3b + 7$$

$$a = 16 - 3b$$

This is a perfect match for (C)!

32. F   Difficulty: High

Category: Algebra

Getting to the Answer: There are several ways to answer this question. You could use polynomial long division to divide the polynomial by each of the choices to determine which one does *not* give a remainder of 0, or you could use synthetic division if

you're familiar with that process. However, the fastest route is to recall that a factor of a polynomial tells you a root of the polynomial, and if you plug that root into the polynomial, the result is 0. The answer choices translate, in order, to roots of 6, 4, 1, −1, and −3. Plug each of these into the polynomial and use your calculator to simplify. Note that you can stop as soon as you find a non-zero remainder, but all the calculations are presented below.

$$6^4 - 6^3 - 13(6)^2 + 6 + 12 = 630$$

$$4^4 - 4^3 - 13(4)^2 + 4 + 12 = 0$$

$$1^4 - 1^3 - 13(1)^2 + 1 + 12 = 0$$

$$(-1)^4 - (-1)^3 - 13(-1)^2 + (-1) + 12 = 0$$

$$(-3)^4 - (-3)^3 - 13(-3)^2 + (-3) + 12 = 0$$

Based on the calculations, 6 is not a root of the polynomial, so $x - 6$ is not a factor, making (F) the correct answer.

33. A   Difficulty: High

Category: Algebra

Getting to the Answer: To completely factor an expression, you may have to use more than one method. Here, for example, you'll need to factor out the GCF and then use the *difference of squares* rule twice. Factor the expression completely, and then identify the term in the answer choices that is not a factor:

$$x^6 - 81x^2 = x^2\left(x^4 - 81\right)$$

$$= x^2\left(x^2 + 9\right)\left(x^2 - 9\right)$$

$$= x^2\left(x^2 + 9\right)(x + 3)(x - 3)$$

The term $x + 9$, (A), is not a factor of $x^6 - 81x^2$.

34. J   Difficulty: High

Category: Algebra

Getting to the Answer: If the absolute value of something is less than 9, then that something is between −9 and 9. Use this interpretation to rewrite the inequality without the absolute value symbols. Then, solve the resulting compound inequality:

$$|5x + 3| < 9$$
$$-9 < 5x + 3 < 9$$
$$-12 < 5x < 6$$
$$\frac{-12}{5} < x < \frac{6}{5}$$
$$-2.4 < x < 1.2$$

There are four integers in that range: $-2, -1, 0,$ and 1, so (J) is correct.

35. D   Difficulty: High

Category: Algebra

Getting to the Answer: When you get stuck on a question involving variables, look for ways to rewrite the expressions that will produce like terms to work with. Keep an eye out for the classic quadratic equations.

Start with the first equation, $(a - b)^2 = 81$. You cannot directly substitute ab into this equation, so use FOIL (or recognize the classic quadratic) to multiply the binomials on the left side. This equation can also be written as $(a - b)(a - b) = 81$, and the result after multiplying the binomials is $a^2 - 2ab + b^2 = 81$; now you have something you can work with that includes the expressions in the question stem! Substitute in the value of ab that was given into the final equation and simplify:

$$a^2 - 2\left(\frac{3}{2}\right) + b^2 = 81$$
$$a^2 - 3 + b^2 = 81$$
$$a^2 + b^2 = 84$$

Thus, (D) is correct.

36. K   Difficulty: High

Category: Number and Quantity

Getting to the Answer: When faced with a fractional exponent, use the definition $a^{\frac{b}{c}} = \sqrt[c]{a^b}$ ("power over root"). Start by finding a common denominator for the fractional exponents and restating the expression: $x^{\frac{8}{12}} y^{\frac{3}{12}} z^{\frac{30}{12}}$. Now, convert to radical form where the index on the root is 12. The result is $\sqrt[12]{x^8 y^3 z^{30}}$, which is (K).

37. E   Difficulty: High

Category: Algebra

Getting to the Answer: A system of two equations has infinitely many solutions when the two equations actually represent the same line. In other words, their slopes are equal and their y-intercepts are equal. This means writing both equations in slope-intercept form should lead you to the correct answer.

First Equation

$$rx + sy = 7$$
$$sy = -rx + 7$$
$$y = \boxed{-\frac{r}{s}}x + \frac{7}{s}$$

Second Equation

$$10x + 15y = -4$$
$$15y = -10x - 4$$
$$y = \boxed{-\frac{2}{3}}x - \frac{4}{15}$$

The slope of the first equation is $-\frac{r}{s}$, and the slope of the second equation is $-\frac{2}{3}$. For there to be infinitely many solutions to the system, the slopes must be the same, therefore $-\frac{r}{s} = -\frac{2}{3}$. Notice that the question asks for the value of $\frac{r}{s}$, so all you need to do now is multiply both sides by -1 to get $\frac{r}{s} = \frac{2}{3}$. The answer is (E).

38. K   Difficulty: High

Category: Algebra

Getting to the Answer: The question is asking for the value of g in terms of h. The two given equations do not show a direct relationship between g and h, so you must solve for q in the second equation to get q in terms of h, and then substitute this value for q in the first equation. To solve for q in the second equation, isolate q by first adding 8 to both sides of the equation, which gives $h + 8 = 2q$. Divide both sides by 2 to get $\frac{h+8}{2} = q$. Use this value of q in the first equation: $g = 4q + 3$ becomes $g = 4\left(\frac{h+8}{2}\right) + 3$.

Factor out a 2 from the numerator and the denominator of the first term to get $g = 2(h + 8) + 3$. Distributing the 2 gives $g = 2h + 16 + 3$, or $g = 2h + 19$, which is (K).

39. A   Difficulty: High

Category: Algebra

Getting to the Answer: If you don't know how to start a question that involves a quadratic equation, try factoring it.

You are given the value of $a + b$. To make use of it, reverse FOIL the equation $4a^2 + 6ab + 2b^2 = 32$ and try to factor out an $a + b$:

$$4a^2 + 6ab + 2b^2 = 40$$
$$(4a + 2b)(a + b) = 40$$
$$2(2a + b)(a + b) = 40$$

Now substitute 5 for $a + b$ and solve for $2a + b$:

$$2(2a + b)(5) = 40$$
$$10(2a + b) = 40$$
$$2a + b = \frac{40}{10} = 4$$

Therefore, (A) is correct. Alternatively, you could simplify the original quadratic equation first by dividing both sides by 2 to get the lowest possible numbers to work with.

40. K   Difficulty: High

Category: Algebra

Getting to the Answer: You could work out the algebra here, but it's not actually necessary. Because the symbol is $>$, the solution to the inequality will include all numbers that are less than a certain value and all numbers that are greater than a certain value. Regardless of what those values are, there will be infinitely many integers in the solution set. Choice (K) is correct.

41. C   Difficulty: High

Category: Algebra

Getting to the Answer: The given equation is quadratic and in the correct form, $ax^2 + bx + c$, so use the quadratic formula. The values of a, b, and c are $a = 1$, $b = 4$, and $c = -9$. Substitute these values into the quadratic formula.

$$x = \frac{-b \pm \sqrt{b^2 - 4ac}}{2a}$$
$$= \frac{-4 \pm \sqrt{(42 - 4 \times 1 \times -9)}}{2 \times 1}$$
$$= \frac{-4 \pm \sqrt{52}}{2}$$
$$= \frac{-2 \pm \sqrt{52}}{2}$$

Choice (C) is the correct answer.

42. J   Difficulty: High

Category: Algebra

Getting to the Answer: Use the structure of the expression to rewrite it. Ignore the big "1 over" part initially. Rewrite the entire denominator, $\frac{1}{x+2} - \frac{1}{x+4}$, as a single fraction, and then take the reciprocal (flip it) to get the final answer.

To combine the two terms, find the least common denominator, $(x + 2)(x + 4)$, and write each term as a fraction with that denominator. Then, simplify as needed by using FOIL and combining like terms:

$$\frac{1}{x+2} - \frac{1}{x+4} = \left(\frac{x+4}{x+4}\right)\left(\frac{1}{x+2}\right) - \left(\frac{x+2}{x+2}\right)\left(\frac{1}{x+4}\right)$$

$$= \frac{(x+4)-(x+2)}{(x+4)(x+2)}$$

$$= \frac{2}{x^2+6x+8}$$

But wait! Choice F is not correct. You still need to take the reciprocal of the simplified expression, which yields $\frac{x^2+6x+8}{2}$, to perform the final "1 over" part of the original expression, making (J) the correct answer. Note that a quick examination of the answer choices tells you to look carefully at the "1 over" part of the original fraction (because the expressions are reciprocals of each other).

43. B   Difficulty: High

Category: Algebra

Getting to the Answer: You could use Picking Numbers to answer this question, but there are a lot of terms to evaluate, so algebra is actually a more efficient route. Notice that most of the answer choices contain radicals in the denominator, so reduce each term before you find a common denominator and add:

$$\frac{\sqrt{x}}{x} + \frac{\sqrt{y}}{y} = \frac{1}{\sqrt{x}} + \frac{1}{\sqrt{y}}$$

$$= \frac{1}{\sqrt{x}}\left(\frac{\sqrt{y}}{\sqrt{y}}\right) + \frac{1}{\sqrt{y}}\left(\frac{\sqrt{x}}{\sqrt{x}}\right)$$

$$= \frac{\sqrt{y}+\sqrt{x}}{\sqrt{xy}}$$

Reverse the order of the terms in the numerator and you have a match for (B).

Note: If you're not sure about the first step (reducing the original terms), think of the radicals in terms of fractional exponents:

$$\frac{\sqrt{x}}{x} = \frac{x^{\frac{1}{2}}}{x^1} = \frac{1}{x^{1-\frac{1}{2}}} = \frac{1}{x^{\frac{1}{2}}} = \frac{1}{\sqrt{x}}$$

44. H   Difficulty: High

Category: Algebra

Getting to the Answer: The equation and the answers are too complicated to efficiently Backsolve, so straightforward algebra is the best approach to answer this question. You need to isolate the square root, then square both sides of the equation, then solve for the variable. There are a LOT of steps, so take them one at a time.

$$\frac{6}{5}\sqrt{2x+1} - 2 = -\frac{2}{5}$$

$$\frac{6}{5}\sqrt{2x+1} = -\frac{2}{5} + 2$$

$$\frac{6}{5}\sqrt{2x+1} = \frac{8}{5}$$

$$\frac{5}{6} \times \left(\frac{6}{5}\sqrt{2x+1}\right) = \frac{8}{5} \times \left(\frac{5}{6}\right)$$

$$\sqrt{2x+1} = \frac{4}{3}$$

$$\left(\sqrt{2x+1}\right)^2 = \left(\frac{4}{3}\right)^2$$

$$2x+1 = \frac{16}{9}$$

$$2x = \frac{7}{9}$$

$$x = \frac{7}{9} \times \frac{1}{2} = \frac{7}{18}$$

This makes (H) correct.

45. C   Difficulty: High

Category: Algebra

Getting to the Answer: Questions that require you to examine multiple situations take a significant amount of time to answer. These are good questions to skip the first time through to maximize your score. Backsolving is a great idea here, because they're asking you to solve for the maximum possibility, not a single value. Because the question asks for the maximum number of correct questions, start with the largest answer choice. Remember that the number of correct, incorrect, and unanswered questions must add up to 50. Try E: if Charles answered 25 questions correctly, he would earn 25(5) = 125 points. If all of the remaining questions were incorrect, he would lose 25(1) = 25 points. His final score would be 125 − 25 = 100, which is too high. Next, D: if Charles answered 23 questions correctly, he would earn 23(5) = 115 points. If all of the remaining questions were incorrect, he would lose 27(1) = 27 points,

for a total score of 115 − 27 = 88. That's too high. Next, (C): if Charles answered 21 questions correctly, he would earn 21(5) = 105 points. If all of the remaining questions were incorrect, he would lose 29(1) = 29 points, for a total score of 105 − 29 = 76. That's correct, so (C) is correct.

To solve this problem algebraically, consider that the maximum number of correct answers would occur in a situation where all of the questions were answered either correctly or incorrectly. Let x represent the number of questions answered correctly and $50 - x$ represent the number of questions answered incorrectly. Then the following equation can be used to find the number of questions answered correctly:

$$5x - (50 - x) = 76$$
$$5x - (50 - x) = 76$$
$$5x - 50 + x = 76$$
$$6x = 126$$
$$x = 21$$

CHAPTER NINE

Geometry

PRACTICE QUESTIONS

The following test-like questions provide an opportunity to practice Geometry questions.

Use the following information to answer questions 1–2.

In the standard (x,y) coordinate plane, points P and Q have coordinates $(2,3)$ and $(12,-15)$, respectively.

1. If M is the midpoint of $\overline{PQ}$, what are the coordinates of M ?

   A. $(6,-12)$

   B. $(6,-9)$

   C. $(6,-6)$

   D. $(7,-9)$

   E. $(7,-6)$

2. If line L is perpendicular to $\overline{PQ}$, which of the following could be the equation of line L ?

   F. $y = -\dfrac{9}{5}x + \dfrac{33}{5}$

   G. $y = -\dfrac{5}{9}x + \dfrac{5}{33}$

   H. $y = \dfrac{5}{9}x + 3$

   J. $y = \dfrac{9}{5}x + 3$

   K. $y = \dfrac{9}{5}x + \dfrac{33}{5}$

3. In the circle shown below, the length of chord $\overline{AB}$ is 24 and the length of $\overline{OC}$ is 5. What is the radius of the circle with center O ?

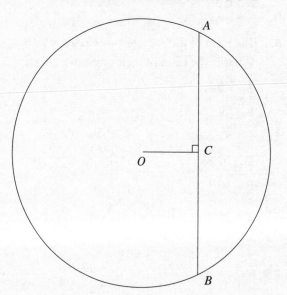

   A. 12

   B. 13

   C. 15

   D. $13\sqrt{2}$

   E. $15\sqrt{2}$

4. The size of a rectangular video screen is usually measured by its diagonal. If a portable DVD player has a screen that measures 7 inches, and the width of the screen is 6 inches, what is the approximate height of the screen, in inches?

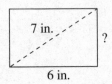

7 in.

?

6 in.

    F.   3.6

    G. 5.0

    H. 5.1

    J.   6.5

    K. 6.6

5. The ratio of the radii of two circles is 9:16. What is the ratio of their circumferences?

    A.   3:4

    B.   9:16

    C. 81:256

    D. 9:18π

    E. 16:32π

6. Ginny wants to prove that $\triangle QRS \cong \triangle STQ$, using the Angle-Side-Angle (ASA) congruence postulate. She knows that $\angle SQR \cong \angle QST$. Which of the following congruences, if established, is sufficient to prove the triangles are congruent?

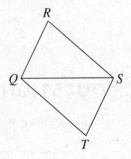

    F. $\angle SQR \cong \angle RQS$

    G. $\angle SQR \cong \angle RSQ$

    H. $\angle SQR \cong \angle TQS$

    J. $\angle RSQ \cong \angle QST$

    K. $\angle RSQ \cong \angle TQS$

7. Which of the following best represents the graph of $y \geq ax + b$ for some negative a and negative b?

A.
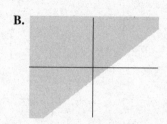

B.
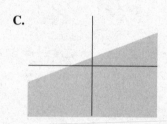

C.

D.

E.

8. In the figure below, $LM = LP$. Which statement must be true?

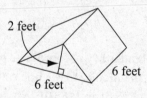

F. $LM = MP$

G. $PN < LM$

H. $MN = PN$

J. $LP < MP$

K. $MN > LP$

9. Margaret made a stage prop that is the shape of a right triangular prism. The prop has a width of 6 feet, a height of 2 feet, and a length of 6 feet. What is the volume, in cubic feet, of the right triangular prism?

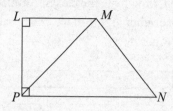

A. 14

B. 36

C. 45

D. 72

E. 144

10. The line graphed below shows the predicted amount of ice sold at a certain store. Which of the following is the closest estimate of this store's predicted rate of ice cream sales, in gallons per day?

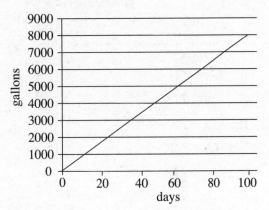

F.   60

G.   72

H.   80

J.   88

K.   100

11. In the standard (x,y) coordinate plane, line m is perpendicular to the line containing the points $(5,6)$ and $(6,10)$. What is the slope of line m ?

A. -4

B. $-\dfrac{1}{4}$

C. $\dfrac{1}{4}$

D. 4

E. 8

12. Polygon $ABCD$ is a square, and the circle centered at point C has a radius of 4. If points B, D, and E lie on the circumference of the circle, what is the area of square $ABCD$?

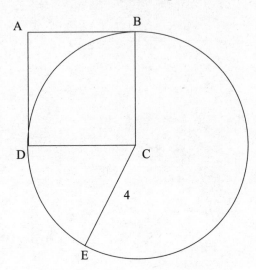

F.   16

G.   20

H. 16π

J.   36

K. 36π

13. The radius of a circle is increased so that the radius of the resulting circle is double that of the original circle. How many times larger is the area of the resulting circle than that of the original circle?

A.   0.5

B.   1

C.   2

D. π

E.   4

14. The equation of a circle is
$(x - 2)^2 + (y + 1)^2 = 14$. What are the
coordinates of the circle's center, and what is
the length of the circle's radius?

   F. Center: $(-1,2)$; Radius: $\sqrt{14}$

   G. Center: $(-1,2)$; Radius: 7

   H. Center: $(2, -1)$; Radius: $\sqrt{14}$

   J. Center: $(2,-1)$; Radius: 7

   K. Center: $(-2,1)$; Radius: 14

15. If $\cos B = \dfrac{12}{13}$, then which of the following
could be $\sin B$?

   A. $\dfrac{5}{13}$

   B. $\dfrac{5}{12}$

   C. $\dfrac{12}{15}$

   D. $\dfrac{13}{12}$

   E. 13

16. Eighteen identical cubes are put together
to form the rectangular solid shown in the
diagram below. How many cubes have
exactly one side that is visible from the
outside of the solid?

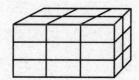

   F. 0

   G. 1

   H. 2

   J. 3

   K. 4

17. A portion of which of the following systems
of inequalities is represented by the shaded
region of the graph below?

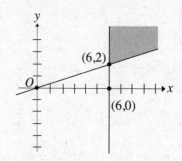

   A. $y \geq \dfrac{1}{3}x$ and $x \geq 6$

   B. $y \geq 3x$ and $x \geq 6$

   C. $y \leq \dfrac{1}{3}x$ and $x \geq 6$

   D. $y \leq 3x$ and $x \geq 6$

   E. $y \leq \dfrac{1}{3}x$ and $x \leq 6$

18. In a rhombus, all 4 sides are the same
length and the diagonals meet at a right
angle. Rhombus $LMNO$ below has vertices
at L (0,0) and N (5,5). What is the slope of
diagonal MO?

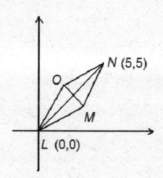

   F. -1

   G. $-\dfrac{1}{2}$

   H. $-\dfrac{1}{5}$

   J. $\dfrac{1}{5}$

   K. 1

19. In the standard (x,y) coordinate plane, what is the distance between the points $(-2,3)$ and $(1,-1)$?

    A. 3

    B. 4

    C. 5

    D. 6

    E. 7

20. The isosceles triangle ABC has an area of 48 square units. If $\overline{AB} = 12$, what is the perimeter of ABC, in units?

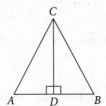

    F. 32

    G. 36

    H. 48

    J. 64

    K. 76

21. What is the value of $x + y$ in the figure below?

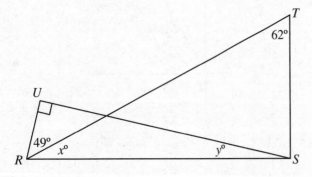

    A. 77°

    B. 62°

    C. 41°

    D. 28°

    E. 13°

22. Sally and Samir left their camp at the same time. Sally walked at a constant rate of 3 miles per hour. She walked 20 minutes north, then 40 minutes east. Samir walked at a constant rate of 2 miles per hour. He walked 20 minutes south, then 40 minutes east. Which of the following is an expression for the number of miles apart Samir and Sally were one hour after they left camp?

    F. $1(3-2)$

    G. $\sqrt{\left(1-\frac{2}{3}\right)^2 + \left(2-\frac{4}{3}\right)^2}$

    H. $\sqrt{\left(1+\frac{2}{3}\right)^2 + \left(2-\frac{4}{3}\right)^2}$

    J. $\sqrt{\left(1+\frac{2}{3}\right)^2 + \left(2+\frac{4}{3}\right)^2}$

    K. $\sqrt{\left(1-\frac{2}{3}\right)^2 + \left(2+\frac{4}{3}\right)^2}$

23. In the standard (x,y) coordinate plane, if the distance between the points $(10,r)$ and $(r,6)$ is 4 coordinate units, which of the following could be the value of r?

    A. 3

    B. 4

    C. 7

    D. 8

    E. 10

24. Which equation represents the line that passes through $(-5,1)$ and is parallel to the line shown below?

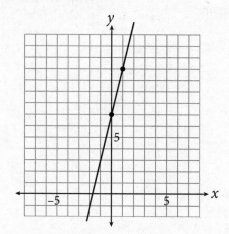

F. $y = x + 20$

G. $y = -5x - 19$

H. $y = 4x + 19$

J. $y = -4x + 20$

K. $y = 4x + 21$

25. In the following triangle, if $\cos \angle BAC = 0.6$ and the hypotenuse of the triangle is 15, what is the length of side BC?

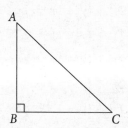

A.   3

B.   5

C.   10

D.   12

E.   15

26. A rectangle has a perimeter of 28, and its longer side is 2.5 times the length of its shorter side. What is the length of the diagonal of the rectangle, rounded to the nearest tenth?

F.   4.0

G.   10.0

H.   10.8

J.   12.4

K.   14.2

27. A zoo has the shape and dimensions, in yards, given in the figure below. The viewing point for the giraffes is halfway between points B and F. Which of the following is the location of the viewing point from the entrance at point A?

(Note: The zoo's borders run east/west or north/south.)

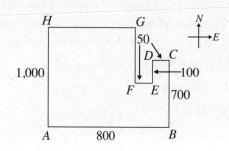

A.   400 yards east and 350 yards north

B.   400 yards east and 500 yards north

C.   600 yards east and 350 yards north

D.   750 yards east and 300 yards north

E.   750 yards east and 350 yards north

28. The figure below is composed of a square and a semicircle. The radius of the semicircle is r and the side of the square is $2r$. Suppose r is doubled. How many times the area of the original figure is the area of the new figure?

    F.   2

    G.   3

    H.   4

    J.   8

    K. 10

29. A farmer wants to enclose a plot of land with a certain amount of fencing. The plot is in the shape of a right triangle, with a base that is 7 yards longer than the height. If the area of the plot is 60 square yards, how many yards of fencing does the farmer need to completely enclose the plot of land?

    A. 34

    B. 40

    C. 46

    D. 80

    E. 96

30. What is the area, in square units, of the square whose vertices are located at the (x,y) coordinate points indicated in the following figure?

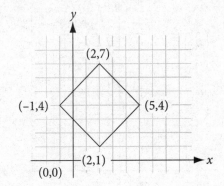

    F.   9

    G. 12

    H. 16

    J.   18

    K. 24

31. Which of the following is an equation of a circle with its center at $(-2,1)$ and tangent to the y-axis in the standard (x,y) coordinate plane?

    A. $(x+2)^2 + (y-1)^2 = 1$

    B. $(x-2)^2 + (y+1)^2 = 1$

    C. $(x-2)^2 + (y-1)^2 = 2$

    D. $(x+2)^2 + (y-1)^2 = 4$

    E. $(x-2)^2 + (y+1)^2 = 4$

32. A painter leans a 35-foot ladder against a house. The side of the house is perpendicular to the level ground, and the base of the ladder is 15 feet away from the base of the house. To the nearest foot, how far up the house will the ladder reach?

    F. 15
    G. 20
    H. 32
    J. 38
    K. 50

33. If $0° \leq n \leq 90°$ and $\cos n = \frac{15}{17}$, then $\tan n = ?$

    A. $\frac{8}{17}$

    B. $\frac{8}{15}$

    C. $\frac{17}{15}$

    D. $\frac{15}{8}$

    E. $\frac{17}{8}$

34. Line segments $\overline{WX}$, $\overline{XY}$, and $\overline{YZ}$, which represent the 3 dimensions of the rectangular box shown below, have lengths of 12 centimeters, 5 centimeters, and 13 centimeters, respectively. What is the cosine of $\angle ZWY$?

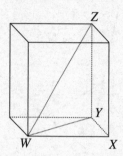

    F. $\frac{13\sqrt{2}}{12}$

    G. 1

    H. $\frac{12}{13}$

    J. $\frac{\sqrt{2}}{2}$

    K. $\frac{5}{13}$

35. In the figure below, M, N, and O are the midpoints of the sides $\overline{DE}$, $\overline{EF}$, and $\overline{DF}$, respectively. If the measure of $\angle EDF$ is 20°, and the measure of $\angle DFE$ is 80°, what is the measure of $\angle OMN$?

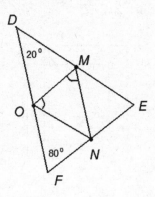

A. 20°

B. 40°

C. 70°

D. 80°

E. 90°

36. If $\cos\theta = -\dfrac{12}{13}$ and $\pi < \theta < \dfrac{3\pi}{2}$, then $\tan\theta = $?

F. $-\dfrac{12}{5}$

G. $-\dfrac{12}{13}$

H. $-\dfrac{5}{12}$

J. $\dfrac{5}{12}$

K. $\dfrac{12}{5}$

37. A formula for the volume V of the rectangular solid shown below is $V = lwh$, where l represents length, w represents width, and h represents height. By halving each of the dimensions (l, w, and h), the volume will be multiplied by what factor?

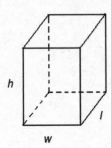

A. $\dfrac{1}{2}$

B. $\dfrac{1}{4}$

C. $\dfrac{1}{6}$

D. $\dfrac{1}{8}$

E. $\dfrac{1}{12}$

38. If $0° < \theta < 90°$ and $\cos\theta = \dfrac{5\sqrt{2}}{8}$, then $\tan\theta = $?

F. $\dfrac{5}{\sqrt{7}}$

G. $\dfrac{\sqrt{7}}{5}$

H. $\dfrac{\sqrt{14}}{8}$

J. $\dfrac{8}{\sqrt{14}}$

K. $\dfrac{8}{5\sqrt{2}}$

39. The figure below shows a square overlapping with a rectangle. One vertex of the rectangle is at the center of the square. What is the area of the shaded region, in square units?

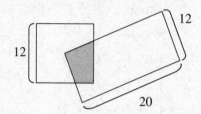

A. 9
B. 18
C. 36
D. 72
E. 144

40. The table below shows several points that lie on the graph of a parabola. Based on the data in the table, what is the value of y when $x = -4$?

x	y
−2	3
0	−3
2	−5
4	−3
6	3
8	13

F. −13
G. −5
H. 5
J. 13
K. Cannot be determined from the given information

41. In the figure below, the circle centered at O has radii $\overline{OA}$ and $\overline{OB}$. $\triangle AOB$ is a right isosceles triangle. If the area of $\triangle AOB$ is 18 square units, what is the area of the circle, in units?

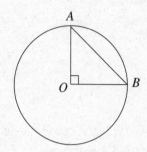

A. 12π
B. 18π
C. 36π
D. 72π
E. 81π

42. In the figure below, DE is the diameter of the circle, F is a point on the circle, and $\overline{EF} \cong \overline{FD}$. What is the degree measure of $\angle DEF$?

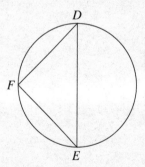

F. 30°
G. 45°
H. 60°
J. 90°
K. Cannot be determined from the given information

43. If the lengths, in inches, of all three sides of a triangle are integers, and one side is 4 inches long, what is the least possible perimeter of the triangle, in inches?

A.   6

B.   8

C.   9

D. 12

E. 16

44. In the standard (x,y) coordinate plane, the graphs of the 3 equations $y - x = 2$, $y + 2x = 5$, and $y = -2$ form the boundary of a triangle. What is the area of this triangle, expressed in square coordinate units?

F.   12.75

G. 15

H. 18.75

J.   37.5

K. 75

45. A circle in the standard (x,y) coordinate plane is tangent to the x-axis at 4 and tangent to the y-axis at 4. Which of the following is an equation of the circle?

A. $x^2 + y^2 = 4$

B. $x^2 + y^2 = 16$

C. $(x - 4)^2 + (y - 4)^2 = 4$

D. $(x - 4)^2 + (y - 4)^2 = 16$

E. $(x + 4)^2 + (y + 4)^2 = 16$

ANSWERS AND EXPLANATIONS

1. E Difficulty: Low

Category: Geometry

Getting to the Answer: The coordinates of the midpoint are the averages of the coordinates of the endpoints. The average of the *x*-values is $\frac{2+12}{2}=7$, and the average of the *y*-values is $\frac{3+(-15)}{2}=-6$, so the coordinates of the midpoint, *M*, are (7,−6), which is (E).

2. H Difficulty: Medium

Category: Geometry

Getting to the Answer: Finding the equation of a line that is perpendicular to another line (or line segment) involves slope. Perpendicular lines have negative reciprocal slopes, so find the slope of $\overline{PQ}$ and then choose the line that has the negative reciprocal slope. (The *y*-intercept doesn't matter in this question, and there is no requirement that line *L* passes through the midpoint found in the previous question.) The slope of $\overline{PQ}$ is:

$$m=\frac{y_2-y_1}{x_2-x_1}$$
$$=\frac{-15-3}{12-2}$$
$$=\frac{-18}{10}$$
$$=-\frac{9}{5}$$

Be careful—don't pick choice F. You want a line that has a slope that is the negative reciprocal of $-\frac{9}{5}$, which is $\frac{5}{9}$, so (H) is correct.

3. B Difficulty: Medium

Category: Geometry

Getting to the Answer: If you're not sure where to get started on a geometry question, try to add a line to the given figure to create a right triangle. Label the figure with all the information given in the question stem. $\overline{OC}$ bisects $\overline{AB}$, so *AC* and *CB* each have a length of 12. Draw in radius *OA*, making a right triangle. In triangle *OCA*, one leg is 12 and the base is 5. This is a 5:12:13 triangle. The hypotenuse, 13, is also the radius of the circle, so (B) is correct.

4. F Difficulty: Medium

Category: Geometry

Getting to the Answer: Some questions look tougher than they really are. This question is only asking you to interpret the figure and apply a familiar formula. The diagonal of the screen forms a right triangle with the sides of the screen. You can use the Pythagorean Theorem to find the height of the screen:

$$c^2=a^2+b^2$$
$$7^2=6^2+b^2$$
$$7^2-6^2=b^2$$
$$\sqrt{7^2-6^2}=b$$
$$\sqrt{49-36}=b$$
$$\sqrt{13}=b$$
$$3.6\approx b$$

The screen is about 3.6 inches tall, which is (F).

5. B Difficulty: Medium

Category: Geometry

Getting to the Answer: Just because a question happens to involve perfect squares doesn't mean that you need to square them or take the square root! One way for the ratio to be 9:16 is for the first radius to be 9 and the second to be 16. Then, the circumference of the first circle is $2\pi r=18\pi$ and the circumference of the second circle is 32π. The ratio of the circumferences is $\frac{18\pi}{32\pi} = \frac{18}{32} = \frac{9}{16}$ or 9:16, which is choice (B). No matter what the radii actually are, as long as they are in this ratio their circumferences will be in the same ratio. The circles could have radii of 18 and 32, 90 and 160, or any other radii in a ratio of 9:16, so (B) is correct.

6. K   Difficulty: Medium

Category: Geometry

Getting to the Answer: To prove triangles congruent by the ASA congruence postulate, two sets of corresponding angles must be congruent, and the corresponding sides included between the angles must be congruent. The given information states that $\angle SQR \cong \angle QST$. Because the triangles share side $\overline{SQ} \cong \overline{QS}$:

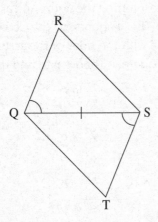

Therefore, to show the triangles are congruent by ASA, Ginny would need to know that $\angle RSQ \cong \angle TQS$. Choice (K) is correct.

7. A   Difficulty: Medium

Category: Geometry

Getting to the Answer: There are three things to consider here: the slope of the line, where the line hits the y-axis, and the direction of the shading (above or below the line). The slope-intercept form of a linear equation is $y = mx + b$, where m is the slope of the line (the change in y over the change in x) and b is the y-intercept. In this particular equation, a is the slope and b is the y-intercept. You

know the slope is negative, so eliminate the answer choices with positive slopes. Choices B and C go up as they go to the right, so they have positive slopes and can be eliminated. You also know the y-intercept is negative, so eliminate any answers that contain lines crossing the y-axis above the origin. Eliminate E. In the inequality, y is greater than or equal to $ax + b$, so the y-value of each shaded point must be greater than or equal to the y-value of the line at the same value of x. Thus, the shading should be above the line. That means (A) is correct.

8. J   Difficulty: Medium

Category: Geometry

Getting to the Answer: Look for familiar shapes within a geometric figure. ΔLMP is an isosceles right triangle with legs LM and LP having equal lengths. Therefore, MP is the hypotenuse of this right triangle. The length of the hypotenuse of any right triangle must be greater than the length of either leg. $LP < MP$ is always true, so (J) is correct.

9. B   Difficulty: Medium

Category: Geometry

Getting to the Answer: The volume of a right triangular prism is equal to the area of its base times its height. Find the area of the triangular base using the equation for the area of a triangle:

$$A = \frac{1}{2}bh = \frac{1}{2} \times 6 \times 2 = 6 \text{ square feet}$$

Then multiply by the height of the prism, or in this case, the dimension that is perpendicular to the prism's base, 6 feet, to get $6 \times 6 = 36$ cubic feet, (B).

10. H   Difficulty: Medium

Category: Geometry

Getting to the Answer: Avoid simple errors on graph questions by drawing horizontal and vertical lines from the axes to the point of interest on a graphed line. To find the most accurate estimate of the rate, look for a point on the graphed line that aligns with tick marks on both axes. The line passes through a point at approximately 8,000 gallons and 100 days, so the per day rate is:

$$\frac{8{,}000 \text{ gallons}}{100 \text{ days}} = 80 \text{ gallons per day}$$

That's (H).

11. B   Difficulty: Medium

Category: Geometry

Getting to the Answer: First, find the slope of the line that contains the given points:

$$\text{Slope} = \frac{y_2 - y_1}{x_2 - x_1} = \frac{10 - 6}{6 - 5} = 4$$

Line m is perpendicular to the above line, so the slope of m is the negative reciprocal of 4, which is $-\frac{1}{4}$. This matches (B).

12. F   Difficulty: Medium

Category: Geometry

Getting to the Answer: In questions that involve multiple figures, look for the relationships between elements that are part of more than one figure. The radius of the circle is also a side of the square. To find the area of the square, square the length of a side: $4^2 = 16$. Choice (F) is correct.

13. E   Difficulty: Medium

Category: Geometry

Getting to the Answer: In the formula for the area of a circle, the radius of the circle is squared. Write the formula for the area of a circle, using r to represent the radius of the original circle in the question: $A = \pi r^2$. This is the area of the original circle. Then write the formula for the area of the resulting circle, using $2r$ as the radius:

$$A = \pi(2r)^2 = \pi(4r^2) = 4\pi r^2$$

Now, divide the two areas $\left(\dfrac{\text{area of resulting circle}}{\text{area of original circle}}\right)$ to find out how many times larger the area of the

resulting circle is compared to the area of the original circle: $\dfrac{4\pi r^2}{\pi r^2} = 4$, which is (E).

14. H   Difficulty: Medium

Category: Geometry

Getting to the Answer: One formula to remember on Test Day is the equation for a circle on a coordinate plane. The formula for a circle $(x - h)^2 + (y - k)^2 = r^2$, where the coordinates (h,k) represent the coordinates of the center of the circle and r is the radius. The value of h is 2. To determine k, think of $(y + 1)^2$ as $(y - (-1))^2$, so $k = -1$. According to the equation, $r^2 = 14$, so $r = \sqrt{14}$. Choice (H) is the correct answer.

15. A   Difficulty: Medium

Category: Geometry

Getting to the Answer: Remembering SOHCAHTOA as well as the commonly tested special triangles, such as 3:4:5 and 5:12:13 triangles, will allow you to breeze through trigonometry questions like this one.

SOHCAHTOA tells you that $\sin\theta = \dfrac{\text{opposite}}{\text{hypotenuse}}$, $\cos\theta = \dfrac{\text{adjacent}}{\text{hypotenuse}}$, and $\tan\theta = \dfrac{\text{opposite}}{\text{adjacent}}$. Because $\cos B = \dfrac{12}{13}$, $\angle B$ is part of a 5:12:13 triangle with the side of length 12 adjacent to B and the hypotenuse of length 13.

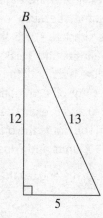

The side with length 5 is therefore opposite to $\angle B$, meaning $\sin B = \frac{5}{13}$. The correct answer is (A). If you are pressed for time, you could strategically guess by recalling that $\sin B$ must always take values between -1 and 1, and eliminate J and K right away. Note that although the sides of the triangle must be in the ratio 5:12:13, they do not necessarily have to be 5, 12, and 13. Multiples such as 10, 24, and 26 would also be possible, and would produce the same answer.

16. H   Difficulty: Medium

Category: Geometry

Getting to the Answer: As you can see in the diagram, there are two layers of 9 cubes each (one in front and one in back). The cubes on the corners each have 3 faces on the outside, the cubes in the middle of each side each have 2 faces on the outside, and the cube in the middle has 1 face on the outside. Since there are two layers, there are two cubes with exactly one face that is visible from the outside of the solid: one in front and one in back. Choice (H) is correct.

17. A   Difficulty: Medium

Category: Geometry

Getting to the Answer: A great way to test inequalities is to plug in a point or two. All the points in the shaded region of the graph should work in *both* inequalities. However, a more algebraic approach may save some time. Because only values of x greater than 6 are shaded, $x \geq 6$ should be one of the inequalities, eliminating E. Because the area *above* the slanted line is shaded, the other inequality should have a $\geq$ symbol, eliminating C and D. To choose between (A) and B, examine the slanted line more closely. From the dot at the origin to the dot at (6,2), the line rises 2 units and runs 6 units, so the slope of the line is $\frac{1}{3}$, making (A) the correct answer.

18. F   Difficulty: Medium

Category: Geometry

Getting to the Answer: Perpendicular lines always have negative reciprocal slopes. All the sides in the rhombus are the same length, and the diagonals of the rhombus are perpendicular. This means $\overline{LN}$ and $\overline{OM}$ are perpendicular. First, use the coordinates to find the slope of $\overline{LN}$:

$$\frac{y_2 - y_1}{x_2 - x_1} = \frac{5-0}{5-0} = \frac{5}{5} = 1$$

Perpendicular lines have negative reciprocal slopes, so the slope of $\overline{OM}$ must be $-\frac{1}{1} = -1$. The correct answer is (F).

19. C   Difficulty: Medium

Category: Geometry

Getting to the Answer: The formula for the distance between two points, $D = \sqrt{(x_2 - x_1)^2 + (y_2 - y_1)^2}$, will be very useful on Test Day. Plug the two points into the distance formula and simplify:

$$D = \sqrt{(1-(-2))^2 + (-1-3)^2} = \sqrt{(3)^2 + (-4)^2}$$
$$= \sqrt{9+16} = \sqrt{25} = 5$$

Choice (C) is correct.

20. F   Difficulty: Medium

Category: Geometry

Getting to the Answer: With only one known side, you cannot find the area directly, as you will need to figure out more sides first. Given the area of triangle ABC and its base, the first step is to find height $\overline{CD}$:

$$\text{Area} = \frac{1}{2}bh$$
$$48 = \frac{1}{2}(12)h$$
$$48 = 6h$$
$$8 = h$$

So $\overline{CD} = 8$. Triangle ABC is an isosceles triangle, so $\overline{CD}$ also happens to be the perpendicular bisector of $\overline{AB}$, meaning $\overline{AD} = \overline{DB} = 6$. With legs of 6 and 8, each of the smaller right triangles must be 3-4-5 right triangles, making the hypotenuse of each triangle— $\overline{AC}$ and $\overline{CB}$—10. (You can also use the Pythagorean Theorem; if x equals the hypotenuse, then $6^2 + 8^2 = x^2$, which simplifies to $36 + 64 = 100 = x^2$. Therefore, x equals 10.) Therefore, the perimeter of triangle ABC is $10 + 10 + 12 = 32$. Choice (F) is correct.

21. C   Difficulty: Medium

Category: Geometry

Getting to the Answer: The sum of the measures of the interior angles of a triangle is 180°. Start with the small triangle on the left. If one angle is a right angle, and the other is 49°, then the third angle can be found using algebra:

$$90 + 49 + (\text{third angle}) = 180$$

$$139 + (\text{third angle}) = 180$$

$$\text{third angle} = 180 - 139 = 41°$$

The supplementary angle to the 41-degree angle is $180 - 41 = 139°$ and is the third angle of the triangle that contains x and y:

$$x + y + 139 = 180$$

$$x + y = 41°$$

Choice (C) is the correct answer.

22. H   Difficulty: High

Category: Geometry

Getting to the Answer: This question combines rates with plane geometry. The first step is to figure out where Samir and Sally have gone. Only then can you come up with an expression that describes the distance between them. Sally walked north for 20 minutes, or $\frac{1}{3}$ of an hour. Since she was walking at a

rate of 3 miles per hour, she went $\frac{1}{3}(3) = 1$ mile north. She walked east for 40 minutes, or $\frac{2}{3}$ of an hour, so she went $\frac{2}{3}(3) = 2$ miles east. Samir walked south at a rate of 2 miles per hour for $\frac{1}{3}$ of an hour, so he went $\frac{1}{3}(2) = \frac{2}{3}$ miles south. Then he went $\frac{2}{3}(2) = \frac{4}{3}$ miles east. A sketch will help you see where they are:

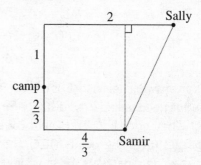

The distance between them is the hypotenuse of a right triangle. The height of the triangle is the north-south distance between them, and the base of the triangle is the east-west distance. The north-south distance is $1 + \frac{2}{3}$, and the east-west distance is $2 - \frac{4}{3}$. Don't bother to simplify these, because the answer choices don't either. Instead, plug them into the Pythagorean Theorem, which can be written as $c = \sqrt{a^2 + b^2}$, to find that the hypotenuse of this triangle must be $\sqrt{\left(1 + \frac{2}{3}\right)^2 + \left(2 - \frac{4}{3}\right)^2}$, which is (H).

23. E   Difficulty: High

Category: Geometry

Getting to the Answer: Backsolving is a great option here if you're not sure how to set this question up algebraically or if you're not confident about your variable manipulation skills. Plug the given coordinates into the distance formula,

$\left(\sqrt{(x_2 - x_1)^2 + (y_2 - y_1)^2}\right)$, set the distance equal to 4, and solve for r:

$$\sqrt{(r-10)^2 + (6-r)^2} = 4$$
$$(r-10)^2 + (6-r)^2 = 16$$
$$\left(r^2 - 20r + 100\right) + \left(36 - 12r + r^2\right) = 16$$
$$2r^2 - 32r + 136 = 16$$
$$2r^2 - 32r + 120 = 0$$
$$r^2 - 16r + 60 = 0$$
$$(r-10)(r-6) = 0$$
$$r = 10 \text{ or } r = 6$$

Only 10 is an answer choice, so (E) is correct. To Backsolve, you still need to know the distance formula to figure out whether A, B, C, and D are correct, but notice that (E) gives the points (10,6) and (10,10). Because the x-coordinates are the same, you can see that the distance between the points is $10 - 6 = 4$ without using the formula.

24. K   Difficulty: High

Category: Geometry

Getting to the Answer: Parallel lines have equal slopes, so start by finding the slope of the line shown in the graph. Using the y-intercept, you can determine that the line rises 4 units and runs 1 unit to the next point, which makes the slope 4. Now you know m in $y = mx + b$, and all you need is the y-intercept of the new line. Use the slope, 4, and the given point, $(-5,1)$, to find b:

$$y = 4x + b$$
$$1 = 4(-5) + b$$
$$1 = -20 + b$$
$$21 = b$$

Therefore, the equation of the line is $y = 4x + 21$, which is (K).

25. D   Difficulty: High

Category: Geometry

Getting to the Answer: You are given the cosine of $\angle BAC$ and the length of the hypotenuse of the triangle, so begin by using these and SOHCAHTOA to find the length of the side adjacent to $\angle BAC$ (which is AB):

$$\cos A = \frac{\text{adjacent}}{\text{hypotenuse}}$$
$$0.6 = \frac{AB}{15}$$
$$AB = 0.6(15) = 9$$

So the adjacent side, $\overline{AB}$, is 9, and triangle ABC is a right triangle with a leg length of 9 and a hypotenuse of length 15. Triangle ABC must therefore be a 3-4-5 right triangle (scaled up by a factor of 3), and $\overline{BC}$ must have a length of 12. Choice (D) is correct.

26. H   Difficulty: High

Category: Geometry

Getting to the Answer: The perimeter of the rectangle is 28, and one of its sides is 2.5 times the length of the other, so call x the shorter side. Our rectangle now has sides of x and $2.5x$. Draw a figure to help visualize this question.

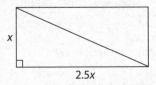

To find x, plug the information into the perimeter formula and solve:

$$\text{Perimeter} = 2l + 2w$$
$$28 = 2(x) + 2(2.5x)$$
$$28 = 2x + 5x$$
$$28 = 7x$$
$$4 = x$$

So $x = 4$, and the dimensions of the rectangle must be $4 \times 1 = 4$ and $2.5 \times 4 = 10$. These values are not parts of a special right triangle, so use the Pythagorean Theorem to find the diagonal:

$$a^2 + b^2 = c^2$$
$$4^2 + 10^2 = c^2$$
$$16 + 100 = c^2$$
$$116 = c^2$$
$$\sqrt{116} = c$$

Because 116 isn't a perfect square but lies between $10^2 = 100$ and $11^2 = 121$, $\sqrt{116}$ must be somewhere between 10 and 11 (it's approximately 10.77). The only choice that fits is (H).

27. D   Difficulty: High

Category: Geometry

Getting to the Answer: Feel free to draw all over your test booklet—that's what it's there for. This question tests your ability to read coordinates and to find a midpoint (although you may not realize this at first glance). Set up a coordinate system to compare points B and F. Because you're trying to find the distance relative to A, make A (0,0). Then B is at (800,0). Use the labeled distances to find the x-value of F, which is 700 ($AB - DC - FE$), and the y-value, which is 600 ($CB - DE$). This means F is at (700,600). The lookout point is at the midpoint of B and F, so you can use the midpoint formula:

$$\left(\frac{800 + 700}{2}, \frac{0 + 600}{2}\right) = (750,300)$$

Using these coordinates, the lookout is 750 yards to the right (east) of point A and 300 yards up (north), which is (D).

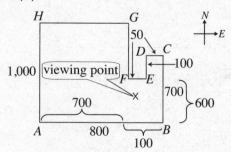

28. H   Difficulty: High

Category: Geometry

Getting to the Answer: The area of the original figure is the area of the square plus the area of the semicircle. The square has sides of length $2r$, so its area is $(2r)^2 = 4r^2$. The area of the semicircle is $\frac{1}{2}\pi r^2$, so the area of the original figure is $4r^2 + \frac{1}{2}\pi r^2$. If r is doubled, the new figure will be composed of a square with sides of length $4r$ and a semicircle with radius $2r$. The new figure's area will be:

$$(4r)^2 + \frac{1}{2}\pi(2r)^2 = 16r^2 + \frac{1}{2}\pi 4r^2 = 16r^2 + 2\pi r^2$$

The new area compared to the original area is:

$$\frac{16r^2 + 2\pi r^2}{4r^2 + \frac{1}{2}\pi r^2} = \frac{2r^2(8 + \pi)}{\frac{1}{2}r^2(8 + \pi)} = \frac{2}{\frac{1}{2}} = 4$$

So, the new figure has 4 times the area of the original figure. Choice (H) is correct.

To make the question more concrete, you could Pick Numbers. If $r = 1$, then the area of the original figure is $2^2 + \frac{1}{2}\pi(1^2) = 4 + \frac{1}{2}\pi$. When r is doubled, it becomes 2, and the area of the new figure is $4^2 + \frac{1}{2}\pi(2^2) = 16 + 2\pi$. This is $\dfrac{16 + 2\pi}{4 + \frac{1}{2}\pi} = 4$ times the area of the original figure.

29. B   Difficulty: High

Category: Geometry

Getting to the Answer: According to the question, the base of the right triangle is 7 yards longer than the height. Use the triangle area formula, $A = \frac{1}{2}bh$, with $b = h + 7$ to determine the value of the height:

$$60 = \frac{1}{2}h(h + 7)$$
$$120 = h(h + 7)$$
$$120 = h^2 + 7h$$
$$0 = h^2 + 7h - 120$$

To find the value of h, factor the polynomial:

$$(h+15)(h-8)=0$$

If either factor is equal to 0, then the product will be 0, so $h=-15$ or $h=8$. Length can't be negative, so the height of the triangle must be 8. Therefore, the base is 15. Use the Pythagorean Theorem $(a^2+b^2=c^2)$ to determine the hypotenuse:

$$8^2+15^2=c^2$$
$$64+225=c^2$$
$$289=c^2$$
$$\sqrt{289}=c$$
$$c=17$$

Add the three sides of the triangle to get the perimeter, or yards of fencing needed: $8+15+17=40$. Choice (B) is correct.

30. J   Difficulty: High

Category: Geometry

Getting to the Answer: Divide the square into two right triangles by drawing the diagonal from (2,7) to (2,1). The area of each triangle is half its base times its height. Treat the diagonal as the base of a triangle. Its length is the distance from (2,7) to (2,1). Because the x-coordinates are the same, that distance is simply the difference between the y-coordinates, $7-1=6$. The diagonal bisects the square, so the height of the triangle is half the distance from (−1,4) to (5,4). You already know that a diagonal of this square is 6, so half the distance is 3. Therefore, the base and height of either triangle are 6 and 3, making the area of each triangle $\frac{6\times3}{2}$, or 9 square units. The square is made up of two such triangles and so has twice the area, or 18 square units, (J).

Alternatively, you could use the distance formula to find the length of one side of the square and then square that side to find the area.

31. D   Difficulty: High

Category: Geometry

Getting to the Answer: Memorize the equations for circles and ellipses. The equation for a circle is $(x-h)^2+(y-k)^2=r^2$, where (h,k) is the center of the circle and r is the radius.

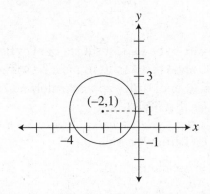

The circle is tangent to the y-axis, which means the radius is 2. The equation for this circle is $(x-(-2))^2+(y-1)^2=2^2$, which simplifies to $(x+2)^2+(y-1)^2=4$, (D).

32. H   Difficulty: High

Category: Geometry

Getting to the Answer: Draw a picture, carefully labeling the sides with the given lengths so that you can see which lengths are the legs and which is the hypotenuse.

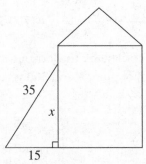

Use the Pythagorean Theorem:

$$15^2+x^2=35^2$$
$$225+x^2=1{,}225$$
$$x^2=1{,}000$$

$x=\sqrt{1{,}000}\approx32$, which matches (H).

33. B   Difficulty: High

Category: Geometry

Getting to the Answer: Don't worry when a trig question doesn't include a diagram. You have all of the information you need, and you can always draw your own triangle if you are confused. Imagine a triangle with angle n. If $\cos n = \dfrac{15}{17}$, then you can assume that the adjacent side is 15 and the hypotenuse is 17, because $\cos \theta = \dfrac{\text{adjacent}}{\text{hypotenuse}}$.

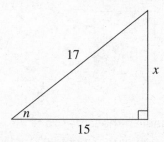

Tangent equals $\dfrac{\text{opposite}}{\text{adjacent}}$, so all you need now is the length of the side opposite angle n. Use the Pythagorean Theorem:

$$15^2 + x^2 = 17^2$$
$$225 + x^2 = 289$$
$$x^2 = 64$$
$$x = 8$$

So, $\tan n = \dfrac{8}{15}$, making (B) the correct answer.

34. J   Difficulty: High

Category: Geometry

Getting to the Answer: If you're not sure where to get started, try working backwards. What are you looking for? The cosine of $\angle ZWY$. What do you need to find that? The lengths of the hypotenuse and the adjacent leg, $\overline{WZ}$ and $\overline{WY}$. How can you find those lengths? By using the given side lengths and your knowledge of right triangles. Now that you've figured out how to get from what you have to what you need, you can go ahead and get there. $\triangle WXY$ is a right triangle. You know that $\overline{WX}$ is 12 and $\overline{XY}$ is 5,

so $\overline{WY}$ must be 13. (If you didn't spot the 5:12:13 triplet, you could have used the Pythagorean Theorem.) $\triangle WYZ$ is also a right triangle. You know that $\overline{WY}$ and $\overline{YZ}$ are both 13, so $\overline{WZ}$ must be $13\sqrt{2}$. (Again, you could have used the Pythagorean Theorem if you didn't spot the 45°-45°-90° triangle.) The cosine of an angle is the adjacent leg over the hypotenuse, so the cosine of $\angle ZWY$ is $\overline{WY}$ over $\overline{WZ}$, or $\dfrac{13}{13\sqrt{2}} = \dfrac{1}{\sqrt{2}} = \dfrac{\sqrt{2}}{2}$. Choice (J) is correct.

35. D   Difficulty: High

Category: Geometry

Getting to the Answer: When you are given a complex figure with multiple triangles, look for similar triangles. Because points M, N, and O are all midpoints of the sides of $\triangle DEF$, the triangles $\triangle DEF$ and $\triangle NMO$ are similar. The interior angles of a triangle add up to 180°, so $\angle E = 180° - 80° - 20° = 80°$. $\angle E$ is equal to $\angle OMN$, so $\angle E$ and $\angle OMN$ both equal 80°. Choice (D) is correct.

36. J   Difficulty: High

Category: Geometry

Getting to the Answer: Most right triangle trig questions will be easier if you draw the triangle. Even though a real triangle couldn't have a side of negative length, drawing a triangle is still a good way to think about trigonometry.

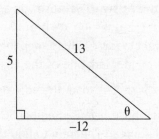

$\cos \theta = \dfrac{\text{adjacent}}{\text{hypotenuse}} = \dfrac{-12}{13}$. Using the 5:12:13 Pythagorean Triplet, the length of the opposite side must be 5. However, the value you need is actually -5 because the question states that θ is in Quadrant III, which means both the cosine and sine values are negative. Thus, $\tan\theta = \dfrac{\text{opposite}}{\text{adjacent}} = \dfrac{-5}{-12} = \dfrac{5}{12}$, which matches (J).

37. D   Difficulty: High

Category: Geometry

Getting to the Answer: Picking Numbers works well for answering abstract questions. Suppose $l = 4$, $w = 2$, and $h = 8$. Original volume $= lwh = (4)(2)(8) = 64$. Halve each dimension and find the new volume: new volume $= (2)(1)(4) = 8$. The original volume is 8 times larger than the new volume. Multiply the original volume by $\dfrac{1}{8}$ to get the new volume. You can also solve the question algebraically. Find the volume when l, w, and h are replaced with $\dfrac{l}{2}$, $\dfrac{w}{2}$, and $\dfrac{h}{2}$. Next, find the ratio between this new volume and the original volume.

$$\text{Original volume} = lwh$$

$$\text{New volume} = \left(\frac{l}{2}\right)\left(\frac{w}{2}\right)\left(\frac{h}{2}\right) = \frac{1}{8}lwh$$

$$\text{Ratio} = \frac{\frac{1}{8}lwh}{lwh} = \frac{1}{8}$$

The correct answer is (D).

38. G   Difficulty: High

Category: Geometry

Getting to the Answer: Because you are not given a diagram for this question, it's best to draw a quick sketch of a right triangle to help keep the sides separate in your mind. Mark one of the acute angles θ. Because $\cos\theta = \dfrac{5\sqrt{2}}{8}$, mark the adjacent side $5\sqrt{2}$ and the hypotenuse as 8. (Remember SOHCAHTOA.) Use the Pythagorean Theorem to find that the side opposite θ is $\sqrt{14}$. The question asks you to find $\tan\theta$. Tangent $= \dfrac{\text{opposite}}{\text{adjacent}}$, so $\tan\theta = \dfrac{\sqrt{14}}{5\sqrt{2}}$, which can be simplified to $\dfrac{\sqrt{7}}{5}$. Choice (G) is correct.

39. C   Difficulty: High

Category: Geometry

Getting to the Answer: Sometimes the answer choices give you a hint about how to answer the question. Here, they are simple enough that you know you don't have to do any fancy calculations. In fact, they're different enough that you might even be able to eyeball the answer. Draw in lines that go from the center of the square to the edge at right angles.

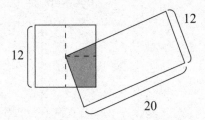

The gray triangle is the same size as the white triangle. (The portion of the upper 90° angle formed by the gray triangle is the same as the portion of the rectangle's 90° angle formed by the gray triangle. Therefore, the portion of the lower 90° angle formed by the white triangle is also the same.) If you move the gray triangle to where the white triangle is, the shaded area is exactly $\dfrac{1}{4}$ of the square.

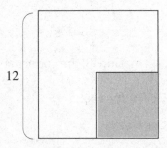

Because the area of the square is $12 \times 12 = 144$ square units, the area of the shaded region is $\dfrac{1}{4}(144) = 36$ square units. Choice (C) is correct.

40. J   Difficulty: High

Category: Geometry

Getting to the Answer: The question states that the points lie on the graph of a parabola (which is a nice, symmetric U shape), so use what you know about parabolas to answer the question. Notice that the x-values in the table increase by 2 each time. To find the y-value when $x = -4$, you just need to imagine adding one extra row to the top of the table. Now, think about symmetry—you can see from the points in the table that $(2, -5)$ is the vertex of the parabola. The points $(0, -3)$ and $(4, -3)$ are equidistant from the vertex, as are the points $(-2, 3)$ and $(6, 3)$. This means the point whose x-value is -4 should have the same y-value as the last point in the table $(8, 13)$. So, when $x = -4$, $y = 13$. Choice (J) is correct.

41. C   Difficulty: High

Category: Geometry

Getting to the Answer: To answer this question, you will have to remember the area formulas for both triangles and circles. To find the area of a circle, use the equation $A = \pi r^2$. You don't know the value of r yet, but you might have noticed that the sides of $\triangle AOB$ are also radii of the circle. Use the area formula for triangles $\left(A = \frac{1}{2}bh\right)$ and the given area, 18, to find the base and height of the triangle. In this case, the base and height are both equal and are both radii of the circle.

$$\frac{1}{2}(r)(r) = 18$$
$$r^2 = 36$$

The area of a circle is πr^2, and you now know that r^2 is 36, so the area of this circle is 36π, which is (C). Even if you were completely stuck, you could narrow down your options and make a strategic guess. The area of the circle must be more than 4 times the area of the triangle, so you can eliminate A and B, which are less than 4 times the area of the triangle.

42. G   Difficulty: High

Category: Geometry

Getting to the Answer: Whenever you see a circle, look for its radius. Let point G represent the midpoint of DE and draw FG into the figure. Because DE is a diameter, G must be the center of the circle.

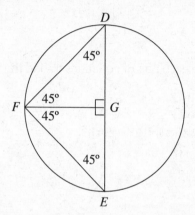

The only way for $\overline{EF} \cong \overline{ED}$ to be true is if FG is perpendicular to DE. Now, GD, EG, and FG are all radii of the same circle, so $\overline{GD} \cong \overline{EG} \cong \overline{FG}$. Therefore, $\triangle FEG$ and $\triangle FDG$ are both isosceles right triangles, so the measure of $\angle DEF$ is 45°, which is (G).

43. C   Difficulty: High

Category: Geometry

Getting to the Answer: Use the Triangle Inequality Theorem here. If the two unknown side lengths are integers, and the sum of the two lengths has to be greater than 4, then the least amount the two unknown sides could add up to would be 5, which would make the perimeter $4 + 5 = 9$. Choice (C) is correct.

44. H   Difficulty: High

Category: Geometry

Getting to the Answer: When you are not given a diagram for a geometry question, draw your own. Sketch a graph of the triangle in the coordinate plane. Find the points of intersection between each pair of equations to find the vertices of the triangle. This will be easier if you write each equation in the same form first.

$$y - x = 2$$
$$y = x + 2$$
$$y + 2x = 5$$
$$y = -2x + 5$$
$$y = -2$$

Combine each pair of equations to find the vertices:

$y = -2$ and $y + 2x = 5$: $(3.5, -2)$
$y = -2$ and $y = x + 2$: $(-4, -2)$
$y = x + 2$ and $y + 2x = 5$: $(1, 3)$

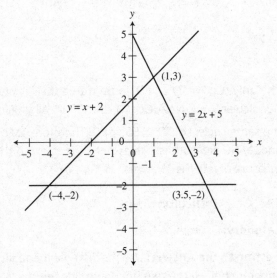

The area of a triangle is $\frac{1}{2}$ (base)(height). The base of this triangle is horizontal, so the difference between the x-coordinates of its endpoints is its length. That's $3.5 - (-4) = 7.5$. Similarly, the height is $3 - (-2) = 5$. The area is $\frac{1}{2}(7.5)(5) = 18.75$, or (H).

45. D   Difficulty: High

Category: Geometry

Getting to the Answer: Concepts such as "tangent to" are less scary if you work on becoming more comfortable with math vocabulary. It also helps to draw a sketch like the one below:

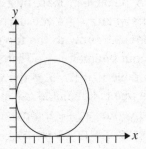

As you can see in the sketch, the center of the circle is at (4,4), and the radius is 4. In the equation of a circle, $(x - h)^2 + (y - k)^2 = r^2$, the center is at (h,k), and the radius is r. Plug in the information you know to get $(x - 4)^2 + (y - 4)^2 = 4^2$, which is (D). If you're stuck, try plugging in a few points. For example, using either (4,0) or (0,4) eliminates all answers except B and (D), and the point (4,8) eliminates B.

CHAPTER TEN

Functions

PRACTICE QUESTIONS

The following test-like questions provide an opportunity to practice Functions questions.

1. Several values for the functions $g(x)$ and $h(x)$ are shown in the tables that follow. What is the value of $g(h(3))$?

x	g(x)
−6	−3
−3	−2
0	−1
3	0
6	1

x	h(x)
0	6
1	−4
2	2
3	0
4	−2

   A. −1

   B. 0

   C. 1

   D. 3

   E. 6

2. If the first four terms of an arithmetic sequence are 25, 21, 17, and 13, respectively, what is the 20th term of the sequence?

   F. −55

   G. −51

   H. −47

   J. −43

   K. −39

3. What is the fifth term in the geometric sequence $-432, 72, -12, 2, \cdots$?

   A. $-\dfrac{1}{3}$

   B. $-\dfrac{1}{6}$

   C. $\dfrac{1}{6}$

   D. $\dfrac{1}{3}$

   E. 1

4. The first and seventh terms in a sequence are 1 and 365, respectively. If each term after the first in the sequence is formed by multiplying the preceding term by 3 and subtracting 1, what is the sixth term?

   F. 40

   G. 41

   H. 121

   J. 122

   K. 123

5. What value of x satisfies the equation $\log_2 x = -3$?

   A. -8

   B. $-\dfrac{1}{8}$

   C. $\dfrac{1}{8}$

   D. 8

   E. 9

6. If $\log_x 100 = 2$, then $x = $?

   F. 1

   G. 10

   H. 50

   J. 100

   K. 200

7. If $x > 0$, $a = x \cos \theta$, and $b = x \sin \theta$, then $\sqrt{a^2 + b^2} = $?

   A. 1

   B. x

   C. $2x$

   D. $x(\cos \theta + \sin \theta)$

   E. $x \cos \theta \sin \theta$

8. If a quadratic function is defined by $q(x) = 2x^2 - x - 15$, for what values of x does the graph of the function cross the x-axis?

   F. $x = -\dfrac{5}{2}, x = -3$

   G. $x = -\dfrac{1}{2}, x = -5$

   H. $x = -\dfrac{3}{2}, x = 5$

   J. $x = -\dfrac{5}{2}, x = 3$

   K. $x = \dfrac{5}{2}, x = 3$

9. The entire graph of a function, F, is shown in the standard (x,y) coordinate plane below. One of the following sets is the range of the function. Which set is it?

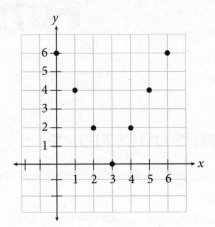

   A. $\{y: y \geq 0\}$

   B. $\{y: 0 \leq y \leq 6\}$

   C. $\{x: 0 \leq x \leq 6\}$

   D. $\{0, 2, 4, 6\}$

   E. $\{0, 1, 2, 3, 4, 5, 6\}$

10. The graph below shows two functions, $f(x)$ and $g(x)$. Which of the following statements is true?

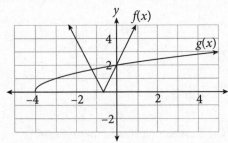

   F. $f(0) = -4$

   G. $g(2) = 0$

   H. $f(x) > g(x)$ for all values of x

   J. $(0,2)$ is a solution for $f(x) = g(x)$

   K. $f(x) = 0$ has exactly two solutions

11. Which of the following statements describes the total of the first n terms of the arithmetic sequence below?

$$1, 3, 5, 7, 9, \cdots$$

A. The total is always equal to 25 regardless of n.

B. The total is always equal to $2n$.

C. The total is always equal to $3n$.

D. The total is always equal to n^2.

E. There is no consistent pattern for the total.

12. Suppose a quadratic function is given by the equation $Q(x) = (x + 4)(x - 1)$. If $R(x)$ is a reflection of $Q(x)$ over the y-axis, through which two points must the graph of $R(x)$ pass?

F. $(-4,0)$ and $(1,0)$

G. $(-1,0)$ and $(4,0)$

H. $(0,-4)$ and $(0,1)$

J. $(0,-1)$ and $(0,4)$

K. $(-4,1)$ and $(4,-1)$

13. If $f(x) = \frac{1}{3}x + 13$ and $g(x) = 3x^2 + 6x + 12$, which expression represents $f(g(x))$?

A. $x^2 + 12x + 4$

B. $\frac{x^2}{3} + 2x + 194$

C. $x^2 + 2x + 17$

D. $x^2 + 2x + 25$

E. $x^2 + 2x + 54$

14. The graph of the quadratic function $f(x) = ax^2 + bx + c$ in the standard (x,y) coordinate plane is shown below.

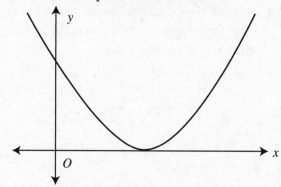

When $f(x) = 0$, which of the following best describes the solution set for x?

F. 2 real solutions

G. 1 double real solution only

H. 1 real and 1 imaginary solution

J. 1 double imaginary solution only

K. 2 imaginary solutions

15. If a function is defined by the rule $r \diamond s = r(r - s)$ for all integers r and s, then $4 \diamond (3 \diamond 5)$ equals which of the following?

A. -8

B. -2

C. 2

D. 20

E. 40

16. In the geometric sequence 3, 12, r, 192, $\cdots$ what is the value of r, the third term?

F. 24

G. 36

H. 48

J. 60

K. 96

17. The following figures show regular polygons and the sum of the degrees of the angles in each polygon. Based on these figures, which equation represents the number of degrees in a regular polygon as a function of the number of sides, n, the polygon has?

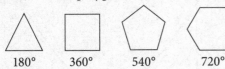

180°   360°   540°   720°

   A. $f(n) = 60n$

   B. $f(n) = 180n$

   C. $f(n) = 180(n - 2)$

   D. $f(n) = 20n^2$

   E. Cannot be determined from the given information

18. Which of the following correctly describes the range of the function $h(x) = 4x^2 - 9$?

   F. All real numbers

   G. All real numbers greater than $-\dfrac{3}{2}$

   H. All real numbers greater than or equal to -9

   J. All real numbers between $-\dfrac{3}{2}$ and $\dfrac{3}{2}$

   K. All real numbers between and including -9 and 9

19. For the 2 functions $f(x)$ and $g(x)$, ordered pairs are shown below. What is the value of $f(g(4))$?

   $f(x)$: $\{(4,1), (5,2), (6,3), (7,4)\}$

   $g(x)$: $\{(-1,-4), (1,0), (2,2), (4,6)\}$

   A. 0

   B. 1

   C. 3

   D. 4

   E. 6

20. If the fifth and sixth terms of a geometric sequence are 3 and 1, respectively, what is the first term of the sequence?

   F. -27

   G. -5

   H. $\dfrac{1}{27}$

   J. 11

   K. 243

Use the following information to answer questions 21–22.

Erin hiked a small mountain over the course of a day. She began at 7 AM at an altitude of 4,000 feet. As she climbed the mountain, Erin climbed at a constant speed during each one-hour interval. She finished her hike back at 4,000 feet at 1 PM. Erin's altitude, as a function of time, is shown in the graph below.

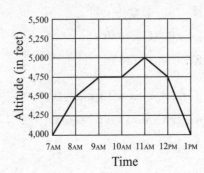

21. For how long, in hours and minutes, was Erin at or above 4,500 feet?

   A. 1 hour 20 minutes

   B. 3 hours

   C. 4 hours

   D. 4 hours 20 minutes

   E. 5 hours

22. Which graph best represents the absolute value of the velocity that Erin traveled, in vertical feet per hour?

(Note: Ignore acceleration and deceleration at the beginning and end of each one-hour interval.)

F.

Absolute Value of Velocity (vertical feet per hour)
(graph, values 0 to 1,500 vs Time 7AM–1PM)

G.

Absolute Value of Velocity (vertical feet per hour)
(graph, values 0 to 1,500 vs Time 7AM–1PM)

H.

Absolute Value of Velocity (vertical feet per hour)
(graph, values 0 to 1,500 vs Time 7AM–1PM)

J.

Absolute Value of Velocity (vertical feet per hour)
(graph, values 0 to 1,500 vs Time 7AM–1PM)

K.

Absolute Value of Velocity (vertical feet per hour)
(graph, values 4,000 to 5,500 vs Time 7AM–1PM)

23. Which of the following is equivalent to $\dfrac{\tan\theta\cos^2\theta + \tan\theta\sin^2\theta}{\sin\theta}$?

   A. $\cos\theta$

   B. $\sin\theta$

   C. $\csc\theta$

   D. $\sec\theta$

   E. $\tan\theta$

24. Which function could have been used to generate the data given in the table below?

x	-3	-2	-1	0	1	2	3
$g(x)$	12	8	6	5	4.5	4.25	4.125

   F. $g(x) = -4x$

   G. $g(x) = -3x - 3$

   H. $g(x) = x^2 + 3$

   J. $g(x) = \left(\dfrac{1}{2}\right)^x + 4$

   K. $g(x) = -2^x + 4$

25. If $f(x) = 3^{3x+3}$ and $g(x) = 27^{\left(\frac{2}{3}x - \frac{1}{3}\right)}$, for what value of x, if any, does the graph of $f(x)$ intersect the graph of $g(x)$?

   A. -4

   B. $-\dfrac{7}{4}$

   C. $-\dfrac{10}{7}$

   D. 2

   E. The graphs do not intersect.

26. Suppose the graph of $g(x)$ passes through the point $(5,-1)$. If $g(x)$ is reflected over the line $y = 3$, through which point must the reflected graph pass?

    F. $(3,-1)$
    G. $(1,-1)$
    H. $(5,1)$
    J. $(5,3)$
    K. $(5,7)$

27. What is the value of the expression $\cos\left(\dfrac{5\pi}{12}\right)$ given that $\dfrac{5\pi}{12} = \dfrac{2\pi}{3} - \dfrac{\pi}{4}$ and that $\cos(x - y) = (\cos x)(\cos y) + (\sin x)(\sin y)$?

    (Note: Use the following table of values.)

θ	$\sin \theta$	$\cos \theta$
$\dfrac{\pi}{4}$	$\dfrac{\sqrt{2}}{2}$	$\dfrac{\sqrt{2}}{2}$
$\dfrac{2\pi}{3}$	$\dfrac{\sqrt{3}}{2}$	$-\dfrac{1}{2}$
$\dfrac{5\pi}{6}$	$\dfrac{1}{2}$	$-\dfrac{\sqrt{3}}{2}$

    A. $-\dfrac{\sqrt{3}}{4}$

    B. $-\dfrac{\sqrt{3}}{2}$

    C. $\dfrac{2 - \sqrt{3}}{4}$

    D. $\dfrac{-1 - \sqrt{2}}{2}$

    E. $\dfrac{\sqrt{6} - \sqrt{2}}{4}$

28. A finite arithmetic sequence has five terms. The first term is 4. What is the difference between the mean and the median of the five terms?

    F. 0
    G. 1
    H. 2
    J. 4
    K. 5

29. If $f(x) = 2(x + 7)$, then $f(x + c) = ?$

    A. $2(x + 7) + c$
    B. $2x + c + 7$
    C. $2x + c + 14$
    D. $2x + 2c + 7$
    E. $2x + 2c + 14$

30. Which of the following piecewise functions could have been used to generate the graph below?

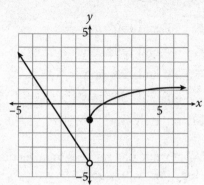

F. $g(x) = \begin{cases} -\dfrac{3}{2}x - 4, & \text{if } x < 0 \\ \sqrt{x} - 1, & \text{if } x \geq 0 \end{cases}$

G. $g(x) = \begin{cases} -\dfrac{3}{2}x - 4, & \text{if } x < 0 \\ x - 1, & \text{if } x \geq 0 \end{cases}$

H. $g(x) = \begin{cases} -\dfrac{3}{2}x - 4, & \text{if } x < 0 \\ -x + 1, & \text{if } x > 0 \end{cases}$

J. $g(x) = \begin{cases} -\dfrac{2}{3}x - 4, & \text{if } x < 0 \\ \sqrt{x} + 1, & \text{if } x \geq 0 \end{cases}$

K. $g(x) = \begin{cases} \dfrac{2}{3}x - 4, & \text{if } x < 0 \\ \sqrt{x} - 1, & \text{if } x \geq 0 \end{cases}$

31. The graph of the function $f(x) = \cos x$ in the standard (x,y) coordinate plane is reflected over the x-axis, shifted right π units, and then shifted down a units. Which of the following functions represents the graph after the 3 transformations have been applied?

A. $f'(x) = -\cos(x - \pi) - a$

B. $f'(x) = -\cos(x + \pi) - a$

C. $f'(x) = -\cos(x + \pi) + a$

D. $f'(x) = \cos(-x - \pi) - a$

E. $f'(x) = \cos(-x + \pi) - a$

32. The graph of $g(x) = \cos(3x)$ is shown below. Which of the following lists represents the values of x for which $g(x) = 0$?

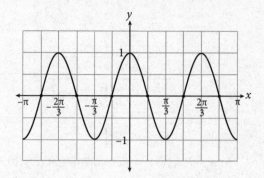

F. $-180°, -120°, -60°, 60°, 120°, 180°$

G. $-165°, -105°, -45°, 45°, 105°, 165°$

H. $-150°, -90°, -30°, 30°, 90°, 150°$

J. $-120°, -80°, -40°, 40°, 80°, 120°$

K. $-105°, -90°, -75°, 75°, 90°, 105°$

33. The function $f(x) = 0.5 \sin(2x)$ is graphed below over the domain $[0, 2\pi]$. What is the period of the function?

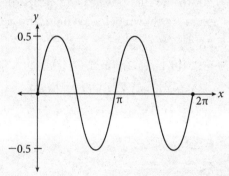

A. $\dfrac{\pi}{4}$

B. $\dfrac{\pi}{2}$

C. π

D. 2π

E. 4π

34. The figure shown here represents the function $g(x) = \sqrt{x}$.

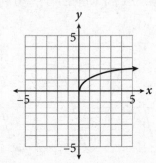

Suppose $h(x)$ is a transformation of $g(x)$ and is given by the equation $h(x) = \sqrt{x+1} + 3$. Which of the following correctly states the domain and range of $h(x)$?

F. Domain: $x \geq -1$; Range: $y \geq 0$

G. Domain: $x \geq -1$; Range: $y \geq 3$

H. Domain: $x \geq 0$; Range: $y \geq 0$

J. Domain: $x \geq 1$; Range: $y \geq -3$

K. Domain: $x \geq 1$; Range: $y \geq 3$

35. For the 2 functions $f(x)$ and $g(x)$, ordered pairs are shown below. What is the value of $f(g(4))$?

$f(x)$: $\{(4,1), (5,2), (6,3), (7,4)\}$

$g(x)$: $\{(-1,-4), (1,0), (2,2), (4,6)\}$

A. 0

B. 1

C. 3

D. 4

E. 6

36. What are the values of θ, between 0° and 360°, when $\sin\theta = \dfrac{\sqrt{3}}{2}$?

F. 30° and 150° only

G. 60° and 120° only

H. 45° and 135° only

J. 60° and 150° only

K. 60° only

37. What value of x satisfies the equation $\log_3(5x - 40) - \log_3 5 = 2$?

A. 17

B. 9

C. 1

D. -9

E. -17

38. For the piecewise function $f(x)$ defined below, what is the value of $f(6)$?

$$f(x) = \begin{cases} x^2 + 5, & \text{if } x \leq 0 \\ 2x - 9, & \text{if } 0 < x \leq 6 \\ 4 + x, & \text{if } x > 6 \end{cases}$$

F. 3

G. 10

H. 41

J. 3 and 10

K. 3, 10, and 41

39. The lengths of the legs of the right triangle below are $5 \sin x$ and $5 \cos x$ respectively. If $0° \leq x \leq 90°$, what is the length of the hypotenuse of the triangle?

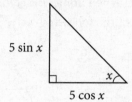

A. 1

B. $\sqrt{5}$

C. 5

D. 25

E. 50

40. If $\log_7 7^{\sqrt{7}} = x$, then x is between which of the following pairs of consecutive integers?

F. 0 and 1

G. 2 and 3

H. 4 and 5

J. 6 and 7

K. 7 and 8

41. For what value of x is the equation $\log_2 x + \log_2 (8x) = 5$ true?

A. 2

B. $\dfrac{32}{9}$

C. 4

D. 8

E. 32

42. The two triangles in the figure below share a common side. What is $\sin (x + y)$?

(Note: For all x and y, $\sin (x + y) = \sin x \cos y + \sin y \cos x$.)

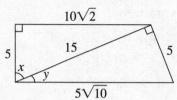

F. $\dfrac{1}{5\sqrt{10}}$

G. $\dfrac{12\sqrt{5} + \sqrt{10}}{30}$

H. $\dfrac{6\sqrt{5} + 3\sqrt{10}}{20}$

J. $\dfrac{2\sqrt{2} + \sqrt{10}}{3}$

K. $5\sqrt{10}$

43. What is the smallest positive value for θ where the graph of $f(x) = \sin 2\theta$ reaches its minimum value?

A. $\dfrac{\pi}{4}$

B. $\dfrac{\pi}{2}$

C. $\dfrac{3\pi}{4}$

D. π

E. $\dfrac{3\pi}{2}$

44. If the first and second terms of a geometric sequence are 6 and 18, what is the expression for the value of the 25th term of the sequence?

F. $a_{25} = 6^{25} \times 3$

G. $a_{25} = 6^{24} \times 3$

H. $a_{25} = 3^{24} \times 6$

J. $a_{25} = 3^{25} \times 6$

K. $a_{25} = 3^{25} \times 18$

45. The graph below shows Aaron's distance from home over a one-hour period, during which time he first went to the library to return some books, then went to the post office, and then returned home. Based on the graph, which of the following statements could be true?

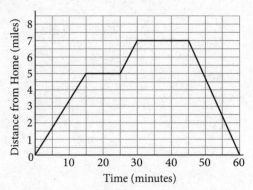

A. The post office is about 5 miles from Aaron's house.

B. Aaron traveled a total of 7 miles from the time he left home until he returned.

C. The post office is 7 miles farther from Aaron's house than the library is.

D. Aaron spent 10 minutes at the library and 15 minutes at the post office.

E. Aaron spent more time at his destinations than he spent traveling to and from his destinations.

ANSWERS AND EXPLANATIONS

1. A   Difficulty: Medium

Category: Functions

Getting to the Answer: The notation $g(h(x))$ indicates a composition of two functions that can be read "g of h of x." It means that the output when x is substituted in $h(x)$, the inner function and the table on the right, becomes the input for $g(x)$, the outer function and the table on the left. First, use the table on the right to find that $h(3)$ is 0. This is your new input. Now, use the table on the left to find $g(0)$, which is -1, making (A) the correct answer.

2. G   Difficulty: Medium

Category: Functions

Getting to the Answer: For arithmetic sequences, use the formula $a_n = a_1 + (n-1)d$, where n is the number of the term you're looking for, a_1 is the first term, and d is the common difference between consecutive terms (the number you're adding to each term to get the next term). Here, n is 20, a_1 is 25, and d is -4. Plug each of these values in the formula and simplify to get:

$$a_{20} = 25 + (20-1)(-4)$$
$$= 25 + (19)(-4)$$
$$= 25 - 76$$
$$= -51$$

Choice (G) is correct.

3. A   Difficulty: Medium

Category: Functions

Getting to the Answer: Only use the geometric sequence formula for questions that ask you about very distant numbers in the sequence. In a geometric sequence, each term is the result of multiplying the previous term by a constant ratio. This question provides the first four terms, so you only need

to determine the ratio to find the fifth term. To find this ratio, divide any term by the term which precedes it: $\frac{2}{-12} = -\frac{1}{6}$. Therefore, the fifth term is $2 \times -\frac{1}{6} = -\frac{1}{3}$. Choice (A) is correct.

4. J   Difficulty: Medium

Category: Functions

Getting to the Answer: Because you're looking for the sixth term of the sequence, call the sixth term x. Every term in this sequence is formed by multiplying the previous term by 3 and then subtracting 1, so the seventh term must be formed by multiplying the sixth term, x, by 3, and then subtracting 1; in other words, the seventh term is equal to $3x - 1$. Because the seventh term is 365, you have $365 = 3x - 1$. You can solve for x by adding 1 to both sides of the equation and then dividing by 3. The result is $x = 122$, which is (J).

5. C   Difficulty: Medium

Category: Functions

Getting to the Answer: Rewrite the logarithm in its exponential form: $2^{-3} = x$. To simplify the left side, recall that a negative exponent indicates taking the reciprocal of the base, so $2^{-3} = \frac{1}{2^3} = \frac{1}{8}$, which is (C).

6. G   Difficulty: Medium

Category: Functions

Getting to the Answer: Remember how to re-write a logarithm as an exponential: The **b**ase of the log becomes the **b**ase of the exponential, and the number on the outer **e**dge becomes the **e**xponent. So, $\log_a c = b$ becomes $a^b = c$, and vice versa.

Using this strategy, you know that $\log_x 100 = 2$ is equivalent to $x^2 = 100$. Simplify by taking the square root of both sides: $\sqrt{x^2} = \sqrt{100}$ gives us $x = 10$, or (G).

7. B   **Difficulty:** Medium

Category: Functions

Getting to the Answer: Substitute the given expressions into the square root for a and b, square each term carefully, and then use trig identities to simplify:

$$\sqrt{a^2 + b^2} = \sqrt{(x\cos\theta)^2 + (x\sin\theta)^2}$$
$$= \sqrt{x^2(\cos^2\theta + \sin^2\theta)}$$
$$= \sqrt{x^2 \times 1}$$
$$= |x|$$

It's given that $x > 0$, so $|x| = x$, which is (B).

8. J   **Difficulty:** Medium

Category: Functions

Getting to the Answer: The graph of a function crosses the x-axis when $q(x) = 0$, so set the given equation equal to 0 and solve for x. You can factor (sometimes) or use the quadratic formula to find x:

$$2x^2 - x - 15 = 0$$
$$a = 2, b = -1, c = -15$$

$$x = -b \pm \frac{\sqrt{b^2 - 4ac}}{2a}$$

$$= -(-1) \pm \frac{\sqrt{(-1)^2 - 4(2)(-15)}}{2(2)}$$

$$= \frac{1 \pm \sqrt{1 + 120}}{4}$$

$$= \frac{1 \pm \sqrt{121}}{4}$$

$$= \frac{1 \pm 11}{4}$$

Simplify to get:

$$x = \frac{1 + 11}{4} = \frac{12}{4} = 3 \text{ or } x = \frac{1 - 11}{4} = \frac{-10}{4} = -\frac{5}{2}$$

Now check the answer choices carefully. Choice (J) is correct.

9. D   **Difficulty:** Medium

Category: Functions

Getting to the Answer: The range of a function is the set of all possible y-values. (Remember, alphabetical order: domain $= x$ and range $= y$.) Eliminate C. The graph consists of discrete points, not continuous segments, so the range will be a set of discrete values, not an interval. Eliminate A and B. To choose between (D) and E, look at the coordinates of the points: The y-coordinates of the points, from left to right, are 6, 4, 2, 0, 2, 4, and 6. Thus, the range is the set {0, 2, 4, 6}. This matches (D). (Note that the set in E is the domain of the function.)

10. J   **Difficulty:** Medium

Category: Functions

Getting to the Answer: Read each answer choice carefully and compare it to the graph. Choice F indicates that the y-value on the graph of f is -4 when the x-value is 0, which is not true (at $x = 0$, the y-value of f is 2). Choice G indicates that the y-value on the graph of g is 0 when the x-value is 2, which is not true (at $x = 2$, the y-value of g is somewhere between 2 and 3). Choice H indicates that the graph of f is above (greater than) the graph of g everywhere, which is not true (the bottom part of the V is below the graph of g). In (J), the notation $f(x) = g(x)$ means the point at which the two graphs intersect. The graphs intersect in two places, one of which is (0,2), so (0,2) is a solution for $f(x) = g(x)$, and (J) is correct.

There is no need to check K, but in case you're curious, the graph of $f(x)$ touches the x-axis in only one place (between -1 and 0), so $f(x) = 0$ has exactly one solution, not two.

11. D   **Difficulty:** Medium

Category: Functions

Getting to the Answer: Test the sum for 2, then 3, then 4, then 5 terms of the sequence to see if a relationship can be determined. If $n = 2$, the sum is $1 + 3 = 4$. If $n = 3$, the sum is $1 + 3 + 5 = 9$. If $n = 4$, the sum is $1 + 3 + 5 + 7 = 16$. If $n = 5$, the sum is $1 + 3 + 5 + 7 + 9 = 25$. The sum is always equal to the square of n. Therefore, the correct answer is (D).

12. G   Difficulty: Medium

Category: Functions

Getting to the Answer: Think this question through logically, one step at a time. The equation for $Q(x)$ is given in factored form, so you know its roots (x-intercepts); they are the values of x that make the equation equal 0, which are -4 and 1. Thus, the graph of $Q(x)$ passes through the points $(-4,0)$ and $(1,0)$. If $R(x)$ is a reflection of $Q(x)$ over the y-axis, which is a horizontal reflection, the x-coordinates of these points will take on the opposite signs. This means the graph of $R(x)$ must pass through $(4,0)$ and $(-1,0)$, which is (G).

13. C   Difficulty: Medium

Category: Functions

Getting to the Answer: With nested functions, work from the inside out. To answer this question, substitute the entire rule for $g(x)$ for x in the function $f(x)$, then simplify:

$$f\big(g(x)\big) = \frac{1}{3}\big(3x^2 + 6x + 12\big) + 13$$
$$= x^2 + 2x + 4 + 13$$
$$= x^2 + 2x + 17$$

Choice (C) is correct.

14. G   Difficulty: Medium

Category: Functions

Getting to the Answer: Don't be intimidated by questions and answers that sound complicated. Ask yourself, "What is this question really asking?" The value of $f(x)$ is equal to 0 when the graph crosses or touches the x-axis. The graphed equation touches the x-axis at one point to the right of the y-axis. Therefore, $f(x) = 0$ for one positive value of x. The graph is a parabola, which typically has two solutions, so this one must be a double real solution, making (G) the correct answer.

15. E   Difficulty: Medium

Category: Functions

Getting to the Answer: Don't panic. This is nothing more than a plug-and-chug question, along with using the correct order of operations. Start in the parentheses (as always), apply the rule, and work your way out: $(3 \diamondsuit 5) = 3(3 - 5) = 3(-2) = -6$; then, $4 \diamondsuit (-6) = 4[4 - (-6)] = 4(10) = 40$. Choice (E) is correct.

16. H   Difficulty: Medium

Category: Functions

Getting to the Answer: A geometric sequence is simply a sequence in which each term except the first is equal to the previous term times some constant. Because the ratio between the second and first term is $\frac{12}{3} = 4$, each term is the previous term times 4, and $12 \times 4 = 48$, which is (H). You can check your answer by seeing whether it gives the correct fourth term: $48 \times 4 = 192$. Yes, this works.

17. C   Difficulty: Medium

Category: Functions

Getting to the Answer: Don't let the function notation throw you. You are looking for an equation that gives the number of degrees in an n-sided regular polygon. One way to answer the question is to make a table and look for a pattern, or a rule, which is exactly what a function is. Notice in the figure that each time the number of sides goes up by 1, the sum of the angle measures goes up by 180°. Make a third column in the table to discover a relationship and a fourth column to express the relationship using function notation.

Number of Sides, n	Sum of the Angles	Pattern	Function Notation
3	180°	180° × 1	$f(3) = 180 \times (3 - 2)$
4	360°	180° × 2	$f(4) = 180 \times (4 - 2)$
5	540°	180° × 3	$f(5) = 180 \times (5 - 2)$
6	720°	180° × 4	$f(6) = 180 \times (6 - 2)$
n			$f(n) = 180 \times (n - 2)$

The final function notation matches (C).

18. H   Difficulty: Medium

Category: Functions

Getting to the Answer: The range of a function is the set of y-values that the function takes on. In other words, the range describes how low and how high the function goes. The graph of this function (which is quadratic) is a parabola that has been shifted down 9 units. The standard parabola, $y = x^2$, has a minimum value of 0 (because its vertex is at the origin and the graph opens upward), so the minimum value of this function is -9. Thus, the range of the function is all real numbers greater than -9, which is (H).

Note that you could also graph the function in your graphing calculator and find the minimum value to identify the range.

19. C   Difficulty: Medium

Category: Functions

Getting to the Answer: Don't let the nested function scare you. Function questions often require little to no math.

Work from the inside out. To find $g(4)$, find $x = 4$ (the first number in the ordered pair) in the data set for $g(x)$ and read off the corresponding y-value, 6. Now repeat the process with the $f(x)$ data set, this time locating 6 in the x position, to find that $f(g(4)) = f(6) = 3$, which is (C).

20. K   Difficulty: Medium

Category: Functions

Getting to the Answer: You could use the general formula for a geometric sequence here, but you only need to go back four terms, so it's probably quicker to work backward. The common ratio (the number you're multiplying by each time to get to the next term) is $\frac{1}{3}$, which means working backward would require multiplying by 3 as you move to the previous term. This means the fourth term is 9, the third term is 27, the second term is 81, and the first term is 243, which is (K).

21. D   Difficulty: Medium

Category: Functions

Getting to the Answer: When a question includes a graph, be sure to fully understand it before trying to answer the question. Erin reached an altitude of 4,500 feet at 8 AM. She stayed at or above 4,500 feet until the final hour of her hike. This suggests that she was at or above 4,500 feet for at least 4 full hours. She descended the final 750 feet at a constant speed in one hour. More specifically, she descended the 250 feet from 4,750 feet to 4,500 feet in 20 minutes. Therefore, she was at or above 4,500 feet for 4 hours 20 minutes, which is (D).

22. F   Difficulty: High

Category: Functions

Getting to the Answer: The question states that during each one-hour interval, Erin traveled at a constant speed. Therefore, a graph showing her speed should remain constant (horizontal on the graph) within each one-hour interval. The only graph that does this is graph (F). All other graphs show a change in speed during each interval, which suggests an acceleration or deceleration and, ultimately, movement at speeds that are not constant.

23. D Difficulty: High

Category: Functions

Getting to the Answer: You should notice two things about the numerator of the expression: There's a tangent in each term (so it can be factored out), and there are squared trig functions. Start with that:

$$\frac{\tan\theta\cos^2\theta+\tan\theta\sin^2\theta}{\sin\theta}=\frac{\tan\theta\left(\cos^2\theta+\sin^2\theta\right)}{\sin\theta}$$

$$=\frac{\tan\theta(1)}{\sin\theta}$$

$$=\frac{\tan\theta}{\sin\theta}$$

Now, take a peek at the answer choices—each one is a single trig function, which means something in the result above must cancel. Use the trig ratios that you learned (SOHCAHTOA) to simplify your answer:

$$\frac{\tan\theta}{\sin\theta}=\frac{\frac{opposite}{adjacent}}{\frac{opposite}{hypotenuse}}$$

$$=\frac{opposite}{adjacent}\times\frac{hypotenuse}{opposite}$$

$$=\frac{hypotenuse}{adjacent}$$

Cosine is $\frac{adj}{hyp}$, and secant is the reciprocal of cosine, so the correct answer is (D).

24. J Difficulty: High

Category: Functions

Getting to the Answer: You could try plugging each pair of values into each answer choice until you find one that works for all the pairs of values in the table, but this is likely to use up valuable time. Instead, examine the patterns in the table and try to eliminate at least 2 or 3 answer choices. The x-values increase by 1 each time, while the y-values decrease

by varying amounts (not a constant change). This means the function cannot be linear, so eliminate F and G. Choice H is a parabola that has been shifted up 3 units, so it should pass through the point (0,3). According to the table, the graph passes through (0,5), so eliminate choice G as well. To choose between (J) and K, choose an easy pair of values from the table, such as (0,5), and check each function. Choice (J) gives $g(0)=\left(\frac{1}{2}\right)^0+4=1+4=5$; choice K gives $g(0)=-2^0+4=-1+4=3$. This means (J) is correct. (Note that -2^0, which equals -1, is not the same as $(-2)^0$, which equals 1.)

25. A Difficulty: High

Category: Functions

Getting to the Answer: Don't let the function notation intimidate you. The graphs of two functions intersect when the function equations are equal. Therefore, you need to set the equations equal to each other and solve for x.

$$f(x)=g(x)$$

$$3^{3x+3}=27^{\left(\frac{2}{3}x-\frac{1}{3}\right)}$$

When the equations have variables in the exponents, you must rewrite one or both of them so that either the bases are the same or the exponents themselves are the same. In this question, the two bases seem different at first glance but, because 27 is actually 3^3, you can rewrite the equation as:

$$3^{3x+3}=3^{3\left(\frac{2}{3}x-\frac{1}{3}\right)}$$

This simplifies to $3^{3x+3}=3^{2x-1}$. Now that the bases are equal, set the exponents equal to each other and solve for x:

$$3x+3=2x-1$$
$$x+3=-1$$
$$x=-4$$

Choice (A) is correct.

197

26. K   Difficulty: High

Category: Functions

Getting to the Answer: A quick sketch is needed to answer this question. You don't need anything fancy, just a graph that includes the given point, $(5, -1)$, and the line $y = 3$ (which is a horizontal line that crosses through the y-axis at 3).

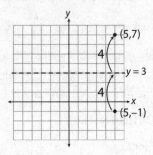

The only real rule to remember here is that if you reflect a point over a line, the distance from the line should remain the same. The point $(5, -1)$ is 4 units below the horizontal line $y = 3$, so the reflected point will be 4 units above the line, or $(5, 3 + 4) = (5, 7)$. Choice (K) is correct.

27. E   Difficulty: High

Category: Functions

Getting to the Answer: Because your calculator can evaluate both $\cos \dfrac{5\pi}{12}$ and each of the answer choices, this is an excellent opportunity to check your work using your calculator. Just make sure you set it to radians instead of degrees. Using the given equation and the table of values, you get:

$$\cos\left(\frac{2\pi}{3} - \frac{\pi}{4}\right) = \left(\cos\frac{2\pi}{3}\right)\left(\cos\frac{\pi}{4}\right) + \left(\sin\frac{2\pi}{3}\right)\left(\sin\frac{\pi}{4}\right)$$

$$= \left(-\frac{1}{2}\right)\left(\frac{\sqrt{2}}{2}\right) + \left(\frac{\sqrt{3}}{2}\right)\left(\frac{\sqrt{2}}{2}\right)$$

$$= -\frac{\sqrt{2}}{4} + \frac{\sqrt{6}}{4} = \frac{\sqrt{6} - \sqrt{2}}{4}$$

This matches (E).

28. F   Difficulty: High

Category: Functions

Getting to the Answer: Fortunately, "cannot be determined" is not one of the answer choices here, because that would be very tempting. There is in fact enough information to answer this question. You just have to use what you know about arithmetic sequences—specifically, that to get from one term to the next, you add the same number each time. Here, you don't know what that number is, so call it n. The five terms in the sequence are:

4

$4 + n$

$4 + n + n$

$4 + n + n + n$

$4 + n + n + n + n$

These terms are already listed in order, so the median is the middle term, which is $4 + n + n$, or $4 + 2n$. The mean is the sum of all the terms divided by the number of terms: $\dfrac{20 + 10n}{5} = 4 + 2n$. Thus, the mean and the median have the same value, making the difference between them equal to 0, which is (F).

29. E   Difficulty: High

Category: Functions

Getting to the Answer: The question asks you to evaluate the function $f(x)$, replacing x with $(x + c)$. Replace any instance of x in the function definition with $x + c$. This means that $2(x + 7)$ will be $2(x + c + 7)$. Use the distributive property and multiply each term in parentheses by 2 to get $2x + 2c + 2(7)$, or $2x + 2c + 14$, which is (E).

30. F   **Difficulty:** High

Category: Functions

Getting to the Answer: Graphing piecewise functions can be tricky. Try describing the graph in words first and then find the matching function. Use words like "to the left of" (which translates to *less than*) and "to the right of" (which translates to *greater than*).

First, notice that both pieces of the graph either start or stop at 0, but one has a closed dot and the other has an open dot. This means you can eliminate H right away because the inequality symbol in both equations would lead to open dots on the graph. To choose among the remaining answers, think about typical functions and transformations. To the left of $x = 0$, the graph is a line with a slope of $-\frac{3}{2}$ and a y-intercept of -4, so you can eliminate choices J and K because the slopes of the lines are incorrect. Now, look to the right of $x = 0$—the graph is a square root function (definitely not a line as in choice G) that has been moved down 1 unit, so its equation is $y = \sqrt{x} - 1$. This means (F) is correct.

31. A   **Difficulty:** High

Category: Functions

Getting to the Answer: Don't spend a lot of time comparing the answer choices. They are very similar and are likely to confuse you. Instead, apply the rules of transformations to the original function, one at a time, and then look for a match. First, a reflection over the x-axis is a vertical reflection, so apply a negative sign to the entire function (not just the x); the result is $-\cos x$. Shifting the graph right π units can be achieved by subtracting π from the x-value only (remember, horizontal translations are the opposite of what you expect); now you have $-\cos(x - \pi)$. Finally, shifting the graph down a units can be achieved by subtracting a from the whole equation to get $-\cos(x - \pi) - a$. Thus, the final function is $f'(x) = -\cos(x - \pi) - a$, which matches (A).

32. H   **Difficulty:** High

Category: Functions

Getting to the Answer: Recall that $g(x) = 0$ means "crosses the x-axis," regardless of the type of function involved, which means you are looking for the x-intercepts. Study the graph carefully: the function crosses the x-axis six times, halfway between each of the labeled grid lines. Rather than finding the points using the radians given in the graph, convert the radians to degrees and then determine the halfway points:

$$-\pi\left(\frac{180°}{\pi}\right) = -180°$$

$$\left(-\frac{2\pi}{3}\right)\left(\frac{180°}{\pi}\right) = -120°$$

$$\left(-\frac{\pi}{3}\right)\left(\frac{180°}{\pi}\right) = -60°, \text{ and so on.}$$

Take a minute now to find the halfway points, because chances are that you don't have to do all the conversions. Halfway between $-180°$ and $-120°$ is $-150°$. Stop—that's all you need to know. The leftmost x-intercept is at $-150°$, which means (H) must be correct. If you want to check another value just to be sure, halfway between $-120°$ and $-60°$ is $-90°$, which is the second value in choice (H), confirming that it is correct.

33. C   **Difficulty:** High

Category: Functions

Getting to the Answer: You don't really have to know anything about trig functions to answer this question. You just need to know the definition of *period*: the period of a repeating function is the distance along the x-axis required for the function to complete one full cycle. For a sine curve, this means one full wave (one up "bump" and one down "bump"). Here, that happens between 0 and π, which means the period is π. Choice (C) is correct.

If you happen to know the normal period of sine, which is 2π, you could also set the x term ($2x$) equal to that period and solve for x. You'll get $2x = 2\pi$, which simplifies to $x = \pi$.

34. G   Difficulty: High

Category: Functions

Getting to the Answer: The fastest route to the correct answer here (because you're given a graph of the parent square root function) is to write the domain and range of $g(x)$ and then adjust the values based on the transformation. The x-values of the curve shown in the graph begin at 0 and extend to the right indefinitely, so the domain is $x \geq 0$. The transformation ($x + 1$) shifts the graph to the left 1 unit, so the domain of $h(x)$ is $x \geq -1$. Eliminate choices H, J, and K. Likewise, the y-values of the curve shown in the graph begin at 0 and extend upward indefinitely, so the range is $y \geq 0$. The transformation ($+3$) shifts the graph up 3 units, so the range of $h(x)$ is $y \geq 3$. This means (G) is correct.

Note that you could also quickly sketch the graph of $h(x)$ to find its domain and range. The graph would look like the dashed curve below:

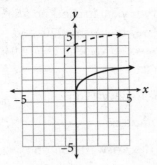

35. C   Difficulty: Medium

Category: Functions

Getting to the Answer: Don't let the nested function scare you. Function questions often require little to no math.

Work from the inside out. To find $g(4)$, find $x = 4$ (the first number in the ordered pair) in the data set for $g(x)$ and read off the corresponding y-value, 6. Now repeat the process with the $f(x)$ data set, this time locating 6 in the x position, to find that $f(g(4)) = f(6) = 3$, which is (C).

36. G   Difficulty: High

Category: Functions

Getting to the Answer: Knowing the basic trig values for benchmark angles (multiples of 30° and 45°) would certainly help here. However, Backsolving also works because there are numbers in the answer choices. Use your calculator to find the sine of each angle (make sure your calculator is in "degree" mode first). Note that $\frac{\sqrt{3}}{2}$ is approximately equal to 0.866.

$$\sin 30° = 0.5$$
$$\sin 45° \approx 0.7071$$
$$\mathbf{\sin 60° \approx 0.866}$$
$$\mathbf{\sin 120° \approx 0.866}$$
$$\sin 135° \approx 0.7071$$
$$\sin 150° = 0.5$$

Choice (G) is correct.

37. A   Difficulty: High

Category: Functions

Getting to the Answer: To solve a logarithmic equation, rewrite the equation in exponential form and solve for the variable. To rewrite the equation, use the translation $\log_b y = x$ means $b^x = y$. The left side of the given equation has two logs, so you'll need to combine them first using properties of logs before you can translate. Don't worry about the right-hand side of the equation just yet.

$$\log_b x - \log_b y = \log_b\left(\frac{x}{y}\right)$$

$$\log_3 (5x - 40) - \log_3 5 = \log_3\left(\frac{5x - 40}{5}\right)$$

$$= \log_3(x - 8)$$

Now the equation looks like $\log_3 (x - 8) = 2$, which can be rewritten as $3^2 = x - 8$. Simplifying yields $9 = x - 8$, or $17 = x$. Choice (A) is correct.

38. F   Difficulty: High

Category: Functions

Getting to the Answer: Don't let piecewise functions intimidate you. The right-hand side of each piece of the function tells you what part of the domain (which x-values) goes with that particular expression. In this function, values of x that are less than or equal to 0 go with the top expression, values of x greater than 0 and less than or equal to 6 go with the middle expression, and values of x that are greater than 6 go with the bottom expression. Because 6 is equal to 6, plug it into the middle expression and simplify:

$$f(6) = 2(6) - 9$$

$$= 12 - 9$$

$$= 3$$

This matches (F).

39. C   Difficulty: High

Category: Functions

Getting to the Answer: Learn trigonometric identities such as $\sin^2 \theta + \cos^2 \theta = 1$ to answer these types of questions more quickly on Test Day. Use the Pythagorean Theorem to set up an equation to find the length of the hypotenuse. Let x represent the length of the hypotenuse:

$$a^2 + b^2 = c^2$$

$$(5 \sin x)^2 + (5 \cos x)^2 = c^2$$

$$25 \sin^2 x + 25 \cos^2 x = c^2$$

$$25(\sin^2 x + \cos^2 x) = c^2$$

$$25(1) = c^2$$

$$c = 5$$

Choice (C) is correct.

40. G   Difficulty: High

Category: Functions

Getting to the Answer: If you remember your properties of logs, this question is very straightforward. Because $\log_b b^x = x$, the value of x is $\sqrt{7} \approx 2.65$, which lies between 2 and 3. Choice (G) is correct.

If you don't remember this property, you'll have to rewrite the logarithmic equation as an exponential equation and solve: $\log_7 7^{\sqrt{7}} = x$ is equivalent to the exponential form $7^x = 7^{\sqrt{7}}$. The bases are the same (7), so the exponents must be equal. This means $x = \sqrt{7} \approx 2.65$, which lies between 2 and 3.

41. A   Difficulty: High

Category: Functions

Getting to the Answer: Use the log property $\log_b x + \log_b y = \log_b(xy)$ to rewrite the left side of the equation. Then rewrite the entire equation in exponential form and solve for x:

$$\log_2 x + \log_2(8x) = 5$$
$$\log_2(8x^2) = 5$$
$$2^5 = 8x^2$$
$$32 = 8x^2$$
$$4 = x^2$$
$$x = \pm 2$$

Because $\log_b x$ is defined only for values of $x > 0$, -2 is not a valid solution. Thus, (A) is correct.

42. G   Difficulty: High

Category: Functions

Getting to the Answer: Use SOHCAHTOA to find the sine and cosine of each angle. The presence of the complicated formula in the note warns you that this question will take a while, so it's a good one to leave for the end of the test. The question stem tells you how to calculate $\sin(x + y)$, so your job is to find $\sin x$, $\cos x$, $\sin y$, and $\cos y$ and plug those values into the given equation.

Because $\sin \theta = \dfrac{\text{opposite}}{\text{hypotenuse}}$,

$\sin x = \dfrac{10\sqrt{2}}{15}$ and $\sin y = \dfrac{5}{5\sqrt{10}}$.

Because $\cos = \dfrac{\text{adjacent}}{\text{hypotenuse}}$,

$\cos x = \dfrac{5}{15}$ and $\cos y = \dfrac{15}{5\sqrt{10}}$.

Plug those values into the formula:

$\sin(x + y) = \sin x \cos y + \sin y \cos x$ to get:

$$\frac{10\sqrt{2}}{15} \times \frac{15}{5\sqrt{10}} + \frac{5}{5\sqrt{10}} \times \frac{5}{15} = \frac{150\sqrt{2}}{75\sqrt{10}} + \frac{25}{75\sqrt{10}}$$
$$= \frac{150\sqrt{2} + 25}{75\sqrt{10}} = \frac{6\sqrt{2} + 1}{3\sqrt{10}} = \frac{\sqrt{10}(6\sqrt{2} + 1)}{\sqrt{10}(3\sqrt{10})}$$
$$= \frac{6\sqrt{20} + \sqrt{10}}{3 \times 10} = \frac{12\sqrt{5} + \sqrt{10}}{30}$$

This matches (G).

43. C   Difficulty: High

Category: Functions

Getting to the Answer: Answering this question requires some knowledge of the unit circle and/or the graph of a sine curve. First figure out where the graph of sine reaches a minimum, then worry about where the 2θ comes in. The sine function first reaches its minimum (of -1) at $\dfrac{3\pi}{2}$, so:

$$2\theta = \frac{3\pi}{2}$$
$$\theta = \frac{3\pi}{2} \times \frac{1}{2} = \frac{3\pi}{4}$$

Choice (C) is correct.

44. H   Difficulty: High

Category: Functions

Getting to the Answer: In a geometric sequence, when you are looking for a term that is fairly far out in the sequence, use the formula $a_n = a_1(r^{n-1})$, where a_n is the nth term in the sequence, a_1 is the first term in the sequence, and r is the amount by which each preceding term is multiplied to get the next term (called the common ratio).

The first two terms in this sequence are 6 and 18, so r is $\frac{18}{6} = 3$. You're given that a_1 is 6 and you're looking for the 25th term, so n is 25. Plug each of these values into the formula and simplify to get $a_{25} = 6(3^{25-1}) = 6 \times 3^{24}$. That's equivalent to (H).

45. D   Difficulty: High

Category: Functions

Getting to the Answer: Compare each answer choice to the graph, eliminating false statements as you go.

Choice A: Aaron went to the library first, so the library (not the post office) is about 5 miles from his home. Eliminate this choice.

Choice B: Aaron traveled 7 miles away from his home (between $t = 0$ minutes and $t = 30$ minutes) but then also traveled 7 miles back (between $t = 45$ minutes and $t = 60$ minutes), so he traveled a total of 14 miles. Eliminate this choice.

Choice C: When Aaron reached the library, he was 5 miles from home; when he reached the post office, he was 7 miles from home. This means the post office must be about $7 - 5 = 2$ miles farther away. Eliminate this choice.

Choice (D): Aaron is the same distance from home (5 miles) between $t = 15$ minutes and $t = 25$ minutes, so he spent 10 minutes at the library. He is stopped once again (at the post office) between $t = 30$ minutes and $t = 45$ minutes, so he spent 15 minutes at the post office. Choice (D) is correct.

There is no need to check E, but in case you're curious or just not sure: Aaron spent $15 + 5 + 15 = 35$ minutes traveling to and from his destinations (represented by the portions of the graph that are not horizontal) and only $10 + 15 = 25$ minutes at his destinations, so E is not a true statement.

CHAPTER ELEVEN

Statistics and Probability

PRACTICE QUESTIONS

The following test-like questions provide an opportunity to practice Statistics and Probability questions.

Use the following information to answer questions 1–2.

The following table shows the amount of trash collected by 30 participants in a litter cleanup drive.

Pounds of trash	10	15	20	25	30
Number of participants	12	9	4	4	1

1. What is the mode of the number of pieces of trash collected by the participants in the litter cleanup drive?

    A. 10

    B. 15

    C. 20

    D. 25

    E. 30

2. What was the average amount of trash collected by each of the 30 participants in the litter cleanup drive?

    F. Between 10 and 11 pounds

    G. Between 11 and 12 pounds

    H. Between 15 and 16 pounds

    J. Between 19 and 20 pounds

    K. Between 20 and 21 pounds

Use the following information to answer questions 3–5.

Phase I clinical trials are run to determine the safety of an investigational drug. Dr. Gibbons is overseeing a treatment-resistant influenza Phase I trial with 400 healthy participants: half are given the drug, and half are given an inert pill. The circle graph below shows a distribution of the severity of common side effects.

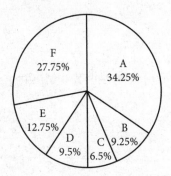

A: inert, mild or no side effects
B: inert, moderate side effects
C: inert, severe side effects
D: drug, mild or no side effects
E: drug, moderate side effects
F: drug, severe side effects

3. What percent of the participants experienced severe side effects?

   A. 6.50%

   B. 21.25%

   C. 27.75%

   D. 34.25%

   E. 65.75%

4. How many more participants experienced mild or no side effects than severe side effects?

   F. 10

   G. 38

   H. 42

   J. 50

   K. 64

5. What percent of the participants who experienced severe side effects were given the drug?

   A. 28%

   B. 50%

   C. 75%

   D. 81%

   E. 90%

6. Six model cars are to be placed on a bookshelf. If all 6 cars are placed on the shelf in order, from left to right, in how many different ways can the cars be placed?

   F. 5

   G. 14

   H. 60

   J. 120

   K. 720

7. The histogram that follows shows the number of vehicles that a car rental agency currently has available to rent, categorized by fuel efficiency ratings. If a customer randomly selects one of the available cars, what is the probability that he will get a car that has a fuel efficiency rating of at least 25 miles per gallon?

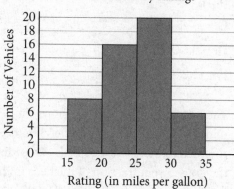

Fuel Efficiency Ratings

A. $\frac{2}{5}$

B. $\frac{12}{25}$

C. $\frac{13}{25}$

D. $\frac{10}{13}$

E. $\frac{21}{25}$

8. The table below shows a summary of a high-density lipoprotein, or HDL, cholesterol study. An HDL level less than 40 mg/dL is considered to be a major risk factor for heart disease. Based on the table, if a single participant is selected at random from all the participants in the study, what is the probability that he or she will be at risk for heart disease and be at least 36 years old?

HDL Cholesterol Study Results

Age Group	< 40 mg/dL	40-60 mg/dL	> 60 mg/dL	Total
18-25	9	22	17	48
26-35	16	48	34	98
36-45	19	35	40	94
Older than 45	12	27	21	60
Total	56	132	112	300

F. $\frac{19}{300}$

G. $\frac{1}{12}$

H. $\frac{31}{300}$

J. $\frac{14}{75}$

K. $\frac{31}{56}$

9. A basketball team made 1-point (free throws), 2-point, and 3-point baskets. Twenty percent of the baskets they made were worth 1 point, 70% of their baskets were worth 2 points, and 10% of their baskets were worth 3 points. To the nearest tenth, what was the average point value of their baskets?

A. 1.4

B. 1.7

C. 1.8

D. 1.9

E. 2.0

10. Set A contains 7 consecutive even integers. If the average of Set A's integers is 46, which of the following is the smallest integer of Set A?

F. 36

G. 38

H. 40

J. 42

K. 44

11. Annette scored an average of 8 points per game on her volleyball team. The numbers of points she scored in each game are shown below.

Game	1	2	3	4	5	6
Points	3	11	6	10	11	?

How many points did Annette score in Game 6?

A. 6

B. 7

C. 8

D. 9

E. 10

12. On her first three geometry tests, Sarah scored an 89, a 93, and an 84. If there are four tests total and Sarah needs at least a 90 average for the four, what is the lowest score she can receive on the final test?

F. 86

G. 90

H. 92

J. 94

K. 96

13. At a district-wide student government convention, 1 female and 1 male will be selected to lead the discussions for the day. If there are 90 females and 125 males at the convention, how many different 2-person combinations of 1 female and 1 male are possible?

A. 35

B. 215

C. 430

D. 5,625

E. 11,250

14. The pictograph that follows shows the number of beds in each of several hotels, rounded to the nearest 50 beds. According to the graph, what fraction of the beds in these four hotels are at the Bedtime Hotel?

F. $\frac{1}{4}$

G. $\frac{1}{3}$

H. $\frac{2}{5}$

J. $\frac{5}{11}$

K. $\frac{1}{2}$

15. In the final round of a trivia competition, contestants were asked to name as many states that begin with the letter M as they could in 30 seconds. The bar graph below shows the number of states the contestants were able to name. Based on the graph, what was the median number of states that contestants were able to name?

Final Trivia Round

(bar graph: x-axis "Number of States Correctly Named" 1–8, y-axis "Frequency" 0–7)

A. 4

B. 5

C. 6

D. 7

E. Cannot be determined from the given information

16. The probability distribution of the discrete random variable X is shown in the table below. Based on the probability distribution, what is the expected value of X?

X	Probability $P(X = x)$
10	$\frac{1}{5}$
11	$\frac{1}{10}$
12	$\frac{3}{10}$
13	$\frac{3}{20}$
14	$\frac{1}{4}$

F. $10\frac{4}{5}$

G. 11

H. 12

J. $12\frac{3}{20}$

K. $13\frac{1}{20}$

17. Based on the circle graph shown below, if there are 1,000 residents in Englebrook who are age 17 or younger, how many residents are 36 through 55 years old?

Age Distribution of Englebrook Residents

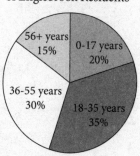

A. 300

B. 700

C. 1,300

D. 1,500

E. 3,000

18. The probability of rain today is 60 percent, and the independent probability of rain tomorrow is 75 percent. What is the probability that it will rain neither today nor tomorrow?

F. 10%

G. 15%

H. 45%

J. 55%

K. 65%

19. The table below shows the results of a study identifying the number of males and females with and without college degrees who were unemployed or employed at the time of the study. If one person from the study is chosen at random, what is the probability that that person is an employed person with a college degree?

	Unemployed	Employed	Totals
Female Degree	12	188	200
Female No Degree	44	156	200
Male Degree	23	177	200
Male No Degree	41	159	200
Totals	120	680	800

A. $\frac{73}{160}$

B. $\frac{10}{17}$

C. $\frac{73}{136}$

D. $\frac{17}{20}$

E. $\frac{73}{80}$

20. For the first 5 passes attempted in a football game, the table below gives the probability, $P(x)$, that a certain quarterback completes x passes. What is the probability that this quarterback will complete at least 1 pass in the first 5 passes he attempts?

x Completed Passes	P(x)
0	0.0219
1	0.0432
2	0.3118
3	0.5288
4	0.0822
5	0.0121

F. 0.0432

G. 0.0651

H. 0.5288

J. 0.9349

K. 0.9781

21. If set A consists of the data values $\{x, x, x, y, y, y, 3x + y, x - y\}$ and the median of set A is 10 where $0 < x < y$, what is the range of set A?

A. 40

B. 30

C. 25

D. 20

E. Cannot be determined from the given information

22. Suppose that m will be randomly selected from the set $\{-2, -1, 0, 1, 2\}$ and that n will be randomly selected from the set $\{-3, -2, -1, 0\}$. What is the probability that $mn < 0$?

    F. $\dfrac{3}{20}$

    G. $\dfrac{1}{5}$

    H. $\dfrac{3}{10}$

    J. $\dfrac{5}{9}$

    K. $\dfrac{3}{5}$

23. A certain baseball stadium has 12,000 seats. Based on several previous years' attendance rates, the owners of the stadium constructed the table below showing the daily attendance rates and their probabilities of occurring for the coming baseball season. Based on the probability distribution in the table, what is the expected number of seats that will be occupied on any given day during the coming baseball season?

Attendance Rate	Probability
0.40	0.15
0.50	0.25
0.60	0.35
0.70	0.15
0.80	0.10

    A. 5,400

    B. 6,240

    C. 6,960

    D. 7,080

    E. 7,200

24. Diane wants to draw a circle graph showing the favorite teachers at her school. When she polled her classmates, 25% said Mr. Green, 15% said Ms. Brown, 35% said Mrs. White, 5% said Mr. Blue, and the remaining classmates said teachers other than Mr. Green, Ms. Brown, Mrs. White, or Mr. Blue. The teachers other than Mr. Green, Ms. Brown, Mrs. White, or Mr. Blue will be grouped together in an Other sector. What will be the degree measure of the sector that represents Other?

    F. 144°

    G. 72°

    H. 36°

    J. 20°

    K. 15°

25. A jar contains 120 red, blue, yellow, green, and purple marbles. The probabilities of randomly selecting any of the given colors (except purple) are shown in the probability distribution table below.

Color	Probability
Red	0.15
Blue	0.25
Yellow	0.05
Green	0.35
Purple	?

    Assuming there are no marbles of any other color in the jar, how many of the marbles in the jar are purple?

    A. 20

    B. 24

    C. 30

    D. 32

    E. 36

Use the following information to answer questions 26–27.

The population of fish in a certain pond from 1985 to 1995 is shown in the graph below.

Population of the Pond

26. Which of the following best describes the percent change in the population from 1985 to 1995?

F. 33.33% increase

G. 33.33% decrease

H. 50% decrease

J. 333.33% increase

K. 333.33% decrease

27. Which of the following years contains the median population for the data?

A. 1986

B. 1989

C. 1990

D. 1991

E. 1995

28. Aneeka and Justin are best friends. They both are saving money for summer vacation. So far, Aneeka has saved $90 and Justin has saved $30 more than Aneeka. Justin's mom gives him a bonus of 20% of what he already has and Justin adds it to his savings. Aneeka's dad tells Aneeka that he will give her a bonus so that she will have the same total as Justin. What percent of Aneeka's current savings must the bonus from her dad be?

F. 45%

G. 52%

H. 60%

J. 64%

K. 70%

29. A baker makes 186 cupcakes. Some have chocolate icing and some have vanilla icing, and both kinds are made with and without sprinkles, as shown in the table that follows. Because they are more popular, the baker used chocolate icing on $\frac{2}{3}$ of the cupcakes. If a cupcake with chocolate icing is chosen at random, what is the probability that it will have sprinkles?

	Chocolate Icing	Vanilla Icing	Total
With Sprinkles		40	
Without Sprinkles			104
Total			186

A. $\frac{21}{93}$

B. $\frac{21}{62}$

C. $\frac{41}{93}$

D. $\frac{21}{41}$

E. Cannot be determined from the given information

30. If an integer is randomly chosen from the first 50 positive integers, what is the probability that an integer with a digit of 3 is selected?

    F. $\frac{1}{10}$

    G. $\frac{7}{25}$

    H. $\frac{3}{10}$

    J. $\frac{2}{5}$

    K. $\frac{3}{5}$

31. At a certain company, the average age of the male employees is 35 and the average age of the female employees is 30. If 20% of the employees are male, what is the average age of all the employees at this company?

    A. 30
    B. 31
    C. 32
    D. 33
    E. 34

32. Which of the following expressions gives the number of distinct permutations of the letters in the word GEOMETRY?

    F. $8!(2!)$

    G. $8!$

    H. $\frac{8!}{2!}$

    J. $\frac{8!}{6!}$

    K. $\frac{8!}{(6!)(2!)}$

33. A state-wide hospital system in a certain state uses patient identifiers that consist of 6 alphanumeric characters (letters A–Z and numbers 0–9) with the constraints that the letters I and O cannot be used and the first character cannot be a zero. Which of the following expressions gives the number of distinct patient identifiers that are possible assuming that repetition of both letters and numbers is allowed?

    A. $24^3 + 9 + 10^2$

    B. $24^3 \times 9 \times 10^2$

    C. $1^{33} \times 5^{34}$

    D. 33×34^5

    E. $33 \times 5 \times 34!$

34. Which of the following expressions gives the number of distinct permutations of the letters in the word STATISTICS?

    F. $10!(3!)$

    G. $10!$

    H. $\frac{10!}{3!}$

    J. $\frac{10!}{5!}$

    K. $\frac{10!}{(3!)(3!)(2!)}$

35. According to a veterinarian's records, the mean weight of 17 puppies who got their first round of vaccines at the vet's office in January was 26 ounces. When the final puppy who got his vaccines on January 31 was added to the data, the mean weight increased to 27 ounces. What was the weight in ounces of the final puppy?

    A. 28
    B. 36
    C. 44
    D. 47
    E. 49

ANSWERS AND EXPLANATIONS

1.   A   Difficulty: Low

Category: Statistics and Probability

Getting to the Answer: The mode is the number that appears most often in a set of data. The largest number of people who collected the same amount of trash was the 12 people who collected 10 pounds of trash, so 10 is the mode of this set of data. That's (A).

2.   H   Difficulty: Medium

Category: Statistics and Probability

Getting to the Answer: The total amount of trash collected by the 30 participants was $12(10) + 9(15) + 4(20) + 4(25) + 1(30) = 120 + 135 + 80 + 100 + 30 = 465$ pounds of trash. Because there were 30 participants, the average amount of trash collected by each one was $\frac{465}{30} = 15.5$ pounds, making (H) the correct answer.

3.   D   Difficulty: Low

Category: Statistics and Probability

Getting to the Answer: A question like this tests your ability to read a graph and its key. Here, you want the percent of the participants who experienced severe side effects, regardless of whether they received the drug or the inert pills. That's sections C and F, so add 6.5% + 27.75% to arrive at the correct answer, 34.25%, which is (D).

4.   G   Difficulty: Medium

Category: Statistics and Probability

Getting to the Answer: There are several different ways to approach this question, but the quickest is to find the percents that fit the two categories (one of which you already calculated in the previous question), subtract, and then multiply by 400. You already know that 34.25% experienced severe side effects. Based on sections F and J of the circle graph,

a total of 43.75% experienced mild or no side effects. That's a difference of 9.5%, so 0.095(400), or 38, more participants experienced mild or no side effects than severe side effects. Choice (G) is correct.

5.   D   Difficulty: High

Category: Statistics and Probability

Getting to the Answer: This question is a bit more involved. It's not asking what percent of *all* the participants were given the drug, so 50% is not the correct answer. Instead, you need to think only of the participants who experienced severe side effects. Of the 34.25% who experienced severe side effects, 27.75% were given the drug. That's 27.75% out of 34.25%, or $\frac{27.75}{34.25} \approx 0.8102$, which is about 81%. Choice (D) is correct.

6.   K   Difficulty: Medium

Category: Statistics and Probability

Getting to the Answer: Permutations are sequences, so order matters. Any of the 6 cars could be placed in the first spot on the shelf. Any of the remaining 5 cars could be placed in the second spot, any of the remaining 4 cars could be placed in the third spot, and so on until there is only 1 remaining car for the sixth spot. You can represent this visually by drawing a line representing each of the shelf's 6 spots, and then writing in how many car choices there are for each spot:

$$\underline{6} \quad \underline{5} \quad \underline{4} \quad \underline{3} \quad \underline{2} \quad \underline{1}$$

Then use the Fundamental Counting Principle to find that the number of possible arrangements is $6 \times 5 \times 4 \times 3 \times 2 \times 1 = 720$, which is (K).

7.   C   Difficulty: Medium

Category: Statistics and Probability

Getting to the Answer: The probability that an event will occur is the number of desired outcomes (number of available cars that have a rating of at least 25 mpg) divided by the number of total possible outcomes (total number of cars). "At least" means that much or greater, so find the number of cars represented by the two bars to the right of 25 in the histogram: $20 + 6 = 26$ cars. Now find the total number of available cars: $8 + 16 + 20 + 6 = 50$.

Finally, divide to find the indicated probability: $\frac{26}{50} = \frac{13}{25}$. That's (C).

8. H   Difficulty: Medium

Category: Statistics and Probability

Getting to the Answer: This question requires careful reading of the table. The first criterion is fairly straightforward—you're looking for a participant with an HDL level in the < 40 range, so focus on that column in the table. The second criterion is a bit trickier—*at least 36 years old* means 36 years old or older, so you'll need to use the values in the rows for 36-45 and Older than 45. There were 19 in the 36-45 age group who were considered at risk, and 12 in the Older than 45 age group, resulting in a total of $19 + 12 = 31$ out of 300 participants (the total in the last row, last column of the table). The probability of randomly selecting one participant from either of these two groups is $\frac{31}{300}$, which is (H).

9. D   Difficulty: Medium

Category: Statistics and Probability

Getting to the Answer: To make the question a little easier to follow, Pick Numbers for the total number of baskets. Imagine that they made a total of 100 baskets. If the team made 100 baskets, then they made 20 1-point baskets, 70 2-point baskets, and 10 3-point baskets. The average point value of all the baskets is the total number of points divided by the total number of baskets:

$$\frac{20(1) + 70(2) + 10(3)}{100} = \frac{20 + 140 + 30}{100}$$
$$= \frac{190}{100}$$
$$= 1.9$$

Choice (D) is correct.

10. H   Difficulty: Medium

Category: Statistics and Probability

Getting to the Answer: Because the integers in Set A are consecutive, their average must equal their middle term. In a set of 7 integers, the middle one is the fourth term. To find the smallest term, count backward from 46: 46, 44, 42, 40. That's (H). You can also answer this question by using Backsolving. Start with (H). If 40 is the smallest integer of Set A, then the next six consecutive integers must be 42, 44, 46, 48, 50, and 52. Take the average of these 7 integers:

$$\frac{40 + 42 + 44 + 46 + 48 + 50 + 52}{7} = \frac{322}{7} = 46$$

This matches the condition in the question stem: The average of these consecutive integers equals 46, so (H) must be the correct answer.

11. B   Difficulty: Medium

Category: Statistics and Probability

Getting to the Answer: Use the formula for finding an average:

$$\text{Average} = \frac{\text{sum of terms}}{\text{number of terms}}$$

Now substitute the given average, 8, and all the number of points, including the unknown number (call it x) into the formula and solve:

$$8 = \frac{3 + 11 + 6 + 10 + 11 + x}{6}$$
$$8 = \frac{41 + x}{6}$$
$$48 = 41 + x$$
$$7 = x$$

Annette scored 7 points in Game 6. Choice (B) is correct.

12. J   Difficulty: Medium

Category: Statistics and Probability

Getting to the Answer: When a question about averages involves a missing value (here, the final test score), it often helps to think in terms of the sum instead. For Sarah's exam scores to average at least a 90, they must sum to at least $90 \times 4 = 360$. She already has an 89, a 93, and an 84, so she needs at least $360 - (89 + 93 + 84)$, which gives $360 - 266 = 94$ points on her final test. Choice (J) is correct.

13. E   Difficulty: Medium

Category: Statistics and Probability

Getting to the Answer: Don't let the word *combination* confuse you. This is a very straightforward question. There are 90 females who could be chosen. For *each* of those 90 females, there are 125 males who could be chosen. That makes $90 \times 125 = 11{,}250$ different pairs of students who could be chosen. Choice (E) is correct.

14. F   Difficulty: Medium

Category: Statistics and Probability

Getting to the Answer: Don't automatically start calculating the actual numbers of beds—the graph is already sufficient to answer this question. Bedtime has 2.5 pictures of beds (each representing 100 actual beds). There's a total of $1.5 + 2 + 4 + 2.5 = 10$ pictures of beds. So the fraction of the total beds that are at Bedtime is $\frac{2.5}{10} = \frac{25}{100} = \frac{1}{4}$, which is (F).

15. B   Difficulty: Medium

Category: Statistics and Probability

Getting to the Answer: The median of a data set is the middle number when the data values are arranged in ascending (or descending) order. If there is an even number of terms, the median is the average of the two middle terms. Use the frequency (along the vertical axis) and the bar heights to list out the values: There is one 1, one 2, two 3s, five 4s, four 5s, four 6s, two 7s, and one 8. The list of data values is:

1, 2, 3, 3, 4, 4, 4, 4, 4, **5, 5,** 5, 5, 6, 6, 6, 6, 7, 7, 8

There are 20 terms in all, so the median is the average of the 10th and 11th terms, which are both 5s. Thus, the median is 5, making (B) the correct answer.

16. J   Difficulty: Medium

Category: Statistics and Probability

Getting to the Answer: The expected value of a random discrete variable is the weighted average of all possible values that the variable can take on. The weights are determined by the probability distribution. To find the expected value, multiply each possible value by its given probability and then add the products:

$$E(X) = \frac{1}{5}(10) + \frac{1}{10}(11) + \frac{3}{10}(12) + \frac{3}{20}(13) + \frac{1}{4}(14)$$
$$= 2 + \frac{11}{10} + \frac{36}{10} + \frac{39}{20} + \frac{14}{4}$$
$$= \frac{40}{20} + \frac{22}{20} + \frac{72}{20} + \frac{39}{20} + \frac{70}{20}$$
$$= \frac{243}{20} = 12\frac{3}{20}$$

Choice (J) is correct.

17. D   Difficulty: Medium

Category: Statistics and Probability

Getting to the Answer: Note that you are given the number of residents in a specific age group here, not the total number of residents, so in this case you will have to work backward to get the total. According to the circle graph, 20% of residents are age 17 or younger, and this corresponds to 1,000 residents. So if x is the total number of residents, you know that 1,000 is 20% of x. Therefore, $1{,}000 = 0.2x$. Divide both sides of this equation by 0.2 to find that $x = 5{,}000$. So there are 5,000 residents total and 30% of them are 36 through 55 years old. Multiply 5,000 by 30% (or 0.3) to determine that 1,500 residents are 36 through 55 years old. That's (D).

18. F   Difficulty: Medium

Category: Statistics and Probability

Getting to the Answer: To find the probability that an event will *not* occur, subtract the probability that it *will* occur from 1. The probability that it will rain today is 60%, so the probability that it will not rain today is $100\% - 60\% = 40\%$. The probability that it will rain tomorrow is 75%, so the probability that it will not rain tomorrow is 100% − 75% = 25%.

To find the probability that two independent events will both occur, multiply the individual probabilities. Thus, to get the probability that it will not rain today or tomorrow, multiply 40% and 25%:

$$(40\%)(25\%) = (0.40)(0.25) = 0.10 = 10\%$$

The answer is (F).

19.   A   Difficulty: Medium

Category: Statistics and Probability

Getting to the Answer: Identify which pieces of information from the table you need. The question asks for the probability that a randomly chosen person from the study is employed and has a college degree, so you need the total of both females and males with college degrees who are employed compared to all the participants in the study. There are 188 employed females with a college degree and 177 employed males with a college degree. That totals 365 employed people with a college degree out of 800 participants, so the probability is $\frac{365}{800}$, which reduces to $\frac{73}{160}$, which matches (A).

20.   K   Difficulty: Medium

Category: Statistics and Probability

Getting to the Answer: Completing at least 1 pass in the first 5 attempts and completing 0 passes are complementary events. Thus,

$$P(x \geq 1) = 1 - P(x = 0)$$
$$= 1 - 0.0219$$
$$= 0.9781$$

Choice (K) is correct.

21.   A   Difficulty: High

Category: Statistics and Probability

Getting to the Answer: This is a very sophisticated question and would be best left until the end of the test. The key is in using the definitions of range and median to see where that takes you.

To find the range, you need to subtract the smallest value from the largest value. Before you can do this, you must identify the smallest and largest values. You are NOT told that the values are listed in increasing order, so you'll need to think logically. The inequality $0 < x < y$ gives you the information you need: Both x and y are positive numbers and x is less than y. This means $x - y$ is a negative number (and is smaller than both x and y) and $3x + y$ is a positive number (and is larger than both x and y). Thus the values written in order are $\{x - y, x, x, x, y, y, y, 3x + y\}$, making the range $(3x + y) - (x - y) = 2x + 2y$.

Now use the definition of median: There are 8 data values in set A, so the median (which you're told is 10) is the average of the two middle terms, x and y. Thus $10 = \frac{x + y}{2}$, which simplifies to $x + y = 20$. The range, $2x + 2y$, is exactly twice $x + y$, so the range is $2(20) = 40$. Choice (A) is correct.

22.   H   Difficulty: High

Category: Statistics and Probability

Getting to the Answer: This question takes a bit of thought: for mn to be less than 0 (a negative number), either the first number selected is negative and the second is positive, or the reverse. These are two independent events, so once you find the probability of each event, you'll need to add them. Also keep in mind that if either number is 0, then the product will not be less than 0 (it will be equal to 0), so selecting a 0 from either set of numbers is not a desired outcome.

$$P(\text{negative then positive}) = \frac{2}{5} \times \frac{0}{4} = 0$$

$$P(\text{positive then negative}) = \frac{2}{5} \times \frac{3}{4} = \frac{6}{20} = \frac{3}{10}$$

The probability that either of these two events will occur is $\frac{3}{10}$, which is (H).

23. C   Difficulty: High

Category: Statistics and Probability

Getting to the Answer: This question actually has two parts: find the expected attendance rate and then use that to find the expected number of occupied seats on any given day. The expected attendance rate is the sum of the products of each attendance rate and its corresponding probability:

$$E(\text{att. rate}) = 0.15(0.4) + 0.25(0.5) + 0.35(0.6)$$
$$+ 0.15(0.7) + 0.10(0.8)$$
$$= 0.58$$

To calculate the expected number of occupied seats, multiply the expected attendance rate by the total number of seats in the stadium. The result is $0.58(12,000) = 6,960$, which is (C).

24. G   Difficulty: High

Category: Statistics and Probability

Getting to the Answer: Once you're strong on the basics, combining two concepts on seemingly complex questions like this one will be a breeze! The percent who chose one of the four named teachers is $25\% + 15\% + 35\% + 5\% = 80\%$. This means that 20% of the answers were grouped under "Other." A circle has 360 degrees, so the measure of the Other sector will be 20% of 360, or $0.2(360) = 72$ degrees, which is (G).

25. B   Difficulty: High

Category: Statistics and Probability

Getting to the Answer: Understanding how a probability distribution table works is the key to answering this question. Because the question states that no other color marble is in the jar, the values in the right-hand column of the table must sum to 1.0. Thus, the probability of randomly selecting a purple marble must be $1.0 - 0.15 - 0.25 - 0.05 - 0.35 = 0.2$. There is a total of 120 marbles in the jar, so $0.2(120) = 24$ of the marbles are purple. That's (B).

26. G   Difficulty: Low

Category: Statistics and Probability

Getting to the Answer: Percent change is calculated by dividing the amount of change by the original amount. In 1985, the population was 3,000; in 1995, the population was 2,000. Thus the amount of change was 1,000. Divide this by the original amount (the 1985 population) to find that the percent change was $1,000 \div 3,000 = 0.3333$, or 33.33%. The population went *down* from 1985 to 1995, so this is a decrease of 33.33%, which is (G).

27. C   Difficulty: Medium

Category: Statistics and Probability

Getting to the Answer: This question requires brute force. You need to list the data value corresponding to each year, order the values from least to greatest, find the median (the middle value), match it to a year in the graph, and then select the correct answer.

85	86	87	88	89	90
3,000	1,000	5,000	5,000	4,000	3,000
91	92	93	94	95	
4,000	1,000	3,000	2,000	2,000	

Order the data, keeping the year labels:

86	92	94	95	85	90
1,000	1,000	2,000	2,000	3,000	3,000
93	89	91	87	88	
3,000	4,000	4,000	5,000	5,000	

The median of this group is the sixth value, or 3,000. The years 1985, 1990, and 1993 all had populations of 3,000. The only one of these years among the answer choices is 1990, which is (C).

28. H   Difficulty: High

Category: Statistics and Probability

Getting to the Answer: This question requires an organized, step-by-step solution. The question asks about Aneeka, so chances are that you'll need to start with the information about Justin. If Justin has saved $30 more than Aneeka, then he has saved $90 + $30 = $120. His bonus, then, is 0.20 times $120 = $24, bringing his total to $144. To get Aneeka's total to the same amount, her dad must give her a bonus of $144 − $90 = $54. As a percentage of her current savings, this equates to $54 ÷ $90 = 0.6, or 60%, which is (H).

29. B   Difficulty: High

Category: Statistics and Probability

Getting to the Answer: The table is not complete, so your first step is to fill in the missing values. Start with what you know and work from there. It may not be necessary to complete the entire table, but rather only what you need to answer the question.

You know there are 186 cupcakes total and that 104 are without sprinkles, which means 186 − 104 = 82 have sprinkles. Because you already know that 40 of those cupcakes have vanilla icing, this means 82 − 40 = 42 of the cupcakes with sprinkles have chocolate icing. You also know that $\frac{2}{3}$ of the total number of cupcakes have chocolate icing, which means there are $\frac{2}{3} \times 186 = 124$ cupcakes with chocolate icing, total, so you can fill this number in the "Total" row of that column. You do not need to fill in any more of the table because the question only asks about cupcakes with chocolate icing that have sprinkles. There are 124 cupcakes with chocolate icing total and 42 of them have sprinkles, so the probability of randomly choosing one with sprinkles is $\frac{42}{124}$, or $\frac{21}{62}$, which is (B).

30. G   Difficulty: High

Category: Statistics and Probability

Getting to the Answer: If an integer is chosen randomly from the first 50 integers, the probability of choosing any particular number is $\frac{1}{50}$, and the probability of choosing an integer with a digit of 3 is the number of integers with a digit of 3 divided by 50. The integers 3, 13, 23, 30, 31, 32, 33, 34, 35, 36, 37, 38, 39, and 43 are the only integers with 3s in them, for a total of 14 different integers, so the probability is $\frac{14}{50}$ or $\frac{7}{25}$, which is (G).

31. B   Difficulty: High

Category: Statistics and Probability

Getting to the Answer: The overall average is not simply the average of the two average ages. Because there are considerably more women than men (80% compared to 20%) and the average age of the women is 30, women carry more weight and the overall average will be closer to 30 than to 35. This means you can eliminate C, D, and E. To choose between A and (B), pick sample numbers for the females and males that meet the criteria that 80% are female and 20% are male. For example, say 8 employees are female and 2 are male. The ages of the 8 females total 8 times 30, or 240, and the ages of the 2 males total 2 times 35, or 70. The average, then, is (240 + 70) divided by 10, or 31. Choice (B) is correct.

32. H   Difficulty: High

Category: Statistics and Probability

Getting to the Answer: Distinct permutations are permutations without repetition. You need to find the number of unique orderings of the letters in the word GEOMETRY. If all eight letters were different, the number of unique orderings would be 8!. The E is repeated, so you must divide by 2! to account for the repeated E. The result is $\frac{8!}{2!}$, which is (H).

Note that this process is the same as using the formula for "indistinguishable" outcomes: $\frac{n!}{a! \times b! \times \cdots}$. The number of letters is 8 (so $n = 8$), and there are 2 indistinguishable Es, so $a = 2$ and there is no b.

33. D   Difficulty: High

Category: Statistics and Probability

Getting to the Answer: Think of each character in the patient identifier as a slot to be filled and use the Fundamental Counting Principle. The first character can be 1 of 24 letters (not 26 because I and O cannot be used) or 1 of 9 numbers (not 10 because the first character cannot be 0), for a total of 33 possibilities for the first character. Each of the remaining characters can be 1 of 24 letters or 1 of 10 numbers, for a total of 34 possibilities for each character. Thus, the total number of possibilities is $33 \times 34 \times 34 \times 34 \times 34 \times 34$, which can be written as 33×34^5. Choice (D) is correct.

34. K   Difficulty: High

Category: Statistics and Probability

Getting to the Answer: Distinct permutations are permutations without repetition. You need to find the number of unique orderings of the letters in the word STATISTICS. If all 10 letters were different, the number of unique orderings would be 10!. However, the S and the T are each repeated three times and the I is repeated twice, so you must divide by 3! to account for the repeated S, by 3! to account for the repeated T, and by 2! to account for the repeated I. The result is $\dfrac{10!}{(3!)(3!)(2!)}$, which is (K).

Note that this process is the same as using the formula for "indistinguishable" outcomes: $\dfrac{n!}{a! \times b! \times \cdots}$. The number of letters is 10 (so $n = 10$), and there are 3 indistinguishable Ss, 3 indistinguishable Ts, and 2 indistinguishable Is (so $a = 3$, $b = 3$, and $c = 2$).

35. C   Difficulty: High

Category: Statistics and Probability

Getting to the Answer: Use the definition of mean and the sum of the weights. Let s = the sum of the weights of the original 17 puppies.

$$\text{mean} = \frac{\text{sum of weights}}{\text{number of puppies}}$$
$$26 = \frac{s}{17}$$
$$s = 442$$

Now, let w be the weight of the final puppy and use the formula again. Don't forget that now there are 18 puppies.

$$27 = \frac{442 + w}{18}$$
$$486 = 442 + w$$
$$w = 44$$

This matches (C).

UNIT THREE

Reading

CHAPTER TWELVE

ACT Reading Test Overview

INSIDE THE ACT READING TEST

The Reading Test is 35 minutes long and includes 40 questions. The test is comprised of four sections, each with either one long passage or two short passages. This means you only have 8–9 minutes to spend on each section. Each section will have 10 multiple-choice questions based on the text. You should spend 3–4 minutes mapping the passage(s) and 4–6 minutes answering the questions. Feel free to skip around within a section and answer the easy questions first. Just make sure to keep track of time so you get to all the questions. The Kaplan Method for ACT Reading will help you answer the questions strategically within the time allowed.

The Format

ACT Reading Passages

The three Reading passages and one Paired Passage set will each be in one of four genres, and these genres will always appear in the same order: Literary Narrative (including prose fiction), Social Science, Humanities, and the Natural Sciences. The Paired Passages will discuss the same or related topics. Always note the genre as you begin reading a passage; your approach will vary slightly according to passage type. Being aware of the genre will also make it easier to identify the passage's central idea, thesis, or theme.

Test Day Directions and Format

Here's what the Reading directions will say on Test Day:

> **DIRECTIONS:** There are several passages in this test. Each passage is accompanied by several questions. After reading a passage, choose the best answer to each question and fill in the corresponding oval on your answer document. You may refer to the passages as often as necessary.

Question Types

ACT Reading questions fall into two general categories: questions that ask about specifically stated information and questions that ask you to make inferences based on the author's intended purpose.

Outside Knowledge

No outside knowledge is required. The answers to every question can be found in the passage.

The Inside Scoop

As noted in the section on test format, the ACT Reading Test always has the same four passage types in the same order. You can expect to see—in order—Literary Narrative (including prose fiction), Social Science, Humanities, and Natural Science passages. Each passage is about 800 words, and the pair of two shorter passages adds up to about 800 words. They are written at the same level of complexity as typical college textbooks and readings.

Paired Passages deal with the same topic or related topics. Some questions ask about only one of the passages, while others ask you to consider both. The passage or passages each question addresses will be clearly labeled. The Paired Passages constitute one of the four sections of the Reading Test, and the questions on these passages will make up about 25% of your Reading score.

The nonfiction passages (Social Science, Humanities, and Natural Science) are written with a clear purpose that you are expected to understand. You'll need to comprehend the author's use of structure as well as the purpose of specific facts relayed in these essays. The Prose Fiction passage, on the other hand, asks about the thoughts, feelings, and motivations of fictional characters, even when these are not explicitly stated in the passage.

The questions *do not* get harder as you proceed through the test.

Timing

Take a few seconds at the beginning of the Reading Test to flip through the four passages, gauging the difficulty of each. Start with the one that best suits your strengths and interests.

Plan to spend 8–9 minutes on each passage. That way, when time is called, you will have looked at all 40 Reading questions and at least gridded in a guess for every question.

Have an organized approach. We recommend that you start with the passage type in which you consistently answer the greatest number of questions correctly. Next, tackle your second and third best passage types, leaving your least successful passage type for last. That way you grab as many points as possible at the beginning, and if you start to run out of time toward the end, you won't be sacrificing points you usually earn on the easier passages.

When You're Running Out of Time

If you have less than five minutes left for the last passage, do the following:

1. Look for questions with specific line references and answer those.
2. Refer to the cited location in the passage and answer the question as best you can, based on what you see there.
3. Make sure you have gridded in an answer for every question before time is called.

Scoring

You will receive a Reading Test score—from 1 to 36—for the entire Reading Test. This score will be averaged into your ACT Composite Score, equally weighted with your scores on the other three major subject tests. You will also receive three other scores based on specific Reading knowledge and concepts. These are called reporting categories and consist of:

*   Key Ideas and Details
*   Craft and Structure
*   Integration of Knowledge and Ideas

QUICK TIPS

Mind-Set

*   **Know where the passage is going.** Read the passage actively, paying attention to structural clues and key words and sentences to predict and evaluate what the passage is "doing." The easiest way to do this is to create a Passage Map.
*   **Conquer the questions.** Look up the answers directly in the passage; don't be tempted by the choices or your memory.
*   **Start with your strengths.** There's no reason to tackle these passages in the order given. Which subject interests you the most? Do you want to do that one first or last? Do you prefer fiction? Science stuff? Passages about people? Get yourself on a roll by starting with the passage that will most help you build confidence and bank your time.

Special Strategies

Paired Passages

If you are tackling a set of Paired Passages, you will want to follow the Kaplan Method for Paired Passages in which you divide and conquer. Here are the steps:

Step 1: Actively read Passage A, then answer its questions

Step 2: Actively read Passage B, then answer its questions

Step 3: Answer questions about both passages

The ACT will make clear which questions relate to Passage A, Passage B, and both Passages A and B, which is very helpful. By concentrating on one passage at a time before you tackle questions that discuss both, you can avoid trap answer choices that refer to the incorrect passage.

Prose Fiction Passages

Pay attention to the characters, especially the main character, and who gets the most (or best) lines. Read between the lines to determine unspoken emotions and attitudes. Ask yourself:

- **Who are these people?** What are they like? How do the characters relate to each other?
- **What is their state of mind?** Are they angry, sad, reflective, excited?
- **What's going on?** What's happening on the surface? What's happening beneath the surface?
- **What is the author's attitude toward the characters?** What words indicate a particular tone? Do any phrases suggest the author is either approving of or critical of one of the characters?

Nonfiction Passages

- **Don't be intimidated by technical vocabulary.** The Natural Science passage may take you into strange territory, but remember: this is the Reading Test, not the Science Test. Everything you need to know will be covered in the passages. If you find a difficult term, odds are the definition will be given to you in context (or else it simply might not matter what the word means).
- **Don't be thrown by unfamiliar topics.** You can get most questions right even if you don't fully understand the passage. Remember, you can find all the answers in the passage.

SMARTPOINTS BREAKDOWN

By studying the information released by the ACT, Kaplan has been able to determine how often certain topics are likely to show up on the test and, therefore, how many points these topics are worth on Test Day. If you master a given topic, you can expect to earn the corresponding number of SmartPoints on Test Day.

Here is a brief overview of what exactly to expect on the ACT Reading Test.

Key Ideas and Details—21 Points

Key Ideas and Details questions make up 55–60% of the Reading Test. The questions in this category require you to determine a text's central ideas and themes, draw logical inferences, and summarize information accurately.

Global—2 Points

The test will require you to identify an author's central idea and purpose. Some concepts you will be tested on include, but are not limited to:

- Choosing a correct summary of the passage as a whole
- Identifying key information within a passage

Inference—5 Points

The test will present both Narrow and Broad Inference questions. Some concepts you will be tested on include, but are not limited to:

- Understanding relationships
- Drawing logical inferences and conclusions

Detail—14 Points

The test will require you to locate key details the author includes in a passage. Some concepts you will be tested on include, but are not limited to:

- Identifying key information within a passage
- Locating specific evidence an author provides

Craft and Structure—11 Points

Craft and Structure questions make up 25–30% of the Reading Test. The questions in this category require an understanding of the author's word choice, text structure, and perspective.

Vocab-in-Context—3 Points

The test will require you to determine word and phrase meanings. Some concepts you will be tested on include, but are not limited to:

- Determining the meaning of a word in context
- Identifying the meaning of a phrase in context

Function—4 Points

The test will require you to demonstrate an understanding of the text structure. You'll need to identify the purpose of portions of a passage. Some concepts you will be tested on include, but are not limited to:

- Analyzing text structure
- Determining the purpose of portions of a passage

Writer's View—4 Points

The test will require you to demonstrate an understanding of an author's perspective. You'll need to identify the author's point of view and differentiate among various perspectives. Some concepts you will be tested on include, but are not limited to:

- Identifying the author's point of view
- Distinguishing among multiple perspectives

Integration of Knowledge and Ideas—4 Points

Knowledge of Language questions make up 13–18% of the Reading Test. The questions in this category are called Synthesis questions, and they require you to understand authors' claims and use facts to make connections between different texts. Some concepts you will be tested on include, but are not limited to:

- Analyzing how authors construct arguments
- Evaluating reasoning and evidence from multiple sources
- Making connections between two short Paired Passages

CHAPTER THIRTEEN

Prose Fiction and Natural Science Passages

GETTING STARTED

Passage Types

In order to read the passage as quickly as possible without missing any information, you should make very short notes in the margin, also known as a Passage Map. Your Passage Map should help you quickly locate information in the passage when you answer questions. Your exact approach to Passage Mapping will vary based on the passage type.

> ✔ *Expert Tip*
>
> **Your Passage Map is an essential part of keeping straight who said what. Use abbreviations and symbols (such as "AM likes EB" or "Sam = hard working") to keep track of the most important ideas within the passage.**

Prose Fiction Passages

Prose Fiction passages are full of characters, relationships, opinions, and themes. Focus on including these important ideas in your **Prose Fiction** Passage Map:

1. Identify the characters and evaluate how the author describes them.
    *   What do the characters want?
    *   What are the characters doing?
    *   What adjectives describe each character?

2. Assess the characters' opinions of each other and themselves.
    *   Do they like each other? Dislike each other?
    *   Why does each character make a particular decision or take a particular course of action?
    *   What do these decisions or actions tell you about a character?

3. Identify the themes of the story.
   - What are the "turning points" in the passage?
   - Is there a moral to the story?

✔ **Expert Tip**

You don't need to memorize the characters and themes of the passage, as you might for the passages you read for your English or Literature classes. Instead, you need to know *where* to go in the passage to find either the answers themselves or the evidence to support the answers.

Natural Science Passages

Natural Science passages are full of details and uncommon terminology. Focus on including these important ideas in your **Natural Science** Passage Map:

1. Locate the central idea in the first paragraph.

✔ **Note**

When you encounter more than one theory or idea, paraphrase each in as few words as possible in your Passage Map.

2. Note how each paragraph relates to the central idea. Does the paragraph . . .
   - Explain?
   - Support?
   - Refute?
   - Summarize?

✔ **Expert Tip**

Note the location of explanations and examples so you can find them quickly if needed for a question.

3. Don't be distracted by jargon or technical terms.
   - Unfamiliar terms will generally be defined within the passage or in a footnote.

4. Don't try to learn or thoroughly understand complicated scientific ideas.
   - Note the *location* of detailed examples/explanations in your Passage Map.
   - Return to the location in the passage if you need the information for a question.

5. Summarize the purpose of the passage.
   - Some common purposes include: to inform, to refute, to promote, to explore, to compare.
   - Note the author's tone. Were there any positive or negative keywords? If not, the author's tone is neutral.
   - Pay particular attention to emphasis and opinion keywords. **Natural Science** passages may discuss how newer studies have modified older theories or different views on a discovery. Keep careful track of the opinions, and be sure to identify the author's opinion.

The different approaches to reading and mapping **Prose Fiction** and **Natural Science** passages are summarized in the table below.

Passage Type(s)	Approach
Prose Fiction (includes **Literary Narrative**)	• Note the author's central ideas and themes • Note characters' personalities, opinions, and relationships with each other
Natural Science	• Identify the author's thesis • Note the main idea of each paragraph • Don't let technical scientific terms intimidate you; no outside science knowledge is needed • Note the definitions of scientific terms that are provided within the passage text (or passage introduction)

IMPROVING WITH PRACTICE

Step 1: Compare Your Notes to the Suggested Prose Fiction or Natural Science Passage Maps

After reading a passage, compare your notes to the suggested Passage Map to be sure you generally included the same important points. Abbreviations and symbols are both very useful when creating Passage Maps, especially if you have a hard time finishing the Reading Test before time is called. Passage Mapping is very personal, and it's just fine if your map is different—even very different!—as long as you captured the following information for these two passage types:

Prose Fiction

- The *location* of the characters
- The *location* of descriptive details
- Major events
- Themes of the passage

Natural Science

- The central idea/theory discussed
- The relationship of each paragraph to the central idea. Is the paragraph explaining, supporting, criticizing, modifying, or applying the central idea?
- Any opinions, especially the author's

- The *location* of descriptive details and examples
- The *reason* the author included details and examples. Is the author using the information to support, modify, or refute the preceding idea?
- Any emphasis or "emotional" keywords. Keywords such as "remarkable," "unfortunate," "unprecedented," and "crucial" are important indicators of the author's tone.

> ✔ *Expert Tip*
>
> Some paragraphs are longer than others. If you are mapping a very long paragraph, you can write two or three short notes rather than trying to fit everything into just one long note.

If you missed important information, go back to the **Prose Fiction** or **Natural Science** passage and identify the keywords that you likely overlooked so you can recognize them more quickly next time. The ACT uses predictable keywords to alert you to the important ideas in the passage. Use these keywords to focus your attention and create strong Passage Maps.

Step 2: Answer the Questions

After you've reviewed and strengthened your **Prose Fiction** or **Natural Science** Passage Map, complete the questions one at a time. Review the Answer and Explanation for every question immediately after completing it. If you got the question correct, congratulate yourself, but take a moment to read the entire explanation to be sure you got the question right for the right reason. The explanation may even point out a more efficient way that you can use on a later question!

> ✔ *Expert Tip*
>
> Prove your answer from the passage before you pick it! You can be as confident of your Reading Test answers as you are of your Math Test answers because you will always be able to support the correct answer from the passage.

Step 3: Review Incorrect Answers

If you get the question incorrect . . . still congratulate yourself! You're about to learn something new that you'll be able to use to improve your performance on Test Day. Don't read the explanation yet; instead, try the question again.

If you get the question correct the second time, read the explanation to see if you solved the question in the most efficient way. Identify the mistake you made the first time, and determine how you're going to avoid making that mistake again.

> ✔ **Expert Tip**
>
> Many top scoring students have an ACT notebook where they write down what they learn from every question. Doing this can be time-consuming, but it can also help you identify the types of mistakes you tend to make.

If you get the question incorrect the second time, use the explanation to learn how to get the question correct. Work through the question again while following the explanation, and identify the steps you will need to take to get a similar question correct. Although the passages and questions will change, the concepts being tested will not. When you encounter unfamiliar questions, take note of them for future study sessions.

> ✔ **Note**
>
> The ACT is a standardized test. While high-difficulty Reading questions are usually more difficult to answer than lower- or medium-difficulty questions, they are often similar in structure and purpose, and the same skills (listed in Chapter 12) are tested on every Reading Test. You actually can predict the types of questions you will see on Test Day!

After all that work, it's time to move to the next question. Reviewing in this way will take time. However, improvement doesn't come from just doing lots and lots of questions; it comes from thinking through your approach and improving it with every question.

RAISING YOUR SCORE EVEN MORE

Once your **Prose Fiction** and **Natural Science** Passage Maps are accurate and quickly leading you to the correct answers, it's time to return to the completed passages and study which sections of the passages were the source of the correct answers. When studying the source of each answer, look for the keywords the author used to indicate that section was important. Recognizing keywords helps you to know when to slow down and read carefully, such as when reading an introductory paragraph or an opinion, and when you can speed up and read superficially, such as when reading the middle of a body paragraph full of details or long explanations. Note the *location* of this information in your map, and if needed, return to this section of the passage if a question asks about it.

> ✔ **Expert Tip**
>
> Unlike the exams you prepare for in your classes, the ACT is an open-book test. You don't need to memorize or thoroughly understand the content of the passage. You need to know the *location* in the passage where you will look up the answers to the exact questions asked.

PRACTICE QUESTIONS

The following test-like question sets provide an opportunity to practice reading Prose Fiction and Natural Science Passages and answering related questions.

PASSAGE I

PROSE FICTION: This passage is adapted from *The Age of Innocence,* by Edith Wharton (1920).

It was generally agreed in New York that the Countess Olenska had "lost her looks."

She had appeared there first, in Newland Archer's boyhood, as a brilliantly pretty little
5 girl of nine or ten, of whom people said that she "ought to be painted." Her parents had been continental wanderers, and after a roaming babyhood she had lost them both, and been taken in charge by her aunt, Medora
10 Manson, also a wanderer, who was herself returning to New York to "settle down."

Poor Medora, repeatedly widowed, was always coming home to settle down (each time in a less expensive house), and bringing with
15 her a new husband or an adopted child, but after a few months she invariably parted from her husband or quarrelled with her ward, and, having got rid of her house at a loss, set out again on her wanderings. As her mother had
20 been a Rushworth, and her last unhappy marriage had linked her to one of the crazy Chiverses, New York looked indulgently on her eccentricities, but when she returned with her little orphaned niece, whose parents had
25 been popular in spite of their regrettable taste for travel, people thought it a pity that the pretty child should be in such hands.

Everyone was disposed to be kind to little Ellen Mingott, though her dusky red cheeks
30 and tight curls gave her an air of gaiety that seemed unsuitable in a child who should still

have been in black for her parents. It was one of the misguided Medora's many peculiarities to flout the unalterable rules that regulated
35 American mourning, and when she stepped from the steamer her family was scandalized to see that the crepe veil she wore for her own brother was seven inches shorter than those of her sisters-in-law, while little Ellen wore a
40 crimson dress and amber beads.

But New York had so long resigned itself to Medora that only a few old ladies shook their heads over Ellen's gaudy clothes, while her other relations fell under the charm of her
45 high spirits. She was a fearless and familiar little thing, who asked disconcerting questions, made precocious comments, and possessed outlandish arts, such as dancing a Spanish shawl dance and singing Neapolitan
50 love-songs to a guitar. Under the direction of her aunt, the little girl received an expensive but incoherent education, which included "drawing from the model," a thing never dreamed of before, and playing the piano in
55 quintets with professional musicians.

Of course no good could come of this, and when, a few years later, poor Chivers finally died, his widow again pulled up stakes and departed with Ellen, who had grown into a tall
60 bony girl with conspicuous eyes. For some time no more was heard of them; then news came of Ellen's marriage to an immensely rich Polish nobleman of legendary fame. She disappeared,

and when a few years later Medora again came
65 back to New York, subdued, impoverished,
mourning a third husband, and in quest of a
still smaller house, people wondered that her
rich niece had not been able to do something
for her. Then came the news that Ellen's own
70 marriage had ended in disaster, and that she
was herself returning home to seek rest and
oblivion among her kinsfolk.

These things passed through Newland
Archer's mind a week later as he watched the
75 Countess Olenska enter the van der Luyden
drawing room on the evening of the momen-
tous dinner. In the middle of the room she
paused, looking about her with a grave mouth
and smiling eyes, and in that instant, Newland
80 Archer rejected the general verdict on her
looks. It was true that her early radiance
was gone. The red cheeks had paled; she was
thin, worn, a little older-looking than her age,
which must have been nearly thirty. But there
85 was about her the mysterious authority of
beauty, a sureness in the carriage of the head,
the movement of the eyes, which, without
being in the least theatrical, struck him as
highly trained and full of a conscious power.
90 At the same time she was simpler in manner
than most of the ladies present, and many people (as he heard afterward) were disappointed
that her appearance was not more "stylish"—
for stylishness was what New York most
95 valued. It was, perhaps, Archer reflected,
because her early vivacity had disappeared;
because she was so quiet—quiet in her move-
ments, her voice, and the tones of her voice.
New York had expected something a good deal
100 more resonant in a young woman with such a
history.

1. The author describes which of the following
practices as undesirable to New York society?

A. Playing the piano

B. Performing Spanish shawl dances

C. Traveling

D. Adopting children

2. With which of the following would the author
most likely agree regarding New York society
as it pertains to Medora?

F. It is rigid and unaccepting of different
behavior.

G. It is usually whimsical, with few solid rules.

H. It is often based on unrealistic
expectations.

J. It is snobbish but occasionally accepting
of less common behavior.

3. It is most reasonable to infer that, after the
death of Medora's third husband, Ellen did
not help her aunt primarily because:

A. Ellen was no longer wealthy, since her
own marriage had failed.

B. Medora had become embittered because
she hadn't heard from Ellen for so long.

C. Ellen resented the incoherent education
she received from her aunt.

D. receiving help from her niece would
interfere with Medora's desire to be
eccentric.

4. Based on the characterization of Newland
Archer in the last paragraph, he can best be
described as:

F. reflective and nonjudgmental.

G. likable but withdrawn.

H. disinterested but fair.

J. stylish and gregarious.

5. In her descriptions of Medora, the author intends to give the impression that Medora is:

    A. eccentric and peripatetic.

    B. impoverished and resentful.

    C. kind and loyal.

    D. precocious and pretty.

6. As it is used in line 34, the word *flout* most nearly means:

    F. eliminate.

    G. exemplify.

    H. disregard.

    J. float.

7. What does the narrator suggest is a central characteristic of Medora Manson?

    A. Arrogance

    B. Immodesty

    C. Non-conformity

    D. Orthodoxy

8. Which of the following characters learns to do something otherwise unheard of by New York society?

    F. Ellen Mingott

    G. Newland Archer

    H. Medora Manson

    J. Count Olenska

9. The author includes reference to Medora's mother and Medora's marriage to "one of the crazy Chiverses" (lines 21-22) in order to indicate that:

    A. she had an unhappy childhood.

    B. her eccentricities were not surprising.

    C. she was the perfect person to raise Ellen.

    D. she was a wanderer.

10. One can reasonably infer from the passage that on the occasion of the dinner, Newland and Ellen:

    F. had not seen each other for some time.

    G. were interested in becoming romantically involved.

    H. were both disappointed with New York society.

    J. had just met, but were immediately attracted to each other.

PASSAGE II

NATURAL SCIENCE: The following is adapted from Wikipedia articles titled "Lemur" and "Ring-tailed Lemur."

Lemurs are part of a suborder of primates known as prosimians, and make up the infraorder Lemuriformes. This type of primate was the evolutionary predecessor of monkeys
5 and apes (simians). The term "lemur" is derived from the Latin word *lemures*, which means "spirits of the night." This likely refers to many lemurs' nocturnal behavior and their large, reflective eyes. It is generically used for
10 the members of the four lemuriform families, but it is also the genus of one of the lemuriform species. The two flying lemur species are not lemurs, nor are they even primates.

Lemurs are found naturally only on the
15 island of Madagascar and some smaller surrounding islands, including the Comoros (where it is likely they were introduced by humans). While they were displaced in the rest of the world by monkeys, apes, and other
20 primates, the lemurs were safe from competition on Madagascar and differentiated into a number of species. These range in size from the tiny 30-gram pygmy mouse lemur to the 10-kilogram indri. The larger species have all
25 become extinct since humans settled on Madagascar, and since the early twentieth century the largest lemurs reach about seven kilograms. Typically, the smaller lemurs are active at night (nocturnal), while the larger
30 ones are active during the day (diurnal).

All lemurs are endangered species, due mainly to habitat destruction (deforestation) and hunting. Although conservation efforts are underway, options are limited because of the
35 lemurs' limited range and because Madagascar is desperately poor. Currently, there are approximately 32 living lemur species.

The ring-tailed lemur is a relatively large prosimian, belonging to the family Lemuridae.
40 Ring-tailed lemurs are the only species within the genus *Lemur* and are found only on the island of Madagascar. Although threatened by habitat destruction and therefore listed as vulnerable by the IUCN Red List, ring-tailed
45 lemurs are the most populous lemurs in zoos worldwide; they reproduce readily in captivity.

Mostly grey with white underparts, ring-tailed lemurs have slender frames; their narrow faces are white with black lozenge-shaped patches
50 around the eyes and black vulpine muzzles. The lemurs' trademark, their long, bushy tails, are ringed in black and white. Like all lemurs, ring-tailed lemurs have hind limbs longer than their forelimbs; their palms and soles are padded with
55 soft, leathery skin, and their fingers are slender and dexterous. On the second toe of their hind limbs, ring-tailed lemurs have claws specialized for grooming purposes.

The very young animals have blue eyes,
60 while the eyes of all adults are a striking yellow. Adults may reach a body length of 46 centimeters (18 inches) and a weight of 5.5 kilograms (12 pounds). Their tails are longer than their bodies, at up to 56 centimeters
65 (22 inches) in length.

Found in the southwest of Madagascar and ranging farther into highland areas than any other lemur, ring-tailed lemurs inhabit deciduous forests with grass floors or forests
70 along riverbanks (gallery forests); some may also inhabit dry, open brush where few trees grow. Ring-tailed lemurs are thought to require primary forest (that is, forests that have

remained undisturbed by human activity) in
75 order to survive; such forests are now being
cleared at a troubling rate.

While primarily frugivores (fruit-eating),
ring-tailed lemurs will also eat leaves, seeds, and
the odd insect. Ring-tailed lemurs are diurnal
80 and primarily arboreal animals, forming troops
of up to 25 individuals. Social hierarchies are
determined by sex, with a distinct hierarchy for
each gender; females tend to dominate the
troop, while males will alternate between
85 troops. Lemurs claim a sizable territory, which
does not overlap with those of other troops; up
to 5.6 kilometers (3.5 miles) of this territory
may be covered in a single day's foraging.

Both vocal and olfactory signals are impor-
90 tant to ring-tailed lemurs' communication: 15
distinct vocalizations are used. A fatty substance
is exuded from the lemurs' glands, which the lemurs run their tails through; this scent is used
by both sexes to mark territory and to challenge
95 would-be rivals amongst males. The males vig-
orously wave their tails high in the air in an attempt to overpower the scent of others.

The breeding season runs from April to
June, with the female fertile period lasting for
100 only a day. Gestation lasts for about 146 days,
resulting in a litter of either one or two. The
young lemurs begin to eat solid food after two
months and are fully weaned after five months.

11. According to the passage, lemurs survived on
the island of Madagascar because:

A. their large, reflective eyes allowed them
to move around at night when predators
were asleep.

B. their ability to mark their territory by
scent gave them adequate territory for
foraging.

C. monkeys, apes, and other primates were
not a threat to them on Madagascar.

D. their strong social hierarchy allowed
them to band together for safety.

12. According to the passage, the social
organization of the ring-tailed lemur:

F. places females at the top of the hierarchy.

G. functions to ensure adequate food supplies.

H. has followed the same structure since
antiquity.

J. is notable for its equality of the sexes.

13. As it is used in line 79, the word *odd* most
nearly means:

A. strange.

B. unusual.

C. eerie.

D. occasional.

14. According to the passage, why are ring-tails
the most populous species of lemurs in zoos?

F. They inhabit deciduous forests, which
make the lemurs' capture relatively easy.

G. They have no difficulty giving birth in a
zoo environment.

H. Their attractive appearance makes them
popular with patrons.

J. Their eating preferences are easily
accommodated.

15. The passage suggests that the rate at which primary forests are being cleared is "troubling" (line 76) because:

    A. it is causing significant soil erosion in the lemurs' primary habitat.

    B. valuable hardwoods are being destroyed.

    C. lemurs' predators inhabit the cleared area.

    D. lemurs need to live in primary forests to survive.

16. All of the following are given as ways in which ring-tailed lemurs use olfactory signals EXCEPT:

    F. to put male challengers on notice.

    G. to mask the scent of other lemurs.

    H. to signify group identification.

    J. to mark their territory.

17. According to the passage, which of the following describes a characteristic of the infraorder Lemuriformes?

    A. They are nocturnal.

    B. They evolved before monkeys and apes did.

    C. They include two species of flying lemurs.

    D. They are found only on Madagascar.

18. Which of the following can reasonably be inferred from information in the second paragraph (lines 14-30)?

    F. The pygmy mouse lemur is diurnal.

    G. The larger species of lemur were hunted for their fur.

    H. The indri lemur is extinct.

    J. Lemurs are descended from monkeys.

19. When ring-tailed lemurs grow from young animals to adults:

    A. they become less aggressive.

    B. they no longer need primary forests.

    C. their eye color changes.

    D. they become known as flying lemurs.

20. Which of the following questions is NOT answered by the passage?

    F. Will conservationists be able to prevent the extinction of lemurs?

    G. Why did lemurs survive on Madagascar?

    H. How many offspring can a female lemur produce per year?

    J. What makes up the lemur's diet?

PASSAGE III

PROSE FICTION: This passage is adapted from *Howard's End*, by E.M. Forster (1910). Two sisters, Helen and Margaret, are attending an orchestra performance with friends and family.

It will be generally admitted that Beethoven's *Fifth Symphony* is the most sublime noise that has ever penetrated into the ear of man. All sorts and conditions are satisfied
5 by it. Whether you are like Mrs. Munt, and tap surreptitiously when the tunes come—of course, not so as to disturb the others—or like Helen, who can see heroes and shipwrecks in the music's flood; or like Margaret, who can
10 only see the music; or like Tibby, who is profoundly versed in counterpoint, and holds the full score of the symphony open on his knee; or like Fraulein Mosebach's young man, who can remember nothing but Fraulein
15 Mosebach: in any case, the passion of your life becomes more vivid, and you are bound to admit that such a noise is cheap at two shillings. It is cheap, even if you hear it in the Queen's Hall, dreariest music-room in London, though
20 not as dreary as the Free Trade Hall, Manchester; and even if you sit on the extreme left of that hall, so that the brass bumps at you before the rest of the orchestra arrives, it is still cheap.

"Whom is Margaret talking to?" said Mrs.
25 Munt, at the conclusion of the first movement. She was again in London on a visit to Wickham Place.

Helen looked down the long line of their party, and said that she did not know.

30 "Would it be some young man or other whom she takes an interest in?"

"I expect so," Helen replied. Music enwrapped her, and she could not be bothered by the distinction that divides young men whom

35 one takes an interest in from young men whom one knows.

"You girls are so wonderful in always having—Oh dear! One mustn't talk."

For the Andante had begun—very beautiful,
40 but bearing a family likeness to all the other beautiful andantes that Beethoven had written, and, to Helen's mind, rather disconnecting the heroes and shipwrecks of the first movement from the heroes and goblins of the third. She
45 heard the tune through once, and then her attention wandered, and she gazed at the audience, or the organ, or the architecture. Then Beethoven started decorating his tune, so she heard him through once more, and then
50 she smiled at her Cousin Frieda. But Frieda, listening to classical music, could not respond. Herr Liesecke, too, looked as if wild horses could not make him inattentive; there were lines across his forehead, his lips were parted,
55 his glasses at right angles to his nose, and he had laid a thick, white hand on either knee. And next to her was Aunt Juley, so British, and wanting to tap. How interesting that row of people was! What diverse influences had gone
60 into the making of them! Here Beethoven, after humming and hawing with great sweetness, said "Heigho," and the Andante came to an end. Applause ensued, and a round of praise volleying from the audience. Margaret
65 started talking to her new young man; Helen said to her aunt: "Now comes the wonderful movement: first of all the goblins, and then a trio of elephants dancing"; and Tibby implored

the company generally to look out for the
70 transitional passage on the drum.

"On the what, dear?"

"On the drum, Aunt Juley."

"No—look out for the part where you think
you are done with the goblins and they come
75 back," breathed Helen, as the music started
with a goblin walking quietly over the universe, from end to end. Others followed him.
They were not aggressive creatures; that was
what made them so terrible to Helen. They
80 merely observed in passing that there was no
such thing as splendor or heroism in the world.
Helen could not contradict them, for once, she
had felt the same, and had seen the reliable
walls of youth collapse. Panic and emptiness!
85 Panic and emptiness! The goblins were right.
Her brother raised his finger; it was the transitional passage on the drum.

Helen pushed her way out during the applause. She desired to be alone. The music had
90 summed up to her all that had happened or
could happen in her life.

She read it as a tangible statement, which
could never be superseded. The notes meant
this and that to her, and they could have no
95 other meaning, and life could have no other
meaning. She pushed right out of the building
and walked slowly down the outside staircase,
breathing the autumnal air, and then she
strolled home.

21. Helen would most likely agree with which of
the following statements about her
relationship with Margaret?

A. Helen disapproves of Margaret's actions.

B. Helen's feelings toward Margaret are
affected by Helen's jealousy of the
attention Margaret receives from suitors.

C. Helen is not interested in Margaret's
actions, at least as long as the music is
playing.

D. They are drawn together principally by
their mutual love of music.

22. Helen can most accurately be characterized
as:

F. creative and effervescent.

G. analytical yet optimistic.

H. imaginative and introspective.

J. curt and insensitive.

23. Which of the following statements does NOT
describe one of Helen's reactions to the
goblins?

A. She feels that their presence is a denial of
the good in the world.

B. She is frightened by the goblins'
aggressive nature.

C. She cannot deny the viewpoint that the
goblins seem to represent.

D. She believes that the goblins will return
after they appear to have left.

24. As it is used in line 48, the word *decorating*
most nearly means:

F. dressing up.

G. glamorizing.

H. awarding.

J. embellishing.

25. Which of the following does the author mention as images the music brings to the listeners' minds?

   A. Wild horses

   B. Shipwrecks

   C. Queen's Hall

   D. Drums

26. According to the passage, when Tibby listens to the symphony he is:

   F. most interested in the technical aspects of the music.

   G. caught up in imagery that the music conveys to him.

   H. distracted from the performance as a whole because of his focus on the drum.

   J. depressed by his dreary surroundings.

27. Which of the following statements most accurately expresses Helen's feelings as she leaves after the symphony?

   A. Helen feels alienated by the indifference of her companions.

   B. Helen is meditative, pondering the music's immutable meaning.

   C. Helen is upset with Tibby's constant focus on the technical aspects of the music.

   D. Helen is relieved to have escaped the crowding and discomfort of the performance hall.

28. It can most reasonably be inferred from the passage that the reason Aunt Juley refrains from tapping along with the music is because:

   F. Aunt Juley is concentrating instead on the drum.

   G. Aunt Juley does not want to distract Helen.

   H. British custom only permits snapping one's fingers along with the music.

   J. Aunt Juley feels it would not be appropriate.

29. All of the following characters are deeply interested in the music EXCEPT:

   A. Herr Liesecke.

   B. Margaret.

   C. Fraulein Mosebach's young man.

   D. Tibby.

30. According to the passage, the reason why Helen's attention returns to the Andante after it had wandered is because she:

   F. hears changes in the tune.

   G. is directed to do so by Tibby.

   H. no longer wishes to speak with Mrs. Munt.

   J. believes the Andante is nearing its end.

PASSAGE IV

NATURAL SCIENCE: The following passage appeared in *Science* magazine as "Pluto: The Planet That Never Was" by Govert Schilling. (© Science, Inc., 1999)

Nearly 70 years ago, Pluto became the ninth member of the sun's family of planets, but now it's on the verge of being cast out of that exclusive clan. The International Astronomical
5 Union (IAU) is collecting votes on how to re-classify the icy body: as the first (and largest) of the so-called trans-Neptunian objects, or as the 10,000th entry in the growing list of minor bodies orbiting the sun. In either case, Pluto
10 may officially lose its planetary status, leaving the solar system with only eight planets.

Children's books and planetariums may not acknowledge the loss. And Brian Marsden of the Harvard-Smithsonian Center for
15 Astrophysics in Cambridge, Massachusetts, who launched the discussion six years ago, says no one is trying to demote Pluto. "If anything, we're going to add to Pluto's status," he says, "by giving it the honor of a very
20 special designation."

Cold comfort for Pluto, maybe, but its reclas-sification will at least end a long identity crisis, which began soon after its 1930 discovery at Lowell Observatory in Flagstaff, Arizona, by
25 Clyde Tombaugh, who died in 1997. Pluto turned out to be much smaller than all the other planets (according to recent estimates, its diam-eter is only 2,200 kilometers), and its orbit is strangely elongated. It didn't belong with either
30 the Earth-like rocky planets or the gas giants.

A clue to its true nature came in 1992, when David Jewitt of the University of Hawaii, Honolulu, and Jane Luu, then at the University of California, Berkeley, discovered a small, icy
35 object beyond the orbit of Neptune. Provisionally cataloged as 1992 QB1, this ice dwarf measures a mere 200 kilometers in diameter. Since then many more trans-Neptunian objects (TNOs) have been detected, some of which move in very Pluto-like
40 orbits around the sun. These "supercomets" populate the Kuiper Belt, named after Dutch-American astronomer Gerard Kuiper, who pre-dicted its existence in the early 1950s. "Pluto fits the picture [of the solar system] much better if it's
45 viewed as a TNO," says Luu, who is now at Leiden University in the Netherlands.

At present, more than 70 TNOs are known, and apparently, Pluto is just the largest mem-ber of this new family, which explains why it
50 was found more than 60 years before number two. If astronomers had known about the other TNOs back in the 1930s, Pluto would never have attained the status of a planet, Luu says: "Pluto was lucky."

55 A couple of months ago, the kinship be-tween Pluto and the TNOs led Richard Binzel of the Massachusetts Institute of Technology to propose that Pluto be made the first entry in a new catalog of TNOs for which precise orbits
60 have been determined. It would then enter the textbooks as something like TN-1 (or TN-0, as some astronomers have suggested).

Marsden agrees that Pluto is a TNO, but he doesn't like the idea of establishing a new
65 catalog of solar system objects, arguing that astronomers already have a perfectly service-able list of numbered minor bodies (mostly asteroids). "The question is: Do we want to recognize [trans-Neptunian objects] with a
70 different designation?" he asks. He points out

that the Centaurs—TNOs that have been nudged well inside Neptune's orbit—have been classified as asteroids and says he sees "no reason for introducing a new designation system
75 for objects of which we have representations in the current [catalog of minor bodies]."

Instead of making Pluto the founding member of a new catalog, Marsden wants to add it to the existing list. "The current number
80 is 9826," he says. "With the current detection rate, we should arrive at number 10,000 some- where in January or February." He notes that asteroids 1000, 2000, 3000, and so on have all been honored by the IAU with special names,
85 including Leonardo and Isaac Newton. "What better way to honor Pluto than to give it this very special number?"

But the prospect of lumping Pluto with the solar system's riffraff outrages supporters of a
90 new TNO category. "It's the most idiotic thing" she's ever heard, says Luu. "Pluto is certainly not an asteroid," she says.

To try to settle the issue, Mike A'Hearn of the University of Maryland, College Park, is
95 collecting e-mail votes from 500 or so members of IAU divisions on the solar system, comets and asteroids, and other relevant top- ics. "I wanted to arrive at a consensus before Christmas [1998]," he says, "but it may take a
100 while, since the community as a whole doesn't seem to have a consensus." Neither proposal has attracted a majority. Although many people opposed Marsden's proposal, a compa- rable number were unhappy with Binzel's idea,
105 A'Hearn says, because Pluto would still be an anomaly, being much larger than the other trans-Neptunian objects. A'Hearn says that if no consensus can be reached, Pluto will probably not end up in any catalog at all, mak-
110 ing it the ultimate outcast of the solar system.

However the debate settles out, Pluto's career as a planet seems to be ending, and even astronomers are wistful at the prospect. "No one likes to lose a planet," says Luu. A'Hearn
115 agrees. "It will probably always be called the ninth planet" by the general public, he says.

31. According to the passage, regarding the view that Pluto should be categorized as an asteroid, Jane Luu expressed which of the following?

  A. Shock

  B. Excitement

  C. Confusion

  D. Forceful opposition

32. It can be inferred that Pluto's original designation as a planet would have never happened if scientists had:

  F. understood its size from the beginning.

  G. seen the icy core of Pluto sooner.

  H. been able to detect the many smaller TNOs when Pluto was discovered.

  J. understood the popular misconceptions about Pluto's planet-hood that would follow.

33. With which of the following statements would the author agree in regard to reclassifying Pluto?

  A. It should be classified as a TNO.

  B. It should be classified as an IAU.

  C. It should remain a planet.

  D. Its future classification is unclear.

34. According to the passage, large objects similar to the makeup and orbit of Pluto found nearer to the sun than Neptune are called:

    F. Centaurs.

    G. IAUs.

    H. TNOs.

    J. ice dwarves.

35. According to lines 68-76, the central issue in the debate over Pluto is:

    A. whether Pluto is more similar to rocky planets or the gas giants.

    B. the distance of Pluto from the sun.

    C. whether or not the unique qualities of Pluto warrant the creation of a new classification category for all TNOs.

    D. scientists' conception of Pluto versus the view of the general public.

36. As used in lines 66-67, the term *serviceable* most nearly means:

    F. able to be fixed.

    G. adequate.

    H. beneficial.

    J. durable.

37. One slightly less scientific concern expressed by most of the scientists in the passage is:

    A. the role of the IAU in making classification decisions.

    B. respect for the views of the public.

    C. who gets the credit for Pluto's reclassification.

    D. the preservation of Pluto's fame and importance.

38. According to the passage, what is the major reason for lack of consensus regarding the status of Pluto?

    F. The general population resists the scientific community's belief that Pluto is not a planet.

    G. Pluto seems very different than the other members of any classification.

    H. Pluto's strange orbit makes it asteroid-like, but its surface more closely resembles a planet.

    J. There have been numerous discoveries of other Pluto-like objects nearer to the sun than to Neptune.

39. Details in the passage suggest that Pluto is much different from other planets in:

    A. its distance from the sun and the shape of its orbit.

    B. its size and the shape of its orbit.

    C. the year of its discovery and its size.

    D. its shape and surface composition.

40. Pluto's size accounts for:

    F. its classification as a TNO.

    G. its dissimilarity to asteroids.

    H. its early discovery relative to other TNOs.

    J. its bizarre orbit.

ANSWERS AND EXPLANATIONS

PASSAGE I

Suggested Passage Map notes:

¶1: Countess Olenska (CO) no longer pretty

¶2: CO 1st in NY as little girl adopted by aunt Medora (M)

¶3: M repeatedly widowed, NY accepting of M's eccentricities

¶4: All kind to Ellen (E) [aka CO], M not follow mourning rules

¶5: E was well-liked, fearless child; E's odd edu.

¶6: E married Polish nobleman, ended in disaster

¶7: NY expected CO to be more stylish and vibrant

1. C   Difficulty: Low

Category: Detail

Getting to the Answer: Remember that the correct answer to Detail questions will be directly stated in the passage. Your notes should guide you as you locate specific references to the details in question. Line 23 mentions Ellen's parents' "regrettable taste for travel" in the context of lines describing what the people of New York thought. Predict something like "travel." Choice (C) matches this prediction. Choice A is a misused detail; Medora does teach her niece to play the piano, but nothing in the passage suggests that this was undesirable. Choice B is a misused detail; Spanish shawl dances are described as *outlandish*, but this is within the context of Medora and Ellen's eccentric, but accepted, behaviors. Choice D is a misused detail; while Medora often adopted children, this is never described as undesirable.

2. J   Difficulty: High

Category: Writer's View

Getting to the Answer: Consider how the author writes about New York society. In lines 26-27, she writes that "people thought it a pity that the pretty child [Ellen] should be in such hands," meaning that they did not feel the eccentric Medora was a good influence on Ellen. People call Medora *misguided* (line 33), and the author notes that she scandalized her family by not adhering to the *unalterable rules* of mourning (line 34). All in all, New York society seems to have some rigid and snobbish rules. On the other hand, New York "looked indulgently on her [Medora's] eccentricities" (lines 22-23) and "resigned itself to Medora," (lines 41-42). The author's view of New York society as it pertains to Medora seems to be mixed, which matches (J). Choice F doesn't take into account New York society's acceptance of Medora's odd behavior, G is opposite, and H is not mentioned in the passage.

3. A   Difficulty: Medium

Category: Inference

Getting to the Answer: To answer Inference questions, you will have to go beyond what is directly stated in the passage. However, the correct answer choice will be supported by evidence from the passage, so make sure you make a prediction that has solid textual support. You can predict, based on lines 56-72, that Ellen was unable to help her aunt because her own marriage to the immensely rich Polish nobleman "had ended in disaster." Choice (A) matches this prediction. Choice B is a distortion; since both Medora and Ellen left New York, their communication over the years is unknown. Choice C is a distortion; while the author tells you that Ellen had an incoherent education, nothing in the passage suggests that she resented this. Choice D is a distortion; though the passage makes it clear that Medora was eccentric, this is in no way related to receiving help from her niece.

4. F   Difficulty: Medium

Category: Global

Getting to the Answer: Global questions require you to synthesize information, sometimes from the entire passage. Predicting an answer is particularly important for questions like this. Make sure you can support your prediction with information in the passage. Lines 73-74 suggest that Newland has spent time thinking about Ellen, and lines 77-95 all describe Newland's observations of Ellen. Newland is not disappointed that Ellen is not as *stylish* as others expected (lines 91-93). You can predict that Newland is thoughtful and, unlike many of the other characters in the passage, non-judgmental. Choice (F) matches this prediction. Choice G is out of scope; it might seem reasonable to conclude that Newland is likeable, but the passage does not provide any evidence to directly support this. Also, there is nothing to suggest that he is withdrawn. Choice H is opposite; Newland's observations about Ellen in the last paragraph clearly indicate that he is interested in her. Choice J is a distortion; Newland's observation that Ellen is not as stylish as New York society might expect says nothing about his own stylishness, nor does the author ever describe his level of sociability.

5. A   Difficulty: Medium

Category: Writer's View

Getting to the Answer: Wharton writes that Medora has "many peculiarities," (line 33), and that "New York looked indulgently on her eccentricities" (lines 22-23). This matches the first part of (A). Since you may not know what peripatetic means, hold on to (A) while you research the other answers. Though Wharton states that each time Medora returns to New York she looks for a less expensive house, indicating reduced circumstances, this doesn't necessarily mean that Medora is impoverished, and there is no suggestion that she is resentful. Eliminate B. Medora may be kind (she does, after all, take in orphaned Ellen), but loyal doesn't describe someone who "invariably parted from her husband or quarrelled

with her ward" (lines 16-17), eliminating C. Choice D mixes up Medora with Ellen; these words describe Ellen as a child, so D is incorrect. Choice (A) must be correct, even if you don't know that peripatetic means "traveling from place to place."

6. H   Difficulty: Medium

Category: Vocab-in-Context

Getting to the Answer: The word *flout* is used in the author's description of Medora wearing a veil considered too short for acceptable mourning and dressing Ellen in "a crimson dress and amber beads" (lines 36-37). Both of these are examples of Medora's "misguided . . . many peculiarities" (line 33), which go against accepted New York behavior. Thus (H), *disregard*, is a good match. Choice F is too strong to describe Medora's behavior, as she does partially follow, rather than totally eliminate, the rules of mourning. Choice G is opposite, and while J looks close to the word *flout*, it doesn't make sense in the passage.

7. C   Difficulty: Medium

Category: Global

Getting to the Answer: Make sure you have good evidence for your prediction, and the right answer choice will be easy to find. Line 23 mentions Medora's *eccentricities*, line 33 mentions her *peculiarities*, and line 48 mentions the *outlandish arts* that Medora teaches Ellen. From these descriptions, you can predict that Medora is unconventional or eccentric. Choice (C) matches this prediction. Choice A is out of scope; although Medora does not adhere to conventions, as indicated by lines 33-35, there is nothing to suggest that this is attributable to arrogance. Choice B is a distortion; the description of the short veil that Medora wore to her brother's funeral in lines 37-39 might suggest immodesty, but the author makes clear that this is evidence of Medora's willingness to flout social conventions and never mentions any immodest dress or behavior. Choice D, which means following established practice, is opposite; you are told in lines 34-35 that one of her peculiarities is to "flout the unalterable rules that regulated American mourning."

8. F   Difficulty: Low

Category: Detail

Getting to the Answer: Detail questions like this one are straightforward, but it can sometimes be difficult to find exactly where in the passage the relevant information comes from. Make sure that you are answering the specific question being asked, so that other details don't distract you. Medora teaches Ellen "drawing from the model" (line 53), which is described as "a thing never dreamed of before," so predict Ellen or Countess Olenska. Choice (F) matches your prediction. Choice G is out of scope; Newland is not described as having learned anything at all, let alone something controversial. Choice H is a distortion; Medora teaches Ellen, but the passage does not mention Medora learning anything herself. Choice J is a distortion; Count Olenska is only mentioned indirectly as the rich nobleman whom Ellen marries. The passage makes it clear that Ellen is Countess Olenska; don't be fooled by this initially tempting, but incorrect, choice.

9. B   Difficulty: Medium

Category: Function

Getting to the Answer: Locate where the author mentions Medora's mother and read the next few lines. The author writes that "her mother had been a Rushworth," (lines 19-20), that Medora married "one of the crazy Chiverses" (lines 21-22), and that because of these two conditions, "New York looked indulgently on her eccentricities" (lines 22-23). In other words, given her mother and her marriage, people were not surprised by Medora's unconventional life, which matches (B). There is no support for A, so it is out of scope. Choice C is opposite; New Yorkers "thought it a pity that the pretty child should be in such hands" (lines 26-27), and D is true but not relevant to Medora's eccentricities.

10. F   Difficulty: High

Category: Inference

Getting to the Answer: Remember that Inference questions will have details in the incorrect answer choices that are meant to throw you off. Making a good prediction before reviewing the choices will guard against this. The beginning of the passage (lines 3-4) implies that Newland knew Ellen when he was young. Lines 60-72 state that no one had heard from Ellen for some time, and after a few years, she came back to New York, as Medora had done before her. Predict that at the dinner, Newland and Ellen had not seen one another for an extended period of time. Choice (F) matches your prediction. Choice G is extreme; although Newland is clearly paying attention to Ellen in the last paragraph, there is nothing to suggest that either of them is interested in a romantic relationship. Choice H is extreme; while Ellen's lack of *stylishness* (lines 92-93) might suggest that she is not interested in New York society's conventions, it goes too far to say that she is disappointed. Choice J is opposite; the passage clearly portrays Ellen and Newland's encounter as a reacquaintance.

PASSAGE II

Suggested Passage Map notes:

¶1: Lemur (L) part of suborder of primates, nocturnal; flying lemurs not primates
¶2: L found on Madagascar, larger are nocturnal, smaller are diurnal
¶3: All L species are endangered b/c deforestation and hunting
¶4: Ring-tailed lemur (RTL) most populous L in zoos
¶5: RTL physical characteristics
¶6: RTL baby v. adult characteristics
¶7: RTL live in forests or open brush, require primary forests
¶8: RTL behavior, territory
¶9: RTL communication
¶10: RTL breeding

11. C   Difficulty: Low

Category: Detail

Getting to the Answer: Incorrect answers on Detail questions often include material relevant to other sections of the passage. Be sure you research the passage carefully to interpret the context correctly. You are looking for a factor that is responsible for the lemurs' survival. Your notes should help you find your way to Paragraph 2, where the author first discusses Madagascar. The author says the lemurs "were safe from competition" on the island. That should factor into the correct choice. Choice A is a misused detail; the author does mention that lemurs have large reflective eyes, but doesn't relate this to survival. Choice B is a misused detail; scent marking is related to their social organization, not their survival. Choice (C) paraphrases the relevant sentence in Paragraph 2. Choice D is a misused detail; the author mentions *hierarchy* later, but not as an explanation for the lemurs' survival.

12. F   Difficulty: Medium

Category: Detail

Getting to the Answer: Taking good notes and marking the passage will help you on Detail questions that lack line references. From your notes, you should see that social organization is discussed in Paragraph 8. The writer states that there are separate hierarchies for each gender and that "females tend to dominate the troop." Look for this among the choices. Choice (F) matches your prediction. Choice G is a distortion; the author does reference *foraging*, but not in the context of social organization. Choice H is out of scope; the author doesn't offer support for such a sweeping statement. Choice J is opposite; the author writes that females tend to dominate the troop.

13. D   Difficulty: Medium

Category: Vocab-in-Context

Getting to the Answer: Since *odd* is a common word, it's important to think about it in the specific

context of what the author has written. He uses the word when describing what ring-tailed lemurs usually eat—fruit, leaves, and seeds, plus an insect every now and then. Thus *odd* refers to occasionally, as (D) says. All other answer choices are possible definitions of *odd*, but none makes sense in the sentence.

14. G   Difficulty: Medium

Category: Detail

Getting to the Answer: The answers to Detail questions are stated directly in the passage—you can find the answer with research. This point is fairly obscure and may not be reflected in your notes. If you have to, skim for *zoo*, which appears in Paragraph 4. The author states that ring-tailed lemurs are the most populous lemurs in zoos and follows that by writing "they reproduce readily in captivity." Use that as your prediction. Choice F is out of scope; the author doesn't make such a contention. Choice (G) is a good paraphrase of the text referenced above. Choice H is out of scope; the author does not make this point. Choice J is a distortion; the author addresses *foraging*, but not in connection with zoos.

15. D   Difficulty: Medium

Category: Inference

Getting to the Answer: When given a line reference, move quickly and read at least that entire sentence to discern context. The author indicates that lemurs need to live in primary forest to survive. The clearing will likely endanger the lemurs' continued survival. Look for a match to this idea. Choice A is out of scope; the author does not refer to this. Choice B is out of scope; the author does not refer to this. Choice C is out of scope; the author doesn't reference such predators here. Choice (D) matches the research above.

16. H   Difficulty: Low

Category: Detail

Getting to the Answer: This is an EXCEPT question. That means you need to find three choices that are mentioned in the text and one that is not mentioned. Don't confuse the two. Your notes can help you to locate *olfactory signals*; they appear in Paragraph 9. Work through the paragraph, crossing off the three choices that do appear. Choice F is opposite; this appears in lines 94-95. Choice G is opposite; this appears in lines 95-97. The author does not reference (H), which makes it the correct answer. Choice J is opposite; this appears in line 94.

17.   B   Difficulty: Medium

Category: Detail

Getting to the Answer: Detail questions are answered directly in the passage. Referencing it before making a prediction will help you avoid misused details. Note that the question concerns all Lemuriformes, not only ring-tailed lemurs. This leads you to the first paragraph, which discusses lemurs in general. You may be unsure exactly which characteristic to predict, so compare this paragraph to the choices. Choice A is a distortion; many lemurs are nocturnal, but not all lemurs are. Choice (B) makes sense. Paragraph 1 states that lemurs represent the *evolutionary predecessor* of monkeys and apes, a paraphrase of what you see here. Choice C is opposite; at the end of Paragraph 1, the author clearly states that these species are not actually lemurs (*Lemuriformes*). Choice D is a distortion; the first sentence in Paragraph 2 states that lemurs are found on Madagascar "and some smaller surrounding islands."

18.   H   Difficulty: Medium

Category: Inference

Getting to the Answer: You need to "read between the lines" to find the correct answer. But don't make too great a logical leap. Check your notes for the second paragraph, and read it again if necessary. The question is very open-ended, so work through the choices and compare them to the information in the paragraph. Choice F is opposite; the author states that the pygmy mouse lemur is the smallest species and that smaller species are typically

nocturnal, not diurnal. Choice G is out of scope; the author does not discuss why certain species of lemur have become extinct. Choice (H) works. The author writes that the indri was the largest lemur. The next sentence states that "the larger species" are all extinct. Therefore, you can infer that the indri is extinct. Choice J is opposite; in Paragraph 1, you learn that lemurs are described as evolutionary *predecessors* of monkeys, meaning monkeys are descended from them.

19.   C   Difficulty: Medium

Category: Detail

Getting to the Answer: Your map should note that Paragraphs 5 and 6 describe the physical attributes of ring-tailed lemurs, and Paragraph 6 states that "the very young animals have blue eyes while the eyes of all adults are a striking yellow." Since there's no other reference to anything else that changes when ring-tailed lemurs become adults, (C) has to be the correct answer. Choice A is out of scope; there's nothing in the passage that supports this. Choice B is contradicted by the sentence "Ring-tailed lemurs are thought to require primary forest" (lines 72-73), and D is opposite; flying lemurs are not lemurs at all, as lines 12-13 state.

20.   F   Difficulty: Medium

Category: Detail

Getting to the Answer: Because this question asks which question is not answered, it functions as an EXCEPT question. Find the issue that is not addressed in the passage. The answers to these questions could fall anywhere in the passage. Your notes, though, should help you find the information you need. The author touches on (F) in Paragraph 3, saying that "options are limited." This implies that the question of survival has not been fully answered. If you're unsure at this point, work through the others to see that they are answered. Choice G is opposite; this is answered in the second sentence of Paragraph 2. Lemurs survived because they did not have to compete with monkeys and apes. Choice H is opposite; looking at the last paragraph, you see that the female is fertile for only one day a year, and that gestation lasts 146 days. So the female can have only one litter, and the author states that a litter consists of one or two babies. Choice J is opposite; this is answered in Paragraph 8. The author states lemurs eat fruit, "leaves, seeds, and the odd insect."

PASSAGE III

Suggested Passage Map notes:

¶1: Audience listens to Beethoven's *5th Symph.* in Queen's Hall

¶2-6: Mrs. Munt (MM) asks Helen (H) who Margaret (M) is talking to, but H doesn't know and doesn't care

¶7-9: H listens to music and observes people around her

¶10: H imagines goblins that represent fleeting youth

¶11: H leaves, wanting to be alone

¶12: H feels music perfectly represented meaning of life

21. C   Difficulty: Medium

Category: Inference

Getting to the Answer: When the passage offers you little information about the subject of the question, make a conservative inference based only on what the text supports. Helen and Margaret interact very little in the passage, though you do see in lines 24-36 that Helen appears uninterested in Margaret's conversation with the young man. Helen is too engrossed in the symphony being played. Don't make too big a leap here; they don't seem that close, but this is just a single incident in the course of a novel. Choice (C) is correct as it captures the sense of this section nicely. Choice A is extreme; Helen "could not be bothered" by Margaret's conversation. She does not express disapproval. Choice B is out of scope; the passage does not suggest that Helen is jealous of Margaret. Choice D is out of scope; the passage doesn't allow you to draw much of a conclusion about what draws them together.

22. H   Difficulty: High

Category: Global

Getting to the Answer: When answer choices consist of pairs of words, both words in a choice have to be correct for that choice to be correct. Consult your notes to come up with a prediction for Helen's personality. She certainly gives the music great consideration, to the exclusion of communing with those in her party. Predict something like "given to deep thought" or "tending to keep to herself." Both of the adjectives in (H) match the prediction and the gist of the text. Choice F is a distortion; her analysis of the music definitely shows creativity, but she does not display an animated personality. Choice G is a distortion; Helen does analyze the music, but the results of her analysis are more pessimistic: "there was no such thing as splendor or heroism in the world . . . Panic and emptiness!" (lines 80-85). Choice J is extreme; Helen doesn't speak much to those around her, but these adjectives are too strong to be supported by the text.

23. B   Difficulty: Low

Category: Detail

Getting to the Answer: With "NOT" questions, find the section that the question draws from, then cross off the three answer choices mentioned there. Your notes should help you see that Helen considers the goblins in depth in lines 73-85. Compare the choices to the description here and work your way to the one NOT mentioned. In lines 78-79, Helen says, "They were not aggressive creatures; that was what made them so terrible to Helen." This line directly contradicts (B), which is the correct choice. Choice A is opposite; in lines 80-81, Helen feels that the goblins communicate the sense that "there was no such thing as splendor or heroism in the world." Choice C is opposite; in lines 82-85, Helen admits she "could not contradict them . . . The goblins were right" in their pessimistic worldview. Choice D is opposite; in lines 73-75, Helen warns her aunt to "look out for the part where you think you are done with the goblins and they come back."

24. J   Difficulty: Medium

Category: Vocab-in-Context

Getting to the Answer: There are several meanings for the word *decorating*, but you're looking for the one which fits into the sentence. In the surrounding lines, the author writes that the Andante portion of the music had "a family likeness to all the other beautiful andantes that Beethoven had written." Because the tune sounded like other music she had heard, Helen's *attention wandered*. She paid attention again when "Beethoven started decorating his tune." In context, this must mean that the music changed, was no longer so familiar, and had new elements. Predict this answer and match it with (J)—*embellishing* means to make more interesting or entertaining. Even if you don't know that definition, you can eliminate all other answer choices because none of them makes sense in a passage about listening to music.

25. B   Difficulty: Medium

Category: Detail

Getting to the Answer: All answer choices are mentioned in the passage, but only one is what listeners imagine when hearing the music, so you'll have to research each answer. In lines 8-9 the author writes that "Helen, . . . can see . . . shipwrecks in the music's flood," making shipwrecks, (B), the correct answer. The wild horses in A are referred to in line 52 to describe how attentive Herr Liesecke is. Queen's Hall, C, is mentioned in lines 18-19 as the "dreariest music-room in London," and drums, D, (lines 68-70) are not in any listener's imagination but are a part of the music to which Tibby wants his fellow listeners to pay particular attention.

26. F   Difficulty: Low

Category: Detail

Getting to the Answer: Remember that "according to the passage" indicates a Detail question; the answer will be a paraphrase of something directly stated in the passage. Your notes can remind you where the author discusses Tibby (Paragraphs 1, 7, and 10). He listens to the symphony with "the full score . . . open on his knee" and draws the company's attention to "the transitional passage on the drum." Predict that he is fascinated by details within the performance. Choice (F) correctly matches the thrust of this prediction and of the text. Choice G is a misused detail; this more correctly defines Helen. Choice H is a distortion; Tibby's attention to the drum exemplifies his focus on the more technical aspects of the music. Choice J is a distortion; the author refers to the hall as dreary, but nothing indicates that this affects Tibby in this way.

27. B   Difficulty: Medium

Category: Inference

Getting to the Answer: Good notes and a good sense of the passage help when you don't receive a line or paragraph reference. The symphony performance takes up most of the passage, so research the last few paragraphs. The symphony leaves Helen with a hopeless feeling, but also feelings of certainty and acceptance of that outcome—a sense of resolution. Look for a match to this idea among the choices. Choice (B) correctly captures Helen's sentiments as she leaves. Choice A is out of scope; the passage paints Helen as unconcerned with her companions, who also seem anything but indifferent. Choice C is also out of scope; the passage does not describe Helen's reaction to Tibby. Choice D is a distortion; though Helen "pushed her way out" of the hall, nothing indicates that conditions in the hall affected her decision to leave.

28. J   Difficulty: Medium

Category: Inference

Getting to the Answer: With Prose Fiction passages, be careful to keep straight which character does or thinks what. This passage contains a number of different characters. Use your notes to find where the author mentions Aunt Juley—principally in line 57. He describes her as "so British, and wanting to tap." You also might have found the reference to Mrs. Munt in lines 5-6: she would tap along with the music, but surreptitiously. You can infer that tapping must be frowned upon, and Aunt Juley is aware of that. Choice (J) is the most reasonable inference based on the text. Choice F is a misused detail; Tibby draws Aunt Juley's attention to the drum, but this comes after her decision not to tap. Choice G is a distortion; the passage does not suggest that Aunt Juley was considering how her tapping might affect Helen. Choice H is out of scope; "snapping one's fingers" is not mentioned in the passage.

29. C   Difficulty: Medium

Category: Detail

Getting to the Answer: Use your notes to whittle down the choices, then research further as needed. In line 14, you read that, though the music enthralls nearly everyone else, Fraulein Mosebach's young man "can remember nothing but Fraulein Mosebach." He must be infatuated with her, and not the music. Choice (C) logically follows from this portion of the passage. Choice A is opposite; the author writes, "wild horses could not make him inattentive" (lines 52-53). Choice B is opposite; though Margaret seems interested in the young man she is speaking with, when the performance is going on, she "can only see the music" (lines 9-10). Choice D is opposite; the author describes Tibby's interest in the music in multiple spots in the passage.

30. F   Difficulty: Low

Category: Detail

Getting to the Answer: If your notes don't help, skim the passage, especially when looking for italicized or capitalized text. The author deals with the Andante in Paragraph 7. Helen listened to the Andante *once more* after "Beethoven started decorating his tune." Predict that she was drawn by a change in the music. Choice (F) matches the prediction nicely. Choice G is a misused detail; Tibby does gesture her way, but this occurs later in the passage.

Choice H is a distortion; the two women had already stopped speaking once the Andante began. Choice J is out of scope; the author doesn't indicate that Helen believed this.

PASSAGE IV

Suggested Passage Map notes:

¶1: 1999, Pluto about to lose planet status
¶2: Marsden says Pluto given special status, not demoted
¶3: Discussion started in 1930, Pluto small & elongated orbit
¶4: 1992 Jewitt and Luu discovered QB1, Luu says Pluto is a TNO
¶5: 70 TNOs are known, Pluto is biggest
¶6: Binzel suggests Pluto be made 1st entry in TNO catalog
¶7: Marsden agrees Pluto is TNO, but doesn't want new way of classifying TNOs
¶8: Marsden wants to give Pluto its own special number in an existing asteroid catalog
¶9: Luu disagrees w/ Marsden
¶10: A'Hearn trying to settle dispute
¶11: general public will still think of Pluto as 9th planet

31. D   Difficulty: Low

Category: Detail

Getting to the Answer: Luu strongly disagrees with the view that Pluto should be labeled an asteroid (lines 90-92). She goes so far as to use the term *idiotic* in reference to others in her profession, so predict something like indignation. Choice (D) matches this prediction. Choice A is a distortion; while "shock" may be an initially tempting choice, it's clear that Luu's surprise stems from her disagreement with the opinion, not her lack of preparation to hear it. Choice B is opposite; excitement suggests some degree of positive response, which Luu clearly does not display. Choice C is opposite; Luu expresses her feelings on the classification controversy quite clearly.

32. H   Difficulty: Medium

Category: Inference

Getting to the Answer: If you get stuck, eliminating answers that have no support in the passage will greatly reduce the number of choices. The passage states that, if astronomers had known about the other TNOs, Pluto would not have been named a planet (lines 51-53). The size of Pluto is indicated as the reason it was discovered before the others. You can infer that a better system of detection would have discovered other TNOs, eliminating Pluto's status as a planet. Account for this in your prediction. Choice (H) matches your prediction. Choice F is a distortion; Pluto's size does indeed make it different from the other planets, but the lack of this knowledge is not cited as the sole reason for its initial classification. Choice G is a distortion; although the icy Pluto is said to belong with neither the *rocky planets* nor the *gas giants* (lines 29-30), this information is included as a way to differentiate Pluto from the planets, and the lack of this knowledge initially is not identified as the reason for Pluto's original classification. Choice J is a distortion; the controversy that would later surround Pluto's initial classification as a planet was never drawn into the discussion of the original classification.

33. D   Difficulty: Medium

Category: Writer's View

Getting to the Answer: As interested as the author is in how to describe Pluto, at no point does the author offer a personal opinion. Because of this, you cannot assume that the author would agree with anything other than a neutral statement, as (D) is. The author does not side with those who would call Pluto a TNO, making A incorrect, nor those who argue that it should remain a planet, C. Choice B is a distortion; IAU stands for International Astronomical Union, not a classification.

34. F   Difficulty: Low

Category: Detail

Getting to the Answer: Your notes on the passage should show the location of key details and terminology so you can quickly find them as you research the question stem. Neptune is mentioned only a few times; the fourth paragraph mentions Neptune in relation to trans-Neptunian objects, and the seventh paragraph mentions Neptune and Centaurs, one of the answer choices. Sure enough, an examination of the description reveals that Centaurs, a great prediction, are asteroids similar to Pluto *nudged* inside Neptune's orbit. Choice (F) matches this prediction. Choice G is a misused detail; the passage states that IAU stands for International Astronomical Union. Choice H is a misused detail; TNO stands for trans-Neptunian objects, things beyond Neptune. Choice J is a misused detail; the term *ice dwarf* is used in connection with the discovery of a TNO.

35. C   Difficulty: Low

Category: Inference

Getting to the Answer: Inference questions such as this ask that you interpret the referenced lines, drawing on your reading of the passage as a whole. The quote making up the majority of the referenced lines comes from a scientist who, in the passage, takes a position against creating a new classification. Your prediction should reflect the issue of whether the existing categories are suitable. Choice (C) matches this prediction. Choice A is a misused detail; this is certainly discussed in the passage, but this doesn't pertain to the cited lines or the speaker in question. Choice B is a misused detail; distance from the sun and from Neptune is significant to certain classification schemes, but this is not the central issue in Pluto's specific case. Choice D is a misused detail; that the scientific community and general public have differing opinions is irrelevant to the cited lines.

36. G   Difficulty: High

Category: Vocab-in-Context

Getting to the Answer: Vocab-in-Context questions require that you understand the context of a cited word or phrase. Locate the reference and focus your research on the text immediately preceding and immediately following the word or phrase in question. Investigating the word in question contextualizes it within the argument of a scientist who "doesn't like the idea of establishing a new catalog of solar system objects" (lines 64-65) and argues that "astronomers already have a perfectly serviceable list of numbered minor bodies" (lines 66-67). Predict something like *sufficient* to replace the word in question. Choice (G) matches this prediction. Choice F invokes the most common meaning of the word, which doesn't make sense in context and is usually a trap answer; the scientist does *not* want to change the system. Choices H and J don't work in context, since describing a particular classification system as *beneficial* or *durable* is awkward.

37. D   Difficulty: Low

Category: Global

Getting to the Answer: Remember that Global questions will attempt to make tempting answer choices out of issues discussed in the passage only briefly. A recurring theme throughout the passage is giving Pluto a "very special designation" (lines 19-20) or *honor* (line 86), which differs from the predominantly scientific concerns over Pluto's classification discussed elsewhere. Predict an answer that touches on this idea of honoring or distinguishing Pluto in some way. Choice (D) matches this prediction. Choice A is out of scope; the role of the IAU is never discussed by the cited experts. Choice B is a misused detail; the author does relay some information about the ways in which public opinion is unlikely to change, but this is not a significant concern for scientists dealing with deeper issues. Choice C is out of scope; none of the cited scientists seems particularly concerned with being credited for solving the problem.

38. G   Difficulty: Medium

Category: Detail

Getting to the Answer: The passage ends with a discussion of one scientist's attempt to find consensus about Pluto's status. In this part of the passage, the major ideas are listed. Binzel's idea is rejected because Pluto "would still be an anomaly." Luu forcefully asserts that "Pluto is certainly not an asteroid." Both criticisms are based on the idea that neither category adequately describes Pluto, so predict that the correct answer will focus on the inadequacy of any categorization scheme. Choice (G) matches this prediction. Choice F is a misused detail; the public's recognition of Pluto's controversial status or a potential change in category are not significant issues to scientists. Choice H is a distortion; Pluto's orbit plays little role in the discussion of its classification, and its surface is never mentioned. Choice J is a misused detail; the existence of Pluto-like objects nearer to the sun than Neptune functions as a criticism of only one theory.

39. B   Difficulty: Medium

Category: Detail

Getting to the Answer: Detail questions will sometimes require a broad approach to information from a variety of locations in the text. Your notes will help you to sort out the specifics. Lines 25-28 discuss Pluto's size in relation to other planets, and lines 28-29 describe its orbit as anomalous. A good prediction will account for both. Choice (B) matches this prediction. Choice A is a misused detail; distance from the sun versus distance from Neptune is significant only in certain classification systems for non-planets. Choice C is out of scope; the year of Pluto's discovery in relation to those of other planets is never discussed. Choice D is out of scope; Pluto's shape is not compared to other planets.

40. H   Difficulty: High

Category: Detail

Getting to the Answer: Tougher Detail questions will require an investigation of several sections of text. Count on your notes to direct you, even when the search is fairly extensive. Lines 25-28 tell you that Pluto is smaller than other planets, which is why scientists need to reclassify it, yet its large size compared to asteroids and TNOs (lines 105-107) is what keeps many scientists confused about its proper category. Lines 48-51 cite Pluto's size as the exact reason that it was found 60 years before the next body like it. Your prediction should account for this classification difficulty as well as Pluto's early discovery. Choice (H) matches this prediction. Choice F is a distortion; categorizing Pluto as a TNO is only a proposed solution to the classification problem and takes into consideration issues other than size, such as Pluto's relation to Neptune. Choice G is opposite; it is Pluto's relatively small size that potentially allows it the same classification as an asteroid. Choice J is a misused detail; the passage never relates Pluto's size to the nature of the planet's orbit.

CHAPTER FOURTEEN

Social Science and Humanities Passages

GETTING STARTED

Passage Types

In order to read the passage as quickly as possible without missing any information, you should make very short notes in the margin, also known as a Passage Map. Your Passage Map should help you quickly locate information in the passage when you answer questions. Your exact approach to Passage Mapping will vary based on the passage type.

Social Science and Humanities Passages

Unlike the **Prose Fiction** and **Natural Science** passage types described in Chapter 13, **Social Science** and **Humanities** passage types have similar structures and can be mapped in similar ways.

Social Science and **Humanities** passages are full of names and dates. Focus on including these important ideas in your **Social Science** and **Humanities** Passage Maps:

1. Identify the topic and scope of the passage.
   - The topic is the broad subject of the passage.
   - The scope narrows the topic to the aspect that is of interest to the author.
   - Always read the "blurb"—the italicized introduction at the top of the passage. The blurb will frequently describe the topic and the scope.
   - If they are not in the blurb, the topic and scope are usually found in the first paragraph. Read carefully until you identify them.
2. Identify the topic sentence of each succeeding paragraph.
   - What does this paragraph accomplish? Does it provide evidence to support a previous statement? Or does it introduce questions about an earlier claim?
   - If the passage is using unfamiliar language, focus on the main idea of the paragraph. You will likely be able to figure out the meaning of unfamiliar terms from the context.

3. Summarize the purpose of the passage.

- Some common purposes include: to inform, to refute, to promote, to explore.

- Note the author's tone. Were there any positive or negative keywords? If not, the author's tone is neutral.

> ✔ **Expert Tip**
>
> Some paragraphs are longer than others. If you are mapping a very long paragraph, you can write two or three short notes rather than trying to fit everything into just one long note.

The approach to reading and mapping **Social Science** and **Humanities** passages is summarized in the table below.

Passage Type(s)	Approach
Social Studies & Humanities	• Identify the author's thesis (often explicitly stated in the first paragraph) • Note the main idea of each paragraph

IMPROVING WITH PRACTICE

Step 1: Compare Your Notes to the Suggested Social Science or Humanities Passage Maps

After reading a passage, compare your notes to the suggested Passage Map to be sure you generally included the same important points. Abbreviations and symbols are both very useful when creating Passage Maps, especially if you have a hard time finishing the Reading Test before time is called. Passage Mapping is very personal, and it's just fine if your map is different—even very different!—as long as you captured the following information for **Social Science** and **Humanities** passage types:

- The main idea of each paragraph

- Any opinions, especially the author's

- The *location* of descriptive details and examples

- The *reason* the author included details and examples. Is the author using the information to support, modify, or refute the preceding idea?

- Any emphasis or "emotional" keywords. Keywords such as "remarkable," "unfortunate," "unprecedented," and "crucial" are important indicators of the author's tone.

If you missed important information, go back to the **Social Science** or **Humanities** passage and identify the keywords that you likely overlooked so you can recognize them more quickly next time. The ACT uses predictable keywords to alert you to the important ideas in the passage. Use these keywords to focus your attention and create strong Passage Maps.

> ✔ *Expert Tip*
>
> Some paragraphs are longer than others. If you are mapping a very long paragraph, you can write two or three short notes rather than trying to fit everything into just one long note.

Step 2: Answer the Questions

After you've reviewed and strengthened your **Social Science** or **Humanities** Passage Map, complete the questions one at a time. Review the Answer and Explanation for every question immediately after completing it. If you got the question correct, congratulate yourself, but take a moment to read the entire explanation to be sure you got the question right for the right reason. The explanation may even point out a more efficient way that you can use on a later question!

> ✔ *Expert Tip*
>
> Resist the temptation to reread large portions of the passage when answering questions. Your Passage Map should help you predict and answer questions correctly without having to dive completely back into the text. Doing this will save you time on Test Day *and* help you get more questions correct!

Step 3: Review Incorrect Answers

If you get the question incorrect . . . still congratulate yourself! You're about to learn something new that you'll be able to use to improve your performance on Test Day. Don't read the explanation yet; instead, try the question again.

If you get the question correct the second time, read the explanation to see if you solved the question in the most efficient way. Identify the mistake you made the first time, and determine how you're going to avoid making that mistake again.

> ✔ *Expert Tip*
>
> Many top scoring students have an ACT notebook where they write down what they learn from every question. Doing this can be time-consuming, but it can also help you identify the types of mistakes you tend to make.

If you get the question incorrect the second time, use the explanation to learn how to get the question correct. Work through the question again while following the explanation, and identify the steps you will need to take to get a similar question correct. Although the passages and questions will change, the concepts being tested will not. When you encounter unfamiliar questions, take note of them for future study sessions.

> **✔ Note**
>
> The ACT is a standardized test. While high-difficulty Reading questions are usually more difficult to answer than lower- or medium-difficulty questions, they are often similar in structure and purpose, and the same skills (listed in Chapter 12) are tested on every Reading Test. You actually can predict the types of questions you will see on Test Day!

After all that work, it's time to move to the next question. Reviewing in this way will take time. However, improvement doesn't come from just doing lots and lots of questions; it comes from thinking through your approach and improving it with every question.

RAISING YOUR SCORE EVEN MORE

Once your **Social Science** and **Humanities** Passage Maps are accurate and quickly leading you to the correct answers, it's time to return to the completed passages and study which sections of the passages were the source of the correct answers. When studying the source of each answer, look for the keywords the author used to indicate that section was important. Recognizing keywords helps you to know when to slow down and read carefully, such as when reading an introductory paragraph or an opinion, and when you can speed up and read superficially, such as when reading the middle of a body paragraph full of details or long explanations. Note the *location* of this information in your map, and if needed, return to this section of the passage if a question asks about it.

> **✔ Expert Tip**
>
> Unlike the exams you prepare for in your classes, the ACT is an open-book test. You don't need to memorize or thoroughly understand the content of the passage. You need to know the *location* in the passage where you will look up the answers to the exact questions asked.

PRACTICE QUESTIONS

The following test-like question sets provide an opportunity to practice reading Social Science and Humanities Passages and answering related questions.

PASSAGE I

HUMANITIES: This passage is adapted from a Wikipedia article titled "Walter Scott."

Born in Edinburgh in 1771, the young Walter Scott survived a childhood bout of polio that would leave him lame in his right leg for the rest of his life. After studying law
5 at Edinburgh University, he followed in his father's footsteps and became a lawyer in his native Scotland. Beginning at age 25, he started dabbling in writing, first translating works from German, then moving on to
10 poetry. In between these two phases of his literary career, he published a three-volume set of collected Scottish ballads, *The Minstrelsy of the Scottish Border*. This was the first sign of his interest in Scotland and history in his writings.

15 After Scott had founded a printing press, his poetry, beginning with *The Lay of the Last Minstrel* in 1805, brought him great fame. He published a number of other poems over the next ten years, including in 1810 the popular
20 *Lady of the Lake*, portions of which (translated into German) were set to music by Franz Schubert. Another work from this time period, *Marmion*, produced some of his most quoted (and most often misattributed) lines, such as

25 *Oh! what a tangled web we weave*
When first we practise to deceive!

When Scott's press became embroiled in financial difficulties, Scott set out, in 1814, to write a successful (and profitable) work. The
30 result was *Waverley*, a novel that did not name its author. It was a tale of the last Jacobite rebellion in the United Kingdom, the

"Forty-Five," and the novel met with considerable success. There followed a large number of
35 novels in the next five years, each in the same general vein. Mindful of his reputation as a poet, he maintained the anonymity he had begun with *Waverley*, always publishing the novels under a name such as "Author of Waverley"
40 or attributed as "Tales of . . . " with no author. Even when it was clear that there would be no harm in coming out into the open, he maintained the façade, apparently out of a sense of fun. During this time, the nickname "The
45 Wizard of the North" was popularly applied to the mysterious best-selling writer. His identity as the author of the novels was widely rumored, and in 1815 Scott was given the honour of dining with George, Prince Regent, who
50 wanted to meet "the author of Waverley."

In 1820, Scott broke away from writing about Scotland with *Ivanhoe*, a historical romance set in twelfth-century England. It too was a runaway success and, as he did with his
55 first novel, he unleashed a slew of books along the same lines. As his fame grew during this phase of his career, he was granted the title of Baronet, becoming Sir Walter Scott. At this time he organized the visit of King George IV
60 to Scotland, and when the King visited Edinburgh in 1822, the spectacular pageantry Scott had concocted to portray the King as a rather tubby reincarnation of Bonnie Prince Charlie made tartans and kilts fashionable and
65 turned them into symbols of national identity.

Beginning in 1825, Scott fell into dire financial straits again, and his company nearly collapsed. That he was the author of his novels became general knowledge at this time as well.
70 Rather than declare bankruptcy he placed his home, Abbotsford House, and income into a trust belonging to his creditors, and proceeded to write his way out of debt. He kept up his prodigious output of fiction (as well as produc-
75 ing a biography of Napoleon Bonaparte) through 1831. By then his health was failing, and he died at Abbotsford in 1832. Though not in the clear by then, his novels continued to sell, and he made good his debts from beyond
80 the grave. He was buried in Dryburgh Abbey; nearby, fittingly, a large statue can be found of William Wallace—one of Scotland's great historical figures.

Scott was responsible for two major trends
85 that carry on to this day. First, he popularized the historical novel; an enormous number of imitators (and imitators of imitators) would appear in the nineteenth century. It is a measure of Scott's influence that Edinburgh's cen-
90 tral railway station, opened in 1854, is called Waverley Station. Second, his Scottish novels rehabilitated Highland culture after years in the shadows following the Jacobite rebellions.

Scott was also responsible, through a series
95 of pseudonymous letters published in the *Edinburgh Weekly News* in 1826, for retaining the right of Scottish banks to issue their own banknotes, which is reflected to this day by his continued appearance on the front of all notes
100 issued by the Bank of Scotland.

1. The main idea of the passage is that:

   A. historical novels can be very successful in rehabilitating a country's culture.

   B. Sir Walter Scott's writings achieved both financial success and cultural impact.

   C. Scott became known more for his financial failures than for his literary talents.

   D. the success of Scott's novels was largely due to the anonymity of the author.

2. According to the passage, Walter Scott turned to writing novels because:

   F. his childhood bout with polio made it difficult for him to continue working as a lawyer.

   G. his printing press business was being sued over copyright violations.

   H. his three-volume set of Scottish ballads did not sell well.

   J. his printing press business was losing money.

3. According to the author, Scott published *Waverley* anonymously because:

   A. he didn't want to damage his reputation as a lawyer.

   B. he had fun watching people try to determine who the author was.

   C. his novels sold faster without an author's name on them.

   D. he was afraid writing fiction would take away from his reputation as a poet.

4. The author would most likely describe Scott's effect on how Scotland was viewed as:

   F. damaging, since Scott degraded Scottish culture by popularizing tartans and kilts.

   G. unimportant, since Scott's novels were no more than popular fiction.

   H. ground-breaking, since Scott was the first to write serious analyses of Scottish history.

   J. positive, since Scott made Scottish culture acceptable again after years of neglect.

5. Based on the passage, it is reasonable to assume that Scott's reputation after his death:

   A. remained favorable.

   B. waned because there were no more of his novels being published.

   C. declined because he died without paying all of his debts.

   D. was debased because of all his imitators.

6. As it is used in line 43, the word *façade* most nearly means:

   F. pretense.

   G. building front.

   H. bluff.

   J. character.

7. The author most likely uses *fittingly* (line 81) when describing the presence of a statue of William Wallace near Scott's grave in Dryburgh Abbey because:

   A. Scott's first major novel was about the achievements of William Wallace.

   B. Scott wrote novels about Scottish history and Wallace is a famous historical figure from Scotland.

   C. Scott was a very religious man and deserved to be buried in an abbey.

   D. Wallace was an avid fan of Scott's poetry.

8. The passage suggests that the author's attitude toward Sir Walter Scott is:

   F. restrained and skeptical.

   G. derisive and contemptuous.

   H. interested and appreciative.

   J. passionate and envious.

9. Based on the fifth paragraph (lines 66-83), it is reasonable to infer that Sir Walter Scott's attitude toward his debts was:

   A. irresponsible, since he left them to be taken care of after his death.

   B. resentful, for he believed that they were caused by his partners.

   C. impatient, because he became annoyed that his creditors hounded him so.

   D. accepting, since he acknowledged his responsibility and tried to pay them back.

10. The author's use of *dabbling* in line 8
    suggests that:

    F. Scott sought to establish himself in a field
    in which he had little experience.

    G. the financial losses eventually suffered by
    Scott's printing press began with this
    activity.

    H. Scott's inexperience led to the poor
    quality of his literary work.

    J. Scott's initial work led to his interest in
    Scottish history.

PASSAGE II

HUMANITIES: This passage is excerpted from "Mr. Bennett and Mrs. Woolf," by Irving Howe. Reprinted by permission of *The New Republic*, © 1990, *The New Republic*, LLC.

Literary polemics come and go, sparking a season of anger and gossip, and then turning to dust. A handful survive their moment: Dr. Johnson's demolition of Soames Jenyn,
5 Hazlitt's attack on Coleridge. But few literary polemics can have been so damaging, or so lasting in consequences, as Virginia Woolf's 1924 essay "Mr. Bennett and Mrs. Brown," about the once widely read English novelists
10 Arnold Bennett, H. G. Wells, and John Galsworthy. For several literary generations now, Woolf's essay has been taken as the definitive word finishing off an old-fashioned school of fiction and thereby clearing the way for liter-
15 ary modernism. Writing with her glistening charm, and casting herself as the voice of the new (always a shrewd strategy in literary debate), Woolf quickly seized the high ground in her battle with Bennett. Against her needling
20 thrusts, the old fellow never had a chance.

The debate has been nicely laid out by Samuel Hynes in *Edwardian Occasions*, and I owe to him some of the following details. It all began in 1917, with Woolf's review of a
25 collection of Bennett's literary pieces, a rather favorable review marred by the stylish snobbism that was becoming a trademark of the Bloomsbury circle. Bennett, wrote Woolf, had a materialistic view of the world—"he had
30 been worrying himself to achieve infantile realisms." A catchy phrase, though exactly what "infantile realisms" meant Woolf did not trouble to say. During the next few years she kept returning to the attack, as if to prepare for "Mr.
35 Bennett and Mrs. Brown." More than personal sensibilities or rivalries of status was involved

here, though both were quite visible; Woolf was intent upon discrediting, if not simply dismissing, a group of literary predecessors who
40 enjoyed a large readership.

In 1923 Bennett reviewed Woolf's novel *Jacob's Room*, praising its "originality" and "exquisite" prose but concluding that "the characters do not vitally survive in the mind."
45 For Bennett, this was a fatal flaw. And for his readers, too—though not for the advanced literary public that by now was learning to suspect this kind of talk about "characters surviving" as a lazy apology for the shapeless
50 and perhaps even mindless Victorian novel.

A year later Woolf published her famous essay, brilliantly sketching an imaginary old lady named Mrs. Brown whom she supplied with anecdotes and reflections as tokens of inner
55 being. These released the sort of insights, suggested Woolf, that would not occur to someone like Bennett, a writer obsessed with dull particulars of setting (weather, town, clothing, furniture, and so on). Were Bennett to write
60 about a Mrs. Brown, he would describe her house in conscientious detail but never penetrate her essential life, for—what a keen polemicist!—"he is trying to hypnotize us into the belief that, because he has made a house,
65 there must be a person living there." (Herself sensitive to the need for a room with a view, Woolf seemed indifferent to what a house might mean for people who had risen somewhat in the world. For a writer like Bennett,
70 however, imagining a house was part of the way to locate "a person living there.") And in a quiet putdown of Bennett's novel *Hilda*

Lessways (not one of his best), Woolf gave a turn of the knife: "One line of insight would have
75 done more than all those lines of description."

From the suave but deadly attack of "Mr. Bennett and Mrs. Brown" Bennett's literary reputation never quite recovered. He remained popular with the general public, but among lit-
80 erary readers, the sort that became the public for the emerging modernists, the standard view has long been that he was a middling, plodding sort of Edwardian writer whose work has been pushed aside by the revolutionary
85 achievements of Lawrence, Joyce, and to a smaller extent Woolf herself.

When Bennett died in 1930, Woolf noted in her diary that "he had some real understand-ing power, as well as a gigantic absorbing
90 power [and] direct contact with life"—all attri-butes, you might suppose, handy for a novelist but for her evidently not sufficient. In saying this, remarks Hynes, "Woolf gave Bennett, perhaps, the 'reality gift' that [she] doubted in
95 herself, the gift that she despised and envied." Yes; in much of her fiction Woolf resembles Stevens's man with the blue guitar who "cannot bring a world quite round/Although I patch it as I can." Still, none of this kept Woolf from
100 steadily sniping at Bennett's "shopkeeping view of literature." Bennett was a provincial from the Five Towns; Bennett was commercially successful; Bennett was an elder to be pulled down, as elders must always be pulled down
105 even if they are also admired a little.

11. Which of the following statements best characterizes the author's view of Virginia Woolf?

   A. Woolf criticized others only in areas where she felt strong, leaving her own weaknesses out of the discussion.

   B. Woolf only disparaged Bennett and his school of authors because she envied the strides they had made.

   C. Woolf almost single-handedly changed the prevailing opinion about a particular writer and laid the path for a new school of literature.

   D. Woolf's views toward the venerated authors of the day were abusive, and her reputation has rightly suffered as a result of those attacks.

12. As it is used in line 1, the word *polemics* most nearly means:

   F. attacks.

   G. reviews.

   H. controversies.

   J. friendships.

13. In the first paragraph, the author compares Woolf's polemic against Bennett to other literary attacks. This comparison supports the author's view that:

   A. Bennett's dull style of writing would soon have fallen out of fashion anyway.

   B. many such attacks are remembered as turning points for the arts.

   C. Woolf fought with other authors often.

   D. Woolf's criticisms of Bennett were especially important and memorable.

14. According to the passage, Bennett's literary output was marked by:

    F. description of the scene rather than insight into the characters.

    G. the use of colorful characters who frequently reveal their deepest emotions.

    H. fewer essays than Woolf wrote.

    J. exhaustive description of minute details.

15. It can be reasonably inferred from the passage that the author means to:

    A. demonstrate an effective strategy for writing a literary polemic.

    B. suggest a new interpretation of a well-known literary polemic.

    C. analyze one literary polemic and its effect on the literature of its era.

    D. assess the significance of a literary polemic in the context of similar works.

16. Based on the passage, it is most reasonable to infer that Woolf's phrase *infantile realisms* (lines 30-31) means:

    F. a focus on things rather than on people.

    G. the values of the Bloomsbury Circle.

    H. the type of writing that doesn't survive in the reader's mind.

    J. the superficial details of Mrs. Brown's house.

17. In the final sentence of the passage, the author suggests that Woolf believed that "elders must always be pulled down." This same sentiment is most closely exemplified by which of the following examples from the passage?

    A. The author's view of Woolf's novel *Jacob's Room*

    B. The author's view of *Edwardian Occasions* by Samuel Hynes

    C. The author's comparison of Woolf to "Stevens's man with the blue guitar"

    D. The author's reference to Bennett's *Hilda Lessways* as "not one of his best"

18. Bennett's general opinion of Woolf's novel *Jacob's Room* was that it was:

    F. inferior to other novels published at that time.

    G. a keen example of a new style of literature.

    H. a success, despite one or two minor failings.

    J. generally original and inspired, but with significant problems.

19. It is Woolf's opinion that the thoughts and feelings of characters are more important than the details of a scene because:

    A. scenic descriptions were part of a literary style that she disliked.

    B. scenic details cannot convey a sense of the character within.

    C. good authors know to include at least one line of insight into a character.

    D. scenic details create characters that are easily forgettable.

20. In the last paragraph, the function of the phrase "he had some real understanding power, as well as a gigantic absorbing power [and] direct contact with life" (lines 88-90) is to present:

    F. Woolf retracting her criticism of Bennett.

    G. Woolf excoriating Bennett.

    H. Bennett praising Woolf.

    J. Woolf praising Bennett.

PASSAGE III

SOCIAL SCIENCE: The following passage is excerpted from a magazine article discussing scientific research on traditional methods of predicting the timing and character of the Indian monsoon.

Can traditional rules of thumb provide accurate weather forecasts? Researchers in Junagadh, India, are trying to find out. Most farmers in the region grow one crop of peanuts
5 or castor per year. In a wet year, peanuts give the best returns, but if the rains are poor, the more drought-tolerant castor is a better bet. In April and May, before the monsoon comes, farmers decide what to plant, buy the seed,
10 prepare the soil, and hope for the best. An accurate forecast would be extremely helpful.

Little wonder, then, that observant farmers have devised traditional ways to predict the monsoon's timing and character. One such
15 rule of thumb involves the blooming of the *Cassia fistula* tree, which is common on road-sides in southern Gujarat. According to an old saying which has been documented as far back as the 8th century, the monsoon begins
20 45 days after *C. fistula's* flowering peak. Since 1996, Purshottambhai Kanani, an agronomist at Gujarat Agricultural University, has been collecting data to test this rule. He records the flowering dates of trees all over the university's
25 campus and plots a distribution to work out when the flowering peak occurs. While not perfect, *C. fistula* has so far done an admirable job of predicting whether the monsoon will come early or late.

30 Similarly, with help from local farmers, Dr. Kanani has been investigating a local belief regarding the direction of the wind on the day of Holi, a Hindu festival in spring. The wind direction at certain times on Holi is supposed
35 to indicate the strength of the monsoon that year. Wind from the north or west suggests a

good monsoon, whereas wind from the east indicates drought. Each year before Holi, Dr. Kanani sends out postcards to more than
40 400 farmers in Junagadh and neighbouring districts. The farmers note the wind direction at the specified times and then send the postcards back.

In years of average and above-average mon-
45 soons (1994, 1997, 1998, and 2001), the wind on Holi tended to come from the north and west. In the drier years of 1995 and 1996, the majority of farmers reported wind from the east (Dr. Kanani did not conduct the study in
50 1999 and 2000). As with the *C. fistula* results, the predictions are not especially precise, but the trend is right.

Dr. Kanani first became interested in tradi-tional methods in 1990, when an old saying
55 attributed to a tenth-century sage named Bhadli—that a storm on a particular day meant the monsoon would come 72 days later—proved strikingly correct. This prompted Dr. Kanani to collect other rules
60 from old texts in Gujarati and Sanskrit.

Not all of his colleagues approve. Damaru Sahu, a meteorologist at Gujarat Agricultural University and a researcher for India's director-general of meteorology, says that traditional
65 methods are "OK as a hobby." But, he goes on, they cannot be relied upon, and "may not be applicable to this modern age." Yet Dr. Sahu concedes that meteorological science has failed to provide a useful alternative to traditional
70 methods. For the past 13 years, he notes, the director-general for meteorology has predicted "normal monsoon" for the country. Every year,

the average rainfall over the whole country is calculated, and this prediction is proved cor-
75 rect. But it is no use at all to farmers who want to know what will happen in their region.

Dr. Kanani hopes that his research will put traditional methods on a proper scientific footing. He and his colleagues have even set up
80 a sort of peer-review forum for traditional meteorology. Each spring, he hosts a conference for 100 local traditional forecasters, each of whom presents a monsoon prediction with supporting evidence—the behaviour of a spe-
85 cies of bird, strong flowering in a certain plant, or the prevailing wind direction that season. Dr. Kanani records these predictions and publishes them in the local press.

He has also started a non-governmental or-
90 ganisation, the Varsha Vigyan Mandal, or Rain Science Association, which has more than 400 members. Its vice-president, Dhansukh Shah, is a scientist at the National Directorate of Meteorology in Pune. By involving such main-
95 stream meteorologists as Dr. Shah in his work, Dr. Kanani hopes to bring his unusual research to the attention of national institutions. They could provide the funding for larger studies that could generate results sufficiently robust to
100 be published in peer-reviewed science journals.

21. According to the passage, all of the following traditional methods of weather prediction have been scientifically tested EXCEPT:

A. wind direction during the Hindi festival of Holi.

B. the behavior of certain bird species.

C. the flowering of *Cassia fistula* trees.

D. a tenth-century prediction connecting storm activity to later monsoons.

22. The author uses the phrase *useful alternative* (line 69) in order to show that:

F. modern meteorology rarely provides an accurate forecast.

G. equipment needed for accurate forecasting is too expensive for many in India.

H. modern meteorology doesn't give as reliable predictions as traditional methods do.

J. today's science is not yet able to provide specific meteorological forecasts needed by farmers.

23. According to the passage, a good monsoon is associated with winds from the:

A. north.

B. south.

C. east.

D. southwest.

24. The author's attitude toward traditional methods of weather forecasting may reasonably be described as:

F. curious as to their development.

G. cautious hopefulness that they are useful.

H. skeptical regarding their real scientific value.

J. regretful of the "fad" of interest in these methods.

25. According to the passage, which of the discussed methods gives the most advanced prediction of monsoon arrival?

A. The behavior of the birds

B. The flowering of the fistula tree

C. The wind direction on Holi

D. Bhadli's prediction based on storms

26. The function of the second paragraph in relation to the passage as a whole is most likely to provide:

   F. a reason why farmers need techniques to predict monsoons earlier.

   G. examples of the inexact nature of predictions made from traditional methods.

   H. an explanation of the ancient saying that the rest of the passage will examine.

   J. an introduction to the modern research of traditional methods.

27. According to the passage, the purpose of Dr. Kanani's springtime conferences is to:

   A. record the traditional methods of weather prediction before they disappear.

   B. help gain acceptance for traditional methods in the academic community.

   C. publish the methods in the local press.

   D. facilitate the exchange of ideas between farmers from far-flung regions of India.

28. According to the passage, the reason farmers use traditional methods to predict the weather is that:

   F. traditional methods are more accessible to rural populations.

   G. "normal" monsoons can still be very different from each other.

   H. they need to anticipate the local conditions for the coming growing season.

   J. traditional methods get the basic trends right.

29. The author uses the term *admirable job* (lines 27-28) to indicate that:

   A. the flowering of the fistula tree provides remarkably predictive data on the coming monsoon.

   B. precision isn't everything.

   C. predictions based on the peak of C. fistula's flowering do provide some reliable answers.

   D. sometimes rules of thumb are better than complex formulas.

30. According to Damaru Sahu, traditional weather prediction:

   F. can be curiously accurate.

   G. has a defined place in meteorology.

   H. is useful in some ways despite its lack of scientific foundation.

   J. appeals to an instinct different than the rational brain.

PASSAGE IV

SOCIAL SCIENCE: The following passage is adapted from the article "What Causes Overweight and Obesity" released by the National Heart, Lung and Blood Institute.

The past 10 years have seen a dramatic rise in "diseases of affluence" in the United States. Americans suffer from type II diabetes, obesity, and cardiovascular disease in epidemic
5 proportions. Indeed, American culture is often perceived to be entrenched in fast-food, excessive consumption, and minimal physical exertion. Supermarkets and restaurants in the United States serve a panoply of processed
10 foods loaded with sugar, preservatives, transfats and cholesterol. Children develop poor eating habits—from sugar-laden cereals to school lunches drenched in saturated fat— that, unfortunately, last into adulthood. While
15 changes in diet are partly responsible for American obesity, the primary cause of obesity is the sedentary lifestyle that 40 percent of Americans currently lead.

For most of human history, people worked
20 as farmers, hunters, laborers, and tradesmen— all physically demanding occupations. Blacksmiths hammered metal, servants washed dirty linen, and farmers lifted hay bales by hand. At the time, the only sources of work
25 energy were animals or man power. However, these lifestyles afforded people vast stretches of idle time—winter months, religious holidays, and festivals—to rest and recover. Furthermore, routine and leisure activities also re-
30 quired more physical exertion. For all but the wealthy, everyday life was similar to a balanced gym routine. Despite high mortality from infectious diseases and malnutrition (and debilitating physical injuries suffered in far more
35 hazardous working environments than today's workplace), physical fitness was standard.

Urbanization and industrialization during the 19th and 20th centuries drastically changed people's life-styles. Agricultural ad-
40 vances have led to increasingly larger farms manned by fewer workers. Machines are used for most aspects of farming, from sowing seeds to harvesting. Manufacturing, meanwhile, transformed into a system of mass pro-
45 duction facilitated by machines—a process that does not require the range or degree of physical exertion from workers as was necessitated by preindustrial fabrication. People began to move less and sit more. During the 20th
50 century, increasingly elaborate systems of government and finance brought about the most sedentary workplace of all: the office building. Suddenly, massive complexes peopled by legions of clerks, salespeople, analysts, and sec-
55 retaries manning telephones, computers, and typewriters began to fill the American city. Urbanization condensed all aspects of living into a few square blocks. The conveniences of the modern urban environment are also con-
60 ducive to inactivity. Transportation has also exacerbated the problem by offering city dwellers numerous options for travel, none of which requires any real physical exertion. Therefore, the average 9-to-5 worker can go to work, run er-
65 rands, and seek entertainment with little more effort than what is required to walk to and from a car or a mass transit station.

Leisure has likewise contributed to the obesity epidemic. Watching television and playing
70 video games have supplanted sports, leisurely strolls, and horse-riding as popular pastimes. Pre-studies have revealed a positive correlation

between hours of television viewing and levels of
obesity. In fact, video games are found to play an
75 especially significant role in childhood obesity.

    Despite the proliferation of gimmick diets
and fancy gadgets, losing weight is actually a
simple matter of burning more calories than
one consumes. Active living initiatives are
80 working hard to bring more movement into
the average American's life. Urban planners are
designing cities that include more sidewalks,
crosswalks, parks, and bicycle trails. Education
programs and advertising campaigns seek to
85 reform the deleterious habits of adults and create
more active lifestyles in children. Parents and
nutritionists are working together to banish
some of the more egregious offenders—fries,
pizza, and soda—from public school cafeterias.

90   In the 21st century, the stakes for combating
obesity in the United States are increasingly
high. As an overweight baby boom generation
enters its twilight, insurance providers and
health care professionals are encountering
95 alarming rates of diabetes and heart disease.
American life expectancy has begun to drop
from all-time highs during the late 1990s. Even
more concerning is the earlier onset of obesity
in younger generations. Given that the World
100 Health Organization has estimated 60 percent
of the global population get insufficient exercise, finding a way to get people back in shape
is perhaps the greatest health care issue that
the world currently faces.

31. According to the author, pre-industrial
    revolution farmers faced challenges of:
    A. winter weather.
    B. obesity.
    C. disease.
    D. poor eating habits.

32. According to the passage, all of the following
    are aspects of pre-industrial culture
    responsible for promoting physical fitness
    EXCEPT:
    F. the hazardous conditions of the 19th-
       century workplace.
    G. the variety of physical activity required
       by most occupations.
    H. the absence of alternative energy
       sources for performing tasks.
    J. the vigor of leisure activities.

33. The function of lines 19-36 is to:
    A. provide examples of typical pre-industrial
       occupations that have been rendered
       obsolete.
    B. cite occupations that necessitated human
       energy for successful completion.
    C. recommend jobs that modern Americans
       should pursue to counter obesity.
    D. explain why consuming foods rich in
       calories was more acceptable in past eras.

34. The third paragraph details the effects of
    industrialization on the workplace by:
    F. citing the hazards of the modern
       workplace.
    G. lamenting the working conditions in
       office buildings.
    H. praising the efficiency of modern farming
       and manufacturing.
    J. indicating specific ways in which modern
       workers do less physical work.

35. The author mentions 9-5 workers (lines 63-67) in order to:

    A. give an example of people who do not get a lot of exercise.

    B. prove that pre-industrial revolution farm workers are superior to modern office workers.

    C. criticize urbanization.

    D. support nutritional initiatives to combat obesity.

36. All of the following are cited as those working to make people more active and improve diets EXCEPT:

    F. urban planners.

    G. advertisers.

    H. nutritionists.

    J. physicians.

37. According to the passage, losing weight:

    A. is essential to avoiding health problems in later life.

    B. can be achieved only through excessive levels of physical exertion.

    C. is possible when caloric intake exceeds energy burned through activity.

    D. requires a deficit between consumption and metabolism.

38. The author most likely mentions diets and exercise machines to:

    F. contrast public opinion with the simplicity of losing weight.

    G. give examples of effective weight loss techniques.

    H. critique nontraditional methods of combating obesity.

    J. emphasize the ease of using modern exercise machines.

39. Based on the passage, health-conscious families and experts' attitudes toward public school lunches can best be described as:

    A. ambivalent.

    B. inimical.

    C. apathetic.

    D. enthralled.

40. The author most likely mentions *life expectancy* in line 96 in order to:

    F. emphasize the longevity of Americans during the 1990s.

    G. indicate that obesity has innocuous effects on older Americans.

    H. illustrate long-term effects of obesity in the U.S. population.

    J. contrast American health with the health of people in other countries.

ANSWERS AND EXPLANATIONS

PASSAGE I

Suggested Passage Map notes:

¶1: Walter Scott (S) born in Scotland in 1771, wrote Scottish ballads

¶2: S poetry brought fame

¶3: 1814, S started writing novels anonymously for $

¶4: 1820 S wrote *Ivanhoe* set in England, became Baronet

¶5: wrote for $ until his death in 1832

¶6: S (1) popularized historical novel, (2) rehabilitated Highland culture

¶7: S responsible for Scottish banks retaining right to issue own banknotes

1. B **Difficulty:** Medium

Category: Global

Getting to the Answer: This question focuses on the big picture. You should be predicting the purpose and main idea of every passage so you can deal with questions like this quickly. Your notes should tell you that the author is writing more about Scott's achievements than about his weaknesses. You can predict that the answer will be favorable overall. Choice A is out of scope; this choice lacks a sufficient focus on Scott. Choice (B) matches your prediction. Scott's success is stressed throughout and the last two paragraphs point out Scott's impact in several areas. Choice C is a distortion; although you read that Scott had financial difficulties, the financial aspect is much less important than is the success of his writing. Choice D is a distortion; the passage offers no support for this claim.

2. J **Difficulty:** Medium

Category: Detail

Getting to the Answer: On Detail questions, first find the appropriate section in the passage. Read the question carefully; sometimes a single word can make a major difference in selecting the correct answer. Note that the question asks about why Scott started writing novels, not poetry, so look to Paragraph 3, where the author first talks about Scott's novels. The first line tells you that financial difficulties led Scott to write a novel, which met with great success. Look for a choice that matches this idea. Choice F is out of scope; the author doesn't list this outcome as a result of Scott's polio. Choice G is out of scope; nothing in the passage mentions *copyright violations*. Choice H is out of scope; the author doesn't reference whether the ballads sold well or not. Choice (J) fits the prediction.

3. D **Difficulty:** Low

Category: Detail

Getting to the Answer: If your notes don't help, titles, whether italicized or capitalized, are easier to spot when skimming. In the third paragraph, you see that the author references *Waverley* to mention that Scott left his name off it because he was "mindful of his reputation as a poet." Use this as your prediction. Choice A is a distortion; your research tells you that it was his reputation as a poet, not as a lawyer, that concerned Scott. Choice B is a misused detail; the author tells you that Scott found writing anonymously *fun* only after he believed that it would not damage his reputation as a poet. Choice C is out of scope; although the fact that Scott was *widely rumored* to be the author indicates that there was public interest in the novels' author, there is nothing to suggest that interest spurred sales. Choice (D) matches the prediction.

4. J **Difficulty:** Medium

Category: Writer's View

Getting to the Answer: Use the passage to help you understand the author's view of this concept. First find where he refers to Scott and Scottish history, and then focus on the tone of that discussion. Consider the author's overall attitude toward Scott, which is positive. In Paragraph 4, the author mentions Scott's popularization of the tartan and kilt and writes that he turned them into symbols of national identity. Also, in Paragraph 6, you see in lines 92-93 that Scott's novels "rehabilitated Highland culture after years in the shadows." Choice F is opposite; the author's tone is more admiring than this. Choice G is opposite; to say that Scott "rehabilitated Highland culture" sounds important. Choice H is a distortion; Scott wrote novels, not "serious analyses of Scottish history." Choice (J) matches the research above.

5.   A   Difficulty: Medium

Category: Global

Getting to the Answer: When in doubt, keep in mind the overall tone that the author takes in the passage. This question asks about Scott's reputation after his death. Since the overall structure of the passage is chronological, it is likely that the answer will come toward the end. The last three paragraphs give evidence of Scott's continued popularity: you read that his novels continued to sell after his death, eventually covering his debts; that Edinburgh's central railroad station was named after his first successful novel; and that his picture is on Scottish currency today. You can predict that his reputation has only grown or is still positive. Choice (A) matches the prediction, and a quick check of the other choices shows that this is the only one with a positive description. Choice B is opposite; the passage clearly states that Scott's novels continued to sell well after his death. Choice C is a distortion; his debts were unpaid, but this did not affect Scott's reputation. Choice D is a distortion; the passage does mention such imitators (lines 86-88), but the author doesn't suggest that they damaged Scott's reputation.

6.   F   Difficulty: High

Category: Vocab-in-Context

Getting to the Answer: Sir Walter Scott never put his own name to his novels, but instead attributed them to "the author of Waverley," or to no author at all. He continued to do this even when his novels became so popular that it would not have hurt his reputation to reveal his name. Nevertheless he "maintained the façade," meaning that he continued to hide his own authorship under the pretense that he was not the author of the novels, a match for (F). Choice G is another definition of façade, but it doesn't make sense in the context of the passage. Choice H has a negative connotation, while the author says Scott maintained the pretense "out of a sense of fun." Choice G also doesn't make sense in the sentence.

7.   B   Difficulty: Low

Category: Function

Getting to the Answer: To understand the function of a word in context, reading the entire sentence it appears in should be enough. Ask yourself why the placement of this statue would be fitting—the author has not referred to Wallace before this point. The author has, however, previously stressed Scott's affinity for his native land, Scotland, for which Wallace is a great historical figure. Look for a connection with Scotland among the choices. Choice A is out of scope; nothing in the passage suggests that Scott ever wrote a novel about Wallace. Choice (B) fits your prediction. Choice C is out of scope; this fails to address the choice of Wallace. Choice D is out of scope; the passage doesn't support this.

8.   H   Difficulty: Medium

Category: Writer's View

Getting to the Answer: You will need to answer this question from your overall impression of the passage rather than any specific paragraph. First you need to decide whether the author's attitude is positive or negative. Look to the close of the passage; you know that the author believes Scott was responsible for two major trends. The focus on Scott's achievements indicates that the author admires Scott's work. Choice F is a distortion; nothing indicates that the author is skeptical toward Scott's achievements. Choice G is opposite; both of these adjectives are too negative. Choice (H) matches your prediction. Choice J is out of scope; the passage gives no such indication of jealousy.

9. D   Difficulty: Low

Category: Global

Getting to the Answer: Paragraph references focus your research. Use your notes and reference the passage as needed. The author writes that Sir Walter refused to declare bankruptcy, insisting on putting his home and income into a trust that would eventually pay back his creditors completely. Predict that he was committed to paying his debts back. Choice A is opposite; the passage clearly contradicts this. Choice B is out of scope; the author never discusses the cause of Scott's debts. Choice C is out of scope; the author doesn't mention such annoyance on Scott's part. Choice (D) matches the prediction.

10. F   Difficulty: Low

Category: Writer's View

Getting to the Answer: Read the complete sentence for context. You may need to read the ones before and after as well. The prior sentence states that Scott was working as a lawyer, after which you read the first mention of Scott's writings. The subsequent sentences make clear that the emphasis has shifted to Scott's literary career. So the sentence including *dabbling* deals with Scott's first forays into writing. Look for a choice that captures that idea. Choice (F) matches the thrust of the prediction. Choice G is a misused detail; Scott's printing press is not mentioned until Paragraph 3, and the author draws no connection between his *dabbling* and his financial troubles. Choice H is a distortion; he was certainly inexperienced, but there is no evidence that his work was inferior. Choice J is a distortion; *dabbling* refers to Scott's writing, not to his interest in history.

PASSAGE II

Suggested Passage Map notes:

¶1: Woolf (W) essay "Mr. Bennett and Mrs. Brown" = enduring literary criticism

¶2: Hynes described debate, W said Bennett (B) was materialistic, wanted to discredit B

¶3: 1923 B said W characters don't "survive in the mind"

¶4: W said B obsessed with dull details

¶5: B's literary reputation didn't recover

¶6: W noted after B died that he had some skill, but she felt he had to be pulled down

11. C   Difficulty: High

Category: Writer's View

Getting to the Answer: Questions that encompass the whole passage will often offer choices that distort or misuse details from the passage. Your notes should give you a good read on "big-picture" questions like this. The author seems to feel that Woolf treated Bennett harshly, detracting from her own reputation, at least in his eyes. The passage makes clear that Bennett's career was never the same and that Woolf's essay paved the way for literary modernism. Choice (C) matches that idea. Choice A is a distortion; the author of the passage compares the authors' strengths and weaknesses, but you receive no indication as to what Woolf considered her own advantages or disadvantages compared to Bennett et al. Choice B is a distortion; the passage lists only the slightest of praise on Woolf's part for Bennett and his peers. Choice D is out of scope; the author references no such repercussions for Woolf.

12. F   Difficulty: Medium

Category: Vocab-in-Context

Getting to the Answer: The word *polemic* is used throughout the passage, which focuses on Woolf's criticism of Arnold Bennett. Criticism best matches (F), *attack*. Choice G is too neutral, H implies an opposite side, which isn't in the passage, and J is opposite.

13. D   Difficulty: Medium

Category: Writer's View

Getting to the Answer: Ask yourself what the writer is attempting to accomplish—why he says what he does. In the paragraph, the author claims that only *a handful* of such disputes "survive their moment," after which he lists two presumably famous ones. But he follows that by saying that few others "can have been so damaging, or so lasting in consequences." Predict that the author feels that this polemic may have been the most important one yet. Choice (D) matches this prediction. Choice A is a distortion; the author doesn't indicate this. Choice B is extreme; even among the others in the *handful*, none is characterized by the author as being so pivotal. Choice C is a distortion; the author doesn't use the comparison to make this point.

14. F   **Difficulty:** Medium

Category: Detail

Getting to the Answer: Use your notes to help find the paragraph where the author discusses this. Discussion of Bennett's work appears in several paragraphs, but the most in-depth treatment comes in Paragraph 4: for example, "a writer obsessed with dull particulars of setting" (lines 57-58), and "he would describe her house in conscientious detail but never penetrate her essential life." Choice (F) correctly matches these ideas. Choice G is opposite; this contradicts the information found in Paragraph 4. Choice H is out of scope; you know of the one essay Woolf wrote attacking Bennett, but not any more than that on this subject. Choice J is extreme; the passage indicates that Bennett did focus on certain details, but it doesn't indicate that he did so to the degree suggested here.

15. C   **Difficulty:** Medium

Category: Global

Getting to the Answer: Some questions will be so generally worded that making a prediction won't be feasible. Start working through the choices, and you should see which part of the passage to research. All of the choices reference the term *polemic*. The author deals with this term most directly in the first paragraph. Compare the choices against that paragraph, only researching further as required. The passage deals primarily with Woolf's polemic and its effect on twentieth-century literature, which matches (C). Choice A is out of scope; the author would likely agree that Woolf provides a great

example of a successful polemic, but he never offers advice about formulating such a work. Choice B is a distortion; the author doesn't offer a *new interpretation*. He discusses and expands on the generally understood view of the dispute. Choice D is out of scope; the author mentions other polemics only as an introduction to discussing Woolf's essay. He doesn't rank or compare multiple polemics.

16. F   **Difficulty:** Medium

Category: Vocab-in-Context

Getting to the Answer: Always try to make a prediction based on context before moving to the choices. When you go to the reference, you'll remember that even the author seems unsure of what Woolf means in using this phrase. Directly before this, however, you read that Woolf wrote that Bennett "had a materialistic view of the world." Look for a choice that incorporates this idea. Choice (F) is correct. Choice G is a distortion; this group is mentioned before the comment on Bennett, but there is no indication that he and the group are related in any way. Choice H is a distortion; this quotes a criticism that Bennett made about Woolf. Choice J is a misused detail; this may be an example of the concept, but it is too specific to represent the entire meaning of the phrase.

17. C   **Difficulty:** High

Category: Writer's View

Getting to the Answer: Take the citation given and put it in your own words. Then review each specific example to see if it matches the general idea of your paraphrase. The quotation refers to Woolf's criticism of a writer whom most observers of that era considered well established and successful. Work through the choices, looking for a match to this general idea. The analogy suggests that Woolf tried to achieve something but couldn't. The *Yes* that begins that sentence (lines 96-99) indicates a continuation of the idea in the previous sentence—a criticism of Woolf, who supposedly envied the *reality gift* displayed by Bennett. Choice (C) matches well. Choice A is a distortion; the author doesn't express an opinion of *Jacob's Room*. He only cites Bennett's opinion of it. Choice B is out of scope; the author refers to this book as an authority for his own essay, but expresses no *view* on it. Choice D is a distortion; this parenthetical comment by the author is not strong enough to *pull down* Bennett's reputation.

18. J   Difficulty: Medium

Category: Detail

Getting to the Answer: A good set of notes will help you to move quickly, even when you don't receive a line reference. Your notes should show you that the author addresses *Jacob's Room* in Paragraph 3. Bennett praised the novel's *originality* and writing style but concluded that "the characters do not vitally survive in the mind." Bennett found this to be a serious deficiency. Only (J) matches the thrust of the citation. Choice F is out of scope; Bennett never compares the work to other novels. Choice G is out of scope; the author does not cite Bennett referring to this. Choice H is opposite; Bennett feels the novel does well in small ways but fails where it counts.

19. B   Difficulty: Medium

Category: Inference

Getting to the Answer: Find the relevant spot in the text, and predict an inference that is close to something said in the text. You find Woolf's opinion on "details of scene" in Paragraph 4. As the author paraphrases, Woolf charged that Bennett would describe Mrs. Brown's "house in conscientious detail but never penetrate her essential life." Predict that such details can't capture a character's inner feelings. Choice (B) accurately matches this prediction. Choice A is a distortion; Woolf criticizes much of the work of these writers, but such feelings are not her reason for devaluing details of scene. Choice C is a distortion; this draws from Woolf's quote on one of Bennett's works. Choice D is a distortion; she might feel this way, but this pulls more from a comment made by Bennett.

20. J   Difficulty: Medium

Category: Function

Getting to the Answer: This is the only paragraph in which Woolf gives credit to Bennett, beginning with the quote in the question. Here Woolf is praising Bennett, making (J) correct. Choice F is opposite; Woolf doesn't say she retracts her criticism, but only gives faint praise upon Bennett's death. Choice G is opposite because to excoriate is to severely criticize. Choice H is also opposite; Woolf is praising Bennett, not the other way around.

PASSAGE III

Suggested Passage Map notes:

¶1: Researchers in Junagadh, India attempt accurate forecast

¶2: 1st trad. rule: monsoon begins 45 days after *Cassia fistula* tree blooms

¶3: 2nd trad. rule: north or west wind = good monsoon, east = drought

¶4: Trad. rules not exact, but general trend is correct

¶5: Dr. K started in 1990 when old saying was exactly correct

¶6: Meteorologist Sahu disagrees w/ Dr. K

¶7: Dr. K hopes research will show trad. methods are valid; holds conference

¶8: Dr. K started NGO to support further research

21. B   Difficulty: Medium

Category: Detail

Getting to the Answer: More difficult Detail questions can be approached using elimination and careful reading. Remember the EXCEPT. For "except" questions, review the answer choices methodically, eliminating those which fail to meet the conditions of the question stem. The passage deals in some depth with both the flowering of the fistula tree, C, and the wind during Holi, A, so you can eliminate those first. Paragraph 5 states that Dr. Kanani became interested in traditional methods when a tenth-century rule of thumb "proved strikingly correct," which suggests that D has been tested. In contrast, the bird behavior is merely listed as an example of a rule of thumb uncovered in one of Kanani's conferences, making (B) the correct answer.

22. J   Difficulty: Medium

Category: Function

Getting to the Answer: Identify the paragraph in which these words appear; it ends with the statement that farmers need more precise forecasts than traditional methods provide. However, science has not developed good alternatives for farmers in different regions. Match this with (J). Choice F is opposite; the author writes that "Every year, the average rainfall over the whole country is calculated, and this prediction is proved correct" (lines 72-75). Choice G isn't mentioned in the passage, and H is a distortion.

23. A   Difficulty: Low

Category: Detail

Getting to the Answer: Your map should tell you that information about the winds observed during the Holi festival is in the third paragraph. In that paragraph, the author states that "Wind from the north or west suggests a good monsoon, whereas wind from the east indicates drought" (lines 36-38), which matches (A). Choices B and C are in the wrong direction, and D, southwest, is not mentioned.

24. G   Difficulty: Medium

Category: Writer's View

Getting to the Answer: Writer's View questions encompassing the whole text will draw on evidence from the entire passage. A good prediction depends on your ability to synthesize the major ideas from throughout the passage. The passage mentions several traditional methods and their general accuracy. Even the scientific skepticism described in the passage admits a place for traditional methodology. The passage validates traditional methods, so predict that the author finds these methods to be valuable. Choice (G)

matches this prediction. Choice F is out of scope; while the author briefly discusses the origins of some methods, she never expresses more interest in the development of the methods. Choice H is a distortion; the skepticism gets relatively little treatment and is followed by a detailed discussion of the progress toward making a real science of traditional methods. Choice J is opposite; the author never casts interest in traditional methods as a *fad,* and, as noted before, mentions the success of traditional methods more than once.

25. D   Difficulty: Low

Category: Detail

Getting to the Answer: Look to your notes to find specific locations for tested details. According to Paragraph 5, Bhadli's storm method offers a 72-day warning. None of the other cited methods provides the same sort of accuracy over such a specific and extended time period, so look for Bhadli's method among the choices. Choice (D) matches this prediction. Choice A is a distortion; while the author mentions bird behavior as a possible predictor discussed at a conference, no information is given about the nature of this prediction. Choice B is a distortion; the flowering of the fistula tree does provide a specific and accurate prediction, but it gives only 45 days' advance warning. Choice C is a distortion; while the passage describes a loose correlation between the character of the monsoon and the wind direction on Holi, this method doesn't predict when the monsoon will arrive.

26. J   Difficulty: Low

Category: Function

Getting to the Answer: Beware of answer choices that present details that are narrower than the main point of the paragraph or sum up surrounding paragraphs instead of the target of the question. Focus on the overall topic of the paragraph and how it helps build the story or argument in the passage. The passage in general describes the accuracy of traditional methods of weather prediction. The paragraph provides an example of a traditional method and introduces you to Dr. Kanani and his interest in applying scientific rigor to these methods; this can serve as your prediction. Choice (J) matches this prediction. Choice F is a misused detail; this sums up the first paragraph. Choice G is a misused detail; this accounts only for the last sentence of the cited paragraph. Choice H is a distortion; while the ancient saying is examined in passage, this choice casts this examination as the central issue.

27. B   Difficulty: Low

Category: Detail

Getting to the Answer: For Detail questions, rely on your notes to direct your research to the relevant part of the passage. In the topic sentence of the seventh paragraph, lines 77-80 read: "Dr. Kanani hopes that his research will put traditional methods on a proper scientific footing. He and his colleagues have even set up a sort of peer-review forum." Predict that the conference's goal is this establishment of traditional methods as worthy subjects of scientific inquiry. Choice (B) matches this prediction. Choice A is out of scope; the passage never discusses the disappearance of traditional methods. Choice C is a misused detail; while Dr. Kanani does, in fact, publish the methods in the local press, this is not the objective of the conference. Choice D is out of scope; the passage never mentions the exchange of ideas between geographically distant farmers.

28. H   Difficulty: Medium

Category: Inference

Getting to the Answer: Beware of general answer choices. Attack the question stem, get a good understanding of what it's really asking, and make a solid prediction. The question asks you for the reason farmers predict the weather using traditional methods. What do they hope to accomplish? When the question is rephrased, the answer seems more obvious; predict that the correct choice, according to the first paragraph, will show that they want to know what to plant, so they need to know what's coming. Choice (H) matches this prediction. Choice F

is out of scope; the passage never mentions the accessibility of the methods. Choice G is a distortion; while *normal monsoons* are discussed in Paragraph 6, this is in reference to modern meteorology, not traditional methods of forecasting. Choice J is a distortion; while traditional methods do get the basics right, the question asks why the farmers are trying to get the basics right in the first place.

29. C   Difficulty: Medium

Category: Function

Getting to the Answer: Eliminate answers that are inconsistent with the central concerns of the passage. Reread the specific reference and the surrounding text, which identifies the flowering of *C. fistula* as a monsoon predictor that isn't *perfect*, but still of value and interest. Predict that the correct choice will account for both an appreciation of this traditional method and an awareness of its limitations. Choice (C) matches this prediction. Choice A is extreme; while the author feels that the predictive data are useful and noteworthy, calling them *remarkable* goes too far. Choice B is out of scope; the author never attempts to generalize on the relative value of precision. Choice D is out of scope; again, the author neither casts traditional methods as rules of thumb and scientific methods as complex formulas nor attempts to elevate one over the other.

30. H   Difficulty: Low

Category: Detail

Getting to the Answer: Consult your notes to direct your research to the relevant text. Sahu says in lines 65-67 that traditional prediction may be "OK as a hobby," but "may not be applicable to this modern age," then concedes that modern-era forecasts are not always helpful to farmers in the way traditional methods claim to be. That some utility exists despite scientific skepticism serves as a good prediction and an accurate paraphrase of his attitude. Choice (H) summarizes Sahu's attitude and matches this prediction. Choice F is opposite; the author identifies Sahu as claiming the methods "cannot be relied upon" (line 66). Choice G is opposite; Sahu rejects traditional methods from the scientific view. Choice J is out of scope; Sahu never mentions the *appeal* of the methods, only their trustworthiness as predictors.

PASSAGE IV

Suggested Passage Map notes:

¶1: recent ↑ type II diabetes, obesity, heart disease

¶2: historically people were more active

¶3: urban. & industr. changed lifestyles, more sedentary

¶4: Leisure is less active

¶5: Burning more calories than consuming = lose weight

¶6: Preventing these diseases is extremely important

31. C   Difficulty: Low

Category: Detail

Getting to the Answer: As your map tells you, farmers in this era are discussed in the first paragraph, but the only one of the answers mentioned there is disease, which matches (C). Winter is mentioned as an idle time (line 27), but not having to work so hard is not necessarily a challenge. Obesity and poor eating habits are afflictions of the modern world, not the pre-industrial one.

32. F   Difficulty: Low

Category: Detail

Getting to the Answer: Whenever a question uses the phrase "EXCEPT," eliminating obviously incorrect answer choices first can make finding the correct choice easier. The author lists several aspects of pre-industrial life that contributed to overall physical fitness. The author never suggests that (F), hazardous conditions of the 19th-century workplace, were conducive to being fit. Choice G is incorrect because the author mentions variation in activity in Paragraph 2. Choice H is incorrect because the second paragraph cites animal and manpower as the

primary sources of pre-industrial work energy. Choice J is incorrect because Paragraph 4 discusses the physicality of pre-industrial pastimes.

33. B   Difficulty: Medium

Category: Writer's View

Getting to the Answer: When answer choices begin with verbs, eliminate choices that don't match the author's purpose. Put yourself in the author's shoes and ask yourself, "Why would I include that information?" The author mentions these occupations to support the main idea of the second paragraph—jobs in pre-industrial society required more physical activity. Choice (B) matches the prediction well. Choice A is out of scope; the passage does not mention jobs that are obsolete. Choice C is extreme; while the passage focuses on obesity, the author does not recommend specific occupations for people. Choice D is a misused detail; caloric intake and nutrition are mentioned in the first paragraph, not the second.

34. J   Difficulty: Medium

Category: Inference

Getting to the Answer: It is sometimes helpful to consider information from the author's viewpoint to determine what it implies. The author describes how the modern workplace promotes obesity by showing ways in which modern work requires less energy from people. Choice (J) is correct. Choice F is opposite; the passage describes pre-industrial work as hazardous. Choice G is extreme; the word *lament* is too strong for the context of the passage, which does not refer to grieving. Choice H is extreme; the passage does not praise modern working conditions.

35. A   Difficulty: Medium

Category: Function

Getting to the Answer: Here, 9-5 workers are examples of people who have "numerous options for travel, none of which require any real physical exertion" (lines 62-63), which matches (A). Choice B is a distortion; the word *prove* is too extreme, and the author doesn't write that farmers are superior to office workers. Choice C is also a distortion; though the author seems to blame urbanization for some aspects of obesity, the author doesn't go so far as to criticize it. Choice D is out of scope—initiatives are in Paragraph 4, and nutritional initiatives have nothing to do with making people more active.

36. J   Difficulty: Medium

Category: Detail

Getting to the Answer: By reviewing lines 76-89, you'll see that all answers except (J) are in the paragraph. Although it can be assumed that physicians are also working toward better health, they are not specifically mentioned.

37. D   Difficulty: High

Category: Detail

Getting to the Answer: Incorrect answers on Detail questions often employ language from the passage. Look for the idea that matches your prediction, not the exact wording. Lines 77-79 state that losing weight requires burning more calories than one consumes. Choice (D) expresses the same basic concept. Choice A is out of scope; while the passage suggests that weight loss is beneficial, the author never directly states this information. Choice B is extreme; the passage does not state that excessive levels of exercise are required for weight loss. Choice C is opposite; the passage states that one must burn more calories than are consumed, not consume more calories than are burned.

38. F   Difficulty: High

Category: Writer's View

Getting to the Answer: Writer's View questions require you to figure out why the author does what he does. Consider how the information relates to the paragraph topic and passage as a whole. The paragraph topic relates measures that people could take to combat obesity. The author mentions

gimmick diets and exercise machines as a means of explaining how losing weight is simpler than people realize. Choice (F) matches your prediction. Choice G is opposite; the passage does not suggest that these methods are effective. Choice H is a distortion; the author's purpose is not to criticize these methods, but rather to focus on the simplicity of losing weight. Choice J is a distortion; the passage focuses more on the ease, or rather simplicity, of losing weight, not of using exercise machines.

39. B   Difficulty: High

Category: Inference

Getting to the Answer: Questions that ask about tone often require you to choose between subtle shades of emotion. A little vocabulary study can help make such differences clear. The author states that parents and nutritionists have banished certain foods from public schools, indicating hostility to such foods. Choice (B) fits this prediction. Choice A is incorrect because the passage doesn't mention any uncertainty in feelings. Choice C is incorrect because the passage clearly indicates that parents and nutritionists care and thus are not apathetic. Choice D is incorrect because *enthralled,* or *fascinated,* is not at all mentioned in the passage.

40. H   Difficulty: Medium

Category: Writer's View

Getting to the Answer: Remember that a Writer's View answer will always be consistent with the main idea of the passage. The last paragraph discusses the increasing need to deal with the obesity problem. Choice (H) supports this. Choice F is a misused detail; while Americans during the 1990s lived longer, this choice has nothing to do with the paragraph topic. Choice G is opposite; the passage does not characterize the effects of obesity as innocuous, or harmless. Choice J is out of scope; American health is not directly compared to the health of people in other countries.

CHAPTER FIFTEEN

Paired Passages

GETTING STARTED

Passage Types

The ACT Reading Test includes three long single passages and one Paired Passage set consisting of two shorter passages. The **Paired Passages** can be any of the four passage types. These **Paired Passages** are about a similar topic, but they present different information or points of view. Some questions for **Paired Passages** ask about only one of the passages, while other questions ask about both passages.

You should create a Passage Map for every passage on the Reading Test. You will use the **Paired Passages** passage type to determine which approach to take for Passage Mapping. The different approaches to reading and mapping the four passage types are summarized in the table below. To learn more about the different approaches for each passage type in more depth, review Chapters 13 and 14.

Passage Type(s)	Approach
Prose Fiction (includes **Literary Narrative**)	• Note the author's central ideas and themes • Note characters' personalities, opinions, and relationships with each other
Natural Science	• Identify the author's thesis • Note the main idea of each paragraph • Don't let technical scientific terms intimidate you; no outside science knowledge is needed • Note the definitions of scientific terms that are provided within the passage text (or passage introduction)
Social Science & Humanities	• Identify the author's thesis (often explicitly stated in the first paragraph) • Note the main idea of each paragraph

The key to success with **Paired Passages** is to keep straight who said what. To help you accomplish that task, Kaplan has a specific Method for approaching **Paired Passages.** The Kaplan Method for Paired Passages has three steps:

Step 1: Actively read Passage A, then answer its questions
Step 2: Actively read Passage B, then answer its questions
Step 3: Answer questions about both passages

These steps are to be used along with the Kaplan Method for ACT Reading (Read actively; Examine the question stem; Predict and answer).

By reading Passage A and answering its questions before moving on to Passage B, you avoid falling into incorrect answer traps that reference the text of Passage B. Furthermore, by addressing each passage individually, you will have a better sense of the central idea and purpose of each passage. This will help you answer questions that ask you to synthesize information about both passages.

> ✔ **Note**
>
> Even though the individual passages are shorter in a **Paired Passage** set, you should still map them using the mapping strategy specific to the passage type. Overall, there are too many details and too many questions—not to mention the likelihood of getting the passages mixed up!—to remember effectively in your head. Your Passage Maps will save you time by helping you locate key details and evidence quickly while staying focused on the main ideas in the passages.

Fortunately, questions in a **Paired Passage** set that ask about only one of the passages will be no different from questions you've seen and answered about single passages. Use the same strategies you've been using to answer these questions.

> ✔ **Expert Tip**
>
> After reading Passage A, remind yourself to "forget" it so you can read Passage B independently.

Synthesis Questions

Several questions in a **Paired Passage** set will be Synthesis questions. These questions will ask you about both passages. You may be asked to identify similarities or differences between the passages or to predict how the author of one passage might respond to a point made by the author of the other passage.

Prior to attacking the Synthesis questions, review your map for Passage A, then identify the relationship between the passages. Possible relationships include two complementary views, two opposing views, one view modifying the other, one passage applying an idea discussed in the other, and more. After identifying the relationship between the passages, proceed to answer the questions about both passages.

> ✔ **Expert Tip**
>
> The toughest questions in the **Paired Passages** are usually the Synthesis questions that ask you about both passages. Thinking through, and noting at the end of your Passage Map, the relationship between the passages *before* working on these questions will improve your accuracy.

IMPROVING WITH PRACTICE

Step 1: Compare Your Notes to the Suggested Paired Passage Passage Map

After reading the first passage, compare your notes to the suggested Passage Map and note the ways your map was both similar and different. Because Synthesis questions require you to answer questions about both passages, your Passage Maps for **Paired Passages** are even more important than usual. As usual, the exact notes you will take depend on the genre of the passages.

For **Prose Fiction** passages, take note of:

- The characters
- The characters' emotions and relationships
- The author's opinion of the characters
- The theme of the passage

For **Natural Science** passages, take note of:

- The central idea/theory discussed
- The relationship of each paragraph to the central idea. Is the paragraph explaining, supporting, criticizing, modifying, or applying the central idea?
- Any opinions, especially the author's
- The *location* of descriptive details and examples
- The *reason* the author included details and examples. Is the author using the information to support, modify, or refute the preceding idea?
- Any emphasis or "emotional" keywords. Keywords such as "remarkable," "unfortunate," "unprecedented," and "crucial" are important indicators of the author's tone.

For **Social Science** and **Humanities** passages, take note of:

- The main idea of each paragraph
- Any opinions, especially the author's
- The *location* of descriptive details and examples
- The *reason* the author included details and examples. Is the author using the information to support, modify, or refute the preceding idea?
- Any emphasis or "emotional" keywords. Keywords such as "remarkable," "unfortunate," "unprecedented," and "crucial" are important indicators of the author's tone.

> ✔ *Expert Tip*
>
> Narratives may appear in either Prose Fiction or Humanities passages. In narratives, the most important character is always the narrator. To create the best Passage Map and answer the questions as effectively as possible, be sure to identify as many characteristics of the narrator as possible, including age, gender, background, and more.

If you missed important information, go back to the passage and identify the keywords that you likely overlooked so you can recognize them more quickly next time. The ACT uses predictable keywords to alert you to the important ideas in the passage. Use these keywords to focus your attention and create strong Passage Maps.

After you've checked your Passage Map for Passage A, move on to Step 2 without looking at Passage B. Since you should always tackle the passages one at a time, you should practice them one at a time!

> ✔ *Note*
>
> Remember to divide and conquer **Paired Passages** by first reading and answering questions about Passage A. Then, read and answer questions about Passage B. Finally, answer the questions about both passages.

Step 2: Answer the Questions

Review the Answer and Explanation for each Passage A question as soon as you complete it. If you got the question correct, congratulate yourself! Then, take a moment to read the entire explanation to make sure you got the question correct for the right reason. Sometimes, the explanation may even help you notice a more efficient way to identify the correct answer next time.

Step 3: Review Incorrect Answers

If you got the question incorrect . . . still congratulate yourself! You're about to learn something new that you'll be able to use to improve your performance on Test Day. Don't read the explanation yet; instead, try the question again.

If you get the question correct the second time, read the explanation to see if you solved the question in the most efficient way. Identify the mistake you made the first time, and determine how you're going to avoid making that mistake again.

> ✔ *Expert Tip*
>
> **Many top scoring students have an ACT notebook where they write down what they learn from every question. Doing this can be time-consuming, but it can also help you identify the types of mistakes you tend to make.**

If you get the question incorrect the second time, use the explanation to learn how to get the question correct. Work through the question again while following the explanation, and identify the steps you will need to take to get a similar question correct. Although the passages and questions will change, the concepts being tested will not. When you encounter unfamiliar questions, take note of them for future study sessions.

> ✔ *Expert Tip*
>
> **Be sure to return to any questions you missed a day or two later and work through them again. Don't simply recall the correct answer, but go through the steps described in the explanation to be sure you retained the correct approach. You will never see this exact question again, but you *will* see others just like it on Test Day.**

After all that work, it's time to move to the next question. Once you have answered and reviewed every Passage A question, it's time to move on to Passage B! Go back to Step 1, and follow these steps again for Passage B questions. Finally, go back to Step 2, and follow steps 2 and 3 for the questions that ask about both passages.

Reviewing in this way will take time. However, improvement doesn't come from just doing lots and lots of questions; it comes from thinking through your approach and improving it with every question.

RAISING YOUR SCORE EVEN MORE

Questions that ask about one author's response to another will hinge on the emphasis and opinion keywords used by that author. Be sure to circle, underline, or note these keywords in some other way. For example, the author may be "dismayed" or may identify an opposing view as "mistaken." Strong opinion keywords justify strong, definite answer choices. In the absence of emphatic keywords, a more neutral answer choice will be correct.

> ✔ *Expert Tip*
>
> **Prove your answer using information in the passage before you pick it. If you can't find at least one line number that supports your answer, that answer choice is incorrect.**

PRACTICE QUESTIONS

The following test-like question sets provide an opportunity to practice reading Paired Passages and answering related questions.

PASSAGE I

NATURAL SCIENCE: Fossil fuels are energy-rich substances formed from the remains of organisms. Both coal and petroleum help power commercial energy throughout the world.

Passage A

Coal is a solid fossil fuel formed from the remains of land plants that flourished 300 to 400 million years ago. It is composed primarily of carbon but also contains small amounts of
5 sulfur. When the sulfur is released into the atmosphere as a result of burning, it can form SO_2, a corrosive gas that can damage plants and animals. When it combines with H_2O in the atmosphere, it can form sulfuric acid, one
10 of the main components of acid rain, which has been demonstrated to be an environmental hazard. Burning coal has also been shown to contain trace amounts of mercury and radioactive materials, similarly dangerous sub-
15 stances. The type of coal that is burned directly affects the amount of sulfur that is released into the atmosphere.

The formation of coal goes through discrete stages as, over millions of years, heat and pres-
20 sure act on decomposing plants. Coal begins as peat, partially decayed plant matter, which is still found today in swamps and bogs, and can be burned, but produces little heat. As the decayed plant material is compressed over time,
25 lignite is formed. Lignite is a sedimentary rock with low sulfur content and, like peat, also produces a small amount of heat when burned. With further compaction, lignite loses moisture, methane, and carbon dioxide, and becomes

30 bituminous coal, the form of coal most widely used. Bituminous coal is also a sedimentary rock, but it has a high sulfur content.

Anthracite, or hard coal, is a metamorphic rock formed when heat and pressure are added
35 to bituminous coal. Anthracite coal is most desirable because it burns very hot and also contains a much smaller amount of sulfur, meaning that it burns cleaner.

However, the supplies of anthracite on Earth
40 are limited. In the United States, most anthracite is extracted from the valleys of northeastern Pennsylvania, which is known as the Coal Region. The major American reserve of bitu-minous coal is in West Virginia, while the
45 largest coal producer in the world is The People's Republic of China. The United States and China are also foremost among the world's coal consumers. There are many other coal-producing areas throughout the world, though
50 in some cases, the coal is essentially tapped out, or other, cleaner sources of energy are preferred.

Coal is extracted from mines. For subsurface mines, machines dig shafts and tunnels under-ground to allow the miners to remove the
55 material. Buildup of poisonous gases, explosions, and collapses are all dangers that underground miners must face. The Sago Mine disaster of January 2006 in West Virginia—where only 1

of 13 trapped miners survived an explosion—
60 shows how extracting these underground deposits of solid material is still a very dangerous
process. Strip mining, or surface mining, is
cheaper and less hazardous than underground
mining. However, it often leaves the land
65 scarred and unsuitable for other uses.

Passage B

Petroleum, or crude oil, is a thick liquid that
contains organic compounds of hydrogen and
carbon, called hydrocarbons. The term "crude
oil" refers to both the unprocessed petroleum
70 and the products refined from it, such as
gasoline, heating oil, and asphalt. Petroleum
contains many types of hydrocarbons in liquid,
solid and gaseous forms, as well as sulfur,
oxygen, and nitrogen.

75 When organic material such as zooplankton
and algae settled on the bottoms of oceans
millions of years ago, the material mixed
with mud and was covered in sediment more
quickly than it could decay. Thousands of years
80 later, the sediments that contained the organic
material were subjected to intense amounts of
heat and pressure, changing them into a waxy
material called kerogen. From this substance,
liquid hydrocarbons can be produced to create
85 oil shale. When more heat was added to the
kerogen, it liquefied into the substance we
know as oil. Since hydrocarbons are usually
lighter than rock or water, they migrate upward
through the permeable rock layers until they
90 reach impermeable rocks. The areas where oil
remains in the porous rocks are called reservoirs.

Oil is traditionally pumped out of the layer
of reserves found under the surface of Earth.
In order to penetrate the earth, an oil well is
95 created using an oil rig, which turns a drill bit.

After the hole is drilled, a casing—a metal pipe
with a slightly smaller diameter than the
hole—is inserted and bonded to its surroundings, usually with cement. This strengthens the
100 sides of the hole, or wellbore, and keeps dangerous pressure zones isolated. This process is
repeated with smaller bits and thinner casings,
going deeper into the surface to reach the
reservoir. Drilling fluid is pushed through the
105 casings to break up the rock in front of the bit
and to clean away debris and lower the temperature of the bit, which grows very hot.
Once the reservoir is reached, the top of the
wellbore is usually equipped with a set of
110 valves encased in a pyramidal iron cage called
a Christmas Tree.

The natural pressure within the reservoir is
usually high enough to push the oil or gas up
to the surface. But sometimes, additional
115 measures, called secondary recovery, are
required. This is especially true in depleted
fields. Installing thinner tubing is one solution,
as are surface pump jacks—the structures that
look like horses repeatedly dipping their heads.

120 It is impossible to remove all of the oil in a
single reservoir. In fact, a 30 percent to
40 percent yield is typical. However, technology
has provided a few ways to increase drilling
yield, including forcing water or steam into the
125 rock to "push" out more of the oil. Even with
this technique, only about 50 percent of the
deposit will be extracted.

There are also more unconventional sources
of oil, including oil shale and tar sands. The
130 hydrocarbons obtained from these sources
require extensive processing to be useable,
reducing their value. The extraction process
also has a particularly large environmental
footprint.

Questions 1–3 ask about Passage A.

1. According to the first paragraph, all of the following are released or formed when coal is burned EXCEPT:

   A. SO_2.

   B. sulfuric acid.

   C. hydrocarbons.

   D. mercury.

2. The passage suggests that which of the following has the smallest amount of moisture, methane, and carbon dioxide?

   F. Lignite

   G. Peat

   H. Bituminous coal

   J. Kerogen

3. The author contrasts bituminous coal with anthracite in order to:

   A. indicate that bituminous coal burns cleaner.

   B. compare the amount of mercury in each one.

   C. suggest that burning anthracite is better for the environment.

   D. recommend replacing all coals with oil.

Questions 4–6 ask about Passage B.

4. As it is used in lines 133-134, the phrase *environmental footprint* most likely means:

   F. indentations in the surface of the earth.

   G. the positive environmental results of extracting oil.

   H. the effect that a person or activity has on the environment.

   J. irreversible damage to the earth.

5. According to the passage, the second step in extracting the oil is:

   A. drilling a hole.

   B. pushing in drilling fluid.

   C. topping with valves.

   D. inserting a pipe.

6. What is most likely true about an oil field in which a pump jack is installed?

   F. Oil is being extracted in the safest way.

   G. The oil reserves in the field are greatly diminished.

   H. About 60 percent of the available oil is recovered.

   J. The wellbore is strengthened.

7. Both passages include details regarding all of the following EXCEPT:

    A. the transformation of organic material into usable energy sources.

    B. the lengthy nature of converting organic material into fossil fuel.

    C. the limited supply of fossil fuels.

    D. evidence to support the claim that solar power is a safer energy source than oil or coal.

8. The formation of both coal and oil requires all of the following EXCEPT.

    F. proper extraction techniques.

    G. pressure.

    H. heat.

    J. organic material.

9. Fossil fuel is formed in a multi-step process, as stated in Passage A, where the author writes that "The formation of coal goes through discrete stages. . ." Which sentence in Passage B confirms a similar multi-step process for the formation of oil?

    A. The areas where oil remains in the porous rocks are called reservoirs.

    B. The natural pressure within the reservoir is usually high enough to push the oil or gas up to the surface.

    C. When more heat was added to the kerogen, it liquefied into the subtance we know as oil.

    D. Petroleum contains many different types of hydrocarbons in liquid, solid, and gaseous forms, as well as sulfur, oxygen, and nitrogen.

10. The final sentence in each passage conveys which of the following?

    F. The land cannot recover after fossil fuels have been extracted.

    G. The processes of extracting coal and oil present environmental repercussions.

    H. New technology can reduce the amount of sulfur released into the air.

    J. Lead is as hazardous to both people and the environment as coal and oil.

PASSAGE II

HUMANITIES: One of the most enjoyable ways to analyze culture is through music. By analyzing musical styles and lyrics, one can explore quintessential characteristics of particular cultures.

Passage A

Country music has its roots in the southern portions of the United States, specifically in the remote and undeveloped backcountry of the central and southern areas of the
5 Appalachian mountain range. Recognized as a distinct cultural region since the late nineteenth century, the area became home to European settlements in the eighteenth century, primarily led by Ulster Scots from Ireland. Early inhab-
10 itants have been characterized as fiercely independent, to the point of rudeness and inhospitality. It was in this area that the region's truly indigenous music, now known as country music, was born.

15 Rooted in spirituals as well as folk music, cowboy songs, and traditional Celtic melodies, country music originated in the 1920s. The motifs are generally ballads and dance tunes, simple in form and accompanied mostly by
20 guitar, banjo, and violin. Though today there are many genres of country music, all have their roots in this mélange of sources.

The term "country" has replaced the original pejorative term, "hillbilly." Hillbillies referred
25 to Appalachian inhabitants who were considered poor, uneducated, isolated, and wary; the name change reflects a more accepting characterization of these mountain dwellers.

Hank Williams put country music on the
30 map nationally and is credited with the movement of country music from the South to more national prominence. Other early innovators include the Carter family, Ernest Tubb, Woody Guthrie, Loretta Lynn, and Bill Monroe, father

35 of bluegrass music. More recently, Faith Hill, Reba McEntire, and Shania Twain have carried on the tradition.

What might be considered the "home base" of country music is in Nashville, Tennessee,
40 and the legendary music hall, the Grand Ole Opry. Founded in 1925 by George D. Hay, it had its genesis in the pioneer radio station WSM's program *Barn Dance*. Country singers are considered to have reached the pinnacle of
45 the profession if they are asked to become members of the Opry. While noted country music performers and acts take the stage at the Opry numerous times, Elvis Presley performed there only once, in 1954. His act was so poorly
50 received that it was suggested he return to his job as a truck driver.

The offshoots and relatives of country music highlight the complexity of this genre. In a move away from its mountain origins, and
55 turning a focus to the West, honky-tonk music became popular in the early twentieth century. Its name is a reference to its roots in honky-tonk bars, where the music was played. Additionally, Western Swing emerged as one of the
60 first genres to blend country and jazz musical styles, which required a great deal of skill and creativity. Some of the most talented and sophisticated musicians performing in any genre were musicians who played in bluegrass string
65 bands, another relative of country music.

Country music has always been an expression of American identity. Its sound, lyrics, and performers are purely American, and though the music now has an international audience,
70 it remains American in its heart and soul.

Passage B

A style of music closely related to country is the similarly indigenous music known as bluegrass, which originated in the Appalachian highland regions extending westwards to the
75 Ozark Mountains in southern Missouri and northern Arkansas. Derived from the music brought over by European settlers of the region, bluegrass is a mixture of Scottish, Welsh, Irish, and English melodic forms, infused, over time,
80 with African-American influences. Indeed, many bluegrass songs, such as "Barbara Allen" and "House Carpenter," preserve their European roots, maintaining the traditional musical style and narratives almost intact. Storytelling
85 ballads, often laments, are common themes. Given the predominance of coal mining in the Appalachian region, it is not surprising that ballads relating to mining tragedies are also common.

90   Unlike country music, in which musicians commonly play the same melodies together, bluegrass highlights one player at a time, with the others providing accompaniment. This tradition of each musician taking turns with
95 solos and often improvising, can also be seen in jazz ensembles. Traditional bluegrass music is typically played on instruments such as banjo, guitar, mandolin, bass, harmonica, and Dobro (resonator guitar). Even household
100 objects, including washboards and spoons, have, from time to time, been drafted for use as instruments. Vocals also differ from country music in that, rather than featuring a single voice, bluegrass incorporates baritone and
105 tenor harmonies.

Initially included under the catch-all phrase "folk music," and later referred to as "hillbilly," bluegrass did not come into his own category until the late 1950s, and appeared first in the
110 comprehensive guide, *Music Index*, in 1965. Presumably it was named after Bill Monroe's

Blue Grass band, the seminal bluegrass band. A rapid, almost frenetic pace characterizes bluegrass tempos. Even today, decades after
115 their most active performing era, The Foggy Mountain Boys members Lester Flatt, a bluegrass guitarist and mandolinist, and Earl Scruggs, known for his three-finger banjo picking style, are widely considered the
120 foremost artists on their instruments.

Partially because of its pace and complexity, bluegrass has often been recorded for movie soundtracks. "Dueling Banjos," played in the movie *Deliverance*, exemplifies the skill
125 required by the feverish tempo of the genre. The soundtrack for *O Brother, Where Art Thou?* incorporates bluegrass and its musical cousins folk, country, gospel, and blues. Bluegrass festivals are held throughout the
130 country and as far away as the Czech Republic. Interactive, often inviting audience participation, they feature performers such as Dolly Parton and Alison Krauss.

Central to bluegrass music are the themes of
135 the working class—miners, railroad workers, farmers. The phrase "high, lonesome sound" was coined to represent the bluegrass undertones of intensity and cheerlessness, symbolizing the hard-scrabble life of the American
140 worker. As with so much of a nation's traditional music, and for better or worse, bluegrass music reflects America.

Questions 11–13 ask about Passage A.

11. According to the passage, country music originated from all of the following EXCEPT:

A. Celtic melodies.

B. spirituals.

C. jazz.

D. cowboy songs.

12. Which of the following would be the most logical place to hear the best of country music?

   F. Honky-tonk bars
   G. Ireland
   H. The Appalachian backcountry
   J. The Grand Ole Opry

13. As it is used in line 24, the word *pejorative* most nearly means:

   A. traditional.
   B. accurate.
   C. disparaging.
   D. mountain dwelling.

Questions 14–17 ask about Passage B.

14. If a song were a lament with Welsh and African-American derivation, the author of Passage B would classify it as:

   F. bluegrass.
   G. country.
   H. jazz.
   J. hillbilly.

15. According to the passage, the instruments played in bluegrass music are:

   A. both typical and unusual.
   B. derived from African-American influences.
   C. made famous by the piece "Dueling Banjos."
   D. restricted to those used in the Ozarks.

16. In addition to highlighting one player at a time, bluegrass music differs from country music because it often:

   F. features harmonies sung by bass and tenor voices.
   G. features a single voice.
   H. is characterized by musicians commonly playing the same melodies together.
   J. is played on instruments such as the banjo and guitar.

17. It can be inferred that laments and high, lonesome sounds both reflect:

   A. the influence of Irish music.
   B. the challenges of American life.
   C. songs sung by Shania Twain.
   D. hillbilly music.

Questions 18–20 ask about both passages.

18. As it is used in the introductory information, *quintessential* most nearly means:

   F. old-fashioned.
   G. representative.
   H. charming.
   J. unconventional.

19. Passage A states that there were "talented and sophisticated" (lines 62-63) musicians playing bluegrass music. Which sentence in Passage B suggests this claim?

A. "Central to bluegrass music are the themes of the working class—miners, railroad workers, farmers."

B. "Partially because of its pace and complexity, bluegrass has often been recorded for movie soundtracks."

C. "Lester Flatt, a bluegrass guitarist and mandolinist, and Earl Scruggs, known for his three-finger banjo picking style, are widely considered the foremost artists on their instruments."

D. "A style of music closely related to country is the similarly indigenous music known as bluegrass . . ."

20. It can be inferred that both authors would agree that:

F. country and bluegrass music are popular genres.

G. both genres—country and bluegrass—are showcased at the Grand Ole Opry.

H. music genres can evolve.

J. country and bluegrass music are gaining in acceptance.

PASSAGE III

SCIENCE: The following two passages were written in the early 1990s and present two viewpoints about the ways that the public responds to the results of scientific research.

Passage A

The way that people in present-day industrial societies think about science in the modern world actually tends to cultivate the very unscientific perception that science supplies
5 us with unquestionable facts. If there is one unquestionable fact about science, it is that science is inherently uncertain. Research consists not so much of a search for truth as a search for some degree of certainty in an
10 uncertain world. Every research study, every experiment, and every survey incorporates an extensive statistical analysis that is meant to be taken as qualifying the probability that the results are consistent and reproducible. Yet
15 policy makers, public relations interests, and so-called experts in the popular media continue to treat the results of every latest study as if they were surefire truths.

History is filled with examples of the fallibility
20 of scientific certainties. From the medieval monks who believed the sun orbited around Earth and the world was only 4,000 years old, to the early twentieth-century scientists who thought that X-rays were a hoax and that ex-
25 ploding a nuclear bomb would set off a chain reaction that would destroy all matter in the universe, it has been demonstrated repeatedly that science deals primarily with possibilities and is subject to the same prejudices as other
30 kinds of opinions and beliefs. Yet statistics are complicated, and in our need to feel that we live in a universe of predictable certainties, it is tempting to place our faith in the oversimplified generalities of headlines
35 and sound bites rather than the rigorous application of probabilities. Ironically, even

though the intent of science is to expand the realm of human knowledge, an unfounded prejudice stemming from a desire for scientific
40 constancy can actually discourage inquiry.

Science serves an important practical function; predictability and reproducibility are vital to making sure that our bridges remain standing, our nuclear power plants run
45 smoothly, and our cars start in the morning so we can drive to work. When these practicalities become everyday occurrences, they tend to encourage a complacent faith in the reliability and consistency of science. Yet faced with so
50 many simple conveniences, it is important to remember that we depend on the advance of science for our very survival. With progress expanding into those gray areas at the boundaries of scientific exploration, caution
55 and prudence are just as important as open-mindedness and imagination. As technological advances engage increasingly complex moral questions within fields such as pharmaceutical developments, indefinite
60 extension of life, and the potential for inconceivably potent weapons, an understanding of the limitations of science becomes just as important as an understanding of its strengths.

Passage B

While it is important that scientific knowl-
65 edge be taken into consideration in significant matters of public interest, such consideration must be tempered with critical rigor. In the early days during the ascendance of science as a practical discipline, the public was inclined
70 to view every new advance and discovery with a healthy skepticism. In the late 19th century,

when Italian astronomer Giovanni Schiaparelli
first detected seas and continents on the planet
Mars, many people balked at the idea of Earth-
75 like topography on the Red Planet. Just a few
decades later, when fellow Italian astronomer
Vincenzo Cerulli provided evidence that the
seas and continents Schiaparelli observed were
merely optical illusions, public disbelief proved
80 to be entirely appropriate.

Since then, the historic tendency of the
public to question scientific findings has
unfortunately been lost. Yet in present-day
industrial societies, and especially where
85 public policy is at issue, response to scientific
research needs more than ever to pursue an
informed, critical viewpoint. Who performs a
research study, what kind of study it is, what
kinds of review and scrutiny it comes under,
90 and what interests support it are every bit as
important as a study's conclusions.

Studies of mass media and public policy
reveal that, all too often, scientific findings
presented to the public as objective and con-
95 clusive are actually funded at two or three
degrees of removal by corporate or political
interests with a specific agenda related to the
outcome of those findings. For example, some
critics question the issue of whether a study of
100 the effectiveness of a new drug is more likely
to produce favorable results when the study is
funded by the pharmaceutical company that
owns the drug patent. In cases where such
findings conflict with the interests of the
105 funding parties, analysts sometimes wonder if
information was repressed, altered, or given
a favorable public relations slant in order to
de-emphasize dangerous side effects. Some
critics of company-funded studies argue that
110 the level of misrepresentation included in such
studies borders on immoral.

Part of the problem grows from the public's
willingness to place blind faith in the authority
of science without an awareness of the interests
115 that lie behind the research. Public officials
then, in turn, may sometimes be too willing to
bend in the face of public or private political
pressure rather than pursuing the best interests
of the constituency. Issues such as genetics,
120 reproductive health, and preventative care
are particularly fraught with political angst.
Where the safety of individuals is at stake, a
precautionary principle of allowing for unpre-
dictable, unforeseen negative effects of techno-
125 logical advances should be pursued. It is the duty
of active citizens in a free society to educate
themselves about the real-world application of
risk-assessment and statistical analysis, and to
resist passive acceptance of the reassurances
130 of self-styled scientific authorities. The most
favorable approach to policy decisions based
on realistic assessments finds a middle ground
between the alarmism of political "Chicken
Littles" and the recklessness of profit-seeking
135 risk takers.

Questions 21–23 ask about Passage A.

21. According to the passage, policy makers
consider the results of studies:
A. with concern.
B. as unquestioned truth.
C. as debatable.
D. as false.

22. The word *probabilities* in line 36 is used to express the author's belief that:

    F. scientific theories will eventually be proven true.

    G. current scientific findings will be regarded as outdated by future scientists.

    H. viewing scientific results as possibly wrong is a wise approach.

    J. refusing to question science is unavoidable because people prefer certainty.

23. As it is used in line 48, the word *complacent* most nearly means:

    A. conceited.

    B. dangerous.

    C. unquestioned.

    D. dissatisfied.

Questions 24–26 ask about Passage B.

24. Which of the following is an example of a scientific discovery greeted with skepticism by the public?

    F. A pharmaceutical study funded by the drug patent holder

    G. Schiaparelli's detection of continents on Mars

    H. The statement that X-rays are a hoax

    J. Darwin's theory of evolution

25. The author of Passage B uses the first paragraph to explain:

    A. a new scientific hypothesis.

    B. a historical contrast.

    C. a public policy generality.

    D. the underlying cause of an issue.

26. With which of the following statements would the author of Passage B most likely agree?

    F. People should not unquestioningly accept the results of scientific studies.

    G. More government control and regulation are needed to ensure that science serves the best interests of the public.

    H. Society should place less emphasis on modern conveniences and more on understanding the limitations of science.

    J. The results that scientists derive from research are less reliable now than they were in former times.

Questions 27–30 ask about both passages.

27. What does the author of Passage A believe is the biggest obstacle to reaching the solution described by the author of Passage B in lines 125-130 ("It is the duty . . . authorities")?

    A. Policymakers are too willing to bend to public pressure when it comes to regulating scientific research.

    B. The interests that fund research are the same interests that stand to profit by favorable results, making impartiality impossible.

    C. Statistics are too abstract when compared with the concrete evidence of technological conveniences.

    D. Unanswered ethical questions are increasingly coming under scrutiny at the forefront of our most advanced scientific research.

28. Both passages refer to which of the following in their introductory paragraphs?

 F. Present-day industrial societies

 G. Early twentieth-century scientists

 H. Critics of company-funded studies

 J. Significant matters of public interest

29. According to Passage B, which of the following is an example of the "fallibility of scientific certainties" (lines 19-20) mentioned in Passage A?

 A. Medieval monks who believed the sun orbited around Earth

 B. People who balked at the idea of Earth-like topography on Mars

 C. Issues such as genetics, reproductive health, and preventative care

 D. Early twentieth-century scientists who thought that X-rays were a hoax

30. The authors of both passages mention the term *pharmaceutical* in order to:

 F. highlight a particular scientific field in which moral questions may arise.

 G. point out an example of the recklessness of profit-seeking risk takers.

 H. identify unfounded prejudice stemming from a desire for scientific constancy.

 J. cite the usefulness of the current approach regarding drug testing and analysis.

PASSAGE IV

SOCIAL SCIENCE: The traditional empires of Japan and China had to decide how much they wanted to reform as a new industrial world emerged in the 19th century. They both tried to change with the times, but with varying degrees of success. In both cases, conservative forces came to resist the attempts at reforms.

Passage A

Japan took radical steps in its response to the challenges of reform and reaction, and emerged from this period as a world power. Even as it continued to selectively isolate itself
5 from the rest of the world, it was changing from a feudal to a commercial economy.

Outside forces played a role in the evolution. The Japanese knew of China's humiliation at the hands of the British in the mid-1800s, thus
10 becoming acquainted with the influence of the Western, and more industrialized, powers. After the California Gold Rush of 1849, the United States became more interested in Pacific commerce, sending a mission to con-
15 clude a trade agreement with Japan. It arrived in Edo (Tokyo) Bay in 1853 with a modern fleet of armed steamships. For the Japanese, who had restricted their trade from much of the world for over two centuries, this was an
20 awe-inspiring sight. The Americans were told to leave, but this caused tense polemics between the shogun (military leader appointed by, but separate from, the emperor) and the samurai (military) classes.

25 Two clans in the south—Satsuma and Choshu—supported a new policy to "revere the emperor and repel the barbarians." In essence, this meant the overthrow of the shogun and restoration of the Kyoto emperor's power
30 and a veiled critique of the shogun in Edo, whom they perceived as unable to ward off the Western "barbarians" as opprobrious.

A younger generation of reform-minded samurai from domains distant from Edo made
35 bold plans to undermine the bakufu, the military dictatorship of the shogun. These "men of spirit" banded together to overthrow the shogun and promote Japanese moderniza-tion. They armed themselves with guns from
40 the West, and civil war broke out in 1866. When the rebels showed the superiority of their Western firepower, the momentum began to shift in their favor.

By 1868, the overthrow of the Tokugawa
45 regime was complete when the victorious re-formers pronounced that they had restored the emperor to his throne. They titled him Meiji, or Enlightened One, reflecting their belief that Meiji was a beacon of national revitalization.
50 The nation rallied around the 16-year-old emperor, and plans were made to move the imperial "presence" to the renamed capital of Tokyo. This great transition in Japanese history has been called both a revolution and a resto-
55 ration. Historians debate about which term to use because the Japanese did not overthrow the old order and replace it with something new; rather, they reached into their past and used an older model to transform their nation.

60 In the Meiji period, the rapidity of the industrialization and modernization of Japan proved a marvel to the observing world. Within the first generation of that period, Japan had built a modern infrastructure and
65 military, defeated the Chinese and Russians in war, and begun building an empire in the

Pacific that European powers had to recognize as both legitimate and potentially formidable. This was a clear sign that industrialization
70 was achievable by non-Europeans and that impending power shifts were forthcoming.

Passage B

The Chinese had to deal with issues of reform and reaction in the 1800s. During the Qing dynasty, it is estimated that the Chinese
75 population quadrupled to 420,000,000. This increase placed great strains on the nation, and famines became increasingly common. A series of wars and rebellions that followed further weakened the dynasty.

80 Aggressive British traders began to import opium from India into China, and a customs dispute in Guangzhou led to the first Opium War in 1839. This resulted in two humiliating defeats for China and a series of unequal
85 treaties that gave Britain and other European nations commercial entry into China.

Uprisings such as the Taiping Rebellion placed further stress on China. An obscure scholar named Hong Xiuquan, who believed
90 he was the brother of Jesus Christ, founded an offshoot of Christianity. A social reform movement grew from this movement in the 1850s, which the government began to suppress. Hong established the Taiping Tianguo
95 (Heavenly Kingdom), and his followers created an army that, within two years of fighting, controlled a large territory in central China. Internal disputes within the Taipings finally helped the Qing dynasty defeat them, but the
100 10-year death toll is estimated in the millions, making it the bloodiest civil war in human history.

The government attempted reforms in an effort to change with the times. With

105 government-sponsored grants in the 1860s and 1870s, local leaders built modern shipyards, railroads, and weapon industries, and created academies for the study of science. It was an ambitious effort, but one that brought
110 only minimal change, since it experienced resistance from the imperial bureaucracy.

The last major reform effort was known as the Hundred Days of Reform. The emperor Guangzu instituted a program to change China
115 into a constitutional monarchy, guarantee civil liberties, and encourage foreign influence. These proposed changes were strongly resisted by the imperial household. Particularly upset was the dowager empress Cixi, who cancelled the re-
120 forms and imprisoned the emperor. With that, China's chance for a reformed society ended.

Amidst all of these rebellions and attempts at reform, a revolutionary movement was slowly emerging in China. It was composed
125 of young men and women who had traveled outside Asia and seen the new liberalism and modernization of the West, and who hoped to import it to China. Cells were organized in Guangzhou and overseas in Tokyo and
130 Honolulu, where plots to overthrow the Qing were made.

Under the leadership of Sun Yixian (Sun Yatsen), many unsuccessful uprisings were mounted, but it wasn't until 1911 that the Qing
135 were forced to abdicate. With the dynasty in considerable chaos, the modern Republic of China was proclaimed. Sun dreamed of a progressive and democratic China based on his Three Principles of the People, but his
140 dream would be shattered by a civil war and the subsequent rise of Communist China in the mid-20th century.

Questions 31–33 ask about Passage A.

31. Which phrase in the passage best describes those who wanted to undermine the bakufu?

    A. "Two clans in the south—Satsuma and Choshu—supported a new policy to 'revere the emperor and repel the barbarians.'" (lines 25-27)

    B. "Outside forces played a role in the evolution." (line 7)

    C. "They titled him Meiji, or Enlightened One, reflecting their belief that Meiji was a beacon of national revitalization." (lines 47-49)

    D. "Men of spirit" (line 37)

32. The *tense polemics* (line 21) described in the second paragraph suggest that:

    F. the shogun and the samurai classes were able to reach an agreement.

    G. the shogun and the samurai classes both expressed dissatisfaction at the arrival of American steamships.

    H. the heated dispute caused considerable civil unrest.

    J. the Americans agreed to compromise with the Japanese.

33. According to the author, the debate questioning if the Meiji government was the result of a revolution or a restoration centers on whether:

    A. future power shifts were to be expected.

    B. it took the form of a brand new or an older model of government.

    C. Japan could be an industrial power.

    D. the civil war was justified.

Questions 34–36 ask about Passage B.

34. The author refers to the Taiping Rebellion to:

    F. describe the last major reform effort.

    G. support the Imperial government.

    H. highlight the role of Christianity in China.

    J. provide an example of attempts at reform.

35. In the context of the passage, the word *strains* (line 76) most nearly means:

    A. inherited qualities.

    B. groups of people with shared ancestry.

    C. very small amounts.

    D. widespread distress.

36. In the context of the passage, the word *cells* (line 128) most nearly means:

    F. groups of rebels.

    G. parts of the body.

    H. confinement rooms in jails.

    J. foreign organizations.

Questions 37–40 ask about both passages.

37. Both passages include:

    A. evidence of improved governments as a result of rebellions.

    B. foreign influences that had an extensive effect on domestic governments.

    C. reforms that resulted in democratic governments.

    D. beneficial modernization.

38. In Passage B the author states that the revolutionary movement in China was composed of "young men and women" (line 125). Which statement in Passage A refers to a similar group in Japan?

   F. "The nation rallied around the 16-year-old emperor, and plans were made to move the imperial 'presence' to the renamed capital of Tokyo."

   G. "The last major reform effort was known as the Hundred Days of Reform."

   H. "A younger generation of reform-minded samurai from domains distant from Edo made bold plans to undermine the bakufu . . ."

   J. "Two clans in the south—Satsuma and Choshu—supported a new policy to 'revere the emperor and repel the barbarians.'"

39. Given the focus of each passage, it is likely that both authors are:

   A. sociologists.

   B. experts on Japan.

   C. public policy developers.

   D. historians.

40. Unrest in both China and Japan was partially the result of:

   F. foreign trade.

   G. revolution in China.

   H. the Opium war.

   J. the Meiji restoration.

ANSWERS AND EXPLANATIONS

PASSAGE I

Suggested Passage Map notes:

Passage A

¶1: Type of coal burned affects amt of sulfur released

¶2: Stages of bituminous coal formation

¶3: Anthracite coal is formed from bit. coal, burns cleaner than bit. coal

¶4: Anth. coal limited, US & China biggest consumers

¶5: Subsurface mining is dangerous, strip mining less dangerous but worse for land

Passage B

¶1: Crude oil refers to petroleum and processed products

¶2: Formed from organic material, heat, pressure to create reservoirs

¶3: Oil wells extract oil from reservoirs

¶4: Secondary recovery required if pressure is low

¶5: At most 50% can be extracted

¶6: Unconventional sources less valuable and higher environ. footprint

1. C   Difficulty: Medium

Category: Detail

Getting to the Answer: The best way to approach this kind of question is to eliminate all answers which are in the passage; the one that's left is the correct answer. The question points you to Paragraph 1, where you read that SO_2 and sulfuric acid are formed in the atmosphere, while mercury is released when coal is burned. The only answer left is (C), which, in Passage B, refers to petroleum compounds of hydrogen and carbon.

2. H   Difficulty: High

Category: Inference

Getting to the Answer: The best way to answer a question like this is to research each answer separately, using your notes or scanning the passage for the words. Look for an answer that the author specifically indicates has low levels of moisture, methane, and carbon dioxide. Since the author states, "With further compaction, lignite loses moisture, methane, and carbon dioxide, and becomes bituminous coal," it must be true that the bituminous coal has less moisture, methane, and carbon dioxide than lignite. Since peat is found in swamps and bogs, it would have more moisture than both lignite and bituminous coal. Choice (H) is the best choice. Choice F is a misused detail; lignite is a sedimentary rock that has *more* moisture, methane, and carbon dioxide than bituminous coal. Choice G is a misused detail; peat is found in swamps and bogs, so it would have more moisture than both lignite and bituminous coal. Choice J is out of scope; kerogen is waxy material found in shale that can be heated to produce oil (Passage B), not coal.

3. C   Difficulty: Medium

Category: Function

Getting to the Answer: As your map tells you, the second paragraph describes how bituminous coal is formed, and the third paragraph provides details about anthracite. The author clearly states that anthracite burns cleaner, making A the opposite of the information. Having detailed all the environmental dangers involved in burning bituminous coal (Paragraph 1), a cleaner burning fuel is obviously better for the environment, as (C) states. Choice B is out of scope, since there's no reference to mercury in anthracite, and D is also out of scope; the author never mentions oil (that's in Passage B) and doesn't recommend one fuel over another.

4. H   Difficulty: Medium

Category: Vocab-in-Context

Getting to the Answer: Questions like this require you to consider the meaning of the phrase in the context not only of the sentence in which it appears, but also in terms of the surrounding sentences. The phrase relates to the *extraction process* of oil shale and tar sands. In the last paragraph, the author writes, "The hydrocarbons obtained from these sources require extensive processing to be usable, reducing their value. The extraction process also has a particularly large environmental footprint," which sounds negative. An environmental footprint refers to how much a person or action affects the health of the environment. In this case, it's a big, and seemingly negative, effect, which matches (H). Choice F is a distortion; in this case, "footprint" does not refer to the imprint of a foot, but to the effect on the environment of the extraction of oil. Choice G is opposite; the phrase *extensive processing* seems like a negative one, as it is associated with a reduction in value. Choice J is out of scope; the author does not state that all effects on the environment, even negative ones, are irreversible.

5. D   Difficulty: Medium

Category: Detail

Getting to the Answer: Use your notes to research where to find the details about how oil is pumped from under the Earth's surface. All the information about the process of extracting oil is in Paragraph 3. Look for keywords that signal the steps in the process, such as *after* and "the process is repeated." Paragraph 3 outlines the steps in erecting a well: "An oil well is created using an oil rig, which turns a drill bit. After the hole is drilled, a casing—a metal pipe with a slightly smaller diameter than the hole—is inserted and bonded to its surroundings, usually with cement." In these three steps, drilling the hole is the second one; thus, (D) is the correct answer. Choice A is a misused detail; drilling a hole is the first step in the process. Choice B is a misused detail; draining fluid is pushed in after casings are in place,

one of the last steps in extraction. Choice C is a misused detail; topping the wellbore is the very last part of the procedure.

6. G   Difficulty: High

Category: Inference

Getting to the Answer: It's hard to predict the answer to a question like this, since many things could be inferred. Rather than make a prediction, use the answers to research the passage. Pump jacks are mentioned in Paragraph 4, where it states that they are used in one particular circumstance. Determine what that circumstance is, then match it with the correct answer. When writing about pump jacks in Paragraph 4, the author states, "But sometimes, additional measures, called secondary recovery, are required. This is especially true in depleted fields . . . " Depleted fields are those in which the oil reserves are greatly diminished, meaning very low. Choice (G) correctly matches the circumstances described in Paragraph 4. Choice F is out of scope; the passage does not provide any information about the safety of using pump jacks. Choice H is opposite; Paragraph 5 states that even with new technology, only about 50% of the oil can be recovered. Choice J is a misused detail; the wellbore (Paragraph 3) is the drilling hole, strengthened by metal pipes, not pump jacks.

7. D   Difficulty: Low

Category: Synthesis

Getting to the Answer: Read the question carefully. Though not worded in the most straightforward way, it's really just saying that, given the information in the passage, it can be inferred that both authors would agree on three of the four answers; the one on which the authors would not agree is the correct one. The key here is that the passages must include information relevant to the question. If there is no information given, there is no basis from which to draw an inference. Look for an answer that is not referred to in any part of either passage. Neither author says anything about solar power, so we don't have evidence regarding the safety of solar power; therefore, (D) is correct. Choice A is opposite; here's a point of agreement. Both authors write about organic material being used as an energy source. Choice B is opposite; in Passage A, the author writes: "Coal is a solid fossil fuel formed from the remains of land plants that flourished 300 to 400 million years ago," and in Passage B the author notes that "organic material such as zooplankton and algae settled on the bottom of ocean[s] millions of years ago." Both statements clearly mean that both oil and coal are created from organic material, and the process takes a very long time. Choice C is opposite; in Passage A, the author refers to limited supplies of anthracite (Paragraph 3), while the reference to *depleted fields* in Passage B (Paragraph 4) indicates that, at least in some oil fields, the supply has dwindled.

8. F   Difficulty: Low

Category: Synthesis

Getting to the Answer: Use your notes to research where to find the details about how coal and oil are formed. The information you need regarding the formation of coal and oil is located in the second paragraph of each passage. According to the passages, extraction does not affect the formation of coal and oil since extraction occurs millions of years after the formation of fossil fuels; therefore, (F) is correct. Choice G is opposite; Passage A states, "The formation of coal goes through discrete stages as, over millions of years, heat and pressure act on decomposing plants." Passage B states, "Thousands of years later, the sediments that contained the organic material were subjected to intense amounts of heat and pressure, changing it into a waxy material called kerogen." Choice H is opposite; heat is mentioned in the second paragraphs of both Passages A and B. Choice J is opposite; organic material is mentioned in the second paragraphs of both Passages A and B.

9. C   Difficulty: Medium

Category: Synthesis

Getting to the Answer: The formation of oil is described in the third paragraph, a likely place to research when looking for support for a multi-step process. Though the information in Paragraph 3 is not given in a step-by-step process with key words such as *first* and *then*, look for a phrase that indicates a process which evolves over time, with different steps at different points. The phrase "when more heat is added" means that the addition of heat is a step taken after a previous one. Even though the passage says that this takes a long time, it's still a step-by-step procedure, which results in oil as we know it. Choice (C) matches this description. Choice A is out of scope; this answer is about the terminology for an oil field, not the process of oil formation. Choice B is out of scope; how oil is pushed to the surface is irrelevant to how it is formed. Choice D is out of scope; the components of oil are also irrelevant.

10. G   Difficulty: Medium

Category: Synthesis

Getting to the Answer: When answering Synthesis questions, consider the author's purpose in doing something. Read both final sentences, focusing on each author's tone. Both authors include negative descriptions of the consequences of extracting fossil fuels. In Passage A, the author states, "However, it often leaves the land scarred and unsuitable for other uses." Passage B states "The extraction process also has a particularly large environmental footprint." Given the information that sulfur is dangerous, it is likely that the authors would agree that extracting coal and oil results in negative consequences. Choice (G) matches these descriptions. Choice F is a distortion; both passages mention negative impacts of extracting fossil fuels, but only Passage A conveys the idea that the land may not recover. The *environmental footprint* mentioned in Passage B does not guarantee irreparable harm to the land. Choice H is out of scope; new technology is mentioned only in Passage B, where it is referenced as a way to increase oil recovery. Since it is not discussed at the end of both Passages A and B it cannot be the correct answer. Choice J is out of scope; since neither author writes about lead, you can eliminate this answer choice.

PASSAGE II

Suggested Passage Map notes:

Passage A

¶1: Country music (C) born in central & southern Appalachians

¶2: Originated in 1920s from multiple sources

¶3: The term "country" replaced "hillbilly"

¶4: Hank Williams 1st to take country national; artists

¶5: Nashville, TN = country home w/ Grand Ole Opry (1925)

¶6: C relatives = honky tonk, Western Swing

¶7: C expresses Am. identity

Passage B

¶1: Bluegrass (B) origin and description

¶2: B diff. from C: highlight 1 musician at a time, diff. instruments, vocal harmonies

¶3: own category in late 1950s, named after Bill Monroe's band

¶4: today: movies, festivals

¶5: B themes = working class; reflects Am.

11. C   Difficulty: Medium

Category: Detail

Getting to the Answer: Use your Passage Map to locate this detail; the second paragraph should include the necessary information. Use the list of the sources of country music ("spirituals as well as folk music, cowboy songs, and traditional Celtic melodies") to make your prediction. Choice (C) is correct because country music is not rooted in jazz. Rather, jazz was combined with country music to create Western Swing. Paragraph 6 states, "Additionally, Western Swing emerged as one of the first genres to blend country and jazz musical styles, which required a great deal of skill and creativity." Choice A is opposite; Paragraph 2 describes the many sources of country music with the sentence, "Rooted in spirituals as well as folk music, cowboy songs, and traditional Celtic melodies, country music originated in the 1920s." Choice B is opposite; spirituals influenced the development of country music. Choice D is opposite; country music is rooted in cowboy songs.

12. J   Difficulty: Medium

Category: Detail

Getting to the Answer: The answer to a Detail question is stated in the passage. However, because all answer choices are in the passage, be careful to assess each one in terms of the actual question asked. A look at your notes or a quick scan of the passage should provide enough information to make a prediction about where to find the best country music. Match that prediction to the correct answer. Choice (J) is correct; in Paragraph 5, the author writes "Country singers are considered to have reached the pinnacle of the profession if they are asked to become members of the Opry." To hear the best music, it makes sense to go to the place where those at the pinnacle, or top of their field, perform. Choice F is a misused detail; one would hear honky-tonk music, a derivative of country, but not country music itself, in these bars. Choice G is a misused detail; Ireland is the original home of the Ulster Scots, many of whom settled in Appalachia. Choice H is a misused detail; though country music had its origins in the mixture of music created in Appalachia, the author does not state that it is the place to hear the best music.

13. C   Difficulty: High

Category: Vocab-in-Context

Getting to the Answer: As with all Vocab-in-Context questions, use the surrounding clues to define the word in question. The word appears in Paragraph 3, where the original term *hillbillies* is used to describe "Appalachian inhabitants who were considered poor, uneducated, isolated, and wary." The more accepting word *country* has replaced *hillbillies*, indicating that pejorative is a negative word, an adjective used to highlight the negative characteristics described in the paragraph.

This matches (C), since disparaging means *belittling*, or *bad*. Choice A is a synonym for *original* rather than a word that means *negative*. Choice B is out of scope, as the author never expresses that the negative view is accurate, and D refers to where the people live rather than fitting the context of describing the term (i.e., it is not a "mountain-dwelling term").

14.   F   Difficulty: Low

Category: Writer's View

Getting to the Answer: Both passages introduce several genres of American music, but this question refers to Passage B, so research the passage carefully. In the first paragraph the author introduces bluegrass music and writes that it is "a mixture of Scottish, Welsh, Irish, and English melodic forms, infused, over time, with African-American influences." (lines 78–80), and that laments "are common themes." (line 85). These are exactly the components of the song in the question, making (F) correct. The other answers refer to Passage A and are described as having different derivations.

15.   A   Difficulty: Medium

Category: Detail

Getting to the Answer: Locate the paragraph in which bluegrass instruments are described, and match those descriptions with the correct answer choice. Your notes point to only one paragraph in which musical instruments are mentioned. Scan the answer choices, then re-read the information in that paragraph to determine which answer choice characterizes the information given. Choice (A) is correct; musical instruments are described in the second paragraph and include typical ones such as "banjo, guitar, mandolin, bass, harmonica, and Dobro (resonator guitar)." But the paragraph goes on to include far less typical ones, such as "household objects, including washboards and spoons," which are not usually considered musical instruments, but are sometimes included in a bluegrass band. Choice B is a misused detail; African-American influences are provided as one more source of the bluegrass genre but instrumentation is not referenced. Choice C is a

misused detail; this is an example of a bluegrass piece used in a movie soundtrack. Choice D is out of scope; the reference to the Ozark mountains concerns the origin of bluegrass and has nothing to do with a description of musical instruments.

16.   F   Difficulty: High

Category: Detail

Getting to the Answer: The answer to a Detail question is stated in the passage. Locate the paragraph in which the differences between country and bluegrass music are discussed. Paragraph 2 includes the information you need to answer the question. Be sure to keep straight which details describe each genre of music. Choice (F) is correct. Paragraph 2 details two characteristics of bluegrass music: first, that "bluegrass highlights one player at a time, with the others providing accompaniment," and second, that "bluegrass incorporates baritone and tenor harmonies." Choice G is opposite; country music features a single voice. Choice H is opposite; country musicians commonly play the same melodies together. Choice J is a distortion; which instruments are used is not cited as a difference between the music styles.

17.   B   Difficulty: Medium

Category: Inference

Getting to the Answer: Locate the paragraphs that mention *laments* and "high, lonesome sound," and consider what the author means by including these two details. The reference to *laments* is in the first paragraph and the reference to "high, lonesome sound" in the last paragraph are examples of "the hard-scrabble life of the American worker," which matches (B). Choice A is out of scope; the elements mentioned in the question stem do not necessarily reflect Irish music; bluegrass has multiple sources. Choice C is a misused detail; Shania Twain is an example of a country singer and is mentioned in Passage A only. Choice D is a misused detail; though bluegrass was originally called *hillbilly*, this is the name for the genre, not the theme.

18. G   Difficulty: Medium

Category: Vocab-in-Context

Getting to the Answer: Vocab-in-Context questions require that you understand the context of a cited word or phrase. Locate the reference and focus your research on the text immediately preceding and immediately following the word or phrase in question. The introductory paragraph states, "One of the most enjoyable ways to analyze culture is through music." Look for an answer choice that indicates that music can provide specific insight about a culture as a whole. Choice (G) matches this prediction. Choices F, H, and J are a distortion; *quintessential* does not mean *old-fashioned, charming,* or *conventional* (*typical*).

19. C   Difficulty: Medium

Category: Synthesis

Getting to the Answer: When asked to use a quote to find support in one paragraph for information in another, be sure to read the quote in the context of the paragraph. First find the paragraph in which the quote from Passage A appears, then match the quote to one in Passage B. Choice (C) is correct; Flatt and Scruggs are mentioned in Passage B, Paragraph 3, in which they are characterized as "the foremost artists on their instruments." The best artists are certainly "talented and sophisticated." Choice A is a misused detail; this quote refers to bluegrass themes, whereas the question asks for one that supports talented and sophisticated musicians. Choice B is out of scope; the "pace and complexity" of the music does not necessarily relate to the skill of the musicians themselves. Choice D is out of scope; the relation between bluegrass and country music refers to the kinship of the genres, not the musicians.

20. H   Difficulty: Medium

Category: Synthesis

Getting to the Answer: When looking for something on which both authors would agree, first determine what each one actually states in the passage, then consider what must be true based on those statements. The evolution, or gradual change, in music, as with anything else, must start from somewhere, so look to the parts of each passage that detail the genesis of the music genres, then consider the progression from there. Choice (H) is correct; both authors detail the various music sources that became either country or bluegrass. In the first passage, the author mentions "folk music, cowboy songs, and traditional Celtic melodies," and in the second passage, the author refers to "Scottish, Welsh, Irish, and English melodic forms, infused, over time, with African-American influences." Both authors affirm that the two music genres are "indigenous." Thus, it must be true that both country and bluegrass music have evolved from their various roots to become American music, supporting agreement on the fact that music can evolve. Choice F is out of scope; each passage mentions how its particular music genre is popular (as explained in the next sentence in the explanation—the Czech festivals and international growth), but both authors don't describe why *both* genres are popular, only their own. Choice G is a misused detail; the Grand Ole Opry showcases country music only, not bluegrass. Choice J is out of scope; the passages don't each discuss both genres, only their own.

PASSAGE III

Suggested Passage Map notes:

Passage A

¶1: Present-day people think science is unquestionable

¶2: History shows that science is not always correct

¶3: People think science remains constant, but questioning leads to progress

Passage B

¶1: Historically people were skeptical about science

¶2: Scientific research should be questioned

¶3: Pharma. company studies should be scrutinized

¶4: Policy decisions should be based on balance of faith and doubt

21. B   Difficulty: Low

Category: Detail

Getting to the Answer: The first mention of policy makers is in Paragraph 1, line 15, where the author writes that they "treat the results of every latest study as if they were surefire truths." In other words, they accept the results without question, which matches (B). Choices A, C, and D are opposites.

22. H   Difficulty: Low

Category: Writer's View

Getting to the Answer: Because the question cites a specific part of the passage, reread the relevant text to make a prediction. In line 36, the author uses the word *probabilities* to refer to the scientific discipline that studies the comparative chances of events taking place, which matches (H). Choice F is opposite; the author believes that science is uncertain, so theories will not necessarily be proven true. Choice G is out of scope; the author does not include information about how future scientists will impact current data. Choice J is a distortion; the author does state that "an unfounded prejudice stemming from a desire for scientific constancy can actually discourage inquiry," but that is not related to the idea that science is an implementation of probabilities.

23. C   Difficulty: Medium

Category: Function

Getting to the Answer: The word *complacent* follows examples of predictable events, including a car starting and a power plant running without problems. Since we assume these events will always be the same, we become used to them and don't question them at all. In the same way, we have a "a complacent faith in the reliability and consistency of science" and assume that study results are always correct. Choice (C), *unquestioned,* is a synonym for *complacent.* All other choices are incorrect definitions based on the context provided.

24. G   Difficulty: Medium

Category: Detail

Getting to the Answer: If you have not made notes about various scientific studies in your map, scan through the passage looking for each of the answer choices and eliminate those which were not accepted by the public. Choice F is questioned by *some critics,* who we cannot assume are the general public. Choice H is in Passage A, not Passage B, and J isn't in the passage at all. That leaves (G) as the correct answer.

25. B   Difficulty: Medium

Category: Function

Getting to the Answer: Use your passage notes to help predict an answer for a Function question that refers to an entire paragraph. The first paragraph of Passage B outlines the way that skepticism toward science has changed over time. Choice (B) matches the function of Paragraph 1. Choice A is out of scope; no new hypothesis is introduced in this paragraph. Choice C is a misused detail; Paragraph 2 introduces the issue of public policy, but this question asks specifically about Paragraph 1. Choice D is a misused detail; underlying causes are discussed in the third paragraph, not the first.

26. F   Difficulty: High

Category: Inference

Getting to the Answer: Remember not to make too big a logical leap; the correct inference will not stray far from the text. The author believes that people are too ready to believe the results of scientific studies. Choice (F) fits well with the text and represents a logical, supportable inference. Choice G is out of scope; neither author supports the idea of government control and regulation. Choice H is a misused detail; this idea applies to Passage A. Choice J is out of scope; the belief that the reliability of science has decreased isn't discussed in the passage.

27. C Difficulty: High

Category: Synthesis

Getting to the Answer: Keeping track of each author's primary viewpoints or beliefs can help you to more quickly evaluate and eliminate answer choices. Passage B describes a solution in which people understand enough about science to assess its reliability for themselves, but Passage A claims that people don't do this because they desire a world of certainties. The contrast between striving for more knowledge and clinging to easy beliefs is captured in (C). Choice A is a distortion; the actions and attitudes of policymakers don't prevent people from becoming better educated. Choice B is a misused detail; Passage B discusses the difficulties of obtaining impartial results, but this is not relevant to the question. Choice D is out of scope; the author of Passage A discusses ethical questions, but this is not related to the solution specified in Passage B.

28. F Difficulty: Low

Category: Detail

Getting to the Answer: Remember that the answers to Detail questions are always stated directly. By turning first to the passages, you can accurately predict the correct answer and not be misled by misused details. Passage A includes the phrase "present-day industrial societies" in the first sentence, and Passage B mentions "present-day industrial societies" in the third sentence. Choice (F) matches your research. Choice G is a misused detail; this phrase is from Paragraph 2 in Passage A. Choice H is a misused detail; this is included in Paragraph 3 in Passage B. Choice J is a misused detail; this is mentioned in the first paragraph of Passage B only.

29. B Difficulty: Medium

Category: Detail

Getting to the Answer: Prediction is key in Detail questions. Incorrect answer choices will often reference other details erroneously. In Paragraph 2, the passage directly states "In the late 19th century,

when Italian astronomer Giovanni Schiaparelli first detected seas and continents on the planet Mars, many people balked at the idea of Earth-like topography on the Red Planet," which shows the fallibility, or inaccuracy, of a scientific certainty. Use this as a prediction. Choice (B) matches the prediction. Choice A is a misused detail; this example is mentioned in Passage A, not Passage B. Choice C is a distortion; the author of Passage B discusses this in Paragraph 4, but these are not examples of the fallibility of scientific certainties. Choice D is a misused detail; this example is mentioned in Passage A, not Passage B.

30. F Difficulty: Medium

Category: Synthesis

Getting to the Answer: When a question stem includes a specific line reference, you usually need to read a little before and a little after those particular lines in order to understand the full context of the quoted portion. The word cited in the question stem comes from the third paragraphs of Passage A and Passage B. Passage A says, "technological advances engage increasingly complex moral questions within fields such as pharmaceutical developments" and Passage B states that "Some critics of company-funded studies argue that the level of misrepresentation included in such studies borders on immoral." Choice (F) matches with the references to moral questions in both passages. Choice G is a misused detail; this is mentioned in Passage B only, in the last paragraph. Choice H is a misused detail; this is mentioned in Passage A only, in the third paragraph. Choice J is a misused detail; drug testing and analysis is discussed in Paragraph 3 of Passage A but not in Paragraph 3 of Passage B.

PASSAGE IV

Suggested Passage Map notes:

Passage A

¶1: Japan: feudal → commercial econ.

¶2: history of outside forces (US); shogun vs. samurai

¶3: 2 clans support emperor > shogun

¶4: young samurai fight bakufu, shogun; western guns key

¶5: emperor Meiji back, capital moved, hist. debate

¶6: Meiji period → J. lots of growth

Passage B

¶1: China: 1800s changes, pop. ↑, hard times

¶2: Britain + opium trouble

¶3: Taiping Rebellion (1850s) = 10 yr. civil war

¶4: gov't grants in 1860s and 1870s = min. change

¶5: 100 Days of Reform = ended by emp. family

¶6: young people inf. by West want rev.

¶7: 1911: modern Rep. of C. lasted until Communist C. (mid-1900s)

31.   D   Difficulty: Low

Category: Detail

Getting to the Answer: The answer to a Detail question is always stated in the passage. Your notes should point you to where to go in the passage to research the question. The first sentence of Paragraph 4 introduces samurai intent on undermining the bakufu ("A younger generation of reform-minded samurai from domains distant from Edo"). In the very next sentence, the samurai are characterized by another phrase, one that answers the question. In fact, the phrase in the second sentence, "These 'men of spirit'," is just another name for those samurai. The correct answer is (D). Choice A is a misused detail; it's not the clans themselves which sought to undermine the bakufu, but a "younger generation of reform-minded samurai" from areas far away from the capital. Choice B is out of scope; this phrase refers to the influence of outside forces, such as other countries, on Japan, but is not relevant to Japanese samurai who undermined the shogun. Choice C is a misused detail; Meiji was the title of the newly empowered emperor not those who fought to restore him to power.

32.   H   Difficulty: Medium

Category: Inference

Getting to the Answer: Even when you may not know know the exact meaning of the word *polemics*, it's possible to still get the right answer by reading the word in the context of the sentence in which it appears, as well as in the context of surrounding sentences. Given the angry reaction to the Americans' appearance on Japan's shores, the word *tense,* and the information about rebellion, *polemics* must refer to a heated dispute, serious enough to provoke civil war. Choice (H) matches this prediction. Choice F is opposite. Choice G is a distortion; though dissatisfaction is negative, it is not strong enough to characterize the result of the expulsion of the Americans. Choice J is opposite; a compromise was not reached between the Americans and the Japanese since the Americans were turned away.

33.   B   Difficulty: Low

Category: Detail

Getting to the Answer: Use your notes, or quickly scan the passage, to locate which paragraph discusses the historians' debate. Paragraph 5 presents the two points of view about the Meiji government. Recognizing what those points of view are will provide the answer to the question. In Paragraph 5, the author writes "Historians debate about which term to use because the Japanese did not overthrow the old order and replace it with something new; rather, they reached into their past and used an older model to transform their nation." The two points of view, then, are old versus new, and (B) answers the question. Choice A is a misused detail; future power shifts are referenced in the last paragraph, and have to do with possible future changes, not the Meiji transition of 1868. Choice C is out of scope; the historians are not debating this question, which is actually never posed in the passage. The only reference to industrial power is in the last paragraph, where it mentions "rapidity of the industrialization . . . " Choice D is out of scope; historians were not arguing over the justification of the civil war, but how to characterize the resulting government change.

34. J   Difficulty: Medium

Category: Function

Getting to the Answer: Using your notes, locate the paragraph in which the Taiping Rebellion is described, then consider why it was included in the passage. Prior to writing about the Taiping Rebellion in the third paragraph, the author points to population stress and military defeats, all of which increased unrest in China. The reference to this rebellion functions, then, as an example of efforts to change the government; (J) matches this prediction. Choice F is a misused detail; it is the Hundred Days of Reform, not the Taiping Rebellion, which is noted as the last effort at reform. Choice G is opposite; the Rebellion was mounted in opposition to the Imperial government, not in support of it. Choice H is out of scope; though the Taiping Rebellion was centered around Christianity, it is not included to describe the general role of Christianity in China.

35. D   Difficulty: Medium

Category: Vocab-in-Context

Getting to the Answer: When answering Vocab-in-Context questions, make a prediction based on the context surrounding the word before considering answer choices. Paragraph 1 introduces some of the reasons why the Qing dynasty began to crumble in the 1800s. The word *strains* is used to convey the idea that the Chinese did not have enough resources to meet the needs of their growing population. The population boom caused considerable hardship for the nation. Because "famines were increasingly common," the distress would be considered widespread. The correct answer is (D). Choice A is a distortion; the word *strains* can be used to described characteristics that are inherited, but that definition does not make sense in this context. Choice B is a distortion; this meaning, which refers to the line of ancestors from whom a person is descended, does not fit. Choice C is opposite; the issues China faced

during that time period were extreme and cannot be considered small.

36. F   Difficulty: Medium

Category: Vocab-in-Context

Getting to the Answer: A Vocab-in-Context question asks about the meaning of a word the author uses, which is usually not the common meaning. Read the word in the context of the sentence and think beyond its ordinary definition. The word *cell* is used in Paragraph 6, which introduces Sun Yat-Sen's revolutionary movement and the people who supported it. The author writes that cells were organized to plot the overthrow of the government, which indicates that the author uses the word *cells* to describe groups of rebels. Choice (F) is correct. Choice G is a misused detail; nothing in the passage comes close to talking about the parts of the body, so cells cannot refer to the body. Choice H is a misused detail; though cells can refer to places where jail inmates are confined, the passage doesn't mention confinement of rebels, so this would be the incorrect definition of the word. Choice J is a distortion; though the cells were organized in Tokyo and Honolulu, areas outside of China, the question is not about where the cells were but what the author meant by the use of the word.

37. B   Difficulty: Low

Category: Synthesis

Getting to the Answer: It is very difficult to predict the answer to this type of question, since the answer choices themselves give the clues. Go directly to the choices and research each one in the passages. The correct answer must contain information that both authors included. Choice (B) works because statements in the passages support it. In Passage A, the author states that "Outside forces played a role in the evolution," and follows this up with references to the British humiliation of China, the California Gold Rush, and the arrival of the American steamships. The author of Passage B writes, "Aggressive British traders began to import opium from India into China," and refers to unequal treaties with European nations. Contact with foreign nations produced unrest in both countries, thus influencing rebellions and the overthrow of the existing governments. Choice A is out of scope; neither author comments on how good the new governments were, so it is not possible to find evidence. Choice C is a misused detail; in Passage B, the author writes that Sun Yat-Sen's dream of a democratic China "would be shattered by a civil war and the subsequent rise of Communist China in the mid-20th century." China, at least, did not end up with a democratic government. Choice D is out of scope; both authors note either the hope for modernization (Passage B, Paragraph 6) or actual modernization (Passage A, Paragraph 6), but neither gives a personal opinion about it, so this cannot be the correct answer.

38. H   Difficulty: Low

Category: Synthesis

Getting to the Answer: Since the correct answer will be one of the sentences in the answer choices, scan the choices to see which one in Passage A reflects the same information as the quote from Passage B. Look for an answer choice that says that the rebels in Japan were the equivalent of the young people in China. The reference to "A younger generation of reform-minded samurai . . . " indicates that, like the Chinese revolutionaries and rebels, those in Japan were also young people. Choice (H) is correct. Choice F is a misused detail; this quote is about the young Japanese Emperor, not young rebels. Choice G is out of scope; this quote is from Passage B, and the question asks for a quote from Passage A. Choice J is a distortion; the reference to clans provides no information about the age of the rebels.

39. D   Difficulty: High

Category: Synthesis

Getting to the Answer: The question asks you to determine in what field the authors work. Think about the content of the passages to give you a

clue. Both passages relate the history of political change in a country, referring to domestic and foreign historical events. This supports the fact that both are probably historians. Choice (D) is correct. Choice A is out of scope; sociologists are concerned with social behavior. Though reform and revolution can be seen as social behavior, the forces behind them are the political and economic histories of the two nations, not understanding the social processes. Choice B is a misused detail; only the author of Passage A could be considered an expert on Japan. This leaves out the second author. Choice C is out of scope; neither author provides any thoughts about how to develop public policy in either Japan or China.

40. F   Difficulty: Medium

Category: Synthesis

Getting to the Answer: Research each answer to make sure that the correct one refers to both China and Japan. Look toward the beginning of each passage to locate details about what caused attempts at reform. In Passage A, lines 12-15, the author writes: "After the California Gold Rush of 1849, the United States became more interested in Pacific commerce, sending a mission to conclude a trade agreement with Japan." The paragraph goes on to note that the Americans were expelled, creating dissension between the shogun and the samurai classes. Similarly, in Passage B, lines 83-84 and 88, it is noted that British opium trade caused "two humiliating defeats for China," which "placed further stress on China," resulting in unrest and rebellion. Choice (F) is correct. Choice G is out of scope; this answer refers to Passage B only, while the question asks about both passages. Choice H is out of scope; the Opium war is relevant only to China, not to Japan as well. Choice J is out of scope; the Meiji restoration was a change in Japanese government, thus was not a factor in Chinese unrest.

Science

CHAPTER SIXTEEN

ACT Science Test Overview

INSIDE THE ACT SCIENCE TEST

The Science Test is 35 minutes long and includes 40 questions. The test consists of 6 passages, each accompanied by 6–8 questions. This means you'll have less than 6 minutes per passage and question set. Assuming that it takes you only a couple of minutes on average to read each passage, you'll have about 30–40 seconds per question. Of course, some passages and questions take longer to work through than others.

The Format

ACT Science Passages

Passages in the ACT Science Test are taken from a variety of natural science subjects that you are expected to have studied in high school. These include topics in:

- Earth and Space Science—astronomy, geology, meteorology, etc.
- Biology—botany, genetics, zoology, etc.
- Chemistry—acids/bases, kinetics/equilibria, organic chemistry, etc.
- Physics—electromagnetism, mechanics, thermodynamics, etc.

While the text of Science passages is considerably shorter than what is found in the English and Reading Tests, most Science passages are accompanied by graphs, tables, and/or diagrams, which you will have to interpret and analyze to answer some questions.

ACT Science Questions

ACT Science Test questions follow the same basic multiple-choice format: each question is attached to the passage that precedes it and features four possible answers. Based on the particular question posed, answer choices can vary considerably in appearance—from words, phrases, and sentences to numbers, measurements, and graphs.

Test Day Directions and Format

Here's what the Science directions will look like:

DIRECTIONS: There are several passages in this test. Each passage is followed by several questions. After reading a passage, choose the best answer to each question and fill in the corresponding oval on your answer document. You may refer to the passages as often as necessary.

You are NOT permitted to use a calculator on this test.

There isn't much to these directions—they could be attached to just about any passage-based multiple-choice test. Thus, there's no need to waste your time reading them on Test Day; make the most of your limited time by jumping into the first passage right away.

Passage Types

Passages in ACT Science fall into three basic types:

- Data Representation
- Research Summaries
- Conflicting Viewpoints

Data Representation passages tend to be light on text but heavy on data presented in graphs or tables. Research Summaries passages tend to contain more text, largely consisting of descriptions of multiple experimental procedures, and often feature their own graphs or tables filled with results. Conflicting Viewpoints passages contain accounts of two or more competing theories on a particular phenomenon, typically featuring more text and fewer figures than the other two passage types.

While the order varies in any given ACT Science Test, you can always expect to see 3 Research Summaries passages (accounting for 45–55% of the questions), 2 Data Representation passages (accounting for 30–40% of the questions), and 1 Conflicting Viewpoints passage (accounting for 15–20% of the questions).

Each passage type has a corresponding Kaplan Method, specifically designed to handle that kind of passage and the questions that accompany it. See Chapter 17 for Data Representation, Chapter 18 for Research Summaries, and Chapter 19 for Conflicting Viewpoints.

Question Types

Questions in ACT Science are also divided into three types:

- Interpretation of Data
- Scientific Investigation
- Evaluation of Models, Inferences, and Experimental Results

Interpretation of Data questions require you to work with the information presented in graphs, tables, and other figures. Scientific Investigation questions test your understanding of the scientific method and experimental design. Evaluation of Models questions depend upon your ability to make judgments about theories, data, and other scientific information.

Any type of passage can contain any type of question, but the frequency of question types remains relatively constant across different administrations of the ACT Science Test. Interpretation of Data questions make up 45–55% of the test, or 18–22 questions out of 40. Evaluation of Models questions account for 25–35%, or 10–14 questions. Scientific Investigation questions account for 20–30%, or 8–12 questions.

Interpretation of Data questions are the most common type in Data Representation passages, so they are featured in Chapter 17. (Note, however, that Interpretation of Data questions are also often found with Research Summaries, which typically contain graphs or tables of results.) Scientific Investigation questions are usually found in Research Summaries passages, so they are covered in Chapter 18. Finally, Evaluation of Models questions are the most prevalent question type in Conflicting Viewpoints passages, so they are discussed in Chapter 19.

Outside Knowledge

The ACT Science Test is first and foremost a test of your scientific reasoning ability, not a test of your knowledge of scientific content. Nevertheless, you are expected to have some outside knowledge of the natural sciences. While you won't need to understand advanced concepts or memorize equations, you will need to have knowledge of basic scientific concepts and terminology to answer some of the questions.

If you've completed high school courses in biology, chemistry, earth/space science, and physics, then you should already know everything you'll need to know for Test Day. In fact, you can still do quite well on the ACT Science Test even if you've never taken or you're still in the process of taking one or more of these courses. On Test Day, if you run across a question that requires knowledge you don't have, just skip over it. Spend your time instead working on the vast majority of questions that don't require outside knowledge.

The Inside Scoop

The ACT Science Test relies upon your capacity to think like a scientist: to work with data in a variety of presentations, to understand the design of scientific experiments, to evaluate theories in the light of empirical evidence, and to engage in other kinds of scientific problem-solving.

Science questions are not ordered by difficulty, so they do *not* get harder as you continue working on a passage or as you move from one passage to the next.

Timing

Plan to spend no more than about 6 minutes per passage. Six passages in 35 minutes means you have an average of exactly 5 minutes and 50 seconds to complete each passage and its 6–8 questions. The timing on the ACT Science Test is definitely tight, so be sure to keep yourself moving. Even the lengthiest passages should take you no more than about 3 minutes to read and mark up—whenever possible, try to finish reading in 2 minutes or less to maximize the time you can spend on the questions, where the points are.

Never spend more than a minute on a question. In the ACT Science Test, there are more questions (40) than there are minutes (35) to work with, so even if you didn't have passages to read, your average time working on a question would still have to be less than a minute. While there will be quick and easy questions that allow you to spend more time on some of the harder questions, if you find yourself getting close to about a minute working on a question without an answer immediately in sight, it's time to guess and move on. Aim for completing most questions in 30 seconds or less.

Be organized in your approach. You should generally try to work on the passages and questions in the order they appear, because you're unlikely to have much time remaining at the end to return to previous passages and questions. (Conflicting Viewpoints passages are an exception to the rule of answering questions in order, as explained in the Kaplan Method for these passages in Chapter 19.) Be sure to grid in your answers regularly, either at the end of every page or two or immediately after each question. Don't wait until the very end or you may run out of time.

When You're Running Out of Time

If you find yourself significantly behind on time with multiple passages remaining, you can still make the most of your score by being a bit more selective about how you work on the passages. Say that you have 3 passages remaining, but only 12 minutes left in the section, and the next passage coming up seems harder than any that you've seen so far. If you ever find yourself in such a situation, your best bet is to skip reading the passage entirely and just enter random guesses for all of that passage's questions. Then you can work on the last two passages as you normally would. Just make sure to enter an answer for every question before time expires.

No one wants to deal with tough choices like guessing through an entire passage, so a better approach is to avoid this type of time crunch entirely by being more aggressive with your guessing whenever you start to fall behind in your pacing. Don't forget that every question is worth the same amount in ACT Science, so it simply doesn't pay to use large amounts of time on a single hard question, even if you get it right.

Scoring

Like the other required sections of the ACT, the Science Test is scored on a scale from 1 to 36. This score also accounts for one-quarter of the ACT Composite Score, which is the average of your English, Math, Reading, and Science scores. Unlike the other tests that make up the ACT, however, the Science Test does not contain subscores.

QUICK TIPS

Mind-Set

- **Mark up the passages.** ACT Science questions may seem to come in many varieties, but they are ultimately predictable. With enough practice and the right strategies (like those provided in Chapters 17, 18, and 19), you can learn what questions to expect as you read through a passage. By marking up the passage—underlining key portions of the text and taking brief notes on highly testable material like patterns in data and controls in experiments—you can prepare yourself to answer its questions more quickly.

- **Focus on getting the points.** Remember that your goal is to answer as many Science questions correctly as possible. There are no points awarded simply for making your way through a tough passage. That doesn't mean you should rush through the passages as quickly as possible—that can actually cost you time when you find yourself having to reread more while working on questions—but it does mean that you should read and mark up each passage efficiently. In addition, because hard questions are worth as much as easy ones, you should never take too long on any one question. Know when to give up and make an educated guess, so you can spend your time getting points elsewhere.

- **Don't be afraid to guess.** When you encounter an especially tough question that you think would take you too long to answer, it's usually better to make a random guess than to leave it blank and expect to come back later. You have a 0% chance of getting a Science question right if you leave it blank but a 25% chance of getting it right with a blind guess. Don't worry if you find yourself guessing on a lot of questions, because you can miss quite a few on the Science Test and still get a great score. Keep in mind that the average ACT test taker gets only about half of the Science questions correct!

Special Strategies: If You Get Stuck . . .

If you have the time to spend on a tough question, but aren't sure where to begin, consider the following strategies:

- **Make a prediction first.** Avoid looking at the answer choices when you first start working on a question. Instead, take everything you can from the question stem, including clues about the parts of the passage that are relevant, and approach the question as though it were open-ended rather than multiple-choice. Even if you can't home in on the exact answer, you can often develop some expectations about what the correct response would have to look like. If you know what to expect before looking at the answer choices, you'll be far less likely to fall into a trap.

- **Eliminate answers that contradict the passage.** If you can't figure out what to predict, narrow down the possibilities by ruling out definite incorrect answers. If an answer choice comes into conflict with scientific information from the text or with data from the passage's graphs and tables, it is almost certainly incorrect. In addition, sometimes you can eliminate answer choices that contradict a key piece of information from the question stem itself; in other cases, you can even use common sense and basic logic to rule out choices that are implausible. Using process of elimination like this will either reveal the one answer that must be correct or at least increase your odds of guessing correctly among the remaining options.

- **Don't overthink it.** Remember that the science on the ACT Science Test remains relatively basic. Most relationships in data will be relatively simple linear ones, either direct or inverse—so don't strain your brain looking for something more complex when you don't need to. In addition, you'll never have to bring in advanced scientific concepts or equations, nor will you need to perform elaborate calculations since you aren't allowed to use a calculator. If it seems like answering a question will require advanced knowledge or a complex calculation, you're most likely overthinking it.

SMARTPOINTS BREAKDOWN

By studying the information released by the ACT, Kaplan has been able to determine how often certain topics are likely to show up on the test, and therefore how many points these topics are worth on Test Day. If you master a given topic, you can expect to earn the corresponding number of SmartPoints on Test Day.

Here is a brief overview of what exactly to expect and how much of it you should be expecting.

Interpretation of Data—17 Points

Approximately 45–55% of the questions on the Science Test are Interpretation of Data questions. These questions test skills such as the following:

- Recognizing data, variables, units, and other information in figures
- Understanding scientific terms and other scientific information from texts
- Determining relationships between variables
- Synthesizing data from multiple figures
- Constructing figures from given information
- Interpolating and extrapolating data
- Analyzing information in the light of new data

Scientific Investigation—9 Points

Approximately 20–30% of Science Test questions fall into the Scientific Investigation category. Scientific Investigation questions test skills such as the following:

- Understanding descriptions of experiments, equipment used in experiments, and experimental methods
- Recognizing controls and other aspects of experimental design
- Finding similarities and differences in multiple experiments
- Predicting experimental results
- Identifying hypotheses and methods for testing them
- Evaluating precision and accuracy in experiments

Evaluation of Models, Inferences, and Experimental Results—10 Points

Approximately 25–35% of Science Test questions belong to the final SmartPoints category, typically shortened to Evaluation of Models. These questions test skills such as the following:

- Identifying basic claims, assumptions, and implications of theories
- Evaluating the consistency of information with a theory
- Finding similarities and differences in multiple theories
- Identifying what would strengthen or weaken a theory
- Determining the effect of new information on a theory
- Making predictions based on theories

CHAPTER SEVENTEEN

Data Representation Passages

PRACTICE QUESTIONS

The following test-like question sets provide an opportunity to practice reading Data Representation Passages and answering related questions. Remember, you may refer to the passages as often as necessary. You are NOT permitted to use a calculator on these questions.

PASSAGE I

A *binary star system* consists of two stars that are gravitationally bound to each other. If two stars that orbit each other are viewed along a line of sight that is not perpendicular to the orbital plane, they will alternately appear to eclipse each other. The orbit of *eclipsing binary* System Q is shown in Diagram 1.

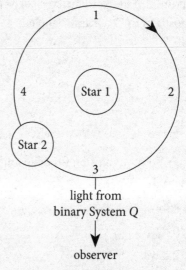

light from
binary System Q

observer

Diagram 1

Notes: Diagram is not drawn to scale. Star 1 is brighter than Star 2.

Astronomers deduce that a given star is an eclipsing binary from its *light curve*—the plot of its surface brightness (observed from a fixed position) against time. The light curve of an eclipsing binary typically displays a deep primary minimum and a shallower secondary minimum. Figure 1 shows the light curve of System *Q*.

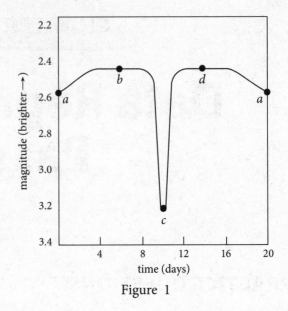

Figure 1

1. The point in Figure 1 labeled *c* corresponds to the position in Diagram 1 labeled:

   A. 1.
   B. 2.
   C. 3.
   D. 4.

2. The period of revolution for eclipsing binary *Q* is about:

   F. 4 days.
   G. 10 days.
   H. 12 days.
   J. 20 days.

3. The stars in eclipsing binary *Q* alternately eclipse each other for periods of approximately:

   A. 2 days and 4 days.
   B. 3 days and 4 days.
   C. 3 days and 8 days.
   D. 5 days each.

4. The light curves for two eclipsing binaries, Systems *X* and *Z*, are shown. Which of the following hypotheses would best account for the deeper primary minimum of System *Z*?

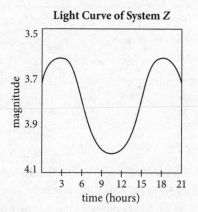

Light Curve of System X

Light Curve of System Z

F. There is a more extreme difference between the magnitudes of the two stars of System *X* than between those of the two stars of System *Z*.

G. There is a more extreme difference between the magnitudes of the two stars of System *Z* than between those of the two stars of System *X*.

H. System *X* has a longer orbital period than does System *Z*.

J. System *Z* has a longer orbital period than does System *X*.

5. The greatest total brightness shown on the light curve of an eclipsing binary star system corresponds to a point in the orbit when:

A. the brighter star in the binary pair is directly in front of the darker star.

B. the larger star in the binary pair is directly in front of the smaller star.

C. the smaller star in the binary pair is directly in front of the larger star.

D. both stars are fully visible.

6. The passage suggests that the light curve shown in Figure 1 assumes that the observer is viewing from a line of sight that is NOT perpendicular to the orbital plane. If the observer were viewing from a line of sight perpendicular to the orbital plane, the light curve of System *Q* would:

F. remain unchanged from Figure 1.

G. show a larger difference between the primary minimum and secondary minimum.

H. suggest a longer duration for the eclipses.

J. indicate no difference in magnitude over time.

PASSAGE II

The utilization and replenishment of Earth's carbon supply is a cyclic process involving all living matter. This cycle is shown in Diagram 1.

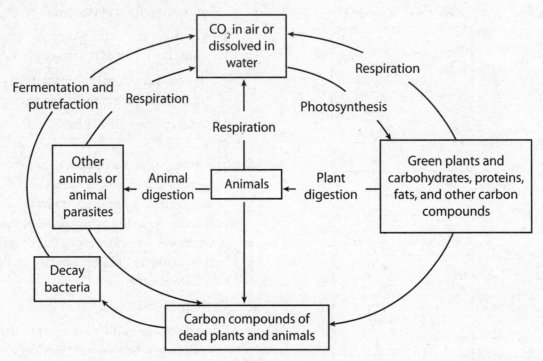

Diagram 1

7. Which of the following can most reasonably be inferred from Diagram 1?

A. An increase in plant photosynthesis would decrease atmospheric carbon, while an increase in animal respiration would increase atmospheric carbon.

B. A decrease in plant photosynthesis would decrease atmospheric carbon, while a decrease in animal respiration would increase atmospheric carbon.

C. An increase in plant photosynthesis would decrease atmospheric carbon, while an increase in animal respiration would decrease atmospheric carbon.

D. A decrease in plant photosynthesis would decrease atmospheric carbon, while an increase in animal respiration would increase atmospheric carbon.

8. Carbon fixation involves the removal of CO_2 from the air and the incorporation of carbon into various compounds. According to the cycle shown, carbon fixation can form which compound(s)?

  I. Fat

 II. Starch

III. Protein

F. II only

G. I and II only

H. II and III only

J. I, II, and III

9. Suppose that scientists discovered a new group of organisms that can impact the carbon cycle in a manner similar to plants. What effect would this have on the model presented in Diagram 1?

    A. The number of pathways to increase atmospheric carbon and the number of pathways to decrease atmospheric carbon would both need to be decreased.

    B. The number of pathways to increase atmospheric carbon would need to be decreased, while the number of pathways to decrease atmospheric carbon would need to be increased.

    C. The number of pathways to increase atmospheric carbon and the number of pathways to decrease atmospheric carbon would both need to be increased.

    D. The number of pathways to increase atmospheric carbon would need to be increased, while the number of pathways to decrease atmospheric carbon would need to be decreased.

10. Based on Diagram 1, can the carbon present in an animal's body return to the atmosphere after the animal dies?

    F. Yes, because animals can engage in the process of putrefaction.

    G. Yes, because bacteria can engage in putrefaction on dead animal bodies.

    H. No, because animals cannot engage in the process of putrefaction.

    J. No, because only plants can return carbon to the atmosphere.

11. Based on Diagram 1, a direct source of CO_2 in the atmosphere is:

    A. the fermentation performed by green plants.

    B. the photosynthesis of tropical plants.

    C. the digestion of plant matter by animals.

    D. the respiration of animal parasites.

12. Which of the following best describes the relationship between animal respiration and photosynthesis?

    F. Respiration and photosynthesis serve the same function in the carbon cycle.

    G. Animal respiration provides vital gases for green plants.

    H. Animal respiration prohibits photosynthesis.

    J. There is no relationship between respiration and photosynthesis.

PASSAGE III

For centuries, physicians attempted to treat patients by transfusion, the transfer of blood from a healthy person to a patient. This was not reliably successful until the discovery of blood groups and blood types in the mid-20th century. A person is said to have a certain blood type if his or her red blood cells have a particular set of molecules, called antigens, on the cells' surfaces. The primary antigens are A and B; if a person's blood cells have neither A nor B antigens, he or she is designated type "O." Also significant is the Rh antigen, which is inherited separately from the A and B antigens; the presence of the Rh antigen is designated by a "+."

A significant complication that can occur from giving blood to someone of a different type is that the recipient's blood contains antibodies (proteins that react with antigens), which recognize and attack any blood group antigen not normally present in the person's blood. A recipient cannot safely receive blood donated by someone with an incompatible blood type. Table 1 presents a sample of transfusion compatibility for some blood types.

The set of antigens present on an individual's red blood cells is an aspect of his or her phenotype, the physical and biochemical properties of that person. The phenotype is determined by the genotype, which is the set of genes that code for those properties. Humans have two copies, or alleles, of each gene; these alleles may be the same or different. For example, the A, B, and o alleles are different versions of the gene for ABO type, while the Rh+ and Rh− alleles are different versions of the gene for Rh type. Each parent passes one allele of each gene on to offspring, so a child's genotype consists of two alleles per gene, one from each parent. Table 2 presents the ABO phenotypes that result from each possible genotype.

Table 2	
Genotype	**Phenotype (ABO type)**
AA	A
Ao	A
BB	B
Bo	B
AB	AB
oo	O

Table 1					
Recipient's blood type		**Compatible with transfusion from:**			
ABO type	**Rh type**	**A−**	**A+**	**B−**	**B+**
AB	+	Yes	Yes	Yes	Yes
AB	−	Yes	No	Yes	No
B	+	No	No	Yes	Yes
B	−	No	No	Yes	No

13. Based on the passage, an individual with A+ blood could safely receive a transfusion from which of the following blood types?

    A. All blood types

    B. All Rh+ blood types

    C. A+ and A−

    D. A+ and B+

14. A child with a blood group phenotype AB+ could have parents with which of the following phenotypes?

    F. O+ and AB+

    G. A− and B−

    H. A+ and B−

    J. A+ and O−

15. Suppose that a patient with blood type B+ is in need of a transfusion, but the blood bank has only A+, A−, B+, and B− available. Based on Table 1, which of those blood types would be suitable for the patient to receive?

    A. A+ only

    B. A+ and A−

    C. B+ only

    D. B+ and B−

16. Based on the information provided in the passage, which of the following blood types would be safe for any transfusion recipient to receive, regardless of the recipient's blood type?

    F. AB−

    G. AB+

    H. O−

    J. O+

17. Which of the following ABO blood types would NOT be possible for the offspring of a woman with type A blood and a man with type AB blood?

    A. O

    B. A

    C. B

    D. AB

18. A physician orders a blood transfusion for a patient with A+ blood and later discovers that her patient was given O+ blood. Should the physician be confident that this is a safe transfusion?

    F. No, because anti-O antibodies in the patient's blood will attack the O antigen in the donor blood, causing an adverse reaction.

    G. No, because anti-Rh antibodies in the patient's blood will attack the Rh antigen in the donor blood, causing an adverse reaction.

    H. Yes, because the O antigen in the donor blood will not react with the anti-A antibodies in the patient's blood.

    J. Yes, because the patient's blood does not contain any antibodies that will attack antigens in the donor blood.

PASSAGE IV

The following chemical equation represents a typical acid-base neutralization reaction:

$$HCl + NaOH \rightarrow H_2O + NaCl$$

Table 1 lists common pH indicators and the pH ranges over which a distinct color change occurs.

Table 1	
Indicator	**pH range**
Methyl yellow	2.9–4.0
Bromocresol green	3.8–5.4
Methyl red	4.4–6.2
Phenol red	6.8–8.4
Phenolphthalein	8.3–10.0
Alizarine	10.1–12.0

In the process of acid-base titration, the *equivalence point* is the point at which equal concentrations of an acid and base are present. When an acid or base is added to a solution at its equivalence point, changes in pH are typically much more drastic than they are at other points in the titration process. Figure 1 shows the pH of Solution A and Solution B versus the amount of an NaOH solution added.

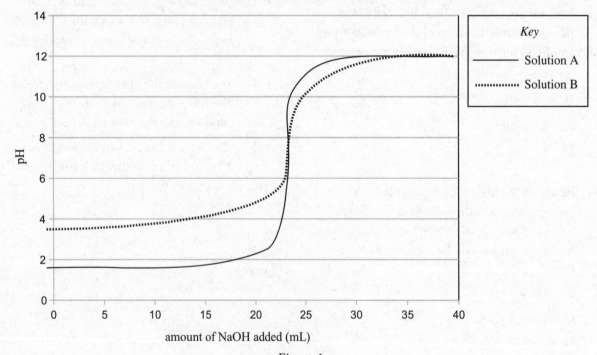

Figure 1

Figure 2 shows the reaction rate for Solutions A and B (as a percentage of the reaction rate at their equivalence point) versus the amount of NaOH solution added.

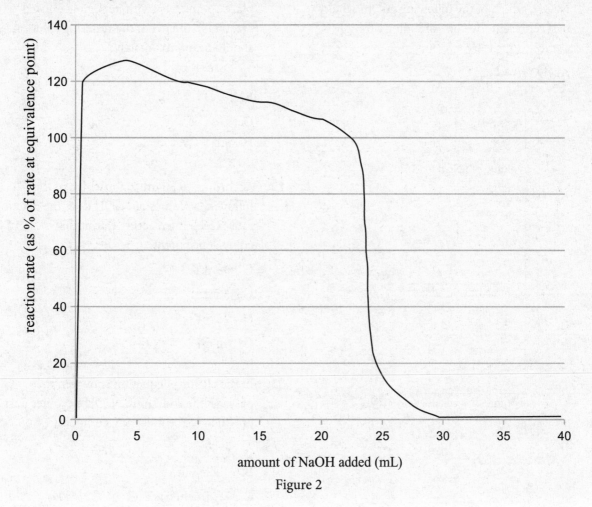

Figure 2

19. If the experimental setup were reversed and Solution A were titrated into a beaker of NaOH, which of the following graphs would best represent the corresponding titration curve?

A.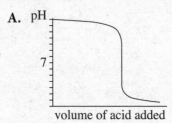
volume of acid added

B.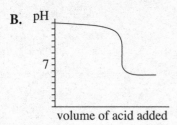
volume of acid added

C.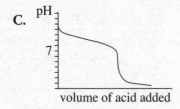
volume of acid added

D.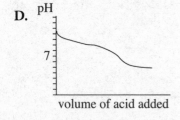
volume of acid added

20. Based on Table 1 and Figure 1, which indicator changes color in a pH range that includes the equivalence point of Solution A?

F. Bromocresol green

G. Methyl red

H. Phenol red

J. Alizarine

21. If the chemical reaction associated with the chemical equation shown in the passage takes place completely (with negligible unused reactants), the pH of the resulting solution should be approximately:

A. 0.

B. 2.

C. 7.

D. 14.

22. According to Figure 2, for which of the following volumes of NaOH does the reaction rate exceed the reaction rate at the equivalence point?

F. 0 mL

G. 5 mL

H. 25 mL

J. 30 mL

23. In the chemical equation shown in the passage, the sodium in NaOH becomes part of which of the following compounds?

A. Water

B. Table salt

C. Hydrochloric acid

D. Sodium hydroxide

24. Based on Figures 1 and 2, the amount of NaOH for which the reaction rate is highest also corresponds to:

F. the equivalence point of Solution A.

G. the equivalence point of Solution B.

H. a high pH in Solution A.

J. a low pH in Solution B.

PASSAGE V

The electrons in a solid occupy *energy states* determined by the type and spatial distribution of the atoms in the solid. The probability that a given energy state will be occupied by an electron is given by the *Fermi-Dirac distribution function*, which depends on the material and the temperature of the solid. Fermi-Dirac distribution functions for the same solid at 3 different temperatures are shown in Figure 1.

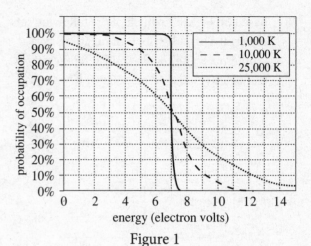

Figure 1

(Note: 1 electron volt (eV) = 1.66×10^{-19} joules (J); eV and J are both units of energy. At energies above 15 eV, the probability of occupation at each temperature continues to decrease.)

25. The information in Figure 1 supports which of the following statements about energy states?

   A. Cooler materials have a larger range of energy states than hotter materials.

   B. Materials have the same range of energy states regardless of temperature.

   C. Cooler materials are more capable of occupying higher energy states than hotter materials.

   D. Hotter materials are more capable of occupying higher energy states than cooler materials.

26. The steepness of the slope of each distribution function at the point where its value equals 50% is inversely proportional to the average *kinetic energy* of the atoms in the solid. Which of the following correctly ranks the 3 functions, from *least* to *greatest*, according to the average kinetic energy of the atoms in the solid?

   F. 25,000 K; 10,000 K; 1,000 K

   G. 25,000 K; 1,000 K; 10,000 K

   H. 10,000 K; 1,000 K; 25,000 K

   J. 1,000 K; 10,000 K; 25,000 K

27. Based on Figure 1, the probability of an electron occupying an energy state of 20 eV at a temperature of 1,000 K is:

   A. less than 5%.

   B. between 5% and 50%.

   C. between 50% and 90%.

   D. greater than 90%.

28. Based on Figure 1, which of the following sets of Fermi-Dirac distribution functions best represents an unknown solid at temperatures of 2,000 K, 20,000 K, and 50,000 K?

F.
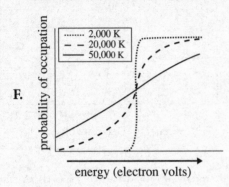

G.
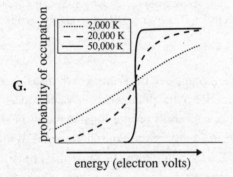

H.
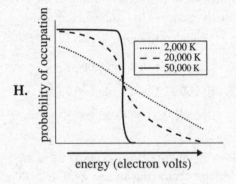

J.
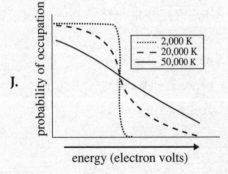

29. Based on Figure 1, the probability of a 5 eV energy state being occupied by an electron will equal 80% when the temperature of the solid is closest to:

A. 500 K.

B. 5,000 K.

C. 20,000 K.

D. 30,000 K.

30. The *de Broglie wavelength* of an electron energy state decreases as the energy of the state increases. Based on this information, over all energies in Figure 1, as the de Broglie wavelength of an electron energy state decreases, the probability of that state being occupied by an electron:

F. increases only.

G. decreases only.

H. increases, then decreases.

J. decreases, then increases.

PASSAGE VI

Wild type *Drosophila melanogaster*, commonly known as the fruit fly, has red eyes and a yellow body. Researchers studied two different recessive mutations: white eyes (ww) and dark bodies (dd). The mode of inheritance (autosomal or X-linked) can be determined by examining two generations following a parent cross and a reciprocal cross. Since males are haploid for the X chromosome, recessive genes on the X chromosome show up more easily in males than in females.

Assuming the white eye mutation is X-linked, researchers crossed white eye, yellow (wild type) body females (X^wX^wDD) with red (wild type) eye, dark body males (X^WYdd). The offspring (F1) from this parental cross (P1) is shown in Table 1. For a reciprocal cross (P2), white eye males (X^wYDD) were crossed with dark body females (X^WX^Wdd). The results are shown in Table 2.

Table 1		
P1 phenotype and genotype	**Wild type eye, dark body male (X^WYdd)**	**White eye, wild type body female (X^wX^wDD)**
F1 phenotype and genotype	**White eye, wild type body males (X^wYDd)**	**Wild type eye and body females (X^WX^wDd)**
Number of flies	41	55
Percentage of total offspring	42.71	57.29

Table 2				
P2 phenotype and genotype	**White eye, wild type body male (X^wYDD)**		**Wild type eye, dark body female (X^WX^Wdd)**	
F1 phenotype and genotype	**White eye, wild type body males (X^wYDd)**	**Wild type eye and body males (X^WYDd)**	**White eye, wild type body females (X^wX^wDd)**	**Wild type eye and body females (X^WX^wDd)**
Number of flies	23	22	19	19
Percentage of total offspring	27.71	26.51	22.89	22.89

The F1 of P1 were then self-crossed to produce a second generation (F2). The results are shown in Table 3. (Note that the general order of a phenotypic ratio, such as 9:3:3:1, is the proportion displaying both dominant traits : the proportion displaying dominant first trait and recessive second trait : the proportion displaying dominant second trait and recessive first trait : the proportion displaying both recessive traits.)

Table 3								
F2 genotype	$X^wYD\_$	$X^WYD\_$	X^wYdd	X^WYdd	$X^wX^wD\_$	$X^WX^wD\_$	X^wX^wdd	X^WX^wdd
Number of flies	74	70	22	22	71	67	24	32
Percentage of total offspring	19.37	18.32	5.76	5.76	18.59	17.54	6.28	8.38

31. According to Table 3, what percentage of the F2 generation is wild type?

    A. 5.76%

    B. 17.54%

    C. 18.32%

    D. 35.86%

32. Upon reviewing the data, the researchers discovered that the results for the reciprocal cross were erroneous because the parents were true-breeding and only two phenotypes should have been produced. Which of the following best explains the reason for the error?

    F. Some of the female flies in P2 died before eggs could be laid.

    G. Some of the male flies in P2 mutated during the experiment.

    H. Some of the female flies in P2 had a different genotype.

    J. Some of the male flies in P2 bred at a faster rate.

33. Based on the data, what percent of F2 males and what percent of F2 females had the same phenotype as P1 males and P1 females, respectively?

	male	female
A	5.76%	17.54%
B	5.76%	18.59%
C	18.59%	5.76%
D	19.37%	8.38%

    A. A

    B. B

    C. C

    D. D

34. Based on the results of the experiments, what is the eye color genotype of the female offspring when a wild type eye male is crossed with a white eye female?

    F. X^wY

    G. X^wY^w

    H. X^WY

    J. X^WY^w

35. Based on Table 3, which of the following phenotypes were expressed by 5.76% of the F2 population?

    A. White eye, wild type body females

    B. Wild type eye, dark body females

    C. White eye, dark body males

    D. Wild type males

36. Which of the following best explains the reason the researchers performed a reciprocal cross (P2)? The researchers wanted to:

    F. determine the mode of inheritance for body color.

    G. verify that the white eye mutation is Y-linked.

    H. examine the offspring of X^wX^wDD crossed with X^WYdd.

    J. investigate mutations in traits other than eye and body color.

37. Evidence shows that if a genetic mutation is X-linked, the F2 phenotypic ratio will be 3:1:3:1. Do the results from the passage support the researchers' assumption that the white-eye mutation is X-linked?

    A. Yes, because both males and females exhibit 3:1:3:1 phenotypic ratios.

    B. Yes, because only the males exhibit a 3:1:3:1 phenotypic ratio.

    C. No, because neither males nor females exhibit 3:1:3:1 phenotypic ratios.

    D. No, because only the males exhibit a 3:1:3:1 phenotypic ratio.

ANSWERS AND EXPLANATIONS

PASSAGE I

1. C   Difficulty: Medium

Category: Interpretation of Data

Getting to the Answer: Point *c* is the point on the light curve in Figure 1 at which the eclipsing binary is the darkest. Take a look at Diagram 1. From the point of view of the observer, System *Q* is going to be darkest when the light from the brighter star, Star 1, is being blocked by the less bright Star 2. Star 2 interposes itself between Star 1 and the observer when Star 2 is in position 3, (C).

2. J   Difficulty: Medium

Category: Interpretation of Data

Getting to the Answer: According to the *x*-axis of the light curve in Figure 1, the complete cycle of changes in the system's surface brightness (from point *a* through points *b*, *c*, and *d* and back to point *a* again) lasts 20 days. This means that Star 2 requires 20 days to complete its orbit around Star 1 (it is this orbit, after all, that is causing the changes in the system's brightness). Choice (J) is correct.

3. C   Difficulty: Medium

Category: Interpretation of Data

Getting to the Answer: The drops in brightness on the light curve in Figure 1 indicate when one star is eclipsing the other. The sharp drop known as the primary minimum—when the darker star eclipses the brighter star—lasts approximately 3 days (days 9 through 11 in Figure 1). The secondary minimum—when the brighter star eclipses the darker star—goes from day 16 through day 20 to day 4, a total of 8 days. Choice (C) is thus correct.

4. G   Difficulty: Medium

Category: Scientific Investigation

Getting to the Answer: This question introduces two new light curve graphs. What gives System *Z* a deeper primary minimum than *X*? The reason *Q* had a deep primary minimum was that one star was brighter than the other; during the time that the brighter star's light was eclipsed by the darker star, the whole system became much darker. You can safely assume that this is the reason *Z* has a deep primary minimum as well. System *X*'s lack of a deep primary minimum must mean, then, that neither of its stars is significantly brighter than the other. As you can see from *X*'s light curve, the drop in brightness of the system is about the same no matter which star is being eclipsed, so the two stars must be about equally bright. Because the more extreme difference in the magnitudes of System *Z*'s stars is the reason for *Z*'s deeper primary minimum, (G) is correct. Choice F states the opposite, while H and J are incorrect because the length of the orbital period has no effect on the depth of the primary minimum.

5. D   Difficulty: Medium

Category: Evaluation of Models, Inferences, and Results

Getting to the Answer: If either star in an eclipsing binary system is in front of the other, the brightness of the system will be reduced because the light from one of the stars will be blocked by the other. The only time the system reaches maximum brightness is when both stars are completely visible—when the full brightness of one star is added to the full brightness of the other. Choice (D) is thus correct.

6. J   Difficulty: High

Category: Evaluation of Models, Inferences, and Results

Getting to the Answer: According to the introductory paragraph of the passage, if a binary star system is "viewed along a line of sight that is not perpendicular to the orbital plane," the two stars "will alternately appear to eclipse each other." This, in turn, causes the brightness to change, because one of the stars will be obscured by the other one at certain points in the orbit. However, if an observer saw System Q from a line of sight that is in fact perpendicular (at a right angle) to the orbital plane, the observer would essentially be seeing the view presented in Diagram 1, in which both stars will always be visible, regardless of Star 2's position in orbit. Thus, the magnitude of the brightness would always stay the same, making (J) correct. Choice F is incorrect because the light curve would change substantially from what is seen in Figure 1, while G is incorrect because the magnitude would remain constant, so there would no longer be a primary minimum and a secondary minimum. Choice H is incorrect because the duration of the eclipses would be reduced to zero.

PASSAGE II

7. A   Difficulty: Medium

Category: Evaluation of Models, Inferences, and Results

Getting to the Answer: Each answer choice includes statements about plant photosynthesis and animal respiration, so consider each process separately. According to Diagram 1, plant photosynthesis removes carbon from the atmosphere. Since a decrease in atmospheric carbon would result from an increase in photosynthesis, not from a decrease in photosynthesis, B and D can be eliminated. Diagram 1 also shows that animal respiration adds carbon to the atmosphere, so an increase in animal respiration would increase, not decrease, atmospheric carbon. Thus, C is incorrect and (A) is the correct answer.

8. J   Difficulty: Medium

Category: Interpretation of Data

Getting to the Answer: The question requires you to identify what is formed when CO_2 leaves the air.

Diagram 1 indicates that CO_2 leaves the air via photosynthesis, which leads to the production in green plants of "proteins, fats, and other carbon compounds." (In fact, carbon fixation is a part of photosynthesis.) Because compounds I and III are both produced through carbon fixation and no other answer choice contains both I and III, (J) must be correct. Compound II, starch, is a complex carbohydrate (a type of carbon compound), which is also produced through carbon fixation—however, it is not necessary to know this outside knowledge to arrive at the correct answer.

9. C   Difficulty: Medium

Category: Interpretation of Data

Getting to the Answer: Diagram 1 shows that plants perform photosynthesis, which decreases atmospheric carbon, and that plants also engage in respiration, which increases atmospheric carbon in the form of CO_2. If a newly-discovered group of organisms behaved in a similar way, the model would need to be modified to add another pathway that increases atmospheric carbon and to add another pathway that decreases atmospheric carbon. Choice (C) is thus correct.

10. G   Difficulty: Medium

Category: Interpretation of Data

Getting to the Answer: According to Diagram 1, the "carbon compounds of dead plants and animals" can be consumed by decay bacteria, which use "fermentation and putrefaction" to return carbon to the atmosphere in the form of CO_2. Choice (G) is thus correct. Choice F is incorrect because the diagram does not suggest that animals can engage in putrefaction themselves; that process requires decay bacteria. Although the reasoning attached to H is a true statement, H is incorrect because it overlooks the fact that decay bacteria *can* engage in putrefaction to return carbon to the atmosphere. Choice J is incorrect because decay bacteria, and not just plants, can return carbon to the atmosphere.

11. D   Difficulty: Low

Category: Interpretation of Data

Getting to the Answer: According to Diagram 1, "other animals and animal parasites" digest animals to acquire carbon and engage in "respiration" to return carbon to the atmosphere. Because the respiration of animal parasites is a direct source of atmospheric CO_2, (D) is correct. Choice A is incorrect because green plants don't perform fermentation; decay bacteria do. Choice B is incorrect because photosynthesis removes carbon from the atmosphere. Choice C is incorrect because the digestion of plants by animals does not directly return carbon to the atmosphere; other processes are required to do that.

12. G   Difficulty: Medium

Category: Interpretation of Data

Getting to the Answer: The arrow signifying animal respiration and the arrow signifying photosynthesis are linked in Diagram 1 by the "carbon dioxide in air or dissolved in water" box. Animal respiration is one of the sources of carbon for carbon dioxide, which in turn provides carbon for the process of photosynthesis. Thus, animal respiration is providing gases that are essential for green plants, making (G) correct. Choice F is incorrect because the 2 processes serve opposite functions. Choice H is incorrect because animal respiration does not inhibit photosynthesis, but enables it. Choice J is incorrect because the 2 processes are related.

PASSAGE III

13. C   Difficulty: Medium

Category: Interpretation of Data

Getting to the Answer: A+ is not one of the recipients listed in Table 1, but its transfusion compatibility can be inferred from the pattern established in the table or from the description in the second paragraph, which states that a recipient's antibodies "recognize and attack any blood group antigen not normally present in the person's blood." An A+ individual's blood cells contain the A and Rh antigens, but not the B antigen. Thus, an A+ individual can safely receive blood of any non-B type. Choices A, B, and D can be eliminated, because they each include at least one blood type containing the B antigen. Choice (C) is correct because it is the only option that exclusively contains blood types without the B antigen.

14. H   Difficulty: High

Category: Interpretation of Data

Getting to the Answer: According to the passage, children receive one allele for ABO type and one allele for Rh type from each parent. In order to have AB blood, a child will need to have one parent passing on the A allele and the other parent passing on the B allele, which means that F and J can be eliminated. To have Rh+ blood, the child will need to have at least one parent who has the Rh antigen, so G can also be eliminated. Choice (H) is correct because the child could receive the A allele and the Rh+ allele from the first parent and the B allele from the second parent.

15. D   Difficulty: Low

Category: Interpretation of Data

Getting to the Answer: Based on Table 1, a recipient with B+ blood can safely receive transfusions from both B+ and B− blood. Choice (D) is thus correct.

16. H   Difficulty: High

Category: Interpretation of Data

Getting to the Answer: According to the second paragraph of the passage, a blood transfusion recipient's antibodies will "recognize and attack any blood group antigen not normally present in the person's blood." Thus, in order for a blood type to be safe for any transfusion recipient, it should completely lack the blood group antigens discussed in the passage. The first paragraph of the passage notes that type O blood cells lack both the A and B antigens and implies that a "−" indicates the lack of the Rh antigen. Thus, type O− blood will completely be lacking in antigens, making it safe for any transfusion recipient. Choice (H) is correct.

17. A   Difficulty: Medium

Category: Interpretation of Data

Getting to the Answer: Based on Table 2, a man with type AB blood would have to have a genotype of AB, while a woman with type A blood could have a genotype of AA or Ao. In order to produce a child with type O blood, both parents would have to be able to pass on an o allele to their offspring, but the father can only pass on an A or a B. Thus, type O blood is not possible for this couple's offspring, making (A) correct. Choice B is incorrect because type A blood would be the result if the father passed on an A allele (the child's genotype would then be AA or Ao). Choice C is incorrect because type B blood would be the result if the father passed on a B allele and the mother passed on an o allele. Choice D is incorrect because type AB blood would be the result if the father passed on a B allele and the mother passed on an A allele.

18. J   Difficulty: Medium

Category: Interpretation of Data

Getting to the Answer: The second paragraph indicates that a transfusion is unsafe when the recipient's antibodies "recognize and attack any blood group antigen not normally present in the person's blood." O+ blood cells include only the Rh antigen because, as noted in the first paragraph, type O simply refers to the absence of A and B antigens. Because the patient has A+ blood, which includes an Rh antigen, he has no anti-Rh antibodies, so it will be safe for him to receive O+ blood. Choice (J) is thus correct. Choices F and G are incorrect because they suggest that the transfusion is unsafe, while H is incorrect because there is no such thing as an O antigen and because A+ blood would not contain anti-A antibodies.

PASSAGE IV

19. A   Difficulty: Medium

Category: Interpretation of Data

Getting to the Answer: As can be seen in Figure 1, titration of a strong base into a strong acid generates a curve that starts with an acidic pH (a value considerably less than 7), followed by a sharp increase to a basic pH (a value considerably greater than 7). Titration of a strong acid into a strong base would show the reverse behavior, starting well above pH 7 and finishing well below pH 7. Choice (A) is thus correct. Choice B has an appropriate appearance, but it is incorrect because it bottoms out near a neutral pH (near 7) instead of an acidic pH. Choices C and D are incorrect because their curves do not match the general shape seen in Figure 1.

20. H   Difficulty: Medium

Category: Interpretation of Data

Getting to the Answer: This question asks about the equivalence point, which is defined in the passage as "the point at which equal concentrations of an acid and base are present." The passage also notes that the change in pH immediately after and immediately before the equivalence point will be drastic, so you should look for the point in the middle of the sharp increase for Solution A in Figure 1. Based on the figure, the equivalence point for Solution A is found at a pH of about 7 (after approximately 24 mL of NaOH have been added). According to Table 1, phenol red has a pH range of 6.8–8.4, making it the only indicator that includes pH 7 in its range. Choice (H) is thus correct. Choices F and G are incorrect because they change colors at too low of a pH, while J is incorrect because it changes colors at too high of a pH.

21. C   Difficulty: Low

Category: Interpretation of Data

Getting to the Answer: This question is easier to answer if you remember from high school chemistry that 7 is a neutral pH. The passage describes the chemical equation as "a typical acid-base neutralization reaction." Thus, if it goes to completion without excess reactants, the resulting solution should have a neutral pH of 7. Choice (C) is correct. Choices A and B present acidic pH values, while D presents a basic pH.

22. G   Difficulty: Medium

Category: Interpretation of Data

Getting to the Answer: Figure 2 presents the reaction rate as a percentage of the rate at the equivalence point. Thus, any percentage value greater than 100% corresponds to a reaction rate that is faster than the rate at the equivalence point. The curve in Figure 2 is above 100% between approximately 1 mL and 24 mL. Choice (G) is correct because it is the only option with a volume in this range.

23. B   Difficulty: Medium

Category: Interpretation of Data

Getting to the Answer: Familiarity with the names of elements and simple compounds will help to answer this question. According to the reaction presented in the passage, sodium (Na) moves from NaOH to NaCl as the reaction proceeds forward. NaCl is sodium chloride, commonly known as table salt. Choice (B) is correct. Choices A and C are incorrect because water (H_2O) and hydrochloric acid (HCl) do not contain sodium. Choice D is incorrect because sodium hydroxide (NaOH) is where the sodium is found before the reaction, not after it.

24. J   Difficulty: Medium

Category: Interpretation of Data

Getting to the Answer: Because the question asks about a reaction rate, look at Figure 2 first. The highest reaction rate (with a value of over 125%) is found after about 5 mL of NaOH have been added. Figure 1 shows low pH values for both solutions at 5 mL of NaOH. Choice (J) is correct because it is the only option that features a low pH. Choices F and G are incorrect because both points are found after about

24 mL of NaOH have been added, when the reaction rate is only 100%. Choice H is incorrect because a high pH in Solution A is only found after about 25 mL or more of NaOH have been added, when the reaction rate drops below 100%.

PASSAGE V

25. D   Difficulty: High

Category: Evaluation of Models, Inferences, and Results

Getting to the Answer: Figure 1 shows how energy relates to the probability of occupation. According to the passage, the figure shows the same solid at 3 different temperatures. The hottest solid (25,000 K) is able to reach energy states beyond 14 electron volts, which is a higher value than the two cooler solids. Choice (D) is thus correct. Choices A and B are incorrect because hotter materials have a larger range of energy states than cooler ones. Choice C is incorrect because it is the opposite of what Figure 1 shows.

26. J   Difficulty: High

Category: Interpretation of Data

Getting to the Answer: All three curves happen to intersect at 50% probability with 7 eV of energy, so look at their slopes at this point. "Inversely proportional" means that the average kinetic energy is lower for steeper slopes. The 1,000 K curve has the steepest slope and therefore the lowest average kinetic energy. The 10,000 K curve has the next steepest slope and therefore the next lowest kinetic energy, while the 25,000 K curve has the least steep slope and the highest kinetic energy. Choice (J) is correct.

27. A   Difficulty: Low

Category: Interpretation of Data

Getting to the Answer: The 1,000 K curve in Figure 1 appears to reach 0% at energies above approximately 8 eV. The note under the graph says that the curves all continue to decrease beyond 15 eV, so the value of the 1,000 K curve should still be approximately 0% at an energy of 20 eV. Clearly, the probability will be less than 5%, so (A) is correct.

28. J   Difficulty: Medium

Category: Interpretation of Data

Getting to the Answer: The temperatures given in the question stem are simply double the values presented in Figure 1, so you can expect the curves to follow the same trends that were seen there. One of the trends in Figure 1 that applies to all three curves is that probability decreases as energy increases. This means that F and G can be eliminated, because both show the opposite. The other trend from Figure 1 is that the curves become shallower as temperature increases. This same trend is evident in (J), so it is the correct answer. Watch out for the trap in H: the solid line is used to represent the hottest material in the answer choices here but the coolest material in Figure 1, so H looks deceptively similar to Figure 1.

29. C   Difficulty: High

Category: Interpretation of Data

Getting to the Answer: Locate the point in Figure 1 corresponding to an 80% probability of occupation for a 5 eV energy state. It lies between the 10,000 K and 25,000 K curves. The temperature of the solid, then, must be between 10,000 K and 25,000 K. Choice (C) must be correct because it is the only option in this range.

30. G   Difficulty: Medium

Category: Interpretation of Data

Getting to the Answer: It doesn't matter whether you've ever heard of the de Broglie wavelength before—or whether you can even pronounce it! Everything you need to know is in the question stem. As the de Broglie wavelength decreases, the energy increases. What happens to probability as energy increases? Figure 1 clearly shows that the values on all three curves decrease with increasing energy. Choice (G), then, is correct.

PASSAGE VI

31. D   Difficulty: Medium

Category: Interpretation of Data

Getting to the Answer: On Table 3, locate the columns that correspond to wild type. Table 3 shows that 18.32% are wild type males ($X^W YD\_$) and 17.54% are wild type females ($X^W X^W D\_$). Thus, the percentage of F2 that is wild type is the sum of the wild type males and wild type females: 18.32% + 17.54% = 35.86%. The correct answer is (D).

32. H   Difficulty: High

Category: Scientific Investigation

Getting to the Answer: The results in Table 2 show that four phenotypes were produced from the cross, instead of the two that would be expected. What would cause additional phenotypes to be expressed in the offspring of the reciprocal cross? If some of the female flies had a different genotype than what was assumed ($X^W X^W dd$), the genotypes and resulting phenotypes of some of the offspring could vary from what is expected. For instance, if a number of the females were actually heterozygous for eye color ($X^W X^w dd$), you could easily see the results obtained in Table 2. Therefore, the correct answer is (H). Choices F and J would not cause additional phenotypes to be produced. Choice G may sound plausible, but the same mutation is highly unlikely to occur naturally in multiple flies within only one generation.

33. B   Difficulty: Medium

Category: Interpretation of Data

Getting to the Answer: According to Table 1, the phenotype of P1 females is white eye, wild type body and of P1 males is wild type eye, dark body. The phenotypes of F2 for P1 are found in Table 3. According to Table 3, 5.76% of the F2 were wild type eye, dark body males ($X^W Ydd$) and 18.59% of the F2 were white eye, wild type body females ($X^w X^w D\_$). Thus, the correct answer is (B). Choice A represents the offspring with the same phenotype as F1, while D is that for P2. Choice C switches the percentages for male and female.

34. J Difficulty: Medium

Category: Interpretation of Data

Getting to the Answer: The cross between a wild type eye male and white eye female can be found in Table 1. Ignoring the second trait (body color), the cross will produce wild type eye females and white eye males. Females have two X chromosomes, so eliminate F and H, which contain the mix of X and Y chromosomes found in males. Choice G presents the homozygous genotype that produces white eyes, while (J) presents the heterozygous genotype (and wild type phenotype) found in all the females of F1. Thus, the correct answer is (J).

35. C Difficulty: Medium

Category: Interpretation of Data

Getting to the Answer: Locate 5.76% on Table 3. That particular value is listed twice and corresponds to X^wYdd and X^WYdd. The genotypes X^wYdd and X^WYdd produce white eye, dark body and wild type eye, dark body phenotypes, respectively. Since XY is the genotype for males, eliminate A and B, which list females. Choice (C) lists one of the two possible phenotypes produced (white eye, dark body males), making it the correct answer.

36. F Difficulty: Medium

Category: Scientific Investigation

Getting to the Answer: According to the introductory paragraphs, "the mode of inheritance (autosomal or X-linked) can be determined by examining two generations following a parent cross and a reciprocal cross . . . recessive genes on the X chromosome show up more easily in males than in females." Whether the dark body mutation is autosomal or X-linked could not be determined from the P1 lineage (F1 and F2) alone. Therefore, the researchers performed a reciprocal cross (P2) in which the mutations were switched for male and female. The correct answer is (F). Choice G is incorrect because Y-linked inheritance is not discussed in the passage or investigated in the experiments. X^wX^wDD and X^WYdd were the genotypes of P1, not of P2, so H is incorrect. Other traits were not considered in the passage, so J is also incorrect.

37. A Difficulty: High

Category: Evaluation of Models, Inferences, and Results

Getting to the Answer: To determine the phenotypic ratios, divide the numbers for each phenotype by the smallest number (you could also use the percentages instead). For males, this would yield $\frac{74}{22}$, $\frac{70}{22}$, $\frac{22}{22}$, and $\frac{22}{22}$. You can round the numbers to make the math easier (for example, round 70 and 74 to 75 and 22 to 25). Reordering the phenotypic ratios to both dominant:first dominant:second dominant: both recessive will give you approximately 3:1:3:1. For the females, you again can round the numbers to estimate the ratios. After reordering, the phenotypic ratio will also be approximately 3:1:3:1. Both the male and female phenotypic ratios match the desired ratio, so the results do support the researchers' assumption. Choice (A) affirms this and supplies the correct reasoning.

CHAPTER EIGHTEEN

Research Summaries Passages

PRACTICE QUESTIONS

The following test-like question sets provide an opportunity to practice reading Research Summaries Passages and answering related questions. Remember, you may refer to the passages as often as necessary. You are NOT permitted to use a calculator on these questions.

PASSAGE I

Preliminary research indicates that dietary sugar may react with proteins in the human body, damaging the proteins and perhaps contributing to the aging process. The chemical effects of glucose on lens proteins in the eye were investigated in the following experiments.

Experiment 1

A human tissue protein sample was dissolved in a glucose and water solution, resulting in a clear yellow solution. After 30 minutes, the solution became opaque. Spectrographic analysis revealed that an *Amadori product* had formed on the protein. It was determined that the Amadori products on one protein had combined with free amino groups on nearby proteins, forming brown pigmented cross-links between the two proteins. The cross-links are termed *advanced glycosylation end products* (AGEs).

Experiment 2

Forty-six samples of human lens proteins taken from subjects ranging in age from 12–80 years were studied under an electron microscope. The lens proteins in the samples from older subjects occurred much more often in aggregates formed by cross-linked bonds than did the lens proteins in the samples from younger subjects. Fluorescent characteristics revealed the cross-links to be of two types: disulfide bonds and an indeterminate formation with brownish pigmentation.

Experiment 3

Two aqueous solutions containing lens proteins from cow lenses were prepared, one with glucose and one without. Only the glucose solution turned opaque. Absorbance measurements for the two solutions are shown in Figure 1. Analysis revealed that the lens proteins in the glucose solution had formed pigmented cross-links with the brownish color and fluorescence characteristics of those observed in Experiment 2.

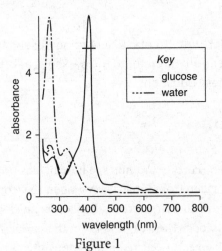

Figure 1

1. Based on Figure 1, what is the approximate wavelength of the maximum absorbance for Amadori products?

   A. 250 nm

   B. 300 nm

   C. 350 nm

   D. 400 nm

2. It was assumed in the design of Experiment 3 that cow lens proteins:

   F. have a brownish pigment.

   G. react with sulfides.

   H. remain insoluble in water.

   J. react similarly to human lens proteins.

3. Based on the results in Experiment 1 only, it can be concluded that:

   A. proteins can form disulfide cross-links.

   B. glucose dissolved in water forms AGEs.

   C. glucose can react with proteins to form cross-links.

   D. Amadori products are a result of glucose metabolism.

4. As people age, the lenses in their eyes sometimes turn brown and cloudy (a condition known as senile cataracts). Based on this information and the results of Experiment 2, which of the following hypotheses is the most likely to be valid?

   F. As people age, the amount of sulfur contained in lens proteins increases.

   G. Senile cataracts are caused by cross-linked bonds between lens proteins.

   H. Lens proteins turn brown with age.

   J. Older lens proteins are more fluorescent than younger lens proteins.

5. Which of the following hypotheses about the brown pigmented cross-links observed in Experiment 2 is best supported by the results of the three experiments?

   A. Their brownish color is caused by disulfide bonds.

   B. They are a natural formation which can be found at birth.

   C. They are caused by glucose in the diet reacting with lens proteins.

   D. They form when proteins are dissolved in water.

6. Based on the experimental results, lens proteins from a 32-year-old man would most likely have:

   F. more cross-links than lens proteins from a 32-year-old woman.

   G. more cross-links than lens proteins from an 18-year-old cow.

   H. fewer cross-links than lens proteins from an 18-year-old man.

   J. fewer cross-links than lens proteins from an 80-year-old man.

7. People with untreated diabetes have excess levels of blood glucose. Based on this information and the results of the experiments, a likely symptom of advanced diabetes would be:

   A. senile cataracts, due to an increase of free amino groups in the urine.

   B. senile cataracts, due to glucose interacting with disulfide cross-links on lens proteins.

   C. senile cataracts, due to AGE cross-links of lens proteins.

   D. kidney failure, due to high levels of free amino groups in the urine.

PASSAGE II

Faraday's Law relates changes in magnetic fields to the production of electric voltage. *Magnetic flux* is a measure of the magnetic field in a region of space. It can be thought of as the mathematical product of the magnetic field and an area defined by a loop of wire in that field. The unit of magnetic flux is the weber, abbreviated Wb. Any instance of change in magnetic flux produces a voltage, also known as an *electromotive force* (emf). This relationship is commonly called *electromagnetic induction*.

Students conducted 3 experiments to study electromagnetic induction.

Experiment 1

A magnet was passed at varying speeds through a coiled wire with a diameter of 2 cm, as shown in Diagram 1. The various speeds created corresponding changes to the magnetic flux within the coil. A voltmeter was used to measure the maximum induced emf in units of volts (V). The results are shown in Table 1.

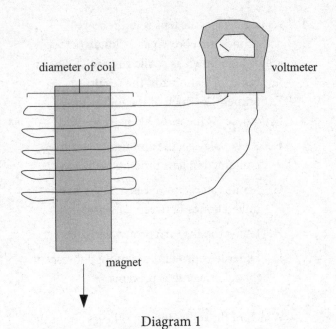

Diagram 1

Table 1		
Trial	**Change in magnetic flux (Wb)**	**Maximum emf (V)**
1	0.3	0.22
2	0.5	0.41
3	0.7	0.63
4	0.9	0.85

Experiment 2

A coiled wire was rotated at various speeds within a constant magnetic field, creating corresponding changes to the magnetic flux within the coil. Special connectors called "slip rings" allow the coil of wire to rotate without tangling the wires. The slip rings also connect the coil electrically to a voltmeter, which was used to measure the maximum resulting emf. This setup is illustrated in Diagram 2 and the results are recorded in Table 2.

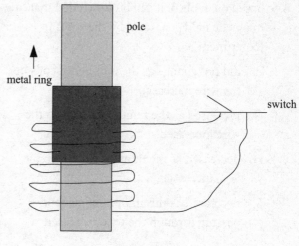

Diagram 3

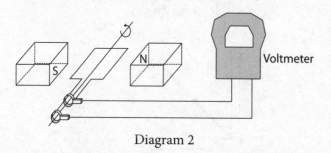

Diagram 2

A current was sent through the wire, producing a magnetic field that caused the metal ring to float up the pole. The students used the same amount of current in each trial and kept the diameter of the coils fixed, but used wires with differing numbers of coils. The height that the metal ring reached on the pole was recorded for each trial. The results are shown in Table 3.

Table 2		
Trial	Change in magnetic flux (Wb)	Maximum emf (V)
5	0.2	0.2
6	0.4	0.4
7	0.6	0.6

Table 3		
Trial	Number of coils	Height (cm)
8	50	1.1
9	100	1.5
10	150	2.1

Experiment 3

A coiled wire was mounted on a pole and a metal ring was placed on the pole, as shown in Diagram 3. (Note that the battery powering the current is not depicted.)

8. Based on Table 3, it can be concluded that the magnetic field generated by the wires in Experiment 3:

    F. did not change as the number of coils in the wire increased.

    G. increased as the number of coils in the wire increased.

    H. decreased as the number of coils in the wire increased.

    J. decreased as the amount of current passing through the wire increased.

9. In Experiment 2, if the coil were slowed down to a rotational velocity of 0 m/s, the resulting emf would correspond to the emf recorded in:

    A. Trial 5.

    B. Trial 6.

    C. Trial 7.

    D. none of the trials.

10. Based on Experiment 1, which of the following would provide the highest maximum emf reading?

    F. Moving the magnet quickly and using a magnet with a strong magnetic field

    G. Moving the magnet quickly and using a magnet with a weak magnetic field

    H. Moving the magnet slowly and using a magnet with a strong magnetic field

    J. Moving the magnet slowly and using a magnet with a weak magnetic field

11. Based on the results of Experiment 1, the relationship between change in magnetic flux and maximum induced emf is best represented by which of the following graphs?

    A.
    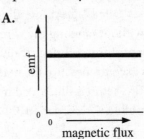

    B.
    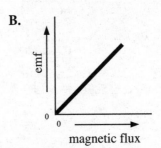

    C.
    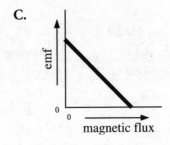

    D.
    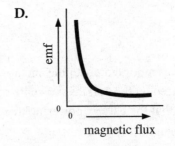

12. In which of the following trials from Experiment 1 was the magnet moved at the slowest speed?

F. Trial 1

G. Trial 2

H. Trial 3

J. Trial 4

13. If a new trial were conducted that repeated the conditions of Trial 9, except with double the current passing through the wire, which of the following would most likely be the recorded height of the metal ring?

A. 0.7 cm

B. 1.1 cm

C. 1.5 cm

D. 2.9 cm

14. Suppose that the students repeated the conditions of Trials 1–4 of Experiment 1, except that they used a coil with a diameter of 4 cm instead of 2 cm. Based on the passage, how would the results of this new experiment most likely compare to the original results of Experiment 1?

F. Maximum emf and change in magnetic flux would both decrease in the new experiment.

G. Maximum emf would decrease but change in magnetic flux would increase in the new experiment.

H. Maximum emf and change in magnetic flux would both increase in the new experiment.

J. Maximum emf would increase but change in magnetic flux would decrease in the new experiment.

PASSAGE III

Carbonated beverages are liquids that have undergone carbonation, a process in which carbon dioxide gas becomes dissolved in them. A group of students proposed a hypothesis that the presence of carbonation in various bottled liquids would affect *balance time* (the time it takes a liquid to reach equilibrium after being initially off-balance). Diagram 1 shows the bottle held by 2 fixed points on a hinged incline. After the hinge is closed and the angle of inclination becomes zero, the liquid in the bottle completes its balance time when it no longer moves within the bottle.

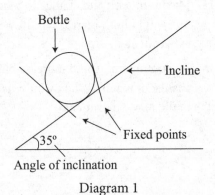

Diagram 1

Each student tested the hypothesis in different trials and recorded average balance times. The initial angle of inclination is 35° for all 3 experiments. Identical 2-L glass bottles were used in all 3 experiments.

Experiment 1

The students added 1 L of clear fruit juice, which is uncarbonated, to an empty bottle. After sealing it, they placed it between the fixed points and closed the hinge. The balance time was then recorded. Next, they added 1 L of the same juice to a second empty bottle, sealed and shook it, and found its balance time. They repeated these 2 procedures with 2 additional liquids: carbonated seltzer that contained a lot of froth, and root beer that was originally carbonated, but was then allowed to become flat (that is, to lose its dissolved carbon dioxide). The results of these trials are shown in Table 1.

Table 1			
		Balance time (seconds)	
Trial	**Liquid**	**Without shaking**	**With shaking**
1	Clear fruit juice	20.01	19.89
2	Carbonated seltzer	21.35	22.97
3	Root beer	20.15	22.48

Experiment 2

The students added 1 L of the flat root beer to an empty bottle. After sealing and shaking the bottle, they set it aside for 10 minutes. After the 10 minutes elapsed, they found the bottle's balance time before and immediately after shaking it again (Trial 4). After conducting these measurements, they set the bottle aside for an additional 90 minutes and found the balance time before and immediately after shaking it a third time (Trial 5). The results can be seen in Table 2.

	Table 2	
	Balance time (seconds)	
Trial	**Before shaking**	**After shaking**
4	20.83	22.67
5	20.04	22.45

Experiment 3

The students added 1 L of the flat root beer to an empty bottle and 1 L of carbonated seltzer to a second empty bottle. They then sealed both bottles. After shaking both bottles and seeing froth form, the students set them aside for observation. At 10 minutes into the experiment, fewer bubbles were visible in the bottle that contained the root beer. At 90 minutes into the experiment, there were no bubbles remaining in the root beer.

15. Which of the following conclusions is most strongly supported by the results of Experiment 3? Ten minutes after being shaken, root beer:

   A. had a lower level of carbonation than seltzer.

   B. had a higher level of carbonation than seltzer.

   C. had a greater quantity of liquid than seltzer.

   D. achieved balance time twice as fast as seltzer.

16. When comparing Trials 1 through 5 in Experiments 1 and 2, in which 2 trials, after shaking, are the balance times the most similar?

   F. Trials 1 and 5

   G. Trials 1 and 3

   H. Trials 2 and 4

   J. Trials 3 and 5

17. In Experiment 2, shaking the bottle of root beer resulted in:

   A. decreasing the number of bubbles in the beverage.

   B. increasing the balance time of the bottle of root beer.

   C. decreasing the balance time of the bottle of root beer.

   D. increasing the mass of the bottle of root beer.

18. Based on the results of the experiments, is it likely that bubbles were present immediately before the bottle was shaken in Trial 4?

   F. Based on Experiment 1, it is likely the bubbles were present before shaking.

   G. Based on Experiment 1, it is unlikely the bubbles were present before shaking.

   H. Based on Experiment 3, it is likely the bubbles were present before shaking.

   J. Based on Experiment 3, it is unlikely the bubbles were present before shaking.

19. Suppose a sixth trial existed in which the same bottle of root beer was set aside for an additional 90 minutes after the fifth trial was completed. Based on the results of Experiment 2, what would the balance time most likely be if the students do not shake the bottle?

   A. Less than 20.83 seconds

   B. Between 20.83 seconds and 22.45 seconds

   C. Between 22.45 seconds and 22.67 seconds

   D. Greater than 22.67 seconds

20. Based on the results of Trials 3–5 and Experiment 3, if the students had added 1 L of the flat root beer to an empty bottle, then sealed the bottle and shook it, how long would it most likely take for the bubbles to become too few to affect the bottle's balance time?

   F. 0 minutes

   G. Between 0 minutes and 10 minutes

   H. Between 10 minutes and 90 minutes

   J. More than 90 minutes

PASSAGE IV

A student performed experiments to determine the relationship between the amount of electrical current carried by a material and the physical dimensions and temperature of a sample of that material. Current is measured in amperes (A) and the resistance to the flow of current is measured in ohms (Ω). Current and resistance are related to voltage, measured in volts (V), by Ohm's law: $V = A \times \Omega$. (Note that Ohm's law can also be written as $V = I \times R$, where V is voltage, I is current, and R is resistance.)

Experiment 1

The student used several lengths of an iron rod with a 1-cm diameter. The rods were heated or cooled to the specified temperatures and used to complete the circuit shown in Diagram 1. The circuit contains a battery and an ammeter, which measures current in milliamperes (mA). The results are presented in Table 1.

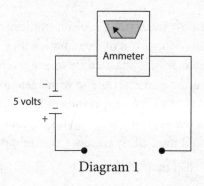

Diagram 1

Table 1			
Trial	Length (cm)	Temperature (°C)	Current (mA)
1	16	80	20
2	16	20	40
3	12	80	27
4	12	20	53
5	10	80	32
6	10	20	64
7	8	80	40
8	8	20	80

Experiment 2

The student then repeated the experiment, this time using 1-cm diameter rods made from either iron or copper. The results are presented in Table 2.

Table 2				
Trial	Material	Length (cm)	Temperature (°C)	Current (mA)
9	Iron	16	80	20
10	Copper	16	80	100
11	Iron	16	20	40
12	Copper	16	20	200
13	Iron	12	80	27
14	Copper	12	80	135
15	Iron	12	20	53
16	Copper	12	20	265

21. Based on the experimental results, which of the following most accurately describes the relationships between current and rod length and between current and temperature?

    A. Current is directly related to length and inversely related to temperature.

    B. Current is inversely related to both length and temperature.

    C. Current is inversely related to length and directly related to temperature.

    D. Current is directly related to both length and temperature.

22. Based on the information from the passage, which of the following rods would have the highest value for resistance?

    F. A 12-cm iron rod at 20°C

    G. A 16-cm copper rod at 20°C

    H. A 16-cm iron rod at 80°C

    J. A 12-cm copper rod at 80°C

23. The *conductivity* of a material is a measure of how readily a length of the material allows the passage of an electric current. Conductivity is represented by σ, the Greek letter sigma, with standard units of siemens per meter (S/m). Siemens are equivalent to inverse ohms (that is, $1/\Omega$). Based on this information, which of the following equations accurately describes the relationship between conductivity and resistance?

    A. $\Omega = \dfrac{1}{\sigma}$

    B. $\sigma = \Omega \times m$

    C. $\sigma = \dfrac{1}{\Omega \times m}$

    D. $\Omega = \sigma \times m$

24. If the rod used in Trial 4 of Experiment 1 were heated to a temperature of 50°C, the current it then conducts would most likely be:

    F. less than 27 mA.

    G. between 27 and 53 mA.

    H. between 53 and 80 mA.

    J. greater than 80 mA.

25. What would happen to the results of Experiment 2 if the student replaced the 5-V battery with a 10-V battery instead?

    A. The recorded current values would increase for both the copper and the iron rods.

    B. The recorded current values would increase for the copper rods but decrease for the iron rods.

    C. The recorded current values would decrease for the copper rods but increase for the iron rods.

    D. The recorded current values would decrease for both the copper and the iron rods.

26. Suppose the student took an iron rod of 8 cm and a copper rod of 8 cm, both with a 1-cm diameter, and attached them end to end, creating a composite rod with a length of 16 cm. Based on the results of Experiment 2, at a temperature of 20°C, this composite rod would most likely conduct a current of:

    F. less than 20 mA.

    G. between 20 and 40 mA.

    H. between 40 and 200 mA.

    J. greater than 200 mA.

27. Which of the following variables was NOT directly manipulated by the student in Experiment 2?

    A. Material

    B. Length

    C. Temperature

    D. Current

PASSAGE V

Microbiologists have observed that certain species of bacteria are *magnetotactic*, that is, sensitive to magnetic fields. Several species found in the bottom of swamps in the Northern Hemisphere tend to orient themselves toward magnetic north (the northern pole of the earth's magnetic field). Researchers conducted the following series of experiments on magnetotactic bacteria.

Study 1

A drop of water filled with magnetotactic bacteria was observed under high magnification. The direction of the first 500 bacterial migrations across the field of view was observed for each of five trials and the tally for each trial recorded in Table 1. Trial 1 was conducted under standard laboratory conditions. In Trial 2, the microscope was shielded from all external light and electric fields. In Trials 3 and 4, the microscope was rotated clockwise 90° and 180°, respectively. For Trial 5, the microscope was moved to another laboratory at the same latitude.

Study 2

The north pole of a permanent magnet was positioned near the microscope slide. The magnet was at the 12:00 position for Trial 6 and was moved 90° clockwise for each of three successive trials. All other conditions were as in Trial 1 of Study 1. The results were tallied and recorded in Table 2.

Table 2				
	Direction			
Trial	12:00	3:00	6:00	9:00
6	470	6	15	9
7	8	483	3	6
8	17	4	474	5
9	5	19	9	467

Table 1				
	Direction			
Trial	North	East	South	West
1	474	7	13	6
2	481	3	11	5
3	479	4	12	5
4	465	9	19	7
5	480	3	11	6

28. What serves as the control in Study 1?

    F. Trial 1

    G. Trial 2

    H. Trial 3

    J. Trial 5

29. The hypothesis that light was NOT the primary stimulus affecting the direction of bacterial migration is:

    A. supported by a comparison of the results of Studies 1 and 2.

    B. supported by a comparison of the results of Trials 1 and 2 of Study 1.

    C. supported by a comparison of the results of Trials 3 and 4 of Study 1.

    D. not supported by any of the results noted in the passage.

30. If the south pole of the permanent magnet used in Study 2 had been placed near the microscope slide, what would the most likely result have been?

    F. The figures for each trial would have remained approximately the same since the strength of the magnetic field would be unchanged.

    G. The bacteria would have become disoriented, with approximately equal numbers moving in each direction.

    H. The major direction of travel would have shifted by 180° because of the reversed direction of the magnetic field.

    J. The bacteria would still have tended to migrate toward Earth's magnetic north but would have taken longer to orient themselves.

31. It has been suggested that magnetic sensitivity helps magnetotactic bacteria orient themselves downward. Such an orientation would be most advantageous from an evolutionary standpoint if:

    A. organisms that consume magnetotactic bacteria were mostly bottom-dwellers.

    B. the bacteria could only reproduce by migrating upwards to the water's surface.

    C. bacteria that stayed in the top layers of water tended to be dispersed by currents.

    D. the nutrients necessary for the bacteria's survival were more abundant in bottom sediments.

32. Researchers could gain the most useful new information about the relationship between magnetic field strength and bacterial migration by repeating Study 2 with:

    F. incremental position changes of less than 90°.

    G. a magnet that rotated slowly around the slide in a counterclockwise direction.

    H. more and less powerful magnets.

    J. larger and smaller samples of bacteria.

33. Which of the following statements is supported by the results of Study 1?

    A. The majority of magnetotactic bacteria migrate toward the Earth's magnetic north pole.

    B. The majority of magnetotactic bacteria migrate toward the north pole of the nearest magnet.

    C. The majority of magnetotactic bacteria migrate toward the 12:00 position.

    D. The effect of the Earth's magnetic field on magnetotactic bacteria is counteracted by electric fields.

34. If each diagram below represents a microscopic field, which diagram best reflects the results of Trial 7 from Study 2?

F.

G.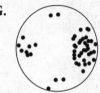

H.

J.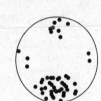

PASSAGE VI

Many proteins undergo denaturation upon heating. A denatured protein is unfolded and can no longer perform its normal biological functions. Denaturation usually occurs over a temperature range. Some proteins can fold back (renature) into their original conformation when the temperature is decreased. A series of experiments was performed to determine the denaturation and renaturation behavior of 3 different proteins.

Experiment 1

Fifteen separate 15-mL samples of each of the proteins ribonuclease (RNase), carboxypeptidase (Case), and hexokinase (Hase) were heated slowly from 20°C to 160°C and cooled slowly back to 20°C. After every 5°C increase in temperature, 0.002 mL of each sample was removed and chemically analyzed to determine the temperature at which denaturation occurred. After every 5°C decrease in temperature, 0.002 mL of each sample was removed and analyzed to determine the temperature at which renaturation occurred. The results of the experiment are shown in Table 1.

Table 1			
Protein	Approximate molecular weight (amu)	Denaturation temperature range (°C)	Renaturation temperature range (°C)
RNase	13,700	135–145	110–135
Case	35,000	150–155	60–140
Hase	100,000	85–95	–

Experiment 2

Solubility is also a measure of protein denaturation. A protein can be considered fully denatured when its solubility drops to zero. Each 0.002-mL sample of ribonuclease, carboxypeptidase, and hexokinase was dissolved in 10 mL of ethyl alcohol, and its solubility was measured. The solubility measurements were taken in 5°C increments as the samples were heated from 20°C to 160°C and again as they were cooled from 160°C to 20°C. The results are shown in Figure 1 and Figure 2.

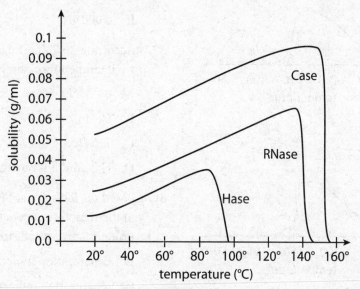

Figure 1

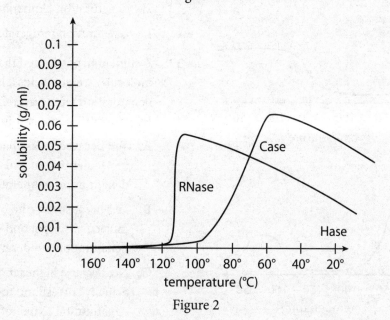

Figure 2

35. If the protein RNase were heated from 40°C to 150°C and then cooled back to 40°C, which of the following plots would its solubility curve most likely resemble?

A.

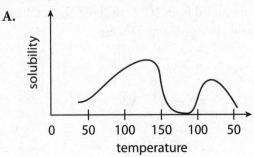

B.

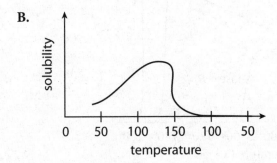

C.

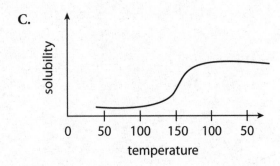

D.

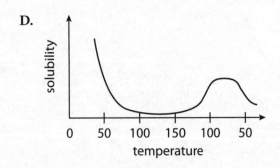

36. According to Figure 1, what would most likely be the solubility of Case in 10 mL of ethyl alcohol at 0°C?

F. 0.055 g/mL

G. 0.045 g/mL

H. 0.015 g/mL

J. 0.000 g/mL

37. According to Table 1, Hase renatured within what temperature range?

A. 85–95°C

B. 60–140°C

C. 110–135°C

D. Hase did not renature.

38. Based on Table 1 and Figure 1, the maximum of the solubility curves for each of the three proteins corresponds to:

F. denaturation molecular weight.

G. renaturation molecular weight.

H. denaturation temperature range.

J. renaturation temperature range.

39. A student hypothesized that a higher molecular weight yields a higher average denaturation temperature. Do the results of Experiment 1 support this hypothesis?

A. Yes, because RNase had the highest molecular weight and the highest average denaturation temperature.

B. Yes, because Case had the highest molecular weight and the highest average denaturation temperature.

C. No, because higher molecular weights actually correspond to lower average denaturation temperatures.

D. No, because there is no correlation between molecular weight and average denaturation temperature.

40. Which of the following best explains why the peak solubility of Case was lower after going through the process of denaturation and renaturation?

    F. Part of the renatured protein formed a precipitate.

    G. The samples before denaturation and after renaturation were taken from different parts of the solution.

    H. Only a fraction of denatured protein renatured back into its native, active form.

    J. There were contaminants in the samples that lowered solubility.

41. A fourth protein, ovalbumin, denaturates between 115°C and 130°C and renaturates between 70°C and 100°C. Based on the results from the passage, if the procedures of Experiment 2 were repeated with ovalbumin, its solubility curve would most likely peak at about:

    A. 85°C.

    B. 95°C.

    C. 105°C.

    D. 115°C.

ANSWERS AND EXPLANATIONS

PASSAGE I

1.   D   Difficulty: Medium

Category: Interpretation of Data

Getting to the Answer: Figure 1 records absorbance measurements from the 2 solutions used in Experiment 3, one which contained glucose and the other that did not. According to the description of Experiment 3, "the lens proteins in the glucose solution had formed pigmented cross-links with the brownish color and fluorescence characteristics of those observed in Experiment 2." These cross-links appear to be the result of Amadori products, as suggested by the results of Experiment 1: "Amadori products on one protein had combined with free amino groups on nearby proteins, forming brown pigmented cross-links between the two proteins." Thus, to answer this question, you merely need to look for the wavelength value in Figure 1 that corresponds to maximum absorbance for the glucose solution. This peak occurs at approximately 400 nm, making (D) correct.

2.   J   Difficulty: Medium

Category: Scientific Investigation

Getting to the Answer: The researchers who designed the experiments were interested in the effect of dietary glucose on lens proteins in the human eye, as suggested in the introductory paragraph. There would be no reason to use cow lens proteins in Experiment 3 if cow lens proteins were expected to react any differently from human lens proteins, especially when human lens proteins were readily available for use—they were used, after all, for Experiment 1. Therefore, it is reasonable to conclude that the researchers assumed that cow lens proteins would react in the same way as human lens proteins. Choice (J) is correct. Choice F is incorrect

because the cross-links that were formed in the experiment were brownish—if the lenses were brownish too, it could interfere with the experiment's results. Choice G is incorrect because sulfides were not discussed in the description of Experiment 3. Choice H is incorrect because the researchers dissolved the proteins in aqueous (water-based) solutions, so they could not have been insoluble in water.

3.   C   Difficulty: Medium

Category: Scientific Investigation

Getting to the Answer: Make sure that you stick to the results of Experiment 1 only when you answer this question. According to the description of the experiment, immersion of the proteins in the glucose solution caused the formation of Amadori products and "the Amadori products on one protein had combined with free amino groups on nearby proteins, forming brown pigmented cross-links between the two proteins." Thus, it is reasonable to conclude that glucose can react with proteins to form cross-links, as in (C). Choice A is incorrect because disulfide cross-links were only mentioned in Experiment 2. Choice B is incorrect because the AGEs did not form without proteins; glucose in water would be insufficient to produce them. Choice D is incorrect because the metabolism of glucose was not discussed in the passage or studied in any of the experiments.

4.   G   Difficulty: Medium

Category: Evaluation of Models, Inferences, and Results

Getting to the Answer: To answer this question, consider the results of Experiment 2. It was found that in the samples from older subjects, the lens proteins often formed cross-linked bonds, some of which were brown. The senile cataracts in the lenses of older people are also brown, according to the question stem. The conclusion suggested by the identical colors of the cataracts and the cross-linked bonds is that the senile cataracts are made up of, or caused by, cross-linked bonds, as in (G). Choice F is incorrect because the passage never suggests that sulfur (as would be found in disulfide bonds) has a brownish pigment. Choices H and J are incorrect because there is no suggestion in the passage that lens proteins by themselves become browner or more fluorescent with age—rather, the browning is caused by the lens proteins reacting with glucose.

5.   C   Difficulty: Medium

Category: Scientific Investigation

Getting to the Answer: You don't know from the results of Experiment 2 alone how the brown pigmented cross-links developed among the lens proteins of older humans. Experiments 1 and 3 indicate, however, that glucose reacts with lens proteins in such a way that brown pigmented cross-links form among the proteins. And remember the main purpose of the experiments noted in the first paragraph: the researchers wanted to investigate "the chemical effects of glucose on lens proteins in the eye." The hypothesis that dietary sugar reacted with lens proteins to cause the brown pigmented cross-links found in older subjects would seem to be supported by the results of the 3 experiments, so (C) is correct. Choice A is incorrect because disulfide bonds are not described as brown in the passage. Choice B is contradicted by the fact that younger subjects had proteins with fewer cross-links. Choice D is contradicted by the results of Experiment 3: the lens proteins in water alone did not appear to form cross-links.

6.   J   Difficulty: Medium

Category: Scientific Investigation

Getting to the Answer: The relevant results are those from Experiment 2: the lens proteins of younger subjects were found to have formed cross-linked aggregates much less frequently than the lens proteins of older subjects did. So you would expect that the lens proteins of a 32-year-old man would have fewer cross-links than the lens proteins of an 80-year-old man, as in (J). Choice F is incorrect because none of the experiments investigated the effect of gender on the formation of cross-links. Choice G is incorrect because humans and cows were not directly compared in any of the experiments. Choice H is incorrect because older subjects were found to have more cross-links than younger ones.

7.   C   Difficulty: High

Category: Evaluation of Models, Inferences, and Results

Getting to the Answer: According to a previous question, senile cataracts are caused by cross-links that form between lens proteins that are brownish in color. The results of the 3 experiments suggested that these brownish cross-links, called AGEs, were in turn caused by glucose reacting with the lens proteins. Thus, it is reasonable to conclude that excess glucose in the blood would lead to the formation of AGE cross-links in lens proteins, which would cause senile cataracts. Choice (C) is therefore correct. Choices A and D are incorrect because the passage never suggests that excess glucose causes higher levels of free amino groups in the urine. Choice B is incorrect because the passage never suggests that there is any interaction between glucose and disulfide cross-links.

PASSAGE II

8.   G   Difficulty: Medium

Category: Interpretation of Data

Getting to the Answer: The description of Experiment 3 states that the current generates a magnetic field, which causes the ring to move up the pole. According to Table 3, as the number of coils in the wire increased, so did the height reached by the metal ring. It follows, then, that a greater number of coils produces a stronger magnetic field, capable of moving the ring up a greater distance. The relationship between magnetic field and number of coils is direct, so (G) is correct. Choices F and H are incorrect because they do not accurately describe the relationship between number of coils and magnetic field. Choice J is incorrect because the amount of current passing through the wire was held constant.

9. D   Difficulty: Medium

Category: Scientific Investigation

Getting to the Answer: In Experiment 2, the rotation of the wire caused a change in magnetic flux, which produced a voltage. If the wire is not rotating, there will be no change in magnetic flux and no voltage produced. Therefore, none of the existing data points accounts for this case. Choice (D) is thus correct.

10. F   Difficulty: High

Category: Scientific Investigation

Getting to the Answer: The introduction to the passage states that magnetic flux depends on the strength of the magnetic field, while the description of Experiment 1 suggests that the speed of the magnet corresponds to changes in magnetic flux. Moreover, Table 1 shows that higher magnetic flux changes correlate with higher emf readings. Thus, in order to produce the highest emf, you need to create the largest change in magnetic flux, which requires moving the magnet more quickly and having a magnet with a stronger magnetic field. Choice (F) is correct.

11. B   Difficulty: Medium

Category: Interpretation of Data

Getting to the Answer: According to Table 1, which provides the results of Experiment 1, maximum induced emf increases as the change in magnetic flux increases. Thus, you are looking for a graph with a positive slope. The only choice that satisfies this requirement is (B).

12. F   Difficulty: Low

Category: Interpretation of Data

Getting to the Answer: According to the description of Experiment 1, the magnet's "various speeds created corresponding changes to the magnetic flux within the coil." In other words, the greater the speed, the greater the change in magnetic flux. To find the trial with the lowest speed, then, you merely need to identify which of the trials had the lowest change in magnetic flux. Trial 1 was lower than any of the other trials in Experiment 1, so (F) is correct.

13. D   Difficulty: Medium

Category: Scientific Investigation

Getting to the Answer: The description of Experiment 3 states that the current sent through the wire produced "a magnetic field that caused the metal ring to float up the pole." From this, it is reasonable to conclude that a larger current would produce a larger magnetic field, which would cause the ring to move farther up the pole. In Trial 9, the ring reached a height of 1.5 cm, so in this new trial the height should be even greater. The only value above 1.5 cm is found in (D), making it the correct answer.

14. H   Difficulty: Medium

Category: Scientific Investigation

Getting to the Answer: According to the introduction of the passage, magnetic flux is "the mathematical product of the magnetic field and an area defined by a loop of wire in that field." Consequently, a larger area (created by a loop with a larger diameter) would create a larger magnetic flux, which means that the changes in magnetic flux caused by passing a magnet through the coil would be greater in the new experiment. Choices F and J can be eliminated because they suggest that the change in magnetic flux would decrease. Because there is a direct relationship between change in magnetic flux and maximum induced emf, as indicated by the results in Table 1, the value for emf could also be expected to increase in the new experiment, which eliminates G. Choice (H) is thus correct.

PASSAGE III

15. A   Difficulty: Low

Category: Evaluation of Models, Inferences, and Results

Getting to the Answer: Experiment 3 does not include a table of results, but the relevant results are described in the text: "At 10 minutes into the experiment, fewer bubbles were visible in the bottle that contained the root beer." This suggests that, 10 minutes after being shaken, the root beer had fewer bubbles and thus a lower level of carbonation than the seltzer. Choice (A) is correct. Choice B is incorrect because it states the opposite. Choice C is incorrect because there was 1 L of liquid in each bottle. Choice D is incorrect because balance time wasn't measured in Experiment 3.

16. J   Difficulty: Low

Category: Interpretation of Data

Getting to the Answer: This question can be answered simply by comparing data in Tables 1 and 2. The question is asking for the most similar balance times after the liquids have been shaken, which is reported in the right-most column of each table. According to the tables, the balance time after shaking for Trial 3 was 22.48 seconds and for Trial 5 was 22.45 seconds. These are by far the closest in value, so (J) is correct.

17. B   Difficulty: Medium

Category: Interpretation of Data

Getting to the Answer: The results for Experiment 2 are found in Table 2. For both of the trials, the balance time after shaking was longer than the balance time before shaking. Thus, it can be concluded that

shaking the bottle of root beer increased its balance time, (B). Choice A is incorrect because the number of bubbles wasn't measured in Experiment 2, though it is more likely that they would have increased, not decreased. Choice C is incorrect because it states the opposite of what the results show. Choice D is incorrect because the bottle was sealed, so its mass should have remained constant.

18. H   Difficulty: Medium

Category: Scientific Investigation

Getting to the Answer: According to the description of Experiment 2, the first measurement of balance time in Trial 4 occurred after setting aside the bottle for 10 minutes, so this question is really asking if bubbles would still be present 10 minutes after the root beer was shaken. This is directly investigated in Experiment 3, when bubbles in the root beer were compared to bubbles in the seltzer: "At 10 minutes into the experiment, fewer bubbles were visible in the bottle that contained the root beer." This suggests that there were still bubbles present before the bottle was shaken in Trial 4, so (H) is correct. Choice F is incorrect because it cites the wrong experiment, while G and J are incorrect because they reach the opposite conclusion.

19. A   Difficulty: Medium

Category: Scientific Investigation

Getting to the Answer: According to the description of Trial 5 in Experiment 2, the bottle of root beer was set aside for 90 minutes after being shaken before having its balance time recorded. The scenario in the question stem merely involves a repetition of the conditions in Trial 5, so similar results should be expected. The original balance time before shaking for Trial 5 was 20.04 seconds, so the balance time in this new trial would likely be slightly above 20 seconds as well. Choice (A) is thus correct.

20. H   Difficulty: Medium

Category: Scientific Investigation

Getting to the Answer: According to the description of Experiment 3, there were no bubbles remaining in the bottle after setting it aside for 90 minutes, although there were bubbles present after setting it aside for only 10 minutes. Moreover, balance time in Trial 4 (after a 10-minute wait) was longer than the original balance time without shaking in Trial 3, while balance time in Trial 5 (after a 90-minute wait) was back to around 20 seconds. It can therefore be inferred that it takes somewhere between 10 and 90 minutes for the bubbles to become too few to affect the balance time. Choice (H) is thus correct.

PASSAGE IV

21. B   Difficulty: Medium

Category: Interpretation of Data

Getting to the Answer: Since the question asks about length and temperature, the simplest data set to consider is Table 1, because Table 2 includes another variable, type of material. Comparing the odd-numbered trials (all conducted at 80°C) or the even-numbered trials (all conducted at 20°C) shows that the shorter the rod, the higher the current, which is an inverse relationship. Choices A and D can be eliminated. Comparing any trials which hold length of the rod constant while changing the temperature, such as Trials 1 and 2, show that as temperature goes down, current through the rod goes up, which is another inverse relationship. Because both length and temperature are inversely related to current, (B) is correct.

22. H   Difficulty: Medium

Category: Interpretation of Data

Getting to the Answer: The passage states that voltage, current, and resistance are related through Ohm's law, $V = A \times \Omega$, where Ω stands for resistance

in ohms and A stands for current in amperes. In the circuit used for these experiments, the voltage is held constant at 5 V, as indicated by the battery in Figure 1. This means that if current goes up, resistance must have gone down. Conversely, the lowest current will result from the highest resistance. Because each of the rods featured in the answer choices was tested in Experiment 2, to find the rod with the highest resistance, you merely need to find the one with the lowest recorded current in Table 2. The rod in Trial 9 conducted a current of only 20 mA, less than any of the others, so it must have the highest resistance. Choice (H) is thus correct.

23. C   Difficulty: High

Category: Interpretation of Data

Getting to the Answer: According to the question stem, conductivity uses the units of siemens per meter (σ = S/m) and siemens are equal to inverse ohms (S = 1/Ω). Putting these two equations together, you can see that the units of conductivity are equivalent to inverse ohms divided by meters (σ = [1/Ω]/m), which simplifies to σ = 1/($\Omega \times$ m). Choice (C) is thus correct.

24. G   Difficulty: Low

Category: Interpretation of Data

Getting to the Answer: According to Table 1, the rod in Trial 4 conducted 53 mA of electricity at 20°C. A rod of the same length was used in Trial 3, but it was heated to 80°C and conducted only 27 mA. Because 50°C is in between these two values, it is reasonable to assume that the current conducted will fall somewhere between 27 and 53 mA. Choice (G) is therefore correct.

25. A   Difficulty: Medium

Category: Scientific Investigation

Getting to the Answer: The introduction to the passage mentions Ohm's law, $V = I \times R$, which shows that voltage and current are directly related. Because the resistance values wouldn't change (the same rods would be used), the increase in voltage with the 10-V battery would lead to higher recorded values for current, regardless of the material of the rods. Thus, since both the copper and iron rods would conduct larger currents with a 10-V battery, (A) is correct.

26. H   Difficulty: Medium

Category: Interpretation of Data

Getting to the Answer: According to the results of Experiment 2, copper conducts electricity more effectively than iron. Thus, a 16-cm composite rod that was half-copper and half-iron would be expected to conduct electricity better than a 16-cm iron rod but worse than a 16-cm copper rod. According to Table 2, a 16-cm iron rod at 20°C conducts 40 mA, while a 16-cm copper rod at that temperature conducts 200 mA. Thus, the composite rod should conduct a current of somewhere between 40 and 200 mA, as in (H).

27. D   Difficulty: Low

Category: Scientific Investigation

Getting to the Answer: The variables that are directly manipulated in an experiment are the independent variables, so this question is asking for the one variable that is not an independent variable. In both experiments, the dependent variable—in other words, the variable that was observed and measured—was the current recorded by the ammeter. Thus, current was not directly manipulated by the student, so (D) is correct.

PASSAGE V

28. F   Difficulty: Low

Category: Scientific Investigation

Getting to the Answer: In any experiment, the control condition is the one used as a baseline, providing a standard of comparison to judge the

experimental effects of the other conditions. In Study 1, there would be no way to know what the effect of, say, rotating the microscope was on bacterial migration if you didn't know how the bacteria migrated before you rotated the microscope. In short, the control condition is the trial that is run without any experimental manipulations. For Study 1, that would be Trial 1, (F).

29. B   Difficulty: Medium

Category: Evaluation of Models, Inferences, and Results

Getting to the Answer: In order to be able to tell whether light was the stimulus affecting the direction of bacterial migration, you have to compare two trials, one with light present and the other with light absent. If there is no difference in the direction of bacterial migration between the two trials, then light does not have an effect and is not the primary stimulus. The two trials you need to compare are Trial 1 and Trial 2 of Study 1, because "Trial 1 was conducted under standard laboratory conditions" (with the light on) but "[i]n Trial 2, the microscope was shielded from all external light." Because the results of the trials differed only minimally, they support the theory that light was not the primary stimulus. Choice (B) is thus correct.

30. H   Difficulty: Medium

Category: Scientific Investigation

Getting to the Answer: The data show that the bacteria are sensitive to magnetic fields and tend to migrate in the direction of magnetic north. In Study 2, this meant that the bacteria moved toward the permanent magnet because the magnet's north pole was facing the slide. If the magnet's south pole faced the slide instead, the magnetic field would be reversed and the bacteria would migrate in exactly the opposite direction, away from the magnet. That makes (H) the correct answer. Choice F is incorrect because the direction, not the strength, of the magnetic field is what determined how the bacteria migrated. Choice G is incorrect because there is no reason to believe that the bacteria could become *disoriented*. Choice J is incorrect because the proximity of the permanent magnet overpowered the effects of the Earth's magnetic field, as can be seen in the results of Study 2.

31. D   Difficulty: Medium

Category: Evaluation of Models, Inferences, and Results

Getting to the Answer: The question stem asks for the reasoning that would be "most advantageous from an evolutionary standpoint," which means that you need to identify the condition that would most aid the survival or reproductive capacity of bacteria that oriented themselves downward. Choice A is incorrect because it concerns the survival of organisms that consume the bacteria, not the bacteria themselves. Choice B is incorrect because it would grant evolutionary advantage to bacteria that oriented themselves upward, not downward. Choice C is incorrect because there is no clear indication of what effect dispersal would have on the bacteria—it could be good or bad, depending on circumstances. Choice (D) is the only remaining option, so it must be correct. And, indeed, if necessary nutrients were more abundant in bottom sediments, bacteria that oriented themselves downward would have an obvious evolutionary advantage in terms of survival.

32. H   Difficulty: Medium

Category: Scientific Investigation

Getting to the Answer: To gain new information about the relationship between magnetic field strength and bacterial migrations, the researchers should vary the magnetic field strength and observe the effect on bacterial migrations. Choice (H) is

correct because it suggests using more and less powerful magnets, which would produce a variety of magnetic field strengths, exactly as required. None of the other choices would create variation in magnetic field strength.

33. A   Difficulty: Medium

Category: Evaluation of Models, Inferences, and Results

Getting to the Answer: In each of the trials of Study 1, bacterial migrations were largely found to be in the direction of magnetic north. Shielding from light and electric fields, rotation of the microscope, and movement of the microscope to another lab all had no distinct effect on the direction of migration. Thus, it is reasonable to conclude from Study 1 that most magnetotactic bacteria migrate towards Earth's magnetic north pole. Choice (A) is correct. Choice B presents a conclusion not supported by the results of Study 2. Choice C is only supported by Trial 6 of Study 2, when the permanent magnet was placed at the 12:00 position. Choice D is incorrect because the first two trials of Study 1 showed that electric fields have no real impact on bacterial migration.

34. G   Difficulty: Medium

Category: Interpretation of Data

Getting to the Answer: To answer this question, refer to Table 2. Based on the data for Trial 7 in the table, 483 bacteria moved in the 3:00 direction on the microscope slide, whereas only a few moved in other directions. Only (G) has a high density of dots at the 3:00 location (that is, to the right) and a low density of dots at other places on the field.

PASSAGE VI

35.   A   Difficulty: Low

Category: Interpretation of Data

Getting to the Answer: This question is essentially asking you to combine parts of the graphs in Figures 1 and 2 into a single graph. Notice that Figure 1 shows the solubility of RNase increasing until it hits a peak at about 135°C, after which it rapidly drops off. Figure 2 shows RNase with no solubility at higher temperatures, but then a rapid increase just before a relatively smaller peak at about 115°C, followed by a more gradual decline as the temperature cools. Thus, the correct graph should look like two hills separated by a valley, with the larger peak coming first. This corresponds to the graph in (A), the correct answer. Choice B is incorrect because it shows only the first peak, but not the second one as RNase renatures. Choice C is incorrect because it shows a single increase followed by a plateau, which corresponds to nothing in Figures 1 and 2. Choice D is incorrect because it places the first peak too high and at too low of a temperature, even though it captures the second peak accurately.

36.   G   Difficulty: Low

Category: Interpretation of Data

Getting to the Answer: Normally, you would draw a line up from where 0°C would be in Figure 1, but 0°C is the *y*-axis. Extend the curve representing Case until it intersects the 0°C line (the *y*-axis). The value at that intersection should be a bit less than 0.05 g/mL. Thus, the correct answer is (G). Choice F can't be correct, because it is higher than the solubility at 20°C, and solubility clearly drops with decreasing temperature. Choices H and J would be too low.

37.   D   Difficulty: Low

Category: Interpretation of Data

Getting to the Answer: According to Table 1, no renaturation temperature range is listed for Hase, so you can infer Hase did not renature upon cooling after heating. The correct answer is (D). Choice A corresponds to Hase's denaturation temperature range, and B and C correspond to the renaturation temperatures of Case and RNase, respectively.

38.   H   Difficulty: Medium

Category: Interpretation of Data

Getting to the Answer: Solubility curves are found in Figure 1, where solubility is a function of temperature, so you can eliminate F and G (also, nothing in the passage suggests that molecular weight changes during denaturation or renaturation). Piecing together Table 1 with Figure 1, you can see that maximum solubility falls within the denaturation temperature range, so the correct answer is (H).

39.   D   Difficulty: Medium

Category: Scientific Investigation

Getting to the Answer: Molecular weight and denaturation temperature can both be found in Table 1. The average denaturation temperature would fall in the middle of the denaturation temperature range. First rank the proteins from highest to lowest molecular weight: Hase is highest, Case is in the middle, and RNase is lowest. Then match the denaturation temperature ranges to the reordered proteins: Hase is 80–95°C, Case is 150–155°C, and RNase is 135–145°C. Case has the highest temperatures in its denaturation range, but its molecular weight falls in the middle, so there is no correlation and the hypothesis is not supported. The correct answer is (D). Choice C is incorrect because it suggests an inverse relationship that is not supported by the data.

40. H   Difficulty: High

Category: Scientific Investigation

Getting to the Answer: What would best explain why the peak solubility is lower after Case denatures and then renatures? The passage states that "some proteins can fold back (renature) into their original conformation when the temperature is decreased," which suggests that not all of the molecules of a particular protein will necessarily renature after denaturing. The correct answer is (H). Choices F, G, and J are not supported by the passage.

41. D   Difficulty: High

Category: Scientific Investigation

Getting to the Answer: This question requires you to predict the results of repeating Experiment 2 with a new protein. You are given its denaturation and renaturation ranges and are asked to figure out where its solubility would peak. For the original experiments, the ranges appear in Table 1 and peak solubility can be found in Figure 1. Each protein's solubility peaks at the lower end of its denaturation range. So, you should expect that the solubility of ovalbumin will peak at the lower bound of its range at 115°C. Thus, the correct answer is (D).

CHAPTER NINETEEN

Conflicting Viewpoints Passages

PRACTICE QUESTIONS

The following test-like question sets provide an opportunity to practice reading Conflicting Viewpoints Passages and answering related questions. Remember, you may refer to the passages as often as necessary. You are NOT permitted to use a calculator on these questions.

PASSAGE I

While the focus (point of origin) of most earthquakes lies less than 20 km below Earth's surface, certain unusual seismographic readings indicate that some activity originates at considerably greater depths. Two scientists discuss the possible causes of deep-focus earthquakes.

Scientist 1

Surface earthquakes occur when rock in Earth's crust fractures to relieve stress. However, below 50 km, rock is under too much pressure to fracture normally. Deep-focus earthquakes are caused by the pressure of fluids trapped in Earth's tectonic plates. As a plate is forced down into the mantle by convection, increases in temperature and pressure cause changes in the crystalline structure of minerals such as serpentine. In adopting a denser configuration, the crystals dehydrate, releasing water. Other sources of fluid include water trapped in pockets of deep-sea trenches and carried down with the plates. Laboratory work has shown that fluids trapped in rock pores can cause rock to fail at lower shear stresses. In fact, at the Rocky Mountain Arsenal, the injection of fluid wastes into the ground accidentally induced a series of shallow-focus earthquakes.

Scientist 2

Deep-focus earthquakes cannot result from normal fractures because rock becomes ductile at the temperatures and pressures that exist at depths greater than 50 km. Furthermore, mantle rock below 300 km is probably totally dehydrated because of the extreme pressure. Therefore, trapped fluids could not cause quakes below that depth. A better explanation is that deep-focus quakes result from the slippage that occurs when rock in a descending tectonic plate undergoes a phase change in its crystalline structure along a thin plane parallel to a stress. Just such a phase change and resultant slippage can be produced in the laboratory by compressing a slab of calcium magnesium silicate. The pattern of deep-quake activity supports this theory. In most seismic zones, the recorded incidence of deep-focus earthquakes corresponds to the depths at which phase changes are predicted to occur in mantle rock. For example, little or no phase change is thought to occur at 400 km, and indeed, earthquake activity at this level is negligible. Between 400 and 680 km, activity once again increases. Although seismologists initially believed that earthquakes could be generated at depths as low as 1,080 or 1,200 km, no foci have been confirmed below 700 km. No phase changes are predicted for mantle rock below 680 km.

1. Suppose that deep-focus earthquakes were found to be the result of rising magma in the asthenosphere, the upper layer of Earth's mantle. Whose view would be supported by this new information?

   A. Scientist 1 only

   B. Scientist 2 only

   C. Both Scientist 1 and Scientist 2

   D. Neither Scientist 1 nor Scientist 2

2. Scientists 1 and 2 agree on which of the following points?

   F. Deep-earthquake activity does not occur below 400 km.

   G. Fluid allows tectonic plates to slip past one another.

   H. Water can exist deep in the Earth's mantle.

   J. Rock below 50 km will not fracture normally.

3. Which of the following would provide the best evidence for Scientist 1's hypothesis?

   A. The discovery that water can be extracted from mantle-like rock at temperatures and pressures similar to those found below 300 km

   B. Seismographic indications that earthquakes occur 300 km below Earth's surface

   C. The discovery that phase changes occur in the mantle rock at depths of 1,080 km

   D. An earthquake underneath Los Angeles that was shown to have been caused by water trapped in sewer lines

4. Both Scientist 1 and Scientist 2 assume that:

   F. deep-focus earthquakes are more common than surface earthquakes.

   G. trapped fluids cause surface earthquakes.

   H. Earth's crust is composed of mobile tectonic plates.

   J. deep-focus earthquakes cannot be detected on Earth's crust without special recording devices.

5. To best refute Scientist 2's hypothesis, a researcher could:

   A. find evidence of underground water sources.

   B. record a deep-focus earthquake below 680 km.

   C. find a substance that does not undergo phase changes even at depths of 680 km.

   D. show that rock becomes ductile at depths of less than 50 km.

6. According to Scientist 1, the earthquake at Rocky Mountain Arsenal occurred because:

   F. serpentine or other minerals dehydrated and released water.

   G. fluid wastes injected into the ground compressed a thin slab of calcium magnesium silicate.

   H. fluid wastes injected into the ground flooded pockets of a deep-sea trench.

   J. fluid wastes injected into the ground lowered the shear stress failure point of the rock.

7. Scientist 2's hypothesis would be strengthened by evidence showing that:

   A. water evaporates at high temperatures and pressures.

   B. deep-focus earthquakes can occur at 680 km.

   C. compression has the same effect on mantle rock that it has on calcium magnesium silicate.

   D. water pockets exist at depths below 300 km.

8. According to Scientist 2, phase changes in the crystalline structure of a descending tectonic plate:

   F. occur only at Earth's surface.

   G. are not possible.

   H. cause certain minerals to release water, which exerts pressure within the plate.

   J. cause slippage that directly results in an earthquake.

PASSAGE II

Two scientists discuss their views about the Quark Model.

Scientist 1

According to the Quark Model, each proton consists of three quarks: two up quarks, which carry a charge of $+\frac{2}{3}$ each, and one down quark, which carries a charge of $-\frac{1}{3}$. All mesons, one of which is the π^+ particle, are composed of one quark and one antiquark, and all baryons, one of which is the proton, are composed of three quarks. The Quark Model explains the numerous different types of mesons that have been observed. It also successfully predicted the essential properties of the Y meson. Individual quarks have not been observed because they are absolutely confined within baryons and mesons. However, the results of deep inelastic scattering experiments indicate that the proton has a substructure. In these experiments, high-energy electron beams were fired into protons. While most of the electrons incident on the proton passed right through, a few bounced back. The number of electrons scattered through large angles indicated that there are three distinct lumps within the proton.

Scientist 2

The Quark Model is seriously flawed. Conventional scattering experiments should be able to split the proton into its constituent quarks, if they existed. Once the quarks were free, it would be easy to distinguish quarks from other particles using something as simple as the Millikan oil drop experiment because they would be the only particles that carry fractional charge. Furthermore, the lightest quark would be stable because there is no lighter particle for it to decay into. Quarks would be so easy to produce, identify, and store that they would have been detected if they truly existed. In addition, the Quark Model violates the Pauli exclusion principle which originally was believed to hold for electrons but was found to hold for all particles of half-integer spin. The Pauli exclusion principle states that no two particles of half-integer spin can occupy the same state. The Δ^{++} baryon, which supposedly has three up quarks, violates the Pauli exclusion principle because two of those quarks, would be in the same state. Therefore, the Quark Model must be replaced.

9. Which of the following would most clearly strengthen Scientist 1's hypothesis?
   A. Detection of the Δ^{++} baryon
   B. Detection of a particle with fractional charge
   C. Detection of mesons
   D. Detection of baryons

10. Which of the following are reasons why Scientist 2 claims quarks should have been detected, if they existed?
   I. They have a unique charge.
   II. They are confined within mesons and baryons.
   III. They are supposedly fundamental particles, and so could not decay into any other particle.
   F. I only
   G. II only
   H. I and III only
   J. I, II, and III

11. Which of the following, if valid, could Scientist 1 use to counter Scientist 2's point about the Pauli exclusion principle?

   A. Evidence that quarks do not have half-integer spin

   B. Evidence that the Δ^{++} baryon exists

   C. Evidence that quarks have fractional charge

   D. Evidence that quarks have the same spin as electrons

12. If Scientist 1's hypothesis is correct, the Δ^{++} baryon should have a charge of:

   F. -1

   G. 0

   H. 1

   J. 2

13. Scientist 2 says the Quark Model is flawed because:

   A. the existence of individual baryons cannot be experimentally verified.

   B. the existence of individual quarks cannot be experimentally verified.

   C. particles cannot have fractional charge.

   D. it does not include electrons as elementary particles.

14. Scientist 1 says that some high-energy electrons that were aimed into the proton in the deep inelastic scattering experiments bounced back because they:

   F. hit quarks.

   G. hit other electrons.

   H. were repelled by the positive charge on the proton.

   J. hit baryons.

15. The fact that deep inelastic scattering experiments revealed a proton substructure of three lumps supports the Quark Model because:

   A. protons are mesons, and mesons supposedly consist of three quarks.

   B. protons are mesons, and mesons supposedly consist of a quark and an antiquark.

   C. protons are baryons, and baryons supposedly consist of three quarks.

   D. protons are baryons, and baryons supposedly consist of one quark and one antiquark.

PASSAGE III

Earth's magnetic field has two distinct poles, labeled North and South. Certain materials, such as iron and steel, are sensitive to Earth's magnetic field. The origin and behavior of the magnetic field is modeled by *dynamo theory*, which links the magnetic field with the geological activity of Earth's molten core. Diagram 1 depicts Earth's geological layers from crust to core.

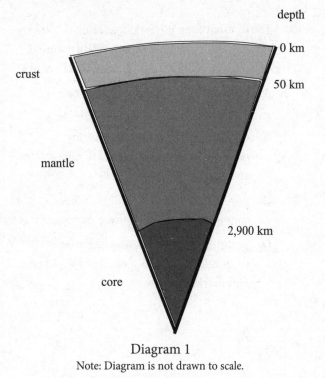

depth

0 km

50 km

2,900 km

crust

mantle

core

Diagram 1
Note: Diagram is not drawn to scale.

Evidence has been found of complete reversals in the polarity of the magnetic field, called *geomagnetic reversals*. Concentrated deposits of rock with reversed magnetic properties have been found on the ocean floor. The magnetic anomalies observed suggest that Earth undergoes a geomagnetic reversal sporadically over time spans of thousands of years (the last geomagnetic reversal occurred approximately 780,000 years ago). Two scientists discuss the possible causes of geomagnetic reversal.

Scientist 1

Dynamo theory suggests that a constantly moving fluid can help maintain a magnetic field. Earth's core is made of molten nickel and iron. The constant motion of this portion of the core creates eddy currents, which in turn help to create Earth's magnetic field. The motions of the molten core can often be chaotic, and, in turn, they disturb the magnetic field. It is this necessary by-product of the dynamo effect that causes spontaneous geomagnetic reversal.

Scientist 2

Earth's molten core is responsible for the creation, maintenance, and shifts of the magnetic field. The motions of the core, in accordance with dynamo theory, create a magnetic field from eddy currents. The motions of tectonic plates and other seismic events can have a powerful effect on Earth's core. Such events can disrupt the motion of the core to such an extent that the magnetic field effectively turns off. When the regular motions of the core resume, the resulting magnetic field will either remain as it was, or emerge as a reversal of its previous state.

16. Dynamo theory can be applied to other planets that have molten cores, and hotter planets are more likely to have molten cores. Based on this information, which of the following planets would the theory most likely NOT apply to?

    F. Neptune

    G. Mars

    H. Venus

    J. Mercury

17. Which of the following pairs of statements best accounts for Earth's geomagnetic reversal according to the viewpoints of the 2 scientists?

Scientist 1	Scientist 2
A. Magnetic field resets after seismic disturbance	Natural consequence of the dynamo effect
B. Seismic disturbance caused by magnetic field	Natural consequence of the dynamo effect
C. Natural consequence of the dynamo effect	Magnetic field resets after seismic disturbance
D. Natural consequence of the dynamo effect	Seismic disturbance caused by magnetic field

    A. A

    B. B

    C. C

    D. D

18. Based on Scientist 2's account, seismic activity that affects Earth's molten core must be able to resonate to depths of at least:

    F. 50 km.

    G. 700 km.

    H. 1,500 km.

    J. 2,900 km.

19. Which of the following statements is most consistent with the ideas expressed by Scientist 1?

    A. The motion of molten nickel and iron creates a magnetic field.

    B. The motion of molten nickel and iron counteracts magnetic fields already in existence.

    C. The melting of nickel and iron creates a magnetic field.

    D. Nickel and iron are found only in Earth's core.

20. Which of the following hypotheses would both scientists agree upon?

    F. The dynamo theory accounts for shifts in Earth's magnetic field.

    G. Eddy currents create seismic disturbances.

    H. Seismic disturbances cause geomagnetic reversal.

    J. The dynamo theory is relevant only every few thousand years.

21. According to the passage, which of the following is a reliable indicator of the polarity of Earth's magnetic field at a particular point in time?

    A. Molten nickel and iron

    B. Deposits of magnetized rock

    C. Seismic activity

    D. Shifts in solar magnetism

22. If it were discovered that the polarity of the Earth's magnetic field can be directly altered only by the activity of the Sun's magnetic field, how would this affect the viewpoints of each scientist?

    F. It would strengthen the viewpoint of Scientist 1 only.

    G. It would weaken the viewpoint of Scientist 2 only.

    H. It would strengthen the viewpoints of both scientists.

    J. It would weaken the viewpoints of both scientists.

23. In a computer simulation, the effect of seismic activity on the motion of Earth's molten core was studied. Which of the following findings would be consistent with Scientist 2's viewpoint? The seismic activity would:

    A. be caused by the motion of the molten core.

    B. cause significant disturbances in the molten core.

    C. have no effect on the motion of the molten core.

    D. cause eddy currents in the molten core.

PASSAGE IV

Straight-chain conformational isomers are simple carbon compounds that differ only by rotation about one or more single carbon bonds. Essentially, these isomers represent the same compound in slightly different positions (or conformations). One example of such isomers can be found with butane (C_4H_{10}), in which the first and last carbon atoms of the chain can be thought of as methyl (CH_3) groups. As bonds in the carbon chain rotate, these 2 methyl groups can occupy different positions in space relative to one another. The conformational isomers of butane are classified into 4 categories, based on the angle between the 2 bonds to the methyl groups. These isomers are depicted as *Newman projections* (a perspective which highlights the angle between the methyl group bonds) in Diagram 1.

1. In the *anti* conformation, the bonds connecting the methyl groups are rotated 180° with respect to each other.

2. In the *gauche* conformation, the bonds connecting the methyl groups are rotated 60° with respect to each other.

3. In the *eclipsed* conformation, the bonds connecting the methyl groups are rotated 120° with respect to each other.

4. In the *totally eclipsed* conformation, the bonds connecting the methyl groups are rotated 0° with respect to each other.

Diagram 1

The anti conformation is the lowest energy and most stable state of the butane molecule since it allows for the methyl groups to maintain maximum separation from each other. The methyl groups are much closer to each other in the gauche conformation, but this still represents a relative minimum or *meta-stable* state, due to the relative orientations of the other hydrogen atoms in the molecule. Molecules in the anti or gauche conformations tend to maintain their shape. The eclipsed conformation represents a relative maximum energy state, while the totally eclipsed conformation is the highest energy state of all of butane's conformational isomers.

Two organic chemistry students offered different hypotheses on the *active shape* (the chemically functional conformation) of a butane molecule.

Student 1

The active shape of a butane molecule is always identical to the molecule's lowest-energy shape. Any other shape would be unstable. Because the lowest-energy shape for a straight-chain conformational isomer of butane is the anti conformation, its active shape is always the anti conformation.

Student 2

The active shape of a butane molecule is dependent upon the energy state of the shape. However, a butane molecule's shape may also depend on temperature and its initial isomeric state. Specifically, in order to convert from the gauche conformation to the anti conformation, the molecule must pass through either the eclipsed or totally eclipsed conformation. If the molecule is not given enough energy to reach either of these states, its active shape will be the gauche conformation.

24. According to the passage, molecules in conformations with relatively low energy tend to:

    F. convert to the totally eclipsed conformation.

    G. convert to the eclipsed conformation.

    H. maintain their shape.

    J. be unstable.

25. The information in the passage indicates that when a compound changes from one straight-chain conformational isomer to another, it still retains its original:

    A. energy state.

    B. shape.

    C. number of single carbon bonds.

    D. temperature.

26. Student 2's views differ from Student 1's views in that only Student 2 believes that a butane molecule's active shape is partially determined by its:

    F. initial isomeric state.

    G. energy state.

    H. stability.

    J. proximity of methyl groups.

27. A student rolls a ball along the curved path shown below. Given that points closer to the ground represent states of lower energy, the ball coming to rest at the position shown corresponds to a butane molecule settling into which conformational isomer?

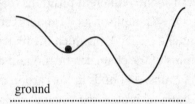

ground

    A. Anti

    B. Gauche

    C. Eclipsed

    D. Totally eclipsed

28. Suppose butane molecules are cooled so that each molecule is allowed to reach its active shape. Which of the following statements is most consistent with the information presented in the passage?

    F. If Student 1 is correct, all of the molecules will be in the anti conformation.

    G. If Student 1 is correct, all of the molecules will have shapes different from their lowest-energy shapes.

    H. If Student 2 is correct, all of the molecules will be in the anti conformation.

    J. If Student 2 is correct, all of the molecules will have shapes different than their lowest-energy shapes.

29. Which of the following diagrams showing the relationship between a given butane molecule's shape and its relative energy is consistent with Student 2's assertions about the energy of butane molecules, but is NOT consistent with Student 1's assertions about the energy of butane molecules?

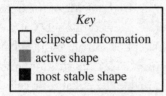

Key
□ eclipsed conformation
▨ active shape
■ most stable shape

A.
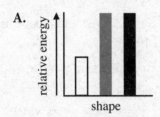

B.
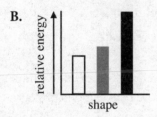

C.
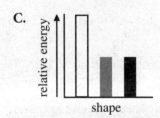

D.
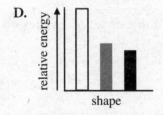

30. Student 2 argues that a butane molecule can sometimes settle into a gauche conformation, even though this is not its lowest energy state. Which of the following findings, if true, would most effectively *counter* the argument he presents for this claim?

F. Once a molecule has settled into a given conformation, all of its single carbon bonds are stable.

G. Enough energy is always available in the environment to overcome local energy barriers.

H. During molecule formation, the hydrogen bonds are formed before the carbon bonds.

J. Molecules that change their isomeric conformation tend to lose their chemical functions.

PASSAGE V

The first prokaryotes (single-celled organisms with no nucleus) appeared two billion years before the first eukaryotes (organisms whose cells contain a nucleus). Most bacteria are prokaryotes, while most complex organisms consist of eukaryotic cells. Eukaryotic cells contain mitochondria, rod-shaped energy-producing organelles. Different from other organelles in the cell, mitochondria are surrounded by two membranes, contain their own DNA, and divide independently from the host cell. Two scientists discuss the evolutionary origin of mitochondria-containing eukaryotes.

Scientist 1

Mitochondria-containing eukaryotes developed from an endosymbiotic relationship between two types of prokaryotes. Early prokaryotes were anaerobic, meaning they did not require oxygen to survive. There was virtually no free oxygen in Earth's atmosphere until prokaryotes began releasing oxygen as a metabolic by-product. As the oxygen levels in the atmosphere rose, some prokaryotes evolved into aerobes to utilize the free oxygen. Since anaerobic prokaryotes could not metabolize oxygen, they engulfed the aerobic prokaryotes. This endosymbiotic relationship resulted in the aerobes gaining a secure environment and a continuous food supply and the anaerobes gaining the ability to survive in an oxygen-rich environment. Over time, the symbiotic partners lost their independence, and the aerobic prokaryotes evolved into mitochondria. For that reason, mitochondrial DNA differs both genetically and structurally from the DNA in the eukaryotic cell's nucleus.

Scientist 2

The DNA, ribosomal proteins, and membranes of mitochondria structurally differ from those of bacteria. Therefore, mitochondria could not have evolved from the endosymbiosis of two prokaryotes.

It is far more likely that eukaryotes first developed directly from a single prokaryote and then the mitochondria developed from the membrane of the cell. Although mitochondria, like prokaryotes, synthesize several of the enzymes necessary for their own function, most mitochondrial proteins are controlled by genes in the nucleus of the eukaryotic cell and are synthesized outside of the mitochondria. Moreover, the key components of mitochondrial DNA replication are more eukaryotic in nature than prokaryotic, indicating mitochondria originated inside the eukaryotic cell.

31. Scientist 1 and Scientist 2 would mostly likely agree that mitochondria:

    A. originated from the membrane of a eukaryotic cell.

    B. originated from aerobic prokaryotes.

    C. contain their own DNA.

    D. cannot self-replicate.

32. According to Scientist 1, an endosymbiotic relationship arose between two prokaryotes because:

    F. aerobic bacteria were not able to utilize free oxygen.

    G. anaerobic bacteria did not require oxygen to survive.

    H. mitochondria use oxygen to generate energy.

    J. the Earth's atmosphere became oxygen-rich.

33. Scientist 1 states that the best evidence that mitochondria evolved from bacteria is that:

   A. mitochondrial DNA is structurally different from DNA in the eukaryotic nucleus.

   B. ribosomal proteins of mitochondria and bacteria are different.

   C. eukaryotes developed directly from a single bacterium.

   D. mitochondria have a single outer membrane.

34. Mitochondrial DNA molecules are circular, having the same structure as prokaryotic DNA. This information, if true, strengthens the viewpoint of:

   F. Scientist 1 only.

   G. Scientist 2 only.

   H. both Scientist 1 and Scientist 2.

   J. neither Scientist 1 nor Scientist 2.

35. Scientist 2 emphasizes the differences between mitochondria and bacteria in order to:

   A. demonstrate the prokaryotic nature of mitochondria.

   B. illustrate the superior aerobic capacity of mitochondria.

   C. prove that bacteria are genetically less complex than mitochondria.

   D. argue that mitochondria could not have evolved from aerobic prokaryotes.

36. Suppose a study shows that mitochondria divide by binary fission, much like bacteria. This study could be used to support the viewpoint of:

   F. Scientist 1, who states mitochondria originated from aerobic eukaryotes.

   G. Scientist 1, who states mitochondria originated from aerobic prokaryotes.

   H. Scientist 2, who states mitochondria originated from an endosymbiotic relationship between prokaryotes.

   J. Scientist 2, who states mitochondria originated from the membrane of eukaryotes.

37. Which of the following arguments could Scientist 1 use to respond effectively to Scientist 2's claim that most mitochondrial proteins originate from outside the mitochondria?

   A. As a result of endosymbiosis, all proteins in a eukaryotic cell are synthesized from genes in the nucleus.

   B. After the two organisms became one, many genes coding for mitochondrial proteins were transferred to the nucleus.

   C. Two billion years ago, prokaryotes evolved into eukaryotes.

   D. Mitochondria do not have the genes to synthesize their own proteins.

PASSAGE VI

Will the universe continue to expand, or will it eventually collapse? The answer to this question depends on the average density of the matter in the universe. If it is greater than a certain critical density (6×10^{-27} kg/m^3), then the universe is "closed" and it will eventually stop expanding and begin contracting. If the average density is less than this critical value, then the universe is "open" and the expansion will continue indefinitely. Two scientists present their views on this issue.

Scientist 1

Astronomers can estimate the average density of the universe by tabulating all the detectable matter over a large volume of the universe. The mass of galaxies, intergalactic stars, and gas has been determined from luminosity (brightness) measurements. From these measurements, the average density of the universe was calculated to be only 3×10^{-28} kg/m^3 or 5% of the critical value. Therefore, the universe is open and will continue to expand.

Scientist 2

There is a great deal more mass in the universe than has been detected. Observations of the motions of stars in other galaxies indicate that the force of gravity is greater than the total mass of the detected matter in those galaxies could possibly exert. The missing mass must be non-luminous matter that cannot be detected by luminosity measurements. Taking this "dark" matter into consideration, the average density of the universe does exceed the critical value. Therefore, the universe must be closed—it will eventually stop expanding and collapse.

38. Scientist 1 and Scientist 2 disagree on the point that:

   F. the universe will be closed if its actual density is greater than the critical density.

   G. luminosity measurements are related to brightness.

   H. some of the matter in the universe has not been detected.

   J. luminosity measurements can be used to calculate the universe's density accurately.

39. Both scientists make the assumption that:

   A. the universe is currently static.

   B. the universe is currently contracting.

   C. the universe is currently expanding.

   D. the critical density cannot be determined.

40. Scientist 2 believes that the missing mass in the universe:

   F. does not exist.

   G. will never be detected.

   H. is made up of non-luminous matter.

   J. is made up of an alien form of matter.

41. According to Scientist 1, the average density of the universe can be determined by:

   I. measuring luminosities.
   II. studying the motions of planets in other galaxies.
   III. determining the mass of non-luminous matter.

   A. I only

   B. II only

   C. I and III only

   D. II and III only

42. To support her hypothesis, Scientist 2 could attempt to:

   F. find a way to measure the mass of non-luminous matter in a large portion of the universe.

   G. show that the universe's average density is exactly 27% of the critical value.

   H. determine the origin of the universe.

   J. develop a method for measuring the temperature at which galaxies come together.

43. Suppose that new measurements were taken, leading to a new scientific consensus that the average density of matter in the universe is greater than the critical density. Which of the following statements could most reasonably be inferred from this new information and the information from the passage?

   A. The new density must come entirely from non-luminous matter.

   B. The new mass accounts for at least 95% of the density of the universe.

   C. The motions of the stars in other galaxies are inconsistent with the new information.

   D. The universe should be considered open.

44. The evidence presented by Scientist 1 supports which of the following conclusions?

   F. The universe is much closer to the critical density than current calculations indicate.

   G. The critical density of the universe is about 20 times greater than its actual density.

   H. The total mass of stars cannot be determined from their brightness.

   J. Non-luminous matter accounts for about 5% of the total mass of the universe.

ANSWERS AND EXPLANATIONS

PASSAGE I

1. D   Difficulty: Medium

Category: Evaluation of Models, Inferences, and Results

Getting to the Answer: Consider the view of each scientist separately. Scientist 1 states that deep-focus earthquakes are due to the release of water from crystalline structures. Because magma in the asthenosphere is not directly related to this release of fluid, it is unlikely to support Scientist 1's viewpoint. That means A and C can be eliminated. Scientist 2 states that deep-focus earthquakes are caused by slippage that occurs when rock in a descending plate undergoes a phase change. The question stem does not mention any kind of phase change, so the new information also fails to support Scientist 2's viewpoint. Because neither scientist is supported, (D) must be correct.

2. J   Difficulty: Medium

Category: Evaluation of Models, Inferences, and Results

Getting to the Answer: Scientist 1 states that "below 50 km, rock is under too much pressure to fracture normally." Scientist 2 gives the fact that "rock becomes ductile at the temperatures and pressures that exist at depths greater than 50 km" as the reason that "deep-focus earthquakes cannot result from normal fractures." Thus, both scientists agree that rock below 50 km will not fracture normally, making (J) correct. Choice F is incorrect because it is directly disputed by Scientist 2. Choice G is incorrect because it attempts to combine the two views discussed in the passage, distorting each one in the process. Choice H is incorrect because Scientist 2 claims that "mantle rock below 300 km is probably totally dehydrated because of the extreme pressure."

3. A   Difficulty: Medium

Category: Evaluation of Models, Inferences, and Results

Getting to the Answer: Scientist 1 maintains that deep-focus earthquakes are caused by fluids that are released from tectonic plates as a result of the increased temperatures and pressures found in the mantle. If researchers could subject mantle-like rock to those temperatures and pressures, and then extract water from it, as in (A), their experimental results would support the hypothesis of Scientist 1. Choice B is incorrect because there could be multiple explanations for earthquakes that occur below 300 km, such as that supplied by Scientist 2. Choice C would contradict a statement made by Scientist 2 but have no impact on Scientist 1's view. Choice D concerns water trapped in sewer lines close to the Earth's surface, not water trapped in rock far beneath the surface, so it is not really relevant to Scientist 1's view.

4. H   Difficulty: Medium

Category: Evaluation of Models, Inferences, and Results

Getting to the Answer: Both scientists believe that the Earth's crust (surface layer) is composed of mobile tectonic plates. In describing the plates as being "forced down into the mantle," Scientist 1 implies that they are normally in the crust, and Scientist 2 similarly makes reference to "a descending tectonic plate." Choice (H) is thus correct. The introductory paragraph says that "most" earthquakes originate less than 20 km below Earth's surface, so F is incorrect. Neither scientist assumes that surface quakes are caused by trapped fluids, as in G; both suggest that such quakes are caused by normal fractures in Earth's crust. Finally, neither scientist discusses how deep-focus earthquakes are detected, so J is not an assumption made by either scientist.

5. B Difficulty: Medium

Category: Evaluation of Models, Inferences, and Results

Getting to the Answer: Scientist 2 believes that deep-focus quakes are the result of slippage caused by phase changes. Scientist 2 also states that "no phase changes are predicted for mantle rock below 680 km." Consequently, if a researcher were able to record a deep-focus earthquake that occurred below that depth, Scientist 2's view would be significantly challenged. Choice (B) is thus correct. Choice A is incorrect because the depth of the underground water sources is not specified and Scientist 2 only denies the existence of water below certain depths. Choice C would be consistent with Scientist 2's view. Choice D would contradict a point made in the first sentence of Scientist 2's account, but it is not relevant to the scientist's hypothesis for the cause of deep-focus earthquakes in particular.

6. J Difficulty: Low

Category: Evaluation of Models, Inferences, and Results

Getting to the Answer: The final sentence of Scientist 1's account mentions that when fluids were injected into the ground at the Rocky Mountain Arsenal, the unintended result was "a series of shallow-focus earthquakes." The opening words "In fact" signal that this final sentence is intended to provide evidence for the previous sentence, which refers to experiments in which trapped fluids caused rock to fail at lower than normal shear stresses. The implication is that the quakes at the Arsenal occurred because the fluid wastes lowered the shear stress failure point of the rock, so (J) is correct. Choice F is incorrect because, even though dehydration is an important part of Scientist 1's explanation, it is not specifically mentioned in the scientist's discussion of the Rocky Mountain Arsenal earthquake. Choice G is incorrect because Scientist 2 mentions that slab of calcium magnesium silicate, not Scientist 1. Choice H confuses the Rocky Mountain Arsenal

incident with the deep-sea trenches that Scientist 1 mentions earlier in the account.

7. C Difficulty: Medium

Category: Evaluation of Models, Inferences, and Results

Getting to the Answer: Scientist 2 claims that the slippage involved in deep-focus quakes results from phase changes. To support this contention, the scientist cites laboratory work that produced similar phase changes and slippage in a slab of calcium magnesium silicate. But neither scientist suggests that mantle rock is composed of calcium magnesium silicate. If the slab is to serve as evidence for Scientist 2's theory, it should at least be similar to mantle rock in its reaction to being compressed, so (C) is correct. Choice A might help refute Scientist 1's viewpoint, but it would not strengthen Scientist 2's theory. Choices B and D would weaken Scientist 2's theory.

8. J Difficulty: Low

Category: Evaluation of Models, Inferences, and Results

Getting to the Answer: According to Scientist 2, "deep-focus quakes result from the slippage that occurs when rock in a descending tectonic plate undergoes a phase change in its crystalline structure along a thin plane parallel to a stress." This directly supports (J). Choices F and G are incorrect because Scientist 2 suggests that these phase changes occur far beneath the Earth's surface. Choice H is incorrect because it is taken from Scientist 1's account.

PASSAGE II

9. B Difficulty: High

Category: Evaluation of Models, Inferences, and Results

Getting to the Answer: Scientist 1 is a proponent of the Quark Model, which says that baryons (including the proton) and mesons are made up of quarks, which have fractional charges. Quarks have never been observed, however. According to Scientist 2, quarks should be easy to distinguish from other particles because they would be the only ones with fractional charge. If a particle with fractional charge were detected, then, it could be a quark, and this would strengthen Scientist 1's hypothesis that the Quark Model is correct. Choice (B) is thus correct. Choice A is incorrect because detection of the Δ^{++} baryon would support Scientist 2, who argues that it violates the Pauli exclusion principle. Choices C and D are incorrect because mesons and baryons have already been detected—the Quark Model does not concern the existence of these particles, but rather concerns what their components are.

10. H   Difficulty: Medium

Category: Evaluation of Models, Inferences, and Results

Getting to the Answer: Scientist 2 argues that "it would be easy to distinguish quarks from other particles using something as simple as the Millikan oil drop experiment because they would be the only particles that carry fractional charge." This confirms statement I, which eliminates G. In addition, Scientist 2 contends that "the lightest quark would be stable because there is no lighter particle for it to decay into." This shows that statement III is also one of Scientist 2's reasons, eliminating F. However, only Scientist 1 claims that isolated "quarks have not been observed because they are absolutely confined within baryons and mesons." Statement II is thus not a reason provided by Scientist 2, so J is incorrect. Because only I and III are reasons given by Scientist 2, (H) is correct.

11. A   Difficulty: High

Category: Evaluation of Models, Inferences, and Results

Getting to the Answer: Scientist 2 says that the Quark Model is wrong because it violates the Pauli exclusion principle, which "states that no two particles of half-integer spin can occupy the same state."

He says that in the Δ^{++} baryon, for example, the presence of two up quarks in the same state would violate the principle, so the model must be incorrect. If Scientist 1 were able to show, however, that quarks do not have half-integer spin, as in (A), she could argue that the Pauli exclusion principle does not apply to quarks and thus counter Scientist 2's objections. Choice B is incorrect because the Δ^{++} baryon is used by Scientist 2 to support his case; Scientist 1 would need to provide an explanation of how the Δ^{++} baryon can be composed of quarks without violating the Pauli exclusion principle. Evidence that quarks have fractional charge, as in C, isn't going to help Scientist 1 because it is not relevant to the Pauli exclusion principle. Choice D is incorrect because evidence that quarks have the same spin as electrons would only support Scientist 2's position.

12. J   Difficulty: Medium

Category: Evaluation of Models, Inferences, and Results

Getting to the Answer: According to Scientist 2, the Δ^{++} baryon is purported to be composed of 3 up quarks. Scientist 1 maintains that each up quark has a charge of $+\frac{2}{3}$, so the 3 quarks together would have a total charge of $3 \times \frac{2}{3} = 2$. Choice (J) is correct.

13. B   Difficulty: Medium

Category: Evaluation of Models, Inferences, and Results

Getting to the Answer: Scientist 2 believes that the Quark Model is flawed for two reasons: 1) quarks have not been detected experimentally (but they would have been if they existed) and 2) the Quark Model violates the Pauli exclusion principle. The first reason is paraphrased in (B), making it correct. Choice A is incorrect because the existence of individual baryons, including protons, has already been verified experimentally. Scientist 2 never says that he thinks particles cannot have fractional charge, nor does he complain that the Quark Model doesn't include electrons as elementary particles, so C and D are incorrect as well.

14. F   Difficulty: Medium

Category: Evaluation of Models, Inferences, and Results

Getting to the Answer: The deep inelastic scattering experiments, according to Scientist 1, showed that the proton has a substructure. Scientist 1 implies that the "three distinct lumps" that were found to bounce high-energy electrons back and scatter them through large angles corresponded to the 3 quarks that make up a proton. Thus, Scientist 1 suggests that the electrons hit quarks, as in (F). Choices G, H, and J are never suggested by Scientist 1.

15. C   Difficulty: Low

Category: Evaluation of Models, Inferences, and Results

Getting to the Answer: According to Scientist 1, who supports the Quark Model, "all baryons, one of which is the proton, are composed of three quarks." Choice (C) is thus correct. All of the other answer choices are incorrect because they include statements that contradict this information.

PASSAGE III

16. F   Difficulty: Low

Category: Evaluation of Models, Inferences, and Results

Getting to the Answer: According to the question stem, hotter planets are more likely to have molten cores, meaning that dynamo theory can be applied to them. Because planets are generally hotter the closer they are to the Sun, the planet that is farthest from the Sun would be the least likely to have a molten core. Neptune is much farther from the Sun than Mercury, Venus, and Mars, so (F) is correct.

17. C   Difficulty: Medium

Category: Evaluation of Models, Inferences, and Results

Getting to the Answer: According to the passage, Scientist 1 believes that geomagnetic reversal is a natural consequence of dynamo theory, whereas Scientist 2 believes it to be caused by seismic events. Choice (C) accurately summarizes the views of both scientists.

18. J   Difficulty: Medium

Category: Interpretation of Data

Getting to the Answer: Scientist 2 suggests that seismic activity can affect the molten core of the Earth. Diagram 1 shows that the core is found at a depth of 2,900 km. Choice (J) is thus correct.

19. A   Difficulty: Medium

Category: Evaluation of Models, Inferences, and Results

Getting to the Answer: Scientist 1 states that the constant motion of molten nickel and iron in the core "creates eddy currents, which in turn help to create Earth's magnetic field." Choice (A) is thus correct.

20. F   Difficulty: Medium

Category: Evaluation of Models, Inferences, and Results

Getting to the Answer: Scientist 1 believes that the dynamo theory, which contends that the Earth's magnetic field is the result of motion in the liquid core, fully accounts for geomagnetic reversal. Scientist 2, while attributing geomagnetic reversal to the effects of seismic activity, does not dispute the dynamo theory itself. Choice (F) is thus correct. Choice G is incorrect because neither scientist attributes seismic disturbances to eddy currents. Choice H is incorrect because only Scientist 2 believes it. Choice J is incorrect because both scientists agree that dynamo theory generally explains the existence of the Earth's magnetic field, not just during times of geomagnetic reversal.

21. B   Difficulty: Medium

Category: Evaluation of Models, Inferences, and Results

Getting to the Answer: The introductory text states that scientists found evidence of geomagnetic reversal in magnetized rock deposits on the ocean floor. Thus, the best evidence of the polarity of the magnetic field at a particular point in time can be found in these deposits, (B).

22. J   Difficulty: Medium

Category: Evaluation of Models, Inferences, and Results

Getting to the Answer: Both scientists argue that geomagnetic reversal is a result of activity within the Earth's molten core. Scientist 1 thinks that these reversals spontaneously arise from the motions of molten nickel and iron, while Scientist 2 believes that seismic disturbances disrupt these motions, sometimes resulting in a geomagnetic reversal. Neither scientist suggests that geomagnetic reversals can be caused by an external source like the Sun's magnetic field, so the information in the question stem would weaken both scientists' accounts. Choice (J) is thus correct.

23. B   Difficulty: Medium

Category: Evaluation of Models, Inferences, and Results

Getting to the Answer: Scientist 2 believes that seismic activity "can disrupt the motion of the core to such an extent that the magnetic field effectively turns off." These disruptions will sometimes result in geomagnetic reversals. Because Scientist 2 contends that seismic activity can significantly disturb the motions of the core, (B) is correct. Choice A is incorrect because it reverses the direction of causality suggested by Scientist 2; seismic activity affects the core, but not vice-versa. Choice C is incorrect because it directly contradicts Scientist 2's account. Choice D is incorrect because Scientist 2 suggests that eddy currents spontaneously arise from the core's motion, but never suggests that these currents are caused by seismic activity.

PASSAGE IV

24. H   Difficulty: Medium

Category: Evaluation of Models, Inferences, and Results

Getting to the Answer: According to the passage, "[t]he anti conformation is the lowest energy and most stable state of the butane molecule," and "[m]olecules in the anti or gauche conformations tend to maintain their shape." Choice (H), then, is a perfect match. Choices F and G are incorrect because they wrongly suggest that molecules in low-energy conformations do change their shapes. Choice J is incorrect because it contradicts the passage's claim that the lowest-energy conformation is the most stable.

25. C   Difficulty: Medium

Category: Evaluation of Models, Inferences, and Results

Getting to the Answer: The first paragraph of the passage states that straight-chain conformational isomers "differ only by rotation about one or more single carbon bonds." The implication here is that, if the only difference is rotation, then the number of single carbon bonds must remain constant. Choice (C) is thus correct. Choice A is incorrect because, as explained in the passage, the different conformational isomers vary with respect to energy, with anti being the lowest energy and totally eclipsed being the highest. Choice B is incorrect because *shape* is just another word for *conformational isomer*. Choice D is incorrect because, according to Student 2, temperature can have an impact on which conformational isomer is favored.

K

26. F   **Difficulty:** Medium

Category: Evaluation of Models, Inferences, and Results

Getting to the Answer: According to the passage, Student 1 believes that a molecule's active shape is *always* identical to its lowest-energy shape. Student 2, however, believes that "a butane molecule's shape may also depend on temperature and its initial isomeric state." Temperature does not appear among the options, but initial isomeric state does, so (F) is correct. The other choices are incorrect because both Student 1 and Student 2 would agree that energy state, stability, and the proximity of methyl groups have an influence on butane's active shape.

27. B   **Difficulty:** High

Category: Interpretation of Data

Getting to the Answer: Try to find structural similarities between the passage and the new situation. The larger valley represents the lowest energy state because it is closest the ground, while the smaller valley is lower in energy than its immediate surroundings, but relatively higher in energy compared to the larger valley. Thus, the larger valley corresponds to the anti conformation, the lowest energy state of butane, while the smaller valley corresponds to the second-lowest energy state, the gauche conformation. Indeed, the passage describes the gauche conformation as "a relative minimum or *meta-stable* state." Choice (B) is thus correct. Choice A is incorrect because anti corresponds to the larger valley. Choice C is incorrect because eclipsed corresponds to the smaller hill. Choice D is incorrect because totally eclipsed corresponds to the larger hills at the far left and far right of the figure.

28. F   **Difficulty:** Medium

Category: Evaluation of Models, Inferences, and Results

Getting to the Answer: According to the passage, Student 1 believes that a molecule's active shape and its lowest-energy shape are the same thing. Therefore, Student 1 believes that all butane molecules in their active shape will be in the anti conformation. Choice (F) is thus correct. Choice G is incorrect because it directly contradicts Student 1's view. Choice H is incorrect because Student 2 believes that the active shape of butane will sometimes be the gauche conformation. Choice J is incorrect because Student 2 believes that the active shape of butane will sometimes be the anti conformation, which is the lowest in energy.

29. D   **Difficulty:** High

Category: Evaluation of Models, Inferences, and Results

Getting to the Answer: According to the passage, Student 2 believes that the energy of a molecule's active shape may be slightly higher than that of its most stable shape, while Student 1 believes that a molecule's most stable shape and its active shape are always the same. Choice (D) depicts a situation in which the active shape has a higher energy than the most stable shape, so it is correct. Choices A and B are incorrect because both students would agree that the energy of the eclipsed conformation is higher than that of either the active or most stable shape. Choice C is incorrect because Student 1 believes that the active shape and most stable shape are always the same, but you're looking for a choice Student 1 would disagree with.

30. G   **Difficulty:** High

Category: Evaluation of Models, Inferences, and Results

Getting to the Answer: Student 2 uses the following argument to contend that the gauche conformation can serve as the active shape of butane: "in order to convert from the gauche conformation to the anti conformation, the molecule must pass through either the eclipsed or totally eclipsed conformation. If the molecule is not given enough energy to reach either of these states, its active shape will be the gauche conformation." Choice (G), however, suggests that the energy to overcome these local barriers is always present in the environment, which would mean that a butane molecule would never settle into a gauche conformation, since it would always have enough energy to convert to anti. Choice (G) is therefore correct. None of the other choices are directly relevant to Student 2's argument.

PASSAGE V

31. C   Difficulty: Low

Category: Evaluation of Models, Inferences, and Experimental Results

Getting to the Answer: Information found in the introductory paragraph of a Conflicting Viewpoints passage can generally be considered as a point of agreement between the different viewpoints. The opening paragraph here states that "mitochondria are surrounded by two membranes, contain their own DNA, and divide independently from the host cell." Therefore, both scientists would agree that mitochondria possess their own DNA, making (C) correct. Choice A is Scientist 2's view, while B is Scientist 1's. Choice D contradicts the opening paragraph, so neither scientist would agree with it.

32. J   Difficulty: Low

Category: Evaluation of Models, Inferences, and Experimental Results

Getting to the Answer: According to Scientist 1, "As the oxygen levels in the atmosphere rose, some prokaryotes evolved into aerobes to utilize the free oxygen. Since anaerobic prokaryotes could not metabolize oxygen, they engulfed the aerobic prokaryotes." This resulted in an endosymbiotic relationship. Therefore, the correct answer is (J). Choice F is a distortion (anaerobic bacteria were the ones that could not utilize free oxygen), and G and H are true but irrelevant.

33. A   Difficulty: Low

Category: Evaluation of Models, Inferences, and Experimental Results

Getting to the Answer: The answer can be found directly stated in the passage. Scientist 1 states that "aerobic prokaryotes evolved into mitochondria. For that reason, mitochondrial DNA differs both genetically and structurally from the DNA in the eukaryotic cell's nucleus." Therefore, the correct answer is (A). Choices B and C correspond to Scientist 2's viewpoint. Choice D contradicts the opening paragraph, which states that mitochondria have 2 membranes.

34. F   Difficulty: Medium

Category: Evaluation of Models, Inferences, and Experimental Results

Getting to the Answer: Scientist 1 states that "aerobic prokaryotes evolved into mitochondria" but Scientist 2 claims that "the DNA . . . of mitochondria differ from those of bacteria." Thus, the statement that mitochondrial DNA has the same structure as prokaryotic DNA would strengthen Scientist 1's viewpoint but weaken Scientist 2's. The correct answer is (F).

35. D   Difficulty: Medium

Category: Evaluation of Models, Inferences, and Experimental Results

Getting to the Answer: Scientist 2 states that mitochondrial DNA and ribosomal proteins differ from those of bacteria, concluding from these facts that "mitochondria could not have evolved from the endosymbiosis of two prokaryotes." This matches (D). Choice A is incorrect because it's the exact opposite of Scientist 2's conclusion. Choice B is incorrect because Scientist 2 never discusses the "aerobic capacity of mitochondria." Choice C is incorrect because genetic complexity is never an issue in the passage.

36. G   Difficulty: High

Category: Evaluation of Models, Inferences, and Experimental Results

Getting to the Answer: What is each scientist's hypothesis? Scientist 1 states that "mitochondria-containing eukaryotes developed from an endo-symbiotic relationship between two types of prokaryotes" and that "aerobic prokaryotes evolved into mitochondria." Scientist 2 claims that "mitochondria developed from the membrane of the [eukaryotic] cell," which evolved from a single pro-karyote. Choice F states that mitochondria originated from aerobic *eukaryotes*, which is a view suggested by neither scientist, making it incorrect. Choice (G) correctly states Scientist 1's view that mitochondria originated from aerobic prokaryotes. Moreover, a study that shows mitochondria divide by binary fission, much like bacteria, would definitely support Scientist 1. Thus, the correct answer is (G). Choice H assigns a view from Scientist 1 to Scientist 2, so it is incorrect. Choice J correctly describes Scientist 2's viewpoint, but it would not be supported by the study.

37. B   Difficulty: High

Category: Evaluation of Models, Inferences, and Experimental Results

Getting to the Answer: Scientist 2's claim is that *most* mitochondrial proteins are synthesized from genes in the nucleus, not *all*, so A is incorrect. Scientist 1 could explain the role of the nucleus in synthesizing mitochondrial proteins by arguing that many mitochondrial genes were transferred to the nucleus after the two independent prokaryotes became one organism. Therefore, the correct answer is (B). Choice C is irrelevant, and D is false because the passage states that mitochondria possess their own DNA and synthesize some of their own enzymes.

PASSAGE VI

38. J   Difficulty: Low

Category: Evaluation of Models, Inferences, and Experimental Results

Getting to the Answer: Scientists 1 and 2 disagree about whether the universe is open or closed, whether mass measurements that have been taken are accurate, and whether luminosity can be used to calculate mass and density. They do not disagree about the fact that a density greater than the critical density results in a closed universe, so eliminate F. *Luminosity* is just a technical term for *brightness* introduced in Scientist 1's account, which Scientist 2 doesn't dispute, so G is also incorrect. The scientists agree that some matter has been detected and some has not (Scientist 1 mentions *detectable matter*, implying that there is also some matter that has not yet been detected), so eliminate H, too. Scientist 1 concludes that the universe is still open based on calculations from luminosity measurements, whereas Scientist 2 concludes that there is some mass that is not revealed by these measurements. Thus, (J) is the correct answer.

39. C   Difficulty: Low

Category: Evaluation of Models, Inferences, and Experimental Results

Getting to the Answer: Scientist 1 argues that the universe "will continue to expand." Scientist 2 argues that the universe "will eventually stop expanding." Both suggest the universe is currently expanding, so (C) is correct. Choice A is incorrect because nothing in the passage suggests a static universe. Choice B is incorrect because the scientists disagree about whether the universe will *eventually* collapse, but neither suggests that it is *currently* collapsing. Neither scientist disputes the value of the critical density provided in the opening paragraph, so D is also incorrect.

40. H   Difficulty: Low

Category: Evaluation of Models, Inferences, and Experimental Results

Getting to the Answer: Scientist 2 states that observations of stars in other galaxies suggest more mass than the value endorsed by Scientist 1 and that this "missing mass must be non-luminous matter that cannot be detected by luminosity measurements." This directly matches (H). Choice F is the opposite of what Scientist 2 suggests, while G is too extreme—just because it has not been detected by luminosity measurements does not mean it will never be detected. Choice J is a distortion: being non-luminous does not necessarily make the matter *alien*.

41. A   Difficulty: Medium

Category: Evaluation of Models, Inferences, and Experimental Results

Getting to the Answer: Scientist 1 determines the average density of the universe by calculating the collected mass of all matter in a large part of the universe detected by luminosity measurements. Statement I is thus true, which allows you to eliminate B and D. Statement II does not appear in the remaining answer choices, so you do not need to evaluate it, but it is false since Scientist 1 never discusses planetary motions. Statement III is false because Scientist 1 never mentions non-luminous matter, so eliminate C. Because only statement I is true, (A) is correct.

42. F   Difficulty: Medium

Category: Evaluation of Models, Inferences, and Experimental Results

Getting to the Answer: What is Scientist 2's hypothesis? The combined density of luminous and non-luminous matter exceeds the critical value. How could Scientist 2 support this hypothesis? If she could determine the mass of non-luminous matter in a large volume of the universe, she could add it to the mass of luminous matter detected and use the

total sum to show that the average density of the universe exceeds the critical value. Choice (F) matches this prediction. Choice G would challenge her hypothesis, while H and J are irrelevant.

43. B   Difficulty: High

Category: Evaluation of Models, Inferences, and Experimental Results

Getting to the Answer: Scientist 1's estimate of the size of the universe comes from evaluating "a large volume of the universe." If this volume is not representative of the whole universe and there are other parts of the universe with greater amounts of luminous matter, then all the new mass need NOT be from non-luminous matter, so eliminate A. Scientist 1's mass calculation accounted for 5% of the critical density. If new measurements show that the universe has passed the critical density, the new mass must account for at least 95% of the critical density. Therefore, the correct answer is (B). Scientist 2 suggests that the motion of the stars in other galaxies was consistent with the idea that the universe had reached critical density, so C is incorrect. Choice D is incorrect because the new information suggests that the universe is closed, not open.

44. G   Difficulty: High

Category: Evaluation of Models, Inferences, and Experimental Results

Getting to the Answer: According to the evidence cited by Scientist 1, the density of the universe is much lower than the critical value, so the universe is open. Choice F is incorrect because Scientist 1 never suggests that there is a discrepancy between the universe's density and current calculations. Scientist 1 concludes that the average density of the universe is currently 5% of the critical value, meaning the critical value is 20 times greater than its actual density, so (G) is correct. Choice H contradicts Scientist 1's viewpoint, which is based on calculating mass (and density) using measurements of brightness. Scientist 1 does not discuss non-luminous matter, so J is also incorrect.

Writing

CHAPTER TWENTY

ACT Writing Test Overview

INSIDE THE ACT WRITING TEST

The ACT Writing Test is designed to gauge your ability to compose a clear and logical argument and effectively present that argument in written form. The Writing Test is 40 minutes long and includes one prompt. You will use that time to read the prompt and then plan, write, and proofread your response.

The writing prompt will present a specific, complex issue and three perspectives on it. You are asked to analyze those multiple perspectives and to arrive at a point of view on the issue. Then, you must state your point of view clearly, support it with clear and relevant examples, and compare it to at least one other perspective.

The Format

Although a different issue will be presented on each ACT Writing Test, the Writing Test directions, prompt format, and essay task will always be the same. This means that, by becoming familiar with the expectations ahead of time, you will save yourself valuable time on Test Day. When other students will be busy wading through the directions and figuring out what to do, you will be able to jump right into reading through the issues and perspectives. The predictable format also means that, with preparation and practice, you can achieve success on the ACT Writing Test.

Test Day Directions and Format

The directions for the ACT Writing Test appear below. Familiarize yourself with the directions ahead of time so you will not need to spend time reading them on Test Day.

This is a test of your writing skills. You will have forty (40) minutes to read the prompt, plan your response, and write an essay in English. Before you begin working, read all material in this test booklet carefully to understand exactly what you are being asked to do.

Your essay will be evaluated on the evidence it provides of your ability to do the following:

- Clearly state your own perspective on a complex issue and analyze the relationship between your perspective and at least one other perspective

- Develop and support your ideas with reasoning and examples

- Organize your ideas clearly and logically

- Communicate your ideas effectively in standard written English

You will write your essay on the lined pages in the answer document provided. Your writing on those pages will be scored. You may use the unlined pages in this test booklet to plan your essay. Your work on these pages will not be scored.

Lay your pencil down immediately when time is called.

The next page in your test booklet will contain the actual **writing prompt** for the specific issue you will be asked to analyze on Test Day. Remember, although the issue will be different on each test, the format of the prompt will be the same:

- The prompt will contain a **paragraph** that summarizes the issue in question. Read this paragraph carefully, marking key words and important ideas. Pay special attention to any questions that are raised, which are usually at the end of the paragraph.

- After the introductory paragraph, there will be three boxes that summarize **three viewpoints** about the issue.

- After the three boxes will be a large box containing the **essay task**. The task will always be the same, so again, familiarize yourself with it before Test Day.

A sample ACT Writing prompt appears below. Note which parts will be the same on every ACT Writing Test and which parts will vary based on the issue given.

American History Curriculum

Educators and curriculum designers continuously debate the best way to teach American history to high school students. Whether students are reading historical interpretations or primary source documents, teachers often put the most emphasis on memorizing important names and dates. Although history is generally regarded as a compilation of facts, should high school students be expected to learn more about history than general information regarding famous people and events? Given the richness of American history, it is worthwhile to explore best practices in presenting the story of the United States to students.

Read and carefully consider these perspectives. Each suggests a particular way of teaching American history.

Perspective One	Perspective Two	Perspective Three
It is important to focus on a nation's prominent historical leaders when studying history. Leaders are representative of the nation as a whole, so studying historical figures provides a full perspective.	The clearest lens through which to view a nation's history is the welfare of its entire population. It is only through an examination of the ways in which society has been affected by historical events that students will truly understand a nation's foundation.	In order to learn the story of America, students need to know what happened, when, and who influenced those events. Becoming familiar with and being tested on important dates and events is the most effective way to study history. Students need to know what happened in years past in order to plan for the future.

Essay Task

Write a unified, coherent essay about the most effective way to teach American history to high school students. In your essay, be sure to:

- clearly state your own perspective on the issue and analyze the relationship between your perspective and at least one other perspective
- develop and support your ideas with reasoning and examples
- organize your ideas clearly and logically
- communicate your ideas effectively in standard written English

Your perspective may be in full agreement with any of those given, in partial agreement, or completely different.

Your test booklet will also include **planning your essay** pages that provide prewriting questions and space for notes. It is helpful to review these prewriting questions ahead of time, but since you will already be familiar with the essay task, don't spend too much time reading the Planning Your Essay questions on Test Day; rather, after carefully reading the essay prompt, begin your planning of the essay according to the Kaplan Method for ACT Writing. Remember that anything you write on these pages will not be scored.

Planning Your Essay

Your work on these prewriting pages will not be scored.

Use the space below and on the next page to generate ideas and plan your essay. You may wish to consider the following as you think critically about the task:

Strengths and weaknesses of the three given perspectives

- What insights do they offer, and what do they fail to consider?
- Why might they be persuasive to others, or why might they fail to persuade?

Your own knowledge, experience, and values

- What is your perspective on this issue, and what are its strengths and weaknesses?
- How will you support your perspective in your essay?

Outside Knowledge

No outside knowledge is required. However, you may choose to strengthen your essay with examples from history, science, literature, or even your own experiences.

The Inside Scoop

The essay is argument-based, not fact-based. That is, you're being tested on what you can effectively argue, not what you know about the topic. Does this mean true examples aren't relevant? Yes and no—you will not be scored based on whether your examples are true or not, but you will be scored based on whether you use examples effectively. In an essay about being active in your community, for example, if you attribute the quote "Ask not what your country can do for you; ask what you can do for your country" to Ronald Reagan, you will be factually wrong, but you will be using an effective piece of evidence anyway. So you will get credit for effective use of information, even though the quote was said by John F. Kennedy.

Timing

With only 40 minutes allotted for the Writing Test, efficient use of time is critical. Divide your time as follows:

- **8 minutes:** Read the prompt and plan your essay
- **30 minutes:** Produce (write) your essay, sticking to the plan
- **2 minutes:** Proofread and correct any errors

When You're Running Out of Time

On the Writing Test, you won't be able to guess on the last few questions when you're running out of time, as you can on the other tests. Thus, practice the timing carefully to avoid losing coherence toward the end. If you do start running out of time, don't write three body paragraphs. Instead, take the time to write a thorough second body paragraph and a clear conclusion paragraph. The conclusion is a necessary component of your essay, and its exclusion will cost you more than a third body paragraph will gain you. Even when you're rushed, allow 1 to 2 minutes to proofread for errors that affect clarity. One or two minor errors can have a dramatic impact on the clarity of your writing as a whole.

Scoring

Your essay will be scored according to four domains: **Ideas and Analysis**, **Development and Support**, **Organization**, and **Language Use and Conventions**. (Notice that these correspond with the four bulleted items in the Essay Task.) What is significant for you, prep-wise, is to make sure you can write an essay that is well developed in each of these four domain areas in order to maximize your Writing Test score.

Two trained readers score your essay on a scale of 1–6 for each of the four Writing Test domains; those scores are added to arrive at your four Writing domain scores (each from 2 to 12). You will also receive an overall Writing Test score ranging from 2 to 12, which is determined by a rounded average of the four domain scores. Essays can receive a zero if they are entirely off-topic, left blank, illegible, or written in a language other than English. If there's a difference of more than 1 point between the two readers' scores (for example, one reader gives the essay a 3 and the other a 5), your essay will be read by a third reader.

Statistically speaking, there will be few essays that score 12 out of 12 for all four Writing Test domains. If each grader gives your essay a 4 or 5 for each of the four domains (making your subscores 8–10), that will place you within the upper range of those taking the exam.

QUICK TIPS

Brainstorm potential examples ahead of time. Sometime before Test Day, refresh your memory about school subjects, historical and current events, personal experiences, activities, or anything else that might provide strong support for multiple essays. By doing so, you strengthen mental connections to those ideas and details, making it easier to use them as specific, relevant support for your thesis on Test Day. Again, the important thing to remember is that real-world evidence is far more powerful than hypothetical stances. Saying "This is right because I believe it" will never be as strong as saying "This is right—here is some evidence."

Practice! Students commonly run into issues with timing on Test Day, so it is imperative to practice the timing ahead of time so you feel comfortable when it counts. Practicing will also help you commit the Method and template to memory so the process is second nature on Test Day. Remember, no matter what issue is raised in the prompt, the directions and task will always be the same. To prepare effectively, read sample essays and practice both planning essay prompts (Steps 1 and 2 of the Method) and writing complete essays (Steps 1–4) multiple times before Test Day. Doing so will enable you to approach the ACT Writing Test with confidence.

CHAPTER TWENTY-ONE

ACT Writing

THE KAPLAN METHOD FOR ACT WRITING

The Kaplan Method for ACT Writing is the method you will use to boost your score on the Writing Test. Use the Kaplan Method for ACT Writing for every ACT Writing Test prompt you encounter, whether you are practicing, completing your homework, working on a Practice Test, or taking the actual exam on Test Day.

The Kaplan Method for ACT Writing has four steps:

Step 1: Prompt (3 minutes)

Step 2: Plan (5 minutes)

Step 3: Produce (30 minutes)

Step 4: Proofread (2 minutes)

Let's take a closer look at each step.

Step 1: Prompt (3 minutes)

- **Read the prompt.** Read about the issue and be sure you clearly understand each of the three core arguments. Getting a high score requires clearly responding to at least one of the three perspectives.
- **Choose a position.** Once you've determined what each perspective is arguing, pick a position on the issue. There is no right or wrong answer, and you can partially or fully agree or disagree with the perspectives provided. You should plan a thesis that you can best defend with evidence and examples, whether it's what you personally believe or not. Be aware that multiple sides can be effectively defended and earn a strong Writing Test score; there's no "easy" or "right" side. The essay graders do not care what position you choose, only that you explain and support it effectively.

✔ *Expert Tip*

Many students find the easiest approach to a high score is to completely agree with one of the stated perspectives and to completely disagree with one of the others. You don't have to come up with a unique point of view.

- **Understanding the issue and addressing the Writing Task are essential to earning a high score.** Do not hurry too quickly through this step: make sure you clearly understand the issue, each of the three perspectives, and which position you are going to argue. You cannot get a high score if you misunderstand the issue and do not address the Writing Task.

> ✔ *Expert Tip*
>
> The task your essay must address is likely to be found in the middle of the prompt. Underline it to be sure you answer the exact question the prompt asks.

Step 2: Plan (5 minutes)

- **Allow up to 8 minutes for Steps 1 and 2.** You must strategically plan your essay before you write. Many students skip this step on Test Day, but strong writers plan their essays carefully. Spend a few minutes planning so you know what you're trying to accomplish and can put forth your best first draft.
- **Use the Kaplan Template for the ACT Essay.** The template will serve as your guide to efficiently plan your essay. In general, the template will help you structure an introduction paragraph, three body paragraphs (two supporting your own perspective and a third explaining how your thesis compares/contrasts with another perspective), and a short concluding paragraph.
- **Write a thesis.** Begin by stating your thesis. Since you already decided upon a stance during Step 1, it should be easy to compose a sentence that clearly states your position.

> ✔ *Expert Tip*
>
> After supporting your thesis, consider addressing a counterexample—a reason an opponent might disagree with your thesis—and then overcoming that objection. Doing this shows that while you've recognized the shortcomings of your thesis, your view withstands criticism.

- **Brainstorm examples.** Start brainstorming examples and reasoning that you can use to support your own position, as well as to support (or refute) at least one of the three perspectives provided in the prompt. Choose the best specific, relevant examples: you'll use these to support your own perspective and argue against competing perspectives.

> ✔ *Expert Tip*
>
> Include enough detail and explanation in your examples to make it clear to the reader how the examples support your reasoning.

Step 3: Produce (30 minutes)

- **Write your essay.** Write your draft, sticking closely to your plan. You're not scored on how many words or paragraphs you write but on the strength of your content, evidence, and organization.

> **✔ Expert Tip**
>
> If you find you have better supporting evidence for a different position from the one you originally thought you would take, just change your position.

- **Write paragraphs with transitions.** Using about 30 minutes, you should aim to produce five well-developed paragraphs with topic sentences and supporting details. Include transition words as you write your essay: do everything you can to make your essay organization and ideas understandable for your readers.

- **Include both an introductory and a concluding paragraph.** Be sure to include an introductory paragraph stating your position and a concluding paragraph that summarizes your position because without those two framing components, you're missing fundamental ingredients your essay needs to earn a high score.

- **Be neat.** As you produce your essay, write as neatly as possible; words that cannot be read cannot be scored.

- **Don't sweat the small stuff.** Finally, do not get caught up in small details or technicalities: do your best and keep writing. It is much more important to write an essay with complete ideas than a technically perfect, but inadequately developed, essay. Even the top-scoring essays contain minor errors. The essay graders understand you are writing a first draft under timed conditions.

Step 4: Proofread (2 minutes)

- **Check your work.** Always leave yourself the last couple of minutes to review your work; this time spent proofreading is definitely to your benefit. Very few of us can avoid the occasional confused sentence or omitted word when we write under pressure, and a missed word can affect the meaning of a sentence. Again, graders can only score what they read, not what you might mean. Therefore, always quickly review your essay to be sure your ideas are clearly stated.

> **✔ Expert Tip**
>
> Use a caret ^ or an asterisk * to insert a word or words, write a backward ¶ to create a new paragraph, and cross out words with one line. Your goal is to stay organized so graders can easily read your essay.

ACT WRITING SCORING RUBRIC

To effectively prepare for the ACT Writing Test, it is important to understand what components are needed for a high-scoring essay. The ACT essay readers will be looking for proficiency in four areas (domains).

The four separate score domains for ACT Writing are Ideas and Analysis, Development and Support, Organization, and Language Use and Conventions. Each of your essay's two readers will assign each domain a score on a scale from 1 to 6. Added together, these individual scores determine your score for each domain on a scale from 2 to 12. The readers use a rubric similar to the following to determine each domain score.

6	5	4
Ideas and Analysis		
• Includes a comprehensive, detailed, and insightful thesis • Establishes thorough context for analysis of the issue and its perspectives • Evaluates implications, intricacies, and/or assumptions	• Includes a detailed, insightful thesis • Establishes effective context for analysis of the issue and its perspectives • Discusses implications, intricacies, and/or assumptions	• Includes a detailed thesis • Establishes adequate context for analysis of the issue and its perspectives • Identifies implications, intricacies, and/or assumptions
Development and Support		
• Provides additional insight and context • Skillfully provides relevant reasoning and significant evidence to support claims • Explores the significance and complexity of the argument • Skillfully analyzes potential counterarguments to strengthen the essay's claims	• Provides additional understanding • Effectively reasons and supports the thesis with evidence • Discusses the significance and complexity of the argument • Analyzes potential counterarguments to give context to the essay's claims	• Provides additional clarity • Adequately reasons and supports the argument • Identifies the significance of the argument • Acknowledges potential counterarguments to the essay's claims
Organization		
• Demonstrates a skillful structure • Focuses on a well-defined main idea throughout the essay • Includes transitions that skillfully connect and deepen understanding between ideas	• Demonstrates an effective structure • Focuses on a main idea • Includes transitions that effectively connect ideas	• Demonstrates an adequate structure • Reflects a main idea • Includes transitions that adequately connect ideas
Language Use and Conventions		
• Features skillful, precise, appropriate word choice that strengthens the argument • Consistently includes varied sentence structure • May include a few minor errors in grammar that do not distract from clarity or readability	• Features precise, appropriate word choice that serves the argument • Often includes varied sentence structure • May include minor errors in grammar that do not distract from clarity or readability	• Features appropriate word choice for the argument • Sometimes includes varied sentence structure • Includes minor errors in grammar that rarely distract from clarity or readability

3	2	1
Ideas and Analysis		
• Includes a thesis • Establishes some context for analysis of the issue and its perspectives • May mention implications, intricacies, and/or assumptions	• Does not include a clear thesis • Does not provide context for analysis of the issue and its perspectives • Does not discuss implications, intricacies, and/or assumptions	• Does not include a thesis • Does not provide context for analysis of the issue and its perspectives • Does not identify implications, intricacies, and/or assumptions
Development and Support		
• Provides general information • Reasons and supports the argument in a redundant or inexact way • Mentions potential counterarguments to the essay's claims	• Weakly provides information • Inadequately reasons and supports the argument • Ignores potential counterarguments to the essay's claims	• Lacks development • Does not reason or support the argument
Organization		
• Demonstrates a basic structure • Contains a main idea • Includes transitions that sometimes connect ideas	• Demonstrates a simplistic structure • May not reflect a main idea • Does not use transitions that adequately connect ideas	• Demonstrates a confusing structure • Does not reflect a main idea • Does not use transitions that adequately connect ideas
Language Use and Conventions		
• Features basic word choice that does not detract from the argument • Rarely includes varied sentence structure • Includes errors in grammar that somewhat distract from clarity and readability	• Features unclear word choice that detracts from the argument • Often includes unclear sentence structure • Includes errors in grammar that distract from clarity and readability	• Features confusing word choice • Often includes unclear, confusing sentence structure • Includes numerous errors in grammar that distract from clarity and readability

Kaplan Template for the ACT Essay

> ✔ *Expert Tip*
>
> **Write several practice essays to memorize the Kaplan template. You can't bring the template—or any other notes—into the testing room on Test Day.**

¶1: **Introductory paragraph**
- **Introductory statement**
- **Thesis**

¶2: **1st body paragraph**
- Describe your **thesis**
- Provide **1st example/reasoning:** include specific, relevant information

¶3: **2nd body paragraph**
- Continue supporting your **thesis**
- Provide **2nd example/reasoning:** include specific, relevant information

—***Time valve:*** *If you are running out of time, don't write a 2nd body paragraph. Instead, take the time to write a thorough 3rd body paragraph and a clear conclusion paragraph.*—

¶4: **3rd body paragraph**
- Explain how your thesis compares and contrasts with **Perspectives One, Two, and/or Three**
- **Strengths/Weaknesses** of the perspective(s)
- Insights offered / Insights not considered
- Persuasive / Not persuasive
- **Example or Reasoning:** provide specific, relevant information

> ✔ *Expert Tip*
>
> **The goal of your 4th paragraph (the 3rd body paragraph) is to evaluate and critique at least one perspective provided, and it is often easiest to discuss a perspective that mostly clearly *contrasts* with your thesis.**

¶5: **Conclusion paragraph**
- Recap your **thesis**
- Recap how your thesis compares and contrasts with **Perspectives One, Two, and/or Three**

PRACTICE QUESTIONS

Essay 1

Directions

This is a test of your writing skills. You will have **forty** (40) minutes to read the prompt, plan your response, and write an essay in English. Before you begin working, read all material in this test booklet carefully to understand exactly what you are being asked to do.

Your essay will be evaluated on the evidence it provides of your ability to do the following:

- Clearly state your own perspective on a complex issue and analyze the relationship between your perspective and at least one other perspective

- Develop and support your ideas with reasoning and examples

- Organize your ideas clearly and logically

- Communicate your ideas effectively in standard written English

You will write your essay on the lined pages in the answer document provided. Your writing on those pages will be scored. You may use the unlined pages in this test booklet to plan your essay. Your work on these pages will not be scored.

Lay your pencil down immediately when time is called.

DO NOT OPEN THIS BOOKLET UNTIL TOLD TO DO SO.

Planning Your Essay

You may wish to consider the following as you think critically about the task:

Strengths and weaknesses of the three given perspectives

- What insights do they offer, and what do they fail to consider?

- Why might they be persuasive to others, or why might they fail to persuade?

Your own knowledge, experience, and values

- What is your perspective on this issue, and what are its strengths and weaknesses?

- How will you support your perspective in your essay?

Access to Technology

To help ready students to become productive members of the workforce, schools concentrate on providing a strong foundation on which students can build their careers. Since job applicants who are proficient in word processing applications, email programs, and storage tools are more likely to be hired than applicants who do not have technology experience, it is to the benefit of students that schools offer technology instruction in high school. Given the importance of technology in today's society, should schools be responsible for providing ongoing access to computers for every student? Since many students will need to use computers in various capacities throughout their lifetimes, how well a school provides access to technology directly affects its student body.

Read and carefully consider these perspectives. Each discusses the importance of student access to technology.

Perspective One	Perspective Two	Perspective Three
Schools should be encouraged to incorporate technology objectives into homework assignments and class projects, but schools do not have an obligation to provide unlimited access to computers. Teachers can provide time during the school day for students to use on-site computer labs, which will allow students the tools they need to complete assignments that require computer technology.	Schools should be required to provide personal computers for students to use at least throughout their high school careers, if not during middle and elementary school as well. Unlimited access to a personal computer for every student will foster continual development of technological abilities, which is a highly valued skill set.	Schools and computer companies should work together to provide significant student discounts so that the majority of parents who have school-age children can afford to purchase at least one personal computer. Students who do not have their own computers can use their schools' computer labs or go to their local libraries to complete homework assignments that require computer technology.

Essay Task

Write a unified, coherent essay about access to technology. In your essay, be sure to:

- clearly state your own perspective on the issue and analyze the relationship between your perspective and at least one other perspective

- develop and support your ideas with reasoning and examples

- organize your ideas clearly and logically

- communicate your ideas effectively in standard written English

Your perspective may be in full agreement with any of those given, in partial agreement, or completely different.

Essay 2

Directions

This is a test of your writing skills. You will have **forty** (40) minutes to read the prompt, plan your response, and write an essay in English. Before you begin working, read all material in this test booklet carefully to understand exactly what you are being asked to do.

Your essay will be evaluated on the evidence it provides of your ability to do the following:

- Clearly state your own perspective on a complex issue and analyze the relationship between your perspective and at least one other perspective

- Develop and support your ideas with reasoning and examples

- Organize your ideas clearly and logically

- Communicate your ideas effectively in standard written English

You will write your essay on the lined pages in the answer document provided. Your writing on those pages will be scored. You may use the unlined pages in this test booklet to plan your essay. Your work on these pages will not be scored.

Lay your pencil down immediately when time is called.

DO NOT OPEN THIS BOOKLET UNTIL TOLD TO DO SO.

Planning Your Essay

You may wish to consider the following as you think critically about the task:

Strengths and weaknesses of the three given perspectives

- What insights do they offer, and what do they fail to consider?

- Why might they be persuasive to others, or why might they fail to persuade?

Your own knowledge, experience, and values

- What is your perspective on this issue, and what are its strengths and weaknesses?

- How will you support your perspective in your essay?

Scientific Research

A great deal of pure research, undertaken without specific goals but generally to further humankind's understanding of themselves and their world, is subsidized at least partly, if not fully, by a nation's government to help drive progress and promote outcomes that improve overall quality of life for citizens. Though pure research often involves considerable time, energy, and money without any assurances of positive outcomes, it can result in economic, medical, and technological benefits. However, it can also result in negative, harmful, and perhaps irreversible outcomes, in which case taxpayer dollars can be wasted and society put at risk. Should governments fund research when the outcome is unclear? Given that taxpayers prefer that their dollars be spent efficiently and effectively, it may be unwise to allocate significant funding to endeavors that may not benefit society as a whole.

Read and carefully consider these perspectives. Each discusses government funding of scientific research.

Perspective One	Perspective Two	Perspective Three
Governments should fund as much pure research as they can afford when the intent is to benefit the mass population. Without the government's money, many research projects would have to cease unless alternative funding is secured. Even research without clear, positive consequences should be pursued because the outcome may prove beneficial, and the research can always be paused or stopped entirely if negative repercussions begin to emerge.	Governments should be very cautious and limit efforts to fund research programs with unclear consequences. Rather, these programs should demonstrate their worth and intended results when seeking government money. Governments should evaluate the merit and benefit of each program on a case-by-case basis and fund only those projects that are designed to create—and will likely achieve—clear and acceptable outcomes.	Governments should partner with private contributors to fund research. Private contributors include companies doing research and development as well as non-profit foundations. These partnerships will distance the government from taking responsibility for any unintended or undesired consequences and relieve the burden on the taxpayer for efforts that do not prove beneficial. Additionally, this approach incentivizes research teams to provide results-based research that can generate private funding, thus increasing the chance that the research will prove useful to multiple entities, including the government.

Essay Task

Write a unified, coherent essay about government funding of scientific research. In your essay, be sure to:

- clearly state your own perspective on the issue and analyze the relationship between your perspective and at least one other perspective

- develop and support your ideas with reasoning and examples

- organize your ideas clearly and logically

- communicate your ideas effectively in standard written English

Your perspective may be in full agreement with any of those given, in partial agreement, or completely different.

Essay 3

Directions

This is a test of your writing skills. You will have **forty** (40) minutes to read the prompt, plan your response, and write an essay in English. Before you begin working, read all material in this test booklet carefully to understand exactly what you are being asked to do.

Your essay will be evaluated on the evidence it provides of your ability to do the following:

- Clearly state your own perspective on a complex issue and analyze the relationship between your perspective and at least one other perspective

- Develop and support your ideas with reasoning and examples

- Organize your ideas clearly and logically

- Communicate your ideas effectively in standard written English

You will write your essay on the lined pages in the answer document provided. Your writing on those pages will be scored. You may use the unlined pages in this test booklet to plan your essay. Your work on these pages will not be scored.

Lay your pencil down immediately when time is called.

DO NOT OPEN THIS BOOKLET UNTIL TOLD TO DO SO.

Planning Your Essay

You may wish to consider the following as you think critically about the task:

Strengths and weaknesses of the three given perspectives

- What insights do they offer, and what do they fail to consider?

- Why might they be persuasive to others, or why might they fail to persuade?

Your own knowledge, experience, and values

- What is your perspective on this issue, and what are its strengths and weaknesses?

- How will you support your perspective in your essay?

Student Loans

Despite the rising cost of higher education, financial experts agree that a college diploma is worth the investment. As students enroll in college to increase their lifetime earning potential, broaden their opportunities, and pursue careers, many worry about the challenge of paying off student loans once they graduate. Student loan repayment includes both the original amount borrowed as well as interest accrued over time, which often takes students years to repay. Should colleges and financial institutions be expected to develop programs and policies to address student concern regarding loans? Given the fact that affording college is a primary factor in deciding whether or not to pursue higher education, it is prudent for institutions to develop practices to better assist students in financing their degrees.

Read and carefully consider these perspectives. Each suggests a particular way of thinking about student loans.

Perspective One	Perspective Two	Perspective Three
Student loans should not be subject to interest rates if a student is able to pay off the loan within a reasonable amount of time. Financial lenders, including the United States government, should not be making a profit on loans that students need to complete their degrees. Should a student request additional time to repay the loan beyond the agreed-upon repayment schedule, interest or a penalty fee can then be applied to the remaining balance.	Higher education is a commodity and is subject to supply and demand principles inherent in a capitalist market. Colleges, financial institutions, and the United States government should not make special accommodations for college students. All loans should be held to the same standard and should not differ according to a borrower's intended use.	The amount of money students can borrow should be proportional to the annual salary they are projected to earn once they graduate. Students should not be allowed to borrow more money than they can pay back in a reasonable amount of time. Reducing or eliminating interest rates does not address the more concerning issue of disproportionate debt and future earning potential.

Essay Task

Write a unified, coherent essay about student loans. In your essay, be sure to:

- clearly state your own perspective on the issue and analyze the relationship between your perspective and at least one other perspective

- develop and support your ideas with reasoning and examples

- organize your ideas clearly and logically

- communicate your ideas effectively in standard written English

Your perspective may be in full agreement with any of those given, in partial agreement, or completely different.

ANSWERS AND EXPLANATIONS

You can evaluate your essay and the model essay based on the following criteria:

- Does the author discuss all three perspectives provided in the prompt?
- Is the author's own perspective clearly stated?
- Does the body of the essay assess and analyze each perspective?
- Is the relevance of each paragraph clear?
- Does the author start a new paragraph for each new idea?
- Is each sentence in a paragraph relevant to the point made in that paragraph?
- Are transitions clear?
- Is the essay easy to read? Is it engaging?
- Are sentences varied?
- Is vocabulary used effectively? Is college-level vocabulary used?

Essay 1—Access to Technology

Level 12 Essay

The question posed is if schools should provide computers to all students so that they can become proficient in using computers, since in today's world, computers are important for jobs and general communication. Since there is no going back to a pre-computer time, and the odds are that computer use will continue to grow, it will be necessary for everyone to know how to use a computer. The question is how schools will contribute to this and the fairest and most workable solution is for schools and business to work together to lower the cost of computers to a point at which most parents can afford to buy them.

When schools and business, presumably those which manufacture and sell computers, such as Apple, work together to lower the cost of computers, most parents who need computers for their children can buy them at a large discount. This will allow most students to have continuous access to computers, and reduce the number of students who still need to use the school computer center. In this way students with their own computers can not only do their schoolwork, but also have the opportunity to explore computer use for a myriad of programs, increasing their computer literacy and thus their competitiveness in the future job market. Indeed, some studies have shown that playing computer games can increase critical thinking, eye-hand coordination, and quick decision-making—all skills which are useful not only in school but in so many other activities. It has been demonstrated, for example, that the best airline pilots play computer games, which promote high-level coordination and decision-making skills.

Furthermore, computers are essentially online libraries—a fount of knowledge in almost every subject, and a boon to students writing research papers or even just looking for an academic site where they can supplement their school program. Computers also offer PowerPoint, illustration programs, and a host of other programs to enhance a presentation. In terms of future employment, a brief scan of newspaper and online job searches shows that many companies require employees to be computer literate. A few hours on a school computer, limited to only the required work, does not provide this comfortable, creative, and, in today's world, necessary tool. Given the volume of computer sales, companies can well afford to reduce their prices in special circumstances. As a marketing tool, this may also ensure a customer for life; one who will purchase the same brand as his purchasing power and need for upgrades allow.

On the other hand, those who posit that students should have access to school computers in a computer lab overlook several problems. School computer labs are open during school hours and an hour or two before and after school, which may not be enough time for all students who need to use computers to take their turns in a lab. Consider also that many students have after-school jobs, sports team practice, or family obligations, and may not be able to take advantage of time in the computer lab. If teachers give students class projects, that work may require that several students work on computers at the same time and in the same place, possibly for hours at a time. This becomes unworkable. In general, this option is not necessarily a poor one, but one which cannot be well-implemented for all students.

Finally, others argue that schools should give computers to all high school students throughout their years in school, and perhaps all middle school and elementary students as well. If all students have computers, there is no doubt that they will be very proficient at using them, and that will be beneficial for their careers in a world of technology. However, I live in Los Angeles and I know from experience that there are problems with giving students their own computers. The school board did just that in Los Angeles and has run into trouble with students using the computers for inappropriate reasons. Also, given the size of the Los Angeles school district and other very large school districts, giving every student a computer, even if it's only for high school students, will cost a great deal of money, and some school districts may not be able to support it. If that is the case, we create two groups: the haves and have-nots. This is inequitable and not something the schools should support.

To reiterate, a partnership between schools and computer companies is the best one because it provides either personal or school computers for all students, and is not a financial burden for parents. It is vital today that all students be computer literate, and this will become even more vital in the future. School is the proper place to prepare students for their working or college careers, and it is incumbent on them to provide all the tools needed for this. Thus, when businesses and schools work together to make computers affordable and available, all students will have the tools they need for school and career success.

Score Explanation (12)

This essay is well-developed, shows a clear focus on the issue, and uses sophisticated language and thought. Ideas are contextualized in several ways, including the importance of computer access for academics, careers, and enhancement of coordination. The writer's point of view is well-expressed, with appropriate support, and all three perspectives are discussed.

Ideas and Analysis (6)

All paragraphs show in-depth understanding of all points of view and give well-thought-out consideration to the perspectives. The thesis is precise: schools and businesses should partner with each other to provide low-cost personal computers. The writer examines the impact of her thesis on school assignments, career skills, and personal growth. Implications of all perspectives are analyzed and the writer's strong support of her point of view shows consistent, persuasive thinking and writing.

Development and Support (6)

The writer's point of view is first stated in the introductory paragraph and developed with strong support in the following two body paragraphs. Critique of other perspectives follows, with a strong return to the thesis in the conclusion. Support is relevant and persuasive: this is a computer world with no going back, computer skills are required for employment, computer use has been shown to be beneficial (referencing airline pilots), and schools need to prepare students for the future by ensuring computer literacy. When critiquing the other perspectives, the author refers to computer and student availability, cost, the failed Los Angeles model, and the inequality of "haves and have-nots." The author makes it clear that access to computers is not only vital for academic use, but also for career training and overall computer literacy.

Organization (6)

The argument is cohesive and logically organized, starting with a restatement of the issue and the author's point of view, moving on to two supporting paragraphs, changing to critiques of alternative perspectives, and closing with reiteration of the thesis. Throughout the essay, the writer maintains focus on the issue while incorporating wider consideration. Transitions are incorporated appropriately ("on the one hand," "other people feel," "finally"), and each paragraph is firmly focused on one perspective, with consideration of several implications.

Language Use (6)

Word choice, grammar, spelling, and sentence construction are sophisticated and correct. Vocabulary is well-chosen and appropriate; the writer correctly incorporated high-level words and phrases such as "posit," "burden," "marketing tool," "inequitable," and "incumbent upon." Sentences are complex, with use of commas, colons, and dashes, though the repetition of "computer" in the first paragraph might have been avoided. Overall, the tone is persuasive, the voice consistent, and excellent communication skills evident.

Level 8 Essay

School is the place to prepare students for the future, and that includes making sure that they have the skills needed in today's world. Thus everybody should have a chance to use a computer, not only for school work but to communicate with friends, have fun in their leisure time, and learn a variety of computer programs. But computers are expensive, so it makes sense for schools and computer companies to be partners in making sure that almost all students can afford a computer by reducing the cost to parents. Such discounts will enable the majority of students to use computers daily, for a variety of projects. Those who do not have personal computers can use school computers for their work.

Many computer companies, such as Apple and Dell, are very prosperous and can afford to make their computers less expensive to parents of school students. It also makes sense for teachers to incorporate computer skills into schoolwork, since schools are intended to prepare students for college and the work world, where computers are in daily use and become almost a necessity. It would obviously be unfair for teachers to insist on computer work if not all students have access to them. A few hours in a crowded school computer lab may not be enough time to complete a project, and the noise and activity in the lab can be distracting. It is far better for students to have individual computers, work at their own pace, concentrate in a quiet space, finish school assignments, but then have the opportunity to use the computer to communicate with friends, research topics of interest to them, and play games if they like.

Some people think that schools should give all students, especially high school kids, their own computers. This is a fine idea but takes a lot of money. Because of the large number of students in many schools, even with a discount most schools won't be able to afford to do this. Access to computers does not mean that schools need to buy them for every student. With a discount parents can buy computers, and schools need only have enough of them in a computer lab for students without their own computers to do their work in the school lab.

Given crowded school computer labs, the amount of money it would take to provide every student with his own computer, and the need for students to learn computer skills in school for their homework and future careers, the best way to fulfill this goal is for schools and computer companies to work together to make computers affordable for almost all students, and to provide school computers in labs for those who still cannot afford their own.

Score Explanation (8)

This essay stays on task throughout its entirety and shows an adequate understanding of the perspectives. The writer's point of view is clearly expressed, with some support provided, and her argument is cogent and consistent.

Ideas and Analysis (4)

The central thesis is stated clearly and reiterated in the conclusion, and the implications of both the thesis and one opposing perspective are discussed. The writer's point of view is analyzed within several contexts: computer use "for a variety of projects," the need for students to have computers for both school use and future job skills, and the benefit of personal computers versus school labs. An opposing view is critiqued on the basis of cost, though the writer does not expand this view but returns to her thesis. The phrase "a fine idea," for example, could be better explained. In general, ideas are relevant and cohesive, if not thoroughly explored. In general, the essay stays on topic, but the writer shows a shallow depth of understanding; she needs to offer a more comprehensive analysis of the issue.

Development and Support (4)

The essay begins with an introduction to school and computers, asserts the author's argument, then moves to well-constructed support centering on the benefits of a school/business partnership that would allow most students to have personal computers. The author makes interesting points about computer use for other than school work and the problems of working in a computer lab. Her support for the partnership references two computer companies, Apple and Dell, and she gives several examples of the use to which computers can be put. The author analyzes only one alternative perspective, and that one in not in much depth. The concluding paragraph reiterates the thesis—the importance of computer literacy. The author could have added more specific examples of computer use and careers which require computer literacy and enlarged the argument beyond the parameter of cost.

Organization (4)

The progression of ideas is logical and cohesive. The writer provides an introduction which presents a general background statement that evolves into her specific thesis. The next paragraph supports the thesis, the following one considers one alternative, and the conclusion returns to the thesis. Though each paragraph is complete in itself, all could benefit from clearer transitions. The thesis, however, is consistent throughout the essay, and she does provide a few transitions appropriately within paragraphs.

Language Use (4)

Word choice is adequate, clearly expressing the author's intent. Despite some flaws—there are a few slang or undefined words ("kids," "fine idea,"), and the last sentence of paragraph is long and somewhat confusing—the author's argument is clearly stated in relatively simple, but appropriate words. The style is generally persuasive and the voice is consistent throughout.

Level 4 Essay

Should schools and businesses give all kids computers by making the price so low that all parents can afford them? I think they should for lots of reasons.

When teachers give homework that has to be done on a computer, its obvious that everyone needs to be able to use one, but school computers break down a lot and there isnt too much time for everyone to use one. Kids can also use computers for fun, which is important for kids to have, and computers even help people learn to share. If you have to share your computer with your brother, you have to figure out a way thats good for both of you. Even more, if every-one has a computer at home, even parents can learn to use them and get better jobs. I know that most jobs today need people who can use computers well. That means that they have to learn early, such as in the school years, so that when their adults they already know a skill they need to make a living.

In conclusion, I think that people who sell computers should cut the price down so all students can have them. This would help with school work, and could also help everyone in the family.

Score Explanation (4)

This essay, though on the topic of computers, displays little attention to the task and almost no understanding of the perspectives. Ideas about the perspectives and their implications are not explored.

Ideas and Analysis (2)

Though there is an author viewpoint about computers, the partnership of schools and businesses is not sup-ported with appropriate or in-depth reasons and centers primarily around the use of computers in the home. Critical thinking is lacking, and there is no development of ideas. The writer's primary opinion is simply restated without movement between general to specific ideas. The majority of the essay is off-topic, completely neglect-ing a discussion of the perspective that businesses and schools should partner to provide low-cost computers. No other perspectives are discussed; thus, the essay lacks any critical thinking about the topic.

Development and Support (2)

The writer's thesis, as stated in the first paragraph, is undeveloped in the rest of the essay, which veers off to general statements about the need for computers in school and their use at home. The author supports her reasons with some evidence (sharing, availability to parents, job skills), but none are relevant to the essay topic or stated thesis.

Organization (2)

There are minimal introduction and conclusion paragraphs and a body statement that neglects to focus on the thesis. The argument is unfocused, without cohesion, and the line of reasoning is inappropriate to that thesis. The writer provides one simplistic transition ("In conclusion") and the concluding paragraph provides a weak ending which, though it connects with previous thoughts, does not do so persuasively.

Language Use (2)

The essay is replete with spelling and grammar mistakes, as well as poorly phrased ideas ("lots of reasons," "figure out a way thats good for both of you," "cut the price down"). Most apostrophes are lacking, word choice is basic, and the tone and style are too informal and personal to be persuasive. The writer displays a lack of coherent and correct writing skills and only a very basic understanding of the issue, with little focus on it.

Essay 2—Scientific Research

Level 12 Essay

I fully agree that pure scientific research is vital to increase our understanding of ourselves and our world, and that this research, even without specific goals, can result in important benefits to society. To fund this research, a consortium of government, pharmaceutical companies, and non-profit agencies should be formed, pooling money but giving no one group entire oversight or responsibility.

Many life-changing discoveries have been found without purposely looking for them. Alexander Fleming did not set out to discover penicilin, but in doing so accidentally saved millions of people from death. Putting a man on the moon did not help people on Earth, but it certainly taught us a lot about our universe. This kind of pure research must continue, and the cost should be shared by the government, drug companies, and non-profit groups. This type of research can be prohibitively expensive; thus, monies must be drawn from various sources, each contributing as much as possible. No single organization can completely fund ongoing research, especially if there is no stated goal other than to hopefully discover something beneficial. Tax payers, pharmaceutical company investors, and non-profit group members expect results, which may be long in coming, or, indeed, continually elusive. However, efforts must continue. As Thomas Edison said, "Just because something doesn't do what you planned it to do doesn't mean it's useless."

Consider also that pharmaceutical companies are always searching for new therapeutic drugs. They send scientists out into the field to come back with anything interesting, which is then researched and, if promising, developed into a new drug. Such is the relation between blood sugar and diabetes, leading to the insulin that my diabetic cousin takes; without insulin, he would not survive. If a drug company develops an important drug, it can make millions of dollars from the sale of it, leading to funding more research. Non-profit organizations also have a stake in pure research, since another accidental discovery could prove to be financially beneficial. Finally, if the government shares the burden of underwriting research, it is not at risk for being fully blamed if the research does not produce positive results. Taxpayers would be more liable to accept a minimal lose in a good cause rather than a major loss in an unsure endeavor. A partnership would ensure continued funding and the funders, as well as all citizens, would benefit from discoveries.

On the other hand, people who say the government should fund only research which has demonstrated its worth do not understand the function of pure research. It is not possible for researchers to say with certainty that they are going to find a cure for cancer. Researchers have to be able to say they are searching for something as yet unknown with the hope that it will be beneficial. And what is a clear and acceptable outcome? If cancer researchers find a cure for diabetes, but not cancer, is that acceptable if it is not the stated intention? A great deal of science is luck and perserverance. According to this perspective, if a researcher wanted government funding to work in the Amazonian rain forest with the general intent of exploring indigenous plants, the government would be unable to fund the project because there is no clearly beneficial objective. But that is exactly how quinine, a now widely-used treatment for malaria, was found, and the general exploration was certainly worth funding. Finally, it is unlikely that pure research, no matter who funds it, will result in disaster. Researchers are very careful to prevent this, and even if a disaster did happen, it would not be the fault of whom is funding the research.

It is quite clear that pure research is invaluable, as the examples of penicilin, quinine, and insulin support. It cannot be dependent on the whims, finances, and oversight of any one group but must be a concerted effort among all and for all who may benefit.

K 427

Score Explanation (12)

This essay is clearly focused on the prompt, shows complete understanding of the issue, logically assesses the implications of all three perspectives, and puts forth the author's point of view in both the first and fifth paragraphs. This is a cohesive, critical analysis of the perspectives, with a solid, well-supported thesis.

Ideas and Analysis (6)

The argument is driven by strong and clear analysis of each perspective, with good examination of implications. The writer's consistent focus on the benefits of pure research makes the essay cohesive and precise: pure research is worth pursuing and, for economic and oversight reasons, must be funded by a consortium of groups. Keeping this focus, the writer is able to explore each perspective, identify pros and cons, and provide strong support for her point of view. Critical, logical thinking is clearly displayed.

Development and Support (6)

The writer introduces her argument with a strong statement supporting pure research in general, and she immediately follows up with her perspective. That perspective is developed through reference to "life-changing discoveries," the cost of research, specific discussion of drug company research and benefits, and what may constitute acceptable risk. Support is strong, referencing Alexander Fleming, penicillin, space exploration, quinine, and insulin, and inserting a relevant quote from Thomas Edison. Reasoning and support are well integrated, and the author never loses sight of the thesis. Both alternatives are discussed. One alternative is discussed in detail, while the other is given only passing, but still strong consideration ("And what is a clear and acceptable outcome?," "Finally, it is unlikely that pure research, no matter who funds it, will result in disaster."). Development moves from the general to the specific, with excellent support for each point, and a clear and consistent perspective.

Organization (6)

There is a clear and strong introduction and a summary conclusion, both of which enlarge the specifics of the prompt to the larger issues involved. Each paragraph begins with a topic sentence, and the contrasting view is signaled with the phrase "On the other hand," while the third paragraph is introduced with a creative transition phrase "Consider also." The essay is cohesive and flows well, ideas are well-connected, and support is explicit, relevant, and well-positioned to enhance the argument.

Language Use (6)

The writing is mostly high-level, with the use of a rhetorical question and words such as "perseverance," "accountable," "consortium," and "pharmaceutical." Several sentences are varied and complex. The grammar and punctuation are mostly correct, though there are some spelling errors ("penicilin," "perserverance"). The writer's style is appropriately formal, even with a personal example, and her word choice is effective in characterizing the perspectives and writing a persuasive argument.

Level 8 Essay

Pure research is done for the purpose of discovery without a specific goal in mind. Even so, it has produced important breakthroughs such as treatment for Alzheimer's disease, and even the development of the GPS. Though scientific research is vitally important, people disagree about who should pay for it. Some people think that the government should fund the research if the goal is a good one. Others think that the government should only give money to research that can be shown will be helpful. Still others believe that the government and private companies should work together to give scientists the money they need, which is the best way to do it, and the perspective I agree with.

I know the importance of research because my little brother has asthma and requires daily medication. Though I don't know who paid for the research that helped make his meds, I'm quite sure that the research behind it took a long time and cost a great deal of money. Though the government may have enough money to fully fund research like this, it has other responsibilities as well and can't afford to fund research alone, especially if the outcome is unsure. However, with other money from drug companies and non-profit agencies, research can continue to be funded without any one entity eating into their finances earmarked for other purposes. Even if the research doesn't show results for many years, a group of funders can provide enough money so that scientists can keep working until they discover something helpful and then continue to develop it.

The government can't do everything on its own and companies shouldn't have to work by themselves either. If they team up, lots of research can get done. Asthma is now manageable, but there are plenty of other illnesses that are very deadly. Everybody is hoping for a cure for cancer one day, and scientists need time and money to find one. Groups working together can give those scientists the time and money they need, since no one group is responsible for an immediate, beneficial result from the research it funds. The government and companies should pick an amount of money they want to spend each year on scientific research and give it to a variety of research groups. Then, if any of the groups make a major discovery, they can earn more money and invest it back into ongoing research.

On the other hand, some people think that scientists should have to show the government that their projects will be helpful in order to get money. That would exclude a lot of past and future research that was done purely in the hopes of discovery but without assurances. Louis Pasture wouldn't have gotten money from his government to make penicillin since it was a total accident. Being able to pinpoint the exact purpose and result of pure research is precisely the opposite of what pure research aims to do.

Like all important things, research requires time, effort and money. The best way to fund it is to gather a group of government, private, and non-profit agencies who can pool their resources to let scientists keep working. Some research may fail miserably, but some may change the course of the world. That possibility is surely worth funding.

Score Explanation (8)

The writer provides a minimal discussion of all three perspectives, but fails to fully consider the implications of the other perspectives. She doesn't fully consider counterarguments, but she does provide relevant support for her opinion.

Ideas and Analysis (4)

Ideas are clearly stated, if redundant. The argument centers around "time, effort, and money," with discussion of each taking up most of the essay. Her perspective is analyzed primarily through a personal anecdote about her brother, which is more related to research in general than to pure research. However, the author is consistent in her argument and able to critique another perspective while returning to her own point of view.

Development and Support (4)

The writer begins with a good statement defining pure research, immediately bringing in the examples of Alzheimer's and the GPS, though a brief explanation of their relevance would enhance the support. The first paragraph also introduces all perspectives. However, when the writer states her own opinion at the end of the introduction, she does not do so forcefully. The argument is developed with a personal statement about her brother's asthma, which leads into further discussion of funding. The writer continues this argument in the next paragraph, again referencing asthma and mentioning cancer, though both statements are fleeting and do not offer strong support. One other alternative is discussed in the fourth paragraph, nicely harking back to the definition of pure research (the incorrect reference to Pasteur and penicillin does not affect the support).

Organization (4)

The writer provides a clear introductory paragraph and a good conclusion, and she is able to tie the essay together by harking back to the initial definition of pure research at the end of the fourth paragraph with "Being able to pinpoint the exact purpose and result of pure research is precisely the opposite of what pure research aims to do." The first paragraph shows good connection between perspectives ("Some," "Others," "Still others"). However, there are few transitions other than the one introducing paragraph four; better use of transitions would make the essay flow more smoothly. The essay is nonetheless cohesive in its perspective.

Language Use (4)

The writing style is adequate, with some spelling and grammar errors. Word choice could be improved by avoiding very informal words and phrases ("eating into their finances," "total accident," "meds," "plenty of other diseases") and expressing ideas with more high-level vocabulary and complex sentence structure. Less use of contractions would also raise the language to a more appropriately formal essay level.

Level 4 Essay

Working with a real goal in mind is the best way to do a project and the goverment has lots of money, so I think the government should pay for research projects but only those which will succeed. I did a school sience project with too other kids but we ended up fighting and not finishing it, which is what would happen if lots of groups got together to fund something.

When my teacher assigns a sience project even though I get to choose which one to do she expects results. The goverment should think the same way because if they don't they will be spending money for something which could be useless. Just like my teacher does when she decides what grade to give my project, the goverment should think about how successful the research might be and save their money for research that will really come up with something important.

Like it says, "to many cooks spoil the broth" which means that when theres a whole group of people, chances are the end result is bad. That goes for the govement partnering with other groups also they should pay for research by themselves but only if it looks like the research will come up with something good.

Score Explanation (4)

Though the author addresses the prompt and takes a side, this essay is very poorly written and supported, and ideas and analysis are weak with little clarity.

Ideas and Analysis (2)

This essay indicates a lack of understanding of the prompt and task, and poor reasoning and writing skills. The author has focused primarily on the issues of money and the negative effects of working with partners, likening the latter to working with others on a science project. She has not analyzed any perspective in depth;

instead, ideas are repetitive, with shallow support. The author has not looked beyond her own school experience, thus her argument is weak and analysis of the prompt is superficial.

Development and Support (2)

The author fails to develop her thesis beyond general, poorly-supported statements which repeat her two ideas that working together is detrimental to a project and government money should be spent on projects with demonstrated success. Her support is weak and irrelevant, focusing on a school project, equating it with pure research, and suggesting that the government should determine its funding in the same way that a teacher determines a grade. The phrase which opens the third sentence is a trite platitude, again lacking any real thought and analysis. The author's reasoning is inadequate and confused, and she fails to examine the argument logically.

Organization (2)

Though there are three separate paragraphs and the conclusion echoes the first paragraph's perspective, each paragraph is weak and disjointed, with no transition phrases to tie the essay together. Ideas are poorly grouped together; the author repeatedly compares a school project to governmental pure research funding.

Language Use (2)

There are numerous spelling and punctuation errors, word choice is simplistic, and the writing fails to be persuasive. "Government" and "science" are consistently misspelled, and there are several instances of improper pronoun/antecedent agreement. The author misuses the word "too," omits the apostrophe from "there's," and follows the missed apostrophe with a run-on sentence. Word choice and sentence structure are rudimentary, and the essay lacks the strength and style of writing which would make it persuasive and engaging.

Essay 3—Student Loans

Level 12 Essay

In today's world the truth of the matter is that a high school diploma no longer makes a job applicant competitive; a college degree is now required for most high-paying jobs which also offer advancement opportunities. Given the high cost of a college education—and even community college fees may be beyond the reach of some students—taking out a student loan is almost a given for the college student. The question is, however, how these loans should be structured. Several options are offered, but the fairest and most workable is that of no-interest government and bank loans.

Firstly, as the issue states, student loans can take years to repay, even when the former students earn good salaries and repay the loan month by month. This is simply because the cost of a college education is so high. The average cost of a four-year college ranges from almost $10,000 per year to over $35,000. For all but the wealthiest of students, paying for college without a loan is prohibitive. My cousin spent years trying to pay off her student loans and, in the long run, defaulted and had to declare bankruptcy. Surely this is not the intention of either the government, other lending institutions, or colleges.

Loans are not special entitlements; they are fundamental to allow students of all economic backgrounds to attend college. As such, the government should not be making money from student loans. Interest is essentially a fee charged for borrowing money, with some sort of collateral insuring repayment. In the case of a college loan, that collateral is the student's future earning capacity. Granted, the principal must be repaid, but beyond that, taking money out of earnings cuts into the former student's ability to use that money for other purchases, including housing, which are so vital in driving the country's economy. Charging only the principal needed to pay for college insures that students can not only pay the yearly tuition, but are also more likely to be able to settle the entire loan and after graduation, contribute to the economy as a whole. In the special circumstance that some students need more time, it is then fair to add some further amount of payment as recognition that the original agreement was not fulfilled. This is the fairest solution and one that provides the greatest opportunity for students to go to college and pay off their loans.

The second option defines a college education as a commodity, which is something that can be bought and sold and also implies choice. Although it can be argued that a college education can be bought, it is not the same as oil or wheat. It is not used for the moment but for the future and it cannot be compared to loans for items that people choose to buy, such as cars or refrigerators. Loans to support an educated populace as the backbone of our society are not the same as car loans and should not be treated as such. If we truly believe in education, we must make allowances for the loans required to fund it. As we have all learned, college is an investment in the future. It has become less and less a personal choice and more of a requirement for job consideration. When considered on a supply and demand basis, it is even more important, since studies show that jobs requiring a college degree are in more and more demand. A capitalist market requires the ability to be competitive and creative; this is exactly what a college education provides. Educated students are far more important than almost anything else a loan can support, and any accommodations, including making college loans less expensive than other loans, is for the benefit of society and the future, and should be promoted, not prohibited.

Finally, the third point of view is simply ridiculous. There is absolutely no way to determine how much money a person will earn in the future. We can make considered guesses—lawyers will earn more than waiters—but there is no guarantee that the lawyer will not be fired and the waiter will not become a restaurant owner. Basing the loan amount on future earnings can also mean that the graduate has no opportunity to change his career from a high-earning one, such as a lawyer, to one that may truly be his heart's desire, such as being an artist. Furthermore, even if one were to train to be a lawyer, it is possible that he will not find a job that pays him the same amount of money the loan projected him to earn. At one time, investment counselors were earning a lot of money, and therefore would have been low-risk borrowers, but after the investment scandal several years ago, many investment counselors are doing other jobs, have no job, or may even be in jail. College graduates are just starting their careers; how well they do, what they earn, and whether they stay in their original jobs are unknown and cannot be used to determine a loan amount.

College loans should be as accessible and easy to repay as possible. There is nothing more important than an educated and far-sighted generation of college graduates. They are the ones who will run the government, captain business, and teach children. To deprive them of their college opportunity by making it too hard for them to either get or repay adequate loans is to deprive this country of those who will steer its future.

Score Explanation (12)

This essay exhibits strong and consistent writing skills. The introduction summarizes the arguments to come and heralds the author's point of view. Each following paragraph then discusses one perspective and its implications, using specific and appropriate examples. The conclusion reiterates the writer's opinion and moves it from specific to general, connecting it to a wider concept.

Ideas and Analysis (6)

The author's ideas are clearly, logically, and persuasively stated: a college-educated populace is the backbone of the country, and since paying for college is difficult, student loans should be granted without adding the financial burden of interest. Ideas are cohesive, build on each other, and are well-developed. Insight and analysis are excellent, examining the issue from both the perspective of the student still in college and the college-educated worker, with implications about the cost of education, the importance of a college education, and the ability of the earner to contribute to the national economy. The conclusion that to make tuition borrowing a heavy burden "is to deprive this country of those who will steer its future" provides both a succinct ending as well as additional insight.

Development and Support (6)

The line of reasoning throughout the essay is clear, consistent, and forceful. Starting out with a general statement about the importance of a college education in today's workplace, the author then enlarges on this idea with specifics about the cost of education (with supporting numbers) that requires most students to take out loans, the argument that college loans are not "special entitlements," cogent reasons why these loans should be interest-free, and well-argued critique of the other two options. Support is excellent, including the example of the writer's cousin and comment that "Surely this [default] is not the intention of either the government or colleges," and reference to a capitalist economy and consumer spending which drives it. The examples of lawyers and investment counselors are highly relevant to the author's critique of the other two perspectives, and show her ability to connect actual events to her thinking.

Organization (6)

The organization is excellent, with good transitions ("Firstly," "The second option," "Finally"). The writer's perspective is firmly introduced in the opening paragraph and reiterated in the conclusion, and all body paragraphs are in logical and persuasive order. The three paragraphs supporting the writer's point of view are persuasive in their individual perspectives on the issue, and contrast well with the two paragraphs critiquing the other viewpoints. There is a central idea, maintained throughout both in direct support and in contrast to other perspectives, and the essay is coherent, flows well, and makes a strong and effective argument.

Language Use (6)

Word choice, writing style, and vocabulary all enhance the argument. High-level vocabulary with words such as "concomitant," "entitlements," and "prohibited" raise the argument to a sophisticated level. There are no grammar mistakes or punctuation errors, and only one spelling error ("insures" for "ensures"). Sentence structure is somewhat varied, particularly with the use of dashes in paragraph five. The phrase "the third point of view is simply ridiculous" begs for more temperate wording, but it does illustrate the author's commitment to her ideas. The tone is appropriately firm and formal for a persuasive essay.

Level 8 Essay

Throughout our school lives, parents and teachers emphasize the importance of going to college. Consequently almost all my friends in my high school are planning on going to college. Some will even be the first in their families to have a higher education, or perhaps even finish high school. They will be better educated than their parents, have more opportunities for better and higher-paying jobs, and perhaps be able to contribute something unique to society. However, the cost of a college education, and the need for loans, means that most students will take out loans. Because the loans are for a good cause, and the end result may benefit all of society, these loans should be readily available and interest free.

I know from the home loan my parents have that it's hard to pay loans back every month, so the less money a borrower has to pay every month, the more likely that the loan will eventually be paid in full. When applying that to college loans, the best way to structure them is to not add anything extra, including interest. The added cost of interest means that students will have to pay more, it will take longer and be harder, and some may not be able to do it at all. The education for a doctor, for example, takes many years, each one involving the cost of schooling. Though a doctor may make a great deal of money over time, this won't happen right away, but the loan payments will and it will all add up to perhaps an unpayable debt. The government makes a great deal of money off taxes, and banks make plenty of money from credit cards; it should not be allowed for them to also make money from student loans.

Those who want to base school loans on future earnings are going to run into a lot of problems. As freshmen and sophomores, how can we be sure of what we will do when we graduate from college, so how can loans for the first two years of college be based on future earnings? And what if a person can't find a job right after school or decides to change his career? Holding a person captive in a career because it's the only way he can make enough money to repay his student loans is unfair to the person and could deprive him from the opportunity to do something else which would benefit society.

Since financial institutions, and the government when it works as one, can get their money back if people actually pay their monthly installments, it makes sense to do what they can to make it easy. Students are borrowing money for something that actually benefits society as a whole. They are not asking for college to be free (although that would be great) but just a fair chance at paying the money they owe without the burden being so much that they can't pay for the necessities of life. If the government and the banks want to get their money back they definitely should make the loans cheaper by not charging interest.

Score Explanation (8)

The writer of this essay remains focused on the issue throughout and develops a clear opinion in the first paragraph. Support is varied, showing some recognition of the complexity of the issue. One alternative perspective is critiqued, followed by reiteration of the author's conclusion. The rhetorical questions in the second paragraph add to the writing quality.

Ideas and Analysis (4)

The author's thesis—loans should be interest-free to enable borrowers to repay them, and banks and the government have no need to add interest—is consistent throughout the essay. The argument recognizes several contexts in which this applies, including children better educated than their parents, the cost of a college education, the burden on the borrower, and not restricting workers to a job simply because they can make enough money to repay the loan. The author analyzes the issue more broadly when discussing the job market, career changes, and possible benefits to society. The author's thoughts are clearly expressed and contribute to a generally persuasive essay.

Development and Support (4)

Though couched primarily in personal terms ("almost all my friends in my high school are planning on going to college,"), the author's reasoning moves from the opening statement, to her perspective, the reasons supporting it (including benefits to society), critique of an alternative, and her conclusion, showing clear and logical development. She expands on her thesis, emphasizing how interest-free loans make it more likely that the borrower can repay with undue burden, and supports this with reference to her parents' home loan, the length and cost of a doctor's education, taxes, and credit cards. Her critique of the third perspective, though somewhat simplistic, is relevant to the thesis.

Organization (4)

The author's thesis is clear and supported by the introductory comments regarding many students planning on going to college. The organizational strategy is clear in the progression of the essay, and ideas are grouped logically. The second paragraph expands on the thesis and is cohesive in its development. The writer then reflects on an alternative perspective, but returns to her thesis in the final paragraph, reiterating the benefit of no-interest loans both to the borrower and possibly to society. There are some internal transition words ("consequently," "however") and paragraph transition words to help the essay flow better. For the most part, the organization is adequate for a persuasive essay.

Language Use (4)

Word choice is correct but simple, with phrases such as "plenty of money," "run into lots of problems," and "make the loans cheaper." Though overall the grammar and spelling are correct, some sentences are awkwardly phrased ("it should not be allowed for them to also make money from student loans") and the phrase "end result" is redundant. Rhetorical questions are well-placed and make good points. Overall, word choice is adequate and occasionally above-average with words such as "burden," "captive," and "unique." Tone and style are generally appropriate.

Level 4 Essay

Everybody knows that the cheaper something is, the more people can afford to buy it. Getting a loan for college isn't exactly buying something but it ends up being the same thing because it means you have to pay for something. With a loan you don't pay the full price rite away but you do in the long run so its better to have to pay less than more which is what happens if theres no interest on the loan. If you have to get a loan, getting a goverment one without interest is best, but you still have to make a lot of money so you can pay your loan and also have money to live.

Even though its not a choice for the essay, I think a better way to get money for college is to get a scholarship because you dont have to pay that back. People who are good at something like sports, like I am, should be rewarded with a college scholarship. I hope I will get a football scholarship because Im the quarterback on the varsity football team and were one of the top three teams in the high school division. If I get a football scholarship I can go to college and still play football and I won't have to pay any money for a loan. It doesnt matter if loans have extra money to pay back like interest because all that money is hard to pay back no matter how much it is. So a scholarship is better and thats what I want so I can go to college.

Score Explanation (4)

Though the essay provides some support for the first perspective, the author then goes off-topic and neglects to consider the prompt from any perspective but his own. Though scholarships are available for college tuition, they are irrelevant to the task, thus the writer has neither understood the task nor fulfilled it in any way. This essay does not show coherent thinking, writing, or attention to the task.

Ideas and Analysis (2)

The writer gives a passing nod to the prompt with a weak response, which is then abandoned in favor of an off-topic thesis. The majority of the essay is irrelevant and even the argument in favor of scholarships lacks any analysis or support. Logic is garbled or non-existent, and no attempt is made to address any alternative perspective for the prompt, though the author does recognize that his perspective is not one of the three given.

Development and Support (2)

There is minimal response to the prompt with no development of ideas. Support is given only in terms of "the cheaper something is." Even the author's own claim is weak, consisting of personal opinion only with no support. But for the brief and somewhat incoherent response to the first perspective, this essay would merit a score of 1.

Organization (2)

The entire essay is contained in two paragraphs with no clear introduction or conclusion. The second paragraph is introduced with a contrast transition ("Even though,") and an argument proceeds from there, but since the argument is irrelevant to the prompt, the entire organization of the paragraph is off-topic. The second-to last sentence somewhat references the task but simply echoes the first paragraph's contention that it is difficult to pay back a loan. This essay does not show appropriate thinking, writing, or attention to the task.

Language Use (2)

Sentence structure and word choice are simplistic, and there are multiple spelling and punctuation errors ("goverment" for "government," "scholaship" for "scholarship," "rite" for "write"). There is a noticeable lack of commas within sentences, and apostrophes are missing from several words. The third sentence is unnecessarily long and should be broken up. The personal and somewhat antagonistic tone and voice are inappropriate for the purpose.